SCRIPTURE AS
REAL PRESENCE

SCRIPTURE AS
REAL PRESENCE

✶

Sacramental Exegesis in the Early Church

HANS BOERSMA

Baker Academic

a division of Baker Publishing Group
Grand Rapids, Michigan

© 2017 by Hans Boersma

Published by Baker Academic
a division of Baker Publishing Group
P.O. Box 6287, Grand Rapids, MI 49516-6287
www.bakeracademic.com

Printed in the United States of America

Library of Congress Cataloging-in-Publication Data is on file at the Library of Congress, Washington, DC.

ISBN: 978-0-8010-1703-2

17   18   19   20   21   22   23   7   6   5   4   3   2   1

To Matthew Levering,
through participatory reading,
a contemporary of the church fathers

CONTENTS

PREFACE

The past several decades have witnessed a remarkable and growing interest in theological interpretation of Scripture. General introductions to theological interpretation, biblical-theological commentaries, and anthologies of patristic exegesis have appeared on the market, and also theological journals, conferences, and seminary courses are devoting themselves to this latest trend in biblical interpretation. In broad terms, the increasing appreciation for theological interpretation stems from the influence both of Karl Barth, via the Yale school, on North American theological scholarship, and of the *nouvelle théologie* movement in France, most notably Henri de Lubac and Jean Daniélou, not only in Catholicism but also among Protestants. To my mind, this two-pronged (ecumenical) impact on biblical exegesis has great promise, as it may mark both a renaissance in biblical studies and a genuine rapprochement between biblical and theological studies.

Advocates of theological interpretation are by no means unanimous, however, on *how* to reappropriate theological (or spiritual) interpretation. We don't need to dig far under the surface to find disagreement about what constitutes theological interpretation of Scripture. Kevin Vanhoozer distinguishes three distinct emphases, and although he adds that they are "more complementary than contradictory," it is probably fair to suggest that they lead to a fair bit of disagreement in practice.[1] Noting divergent attitudes to historical criticism along with ecclesial fragmentation, R. R. Reno is forced to acknowledge in the series preface to the Brazos Theological Commentary on the Bible that "the Nicene tradition, *in all its diversity and controversy*, provides the proper

1. Vanhoozer, "Introduction," 23.

basis for the interpretation of the Bible" and that "we cannot say in advance how doctrine helps the Christian reader assemble the mosaic of scripture."[2] The general editor's modesty with regard to the series' homogeneity illustrates the wide range of approaches in theological interpretation. Clearly, we are in need of continuing discussion about the nature of theological interpretation.

Indeed, the term "theological interpretation" is not without its drawbacks. As I just noted, the term is a catchall for a variety of approaches to the Scriptures, not all of which are compatible with each other. What is more, by speaking of "theological interpretation," we may give the impression that other kinds of interpretation (such as "historical exegesis") approach the biblical text simply from a different angle and that both are equally independent and equally valid. To be sure, the Christian faith is rooted in history, and historical exegesis is indispensable for a proper understanding of the Scriptures. However, historical reading is never *purely* historical, as if there were a purely natural or factual substructure on which one would subsequently build a separate or distinct theological reading. As I will make clear throughout this book (particularly in chap. 2), the church fathers understood even a literal reading of the text theologically. That is to say, historiography is always theologically shaped—or, to put it perhaps better, the writing of history is itself undergirded by Jesus Christ, whom we have come to know in faith through the proclamation of the Word. Just as there is no pure nature (*pura natura*), so there is also no pure history (*pura historia*). Although I will use the term "theological interpretation" both in this preface and elsewhere in the book, I mean by that simply a reading of Scripture *as Scripture*, that is to say, as the book of the church that is meant as a sacramental guide on the journey of salvation—and one aspect of reading Scripture as Scripture is to take history seriously as anchored in Jesus Christ, who is the Alpha and the Omega of history (Rev. 1:8; 21:6; 22:13).[3]

This book is meant as a contribution to such a discussion on the nature of biblical interpretation. It presents my own approach and does so through interaction with patristic sources. Apart from the first chapter, the book simply follows the canonical sequencing of the biblical books as most Christian readers will be familiar with it. In each chapter, I take a portion (or portions) of Scripture and look at how various church fathers approached the Scriptures in their reading of a certain passage or biblical book. Each of the chapters makes a distinct argument and can, in principle, be read and understood on its own terms. At the same time, it is the cumulative effect of the chapters

2. Reno, "Series Preface" (emphasis added).
3. For these insights, I am particularly indebted to correspondence with Fr. John Behr.

together that lends credence to the overall argument of the book, namely, *that the church fathers were deeply invested in reading the Old Testament Scriptures as a sacrament, whose historical basis or surface level participates in the mystery of the New Testament reality of the Christ event.* The underlying message of my argument is that this sacramental approach to reading the Scriptures is of timeless import and that it is worthy of retrieval today. The chapter titles are more or less playful references to various "kinds" of reading (e.g., "Hospitable Reading," "Harmonious Reading"). In each case, I attempt to show that the kind of reading discussed in that chapter is sacramental in nature. In other words, I attempt to show how it is that the hospitable reading, harmonious reading, and so on, all give some indication of what it means for biblical reading to be sacramental in character.

This advocacy of sacramental reading is not without its predecessors. Most notably, mid-twentieth-century patristics scholar Henri de Lubac tirelessly promoted an understanding of "spiritual interpretation" that focused on the biblical text as being sacramental in character: "The entire New Testament is a great mystery hidden within this sacrament, or signifies by means of this sacrament which is the Old Testament."[4] Andrew Louth defends particularly the use of allegory, with an appeal to participation and to mystery: "Allegory is a way of holding us before the mystery which is the ultimate 'difficulty' of the Scriptures—a difficulty, a mystery, which challenges us to revise our understanding of what might be meant by meaning."[5] And Matthew Levering suggests: "Time or history as understood biblically, as Christologically and metaphysically participatory, challenges the modern understanding of eisegesis by understanding biblical realities from within their ongoing 'conversation' with God."[6] Each of these authors has been deeply influential in shaping my own reading of Scripture. This book will betray my debt to them on pretty much every page.

My turn to the patristic practice of reading Scripture sacramentally represents a fairly major shift in my thinking, one that has taken place gradually over the past fifteen years. The confessional Reformed tradition in which I grew up taught me to read the Scriptures historically, though always with a view to Christ. Our preachers loved the Old Testament inasmuch as it witnesses to Christ's coming. Twentieth-century Dutch theologians such as Benne Holwerda and Klaas Schilder emphasized the need for thorough grammatical-historical exegesis, reading against the backdrop of the original

---

4. De Lubac, *Medieval Exegesis*, 22. See also H. Boersma, *Nouvelle Théologie*, 149–90.
5. Louth, *Discerning the Mystery*, 111.
6. Levering, *Participatory Biblical Exegesis*, 35.

context, and carefully taking into account the literary genre of the passage under consideration. The so-called redemptive-historical method of Holwerda and others staunchly opposed the moralizing and fragmentary use of the Old Testament that they encountered in "exemplaric" preaching, in which the *dramatis personae* of the Old Testament were reduced to the function of positive or negative role models. Over against this approach, the redemptive-historical method took as its starting point the centrality of history in the narrative of salvation: in Old Testament narratives God shows us how he prepares Israel and the world for the coming of the Christ.[7] The result of Holwerda's approach was thoroughly Christocentric preaching without a whiff of moralism (but also, some complained, without real concern for personal application). Every Old Testament text was analyzed in terms of its historical relationship to Jesus Christ.

For several years I served as a pastor in this denominational tradition, and during this time I became acquainted with N. T. Wright's theology. I devoured his books, which advocate the so-called new perspective on Paul.[8] Although at crucial points Wright's theology is incompatible with the Reformed tradition (notably in the way he treats the doctrines of predestination and justification), at the same time his hermeneutic is "redemptive historical" in the very same sense as advocated by the Dutch Reformed tradition of Holwerda and Schilder—only more emphatically so (and, as I think of it now, more reductively so). For Wright—and for an increasingly large number of evangelical biblical scholars—exegesis is primarily a historical discipline, one that escapes the "abstract" and "timeless" theology of Western, Platonized Christianity.

One of the greatest pastoral drawbacks of both the redemptive-historical method and the new perspective on Paul is that it's hard to see how, with these approaches, readers of the Old Testament are able to relate the historical narrative to their own lives. It seems that in both these hermeneutical frameworks, the only way to arrive at a personal appropriation is by moving *from* the Old Testament, *via* Christ, *to* the situation of today. In the end, one is forced to leave the Old Testament behind. For example, on Wright's understanding of exile, if one preaches on an Old Testament exilic text—say, one of Jeremiah's warnings regarding the impending Babylonian invasion—the interpreter will first carefully read the text in a (grammatical-)historical manner and then move *from* Jeremiah *to* Christ as the one who, as the new Israel, took the exilic curse upon himself. By traversing six hundred years, from Jeremiah to the life of Christ and the origin of the church, we discover at the end of the journey

---

7. For the foregoing, see Greidanus, *Sola Scriptura*, 131–37.
8. The impact of N. T. Wright is obvious in my book *Violence, Hospitality, and the Cross*.

that in and through Christ the exile has now come to an end, and we have been placed into the freedom of the children of God. On this understanding, the book of Jeremiah is of significance today only inasmuch as we leave the prophet (and the exile he announced) behind us in the historical record of the book that bears his name. Strictly historical readings of Scripture separate the reader from the original event described in the biblical text.

I won't gainsay the important exegetical insights that such historical approaches yield. The weakness of historical exegesis, however, is that it doesn't treat the Old Testament as a sacrament (*sacramentum*) that *already contains* the New Testament reality (*res*) of Christ. Or, as Irenaeus and others would have put it, strictly historical exegesis doesn't see Christ as the treasure hidden in the field of the Old Testament (Matt. 13:44) and, therefore, as already really present within it.[9] The fathers detected this presence of Christ throughout the Old Testament, and perhaps nowhere more clearly than in the Old Testament theophanies (divine appearances). The burning bush (Exod. 3), for instance, was typically interpreted as Christ manifesting himself to Moses. As the cover of this book makes clear, this reading continued into the Middle Ages, when around the year 1210 the Psalter of Ingeborg of Denmark, the Queen of France, depicted Moses as contemplating Christ in front of the burning bush. These kinds of interpretations directly result from a sacramental approach to reading the Scriptures.

This sacramental mode of interpretation has rich spiritual and pastoral implications. After all, if it is true that the mystery, or the New Testament reality, of the Christ event is already present in the historical basis or surface level of the Old Testament, then this allows the Old Testament to speak directly into the lives of believers today—both personally and corporately. While in some way believers today may be separated from the Old Testament by several millennia, they are also actually present in the hidden dimension of the Old Testament. If Christ is genuinely present in the Old Testament, then believers—who are "in Christ"—are as well. Because believers are "in Christ," when they locate his real presence in the Old Testament, they also find their own lives and realities reflected there. Put differently, when Christian readers find the treasure in the field, they discover themselves—their own

9. Throughout this book I refer to the Hebrew Scriptures as the "Old Testament," even though this is a somewhat anachronistic designation, since the church fathers only knew of the "Scriptures." Cf. Allert, *High View of Scripture?* Still, the term "Hebrew Scriptures" is unsuitable because the church fathers often used the Septuagint or a Latin translation as their Scriptures, and so for the sake of easy reference I have thought it best simply to use the term "Old Testament."

identity—within the treasure. Why? Because it is in finding the presence of Christ that we most deeply come to know ourselves.

Although the theological direction advocated in this book has been percolating in my mind for years, its more immediate origin is a course on patristic exegesis that I started teaching at Regent College in Vancouver in 2010. I have very much enjoyed reading and discussing patristic commentaries and sermons together with my students; none of the material in this book would have seen the light of day were it not for their love for the Scriptures and their eagerness to read them with Spirit-filled passion and skill. I am grateful to Alec Arnold, Lewis Ayres, Fr. John Behr, Corine Boersma, Gerald Boersma, Silvianne Aspray, Norm Klassen, Peter Martens, Tracy Russell, Karl Shuve, Matthew Thomas, and George Westhaver for the numerous insightful comments and corrections they offered on the manuscript. I also appreciate the hard work and efficiency of my research assistants: Phillip Hussey not only read the manuscript but also put together the bibliography, and Austin Stevenson put together an excellent set of indexes.

I put the finishing touches on this book during the early stages of my appointment as the Danforth Visiting Chair in Theological Studies at Saint Louis University (2015–2016). I am indebted to the president and board of Regent College for granting me an extended leave of absence. I want to thank my colleagues in the Department of Theological Studies at SLU both for the honor of inviting me to spend a year in their midst and for their gracious hospitality. It was a particular pleasure to deliver the Danforth Lecture, which subsequently has turned into chapter 3, "Hospitable Reading."

Many additional opportunities to present and discuss the ideas in this book have helped to improve its contents. I'd like to thank George Westhaver for inviting me twice to speak at Pusey House, Oxford. George introduced me to Edward Pusey's work on biblical interpretation, from which I have benefited greatly. I also thank Ephraim Radner for asking me to do a presentation at Wycliffe College in Toronto; Joseph Clair for the opportunity to try out some of my ideas at the William Penn Honors Program at George Fox University; Jens Zimmermann for inviting me to be part of his lecture series "Scripture, Theology and Culture" at Trinity Western University; Craig Hovey and Cyrus Olsen for organizing a panel on "The Hermeneutics of Tradition" at the American Academy of Religion; George Kalantzis and Dan Williams for organizing a colloquium on evangelical *ressourcement* at Wheaton College; and Bill Wilder and Fitz Green for asking me to speak at the Center for Christian Study in Charlottesville, Virginia.

It has been a real pleasure to work once again with Dave Nelson, Eric Salo, and their colleagues at Baker Academic. I thank them for their confidence in the project and for the kind support they have shown at every stage of its development. I also would like to acknowledge the permission to republish my articles from the *Journal of Theological Interpretation*, *Calvin Theological Journal*, the *Canadian Theological Review*, and *Crux* (2012), as well as chapters from *Imagination and Interpretation: Christian Perspectives* (Regent College Publishing) and from *Living Waters from Ancient Springs: Essays in Honor of Cornelis Van Dam* (Pickwick). Each of these articles and chapters are mentioned in the bibliography.

Finally, my wife, Linda, has lovingly treasured me for many years; she is, in turn, a treasure whose riches I'm still only learning to discover as she makes Christ really present in my life.

ABBREVIATIONS

ACW   Ancient Christian Writers

ANF   *Ante-Nicene Fathers*

CA   Athanasius, *Orationes contra Arianos*

CSEL   Corpus Scriptorum Ecclesiasticorum Latinorum

FC   Fathers of the Church

LCL   Loeb Classical Library

NPNF¹   *Nicene and Post-Nicene Fathers*, Series 1

NPNF²   *Nicene and Post-Nicene Fathers*, Series 2

WGRW   Writings from the Greco-Roman World

WSA   The Works of Saint Augustine: A Translation for the 21st Century (Hyde Park, NY: New City)

PATRISTIC READING

The Church Fathers
on Sacramental Reading of Scripture

Scripture as Sacrament

This book is about the church fathers' sacramental reading of Scripture. The main argument is that they saw the Scriptures as a sacrament and read them accordingly. In this introductory chapter I want to explain in broad terms what this claim entails. I have long been convinced that the notion of sacrament should not be limited to the ecclesial rites of baptism and Eucharist. My Christian Platonist convictions persuade me that everything around us is sacramental, in the sense that everything God has created both points to him and makes him present. Robin Parry, in his recent book *The Biblical Cosmos*, makes exactly this point, arguing that for the Old Testament everything in creation is in some way sacramental. Everything that God has made, explains Parry, participates in his life: "Creation participates in this divine Life just as it participates in Being, Beauty, Truth, and Goodness. So in some *analogical* sense all things, even rocks, have some sharing in life, albeit at a very far remove from the divine Source."[1] I will elaborate on this in a moment in connection with Origen, but for now this is enough to explain that, in some sense, everything created is sacramental in character.

1. Parry, *Biblical Cosmos*, 205 (emphasis original).

To be sure, we do need to make a distinction between such "general" sacramentality and the sacraments of the church. The distinction between general and special revelation, between nature and grace, between world and church, is by no means theologically inconsequential.[2] But also when it comes to the church and to the gift of new life through the Spirit, it doesn't seem quite right to limit the language of "sacrament" to the two rites of baptism and Eucharist—or to the seven rites that count as sacraments in the Catholic Church.[3] Saint Augustine uses the term to describe liturgical feasts (such as Easter and Pentecost), ecclesial rites (including exorcisms and penance), worship activities (singing, reading, prayer, the sign of the cross, bowing of the head), and objects used in church (such as penitential garments, the font, and salt).[4] Moreover, he regularly refers to scriptural texts as *sacramenta*, much as I will do throughout this book.[5] I do not mean to suggest that there is no difference between such sacraments and, say, baptism and Eucharist. Clearly, there is. Throughout the church's history, these latter two rites have been recognized as central to the church's life and as making the grace of God present in a unique way—they are authoritatively given by Christ himself for the renewal of his people.[6] At the same time, the early church's fluidity with regard to the term "sacrament" is helpful in reminding us that God uses not only baptism and Eucharist but also many other activities, rites, objects, people, and celebrations to fill the church's saints with grace. It wouldn't seem out of place, therefore, to add to Augustine's list of ecclesial sacraments the Scriptures themselves. Holy Scripture too is a sacrament, inasmuch as it renders Christ present to us—but more about that anon.

2. Upon reading my book *Heavenly Participation*, some have wondered whether I believe this distinction matters at all. The book presents a plea for a reintegration of nature and the supernatural, which may of course fuel the objection: if everything is a sacrament, then nothing is a sacrament. I don't think the book undermines the unique way in which God makes his grace available through the church—it has an entire chapter on the centrality of the Eucharist—but I do want to be on record as noting that the distinction (as opposed to separation) between nature and the supernatural is crucially important.

3. Twentieth-century Catholic scholar Marie-Dominique Chenu lamented the limitation of the number of the sacraments to merely seven, arguing that this twelfth-century "operation of delimiting the seven major sacraments manifested a desacralizing tendency." *Nature, Man, and Society*, 127. For similar criticism, see Brown, "Sacramental World," 605.

4. Cutrone, "Sacraments," 742.

5. See Dodaro, *Christ and the Just Society*, 147–59. I owe this reference to Lewis Ayres.

6. The Catholic *Catechism* distinguishes the seven sacraments from "sacramentals": "These are sacred signs which bear a resemblance to the sacraments. They signify effects, particularly of a spiritual nature, which are obtained through the intercession of the Church. By them men are disposed to receive the chief effect of the sacraments, and various occasions in life are rendered holy." *Catechism of the Catholic Church*, par. 1667 (p. 415).

Metaphysics and Hermeneutics: Origen, Hobbes, and Spinoza

The brilliant third-century biblical interpreter Origen (ca. 185–ca. 254) pauses in book 3 of his *Commentary on the Canticle of Canticles* to explain what he believes allegorical interpretation is all about. Interestingly, he doesn't begin by talking about exegesis at all. Instead, he starts off with a lengthy discussion of metaphysics—Paul's teaching "that the invisible things of God are understood by means of things that are visible and that the things that are not seen are beheld through their relationship and likeness to things seen" (cf. Rom. 1:20; 2 Cor. 4:18).[7] Origen clarifies how he views this relationship between the visible and the invisible. "God," he writes, "thus shows that this visible world teaches us about that which is invisible, and that this earthly scene contains certain patterns (*exemplaria*) of things heavenly. Thus it is to be possible for us to mount up (*ascendere*) from things below to things above, and to perceive and understand from the things we see on earth the things that belong to heaven."[8] Origen maintains that earthly things contain patterns (*exemplaria*) of heavenly things, and it is their purpose to enable us to go up (*ascendere*). Origen has in mind that in an important sense not just human beings are created in God's image and as such have a divine character stamped upon them. Other creatures, he insists, must also have something in heaven whose image and likeness they bear.[9] Even the smallest of creatures, a mustard seed, has a likeness to heavenly things; in this case the prototype is nothing less than the kingdom of heaven itself (cf. Matt. 13:31).[10] Origen observes that though it's true that flora and fauna "do serve the bodily needs of men," they also have the "forms and likenesses" (*formas et imagines*) of incorporeal things, so that the soul can be taught by them "how to contemplate those other things that are invisible and heavenly."[11] For Origen, it seems, a mustard seed doesn't just point to the kingdom of heaven as something far away; it contains the very pattern of the kingdom and in some way already makes it present.

The key passage for Origen is Wisdom 7:17–21, which he says "perhaps" refers to just the kind of thing he has in mind.[12] Here King Solomon lists many

---

7. Origen, *Commentary on the Canticle of Canticles* 3.12 (ACW 26:218).

8. Ibid. Here and throughout, unless otherwise indicated, Latin and Greek terms in round brackets are my own addition.

9. Ibid., 3.12 (ACW 26:219).

10. Origen observes that the mustard seed is also a likeness or image of perfect faith (cf. Matt. 17:20), so that it is possible to bear the likeness of heavenly things in several respects. Ibid.

11. Ibid., 3.12 (ACW 26:220). I have changed the translation of *formas* from "shapes" to "forms."

12. Ibid.

aspects of the world around him, about which God has given him knowledge, and the king ends the list with "all such things as are hid and manifest (*occulta et manifesta*)."[13] Origen takes the phrase as applying to each of the foregoing items in the list, for the expression shows, so he claims, that everything visible or "manifest" on earth has its invisible or "hidden" complement in heaven: "He who made all things in wisdom so created all the species of visible things upon earth, that He placed in them some teaching and knowledge of things invisible and heavenly, whereby the human mind might mount (*ascenderet*) to spiritual understanding (*spiritalem intelligentiam*) and seek the grounds of things in heaven."[14] Created things, for Origen, contain heavenly teaching and knowledge, and the human mind is meant to go up to discover what this spiritual or heavenly knowledge is that God has placed in created things.

Origen goes through each of the items in Solomon's list, showing from Scripture how each is a copy of a heavenly exemplar and so contains heavenly knowledge.[15] A few examples will suffice to illustrate what the theologian from Alexandria has in mind. When the Book of Wisdom mentions that Solomon knows "the natures of animals and the rages of beasts" (Wis. 7:20), Origen points out that in Scripture human beings are referred to as a "fox" (Luke 13:32), as a "brood of vipers" (Matt. 3:7), as "stallions" (Jer. 5:8), as "senseless beasts" (Ps. 48:13 [49:12]), and as a "deaf adder" (Ps. 57:5 [58:4]).[16] Origen's point seems to be that when, with our physical eyes, we see animals acting in certain ways, we can then mentally transfer these characteristics to human beings. Similarly, when Solomon claims he knows "the forces of the winds" (Wis. 7:20), Origen turns to Paul's language of "winds of doctrine" (Eph. 4:14) to make clear that on the visible side there are "winds and breezes of the air," while on the invisible side there are "forces of the unclean spirits."[17]

13. Ibid. The Greek text speaks of *krypta kai emphanē*. I have left out the italics that Lawson uses to render Origen's biblical quotations.

14. Ibid.

15. Ibid., 3.12 (ACW 26:220–21).

16. The numbering of the psalms follows the Septuagint. Modern (Hebrew) numbering is given in brackets.

17. Origen, *Commentary on the Canticle of Canticles* 3.12 (ACW 26:222). The first set of metaphors (where Origen moves from animals to human beings) is different from the second (where he actually moves from sensible to spiritual realities). Origen doesn't elaborate on the difference; I suspect his point is that a metaphor, in its very nature, takes a characteristic observed with the senses and then mentally applies it to a different object. The difference between the two kinds of metaphors is important, however, in connection with patristic exegesis. Here one of the questions is whether historical types in the Old Testament only point forward to future historical antitypes (like visible animals metaphorically representing visible human beings) or whether they also point upward to eternal realities (like sensible wind pointing up to the spiritual reality of "winds of doctrine"). Origen's exegesis sees Old Testament types functioning in both ways, as we will see.

Origen concludes from his discussion that God's wisdom teaches us "from actual things and copies" (*rebus ipsis et exemplis*), "things unseen by means of those that are seen," and that in this way God "carries us over" (*transferat*) from earthly to heavenly things.[18]

It is at this point that Origen finally moves from metaphysics to hermeneutics. Until now—and it has occupied by far the longest part of his discussion of allegorizing—all he has dealt with is metaphysics: the question of the relationship between visible and invisible things. (To be sure, it is clearly a *theological* metaphysic that he advocates, one that he believes is both taught and assumed in the Scriptures.) Origen obviously believes that attention paid to metaphysics is time well spent: good metaphysics leads to good hermeneutics. Metaphysics prepares us, Origen thinks, to grasp how we should read the Song of Songs (and, for Origen, much of the rest of Scripture as well):

> But this relationship [between earthly and heavenly things] does not obtain only with creatures; the Divine Scripture itself is written with wisdom of a rather similar sort. Because of certain mystical and hidden (*occulta et mystica*) things the people is visibly led forth from the terrestrial Egypt and journeys through the desert, where there was a biting serpent, and a scorpion, and thirst, and where all the other happenings took place that are recorded. All these events, as we have said, have the aspects and likeness (*formas et imagines*) of certain hidden things (*occultorum*) [19]

What biblical interpretation does, on Origen's explanation of it here, is to move from the visible event to the "mystical and hidden things." The events in the desert did occur—Origen displays no suspicion about the historical narrative—but they did so in order to portray hidden, mystical things. And it is these hidden, mystical things that we are particularly concerned with in our reading of the Scriptures.

I have chosen this passage from Origen because it illustrates that he regards metaphysics and biblical interpretation as closely connected. The way we think about the relationship between God and the world is immediately tied up with the way we read Scripture. This is something easily lost sight of, yet of crucial significance. I suspect we often treat biblical interpretation as a relatively value-free endeavor, as something we're equipped to do once we've acquired both the proper tools (biblical languages, an understanding of how grammar and syntax work, the ability to navigate concordances and computer programs, etc.) and a solid understanding of the right method

18. Ibid., 3.12 (ACW 26:223).
19. Ibid.

(establishing the original text and translating it, determining authorship and original audience, studying historical and cultural context, figuring out the literary genre of the passage, and looking for themes and applicability). Such an approach, even when it does recognize the interpreter's dependence upon the Spirit's guidance, treats the process of interpretation as patterned on the hard sciences.[20] In other words, the assumption is that the way to read the Bible is by following certain exegetical rules, which in turn are not affected by the way we think of how God and the world relate to each other. Metaphysics, on this assumption, doesn't affect interpretation. In fact, many will see in the way Origen links metaphysics and exegesis the root cause of why his exegesis is wrongheaded: the Bible ought to be read on its own terms, without an alien, philosophically derived metaphysical scheme being imposed on it.

For Origen, metaphysics does affect one's interpretation, and it seems to me that he gives us much food for thought, whereas modern attempts to separate biblical interpretation from metaphysics appear to me misguided. Historically, it is clear that changes in metaphysics and hermeneutics have gone hand in hand. The separation between nature and the supernatural—or, we might say, between visible and invisible things—first philosophically advocated by William of Ockham (ca. 1287–ca. 1347), led to attempts to isolate biblical interpretation from metaphysics. On Ockham's understanding, individual things are not related to other things through their common source of origin. Adrian Pabst, in his fascinating book *Metaphysics: The Creation of Hierarchy*, comments that, with Ockham, "relations between individual things are severed from relations with God. Things entertain real (extra-mental) relations between one another, not in virtue of a common source to which they are ordered, but on the basis of an intrinsic similarity."[21] For Ockham, visible things may be like one another (e.g., the similarity that a variety of cats have to each other), but this doesn't mean that they contain patterns (*exemplaria*) of heavenly things sustaining their creaturely individuality, as Origen would have thought of it. Ockham's philosophy decisively abandons the earlier Christian Platonist assumption of eternal patterns or "forms" expressing themselves within the objects of the empirical world around us.

Ockham's philosophical position, commonly known as nominalism, was to have profound consequences for biblical interpretation.[22] These became manifest most clearly in the seventeenth century with Thomas Hobbes (1588–1679)

20. Louth, *Discerning the Mystery*, 26–27, 45–72.
21. Pabst, *Metaphysics*, 290.
22. I give a somewhat more extended discussion in H. Boersma, *Heavenly Participation*, 79–81.

and Baruch Spinoza (1632–1677).[23] Hobbes's book *Leviathan* (1651) suggests that the underlying cause of the wars of religion was a slavish following of Aristotle over Scripture. Aristotle's claim that "being" and "essence" have real existence lies at the root of the problem, according to Hobbes.[24] He counters Aristotelian philosophy by insisting that universal notions are just words and that we should treat them accordingly. Though we employ such notions—"man," "horse," and "tree"—Hobbes urges his readers to keep in mind that these are merely names "of divers particular things; in respect of all which together, it is called an Universall; there being nothing in the world Universall but Names; for the things named, are every one of them Individuall and Singular."[25] Put differently, Hobbes's metaphysics follows that of Ockham: both reject the notion that visible things have real relations to invisible things.

The result is that, for Hobbes, good and evil are simply words that we assign to the objects of our desire and hatred, respectively.[26] We rely on political authorities—not on universal, Aristotelian truth claims—to determine right and wrong.[27] According to Hobbes, had the Christian tradition simply followed Scripture instead of Aristotle, the church would never have been able to override the proper authority of the king.[28] Hobbes therefore suggests that there is but one solution to restoring the proper role of the king vis-à-vis papal power: "a proper reading of Scripture," under the authority of the royal sovereign, who alone has the authority to determine what it is that Scripture demands.[29] It is obvious that this "proper reading" was politically motivated. Hobbes's exegesis, suggest Scott Hahn and Benjamin Wiker, "was, first to last, entirely politicized, offering a nearly endless arsenal of support

23. For the following account, I am indebted particularly to Levering, *Participatory Biblical Exegesis*, 108–18, and to Hahn and Wiker, *Politicizing the Bible*, 285–393.

24. Hobbes, *Leviathan* 4.46 (pp. 533–36).

25. Ibid., 1.4 (p. 28). Cf. Levering, *Participatory Biblical Exegesis*, 108–9; Hahn and Wiker, *Politicizing the Bible*, 301–2.

26. "But whatsoever is the object of any mans Appetite or Desire; that is it, which he for his part calleth *Good*: And the object of his Hate, and Aversion, *Evill*; And of his Contempt, *Vile*, and *Inconsiderable*. For these words of Good, Evill, and Contemptible, are ever used with relation to the person that useth them: There being nothing simply and absolutely so; nor any common Rule of Good and Evill, to be taken from the nature of the objects themselves; but from the Person of the man (where there is no Common-wealth;) or, (in a Common-wealth,) from the Person that representeth it; or from an Arbitrator or Judge, whom men disagreeing shall by consent set up, and make his sentence the Rule thereof." Hobbes, *Leviathan* 1.6 (p. 44).

27. According to Hobbes, it is the notion of "separated essences," "built on the Vain Philosophy of Aristotle," that "would fright them from Obeying the Laws of their Countrey, with empty names; as men fright Birds from the Corn with an empty doublet, a hat, and a crooked stick." Ibid., 4.46 (p. 536).

28. Levering, *Participatory Biblical Exegesis*, 109–10.

29. Ibid., 109. See Hobbes, *Leviathan* 3.33 (p. 306).

for the subordination of every aspect of Scripture, from canon to interpretation, to the arbitrary authority of the civil sovereign."[30] For Hobbes, then, a
proper reading of Scripture is one that is freed from ecclesial constraints and
one that abandons the metaphysical notion that earthly things are linked to
heavenly things. Having rejected the sacramental link between heaven and
earth, Hobbes turned the reading of Scripture into a purely natural exercise
of historical scholarship.[31]

Spinoza, much like Hobbes, was concerned with the recent past of religious violence, and he too reconfigured biblical interpretation so as to serve
political ends. In his *Tractatus theologico-politicus* (1670), Spinoza outlined
a pantheistic view of reality, which had the effect of placing the methods of
natural science in control of biblical exegesis. God was not so much shut
out from the natural order (as in Hobbes's understanding) as he was simply
equated with it. As Hahn and Wiker put it: "What Hobbes achieved by *excluding* God from his amoral mathematical-mechanical account of nature,
Spinoza obtained by *identifying* God with his amoral mathematical account
of nature."[32] The effect was similar: biblical scholarship became a purely
natural, empirical endeavor that served political aims—in Spinoza's case, the
establishment of a tolerant, peaceful, liberal democratic system, in which it is
fine for the plebs to be governed by revealed religion, imagination, opinion,
and ignorance, while scholarly elites go about finding the truth, establishing
the historical origins of Scripture's original sources.[33]

According to Spinoza, therefore, the scholarly task was to establish the true
meaning of Scripture. This was to be accomplished by reason—not ecclesial
authority.[34] Human reason has the ability to investigate history, and so Scripture should be read historically rather than allegorically.[35] As a result, Spinoza
claimed that Scripture must be treated like any other ordinary, visible thing:
it must be analyzed empirically, and one must not allow higher, invisible
realities to determine one's natural understanding of the Bible.[36] Matthew
Levering describes the basis of Spinoza's interpretive approach as follows:
"Separated from metaphysical judgment, Scripture can be evaluated on its
own terms. The difference with patristic-medieval interpretation thus begins

---

30. Hahn and Wiker, *Politicizing the Bible*, 336.
31. See Malcolm, "*Leviathan*," 241–64.
32. Hahn and Wiker, *Politicizing the Bible*, 381.
33. Ibid., 375–77, 388–90.
34. Harrisville and Sundberg, *Bible in Modern Culture*, 40.
35. Bartholomew, *Reading Ecclesiastes*, 10.
36. Harrisville and Sundberg comment: "Spinoza reduces the rationality of Scripture—that
is, its truth—to what agrees with the understanding of the autonomous biblical critic free of
dogmatic commitments." *Bible in Modern Culture*, 39.

with a different understanding of 'nature': for the patristic-medieval tradition, nature is a created participatory reality that signifies its Creator and possesses a teleological order; for Spinoza nature simply yields empirical data within the linear time-space continuum."[37] Spinoza, in other words, came to reject the kind of connection between visible and invisible things that Origen had posited as real; Spinoza could no longer see the universe as sacramental. Interpretation, therefore, was no longer driven by the search for (participatory) correspondences between things that are manifest and those that are hidden. Spinoza was among the first instead to look behind the biblical text for historical origins, arriving at positions that adumbrated viewpoints commonly associated with the later higher biblical criticism of nineteenth-century German scholarship.

Both Hobbes and Spinoza recognized that there is, in fact, a close link between metaphysics and interpretation, and that treating interpretation of Scripture as a historical investigation of empirical (visible) realities by means of purely natural, rational abilities has inescapable metaphysical implications. It is only possible to pull off such a drastic restriction of interpretation to visible things by denying their sacramental connection to heavenly, invisible realities—in Hobbes's case by excluding the latter, and in Spinoza's case by radically immanentizing them. Put differently, modern hermeneutics in the tradition of Hobbes and Spinoza is predicated on a radical dichotomizing between visible and invisible things, between heaven and earth—or, we could also say, between nature and the supernatural.[38] The notion that the Bible can—perhaps even ought to—be read without metaphysical assumptions seems to me seriously mistaken. Today's heirs of Hobbes and Spinoza—for all their clamoring about "objectivity"—are unable to escape metaphysical assumptions when interpreting Scripture. Even when we're not aware of it, we still do metaphysics.

Sacramental Reading in Origen: Discerning Heavenly Patterns

Let's return to Origen's explanation of biblical interpretation. I have argued that, on his understanding, there's a close connection between earthly and heavenly things. But is Origen consistent in affirming such an intimate, relational unity of the two? After all, there is little doubt that he treats invisible,

---

37. Levering, *Participatory Biblical Exegesis*, 115.

38. Spinoza, of course, did not dichotomize visible and invisible things; he identified them in pantheistic fashion. Modern biblical scholarship, it seems to me, has more commonly followed the trajectory of Hobbes's exclusion of God from nature than Spinoza's merging of the two.

spiritual realities as far more significant than visible, material things. Origen's logic is unmistakably anagogical: he believes that we are to "mount up" (*ascendere*) from the created order. The language of ascent (*anagōgē*) is dear to the Alexandrian theologian. We must be carried over (*transferre*) from earth to heaven, from visible things to invisible things. The distinction he draws between visible and invisible things, or between manifest and hidden things (Wis. 7:21), underscores the sense of duality that characterizes Origen's thinking. This distinction between visible and invisible things (along with the priority of the latter) is something Origen has in common with the Platonic tradition, and some may suspect him of falling prey to a Platonic dualism that runs counter to the holistic biblical understanding of reality.

It seems to me, however, that this would be a misreading of Origen. It is true that his use of the distinction between *manifesta* and *occulta*—or between visible and invisible things—is congenial to his Platonic metaphysical assumptions. But Origen gives numerous indications that he doesn't regard invisible things as separate from visible things. As we have seen, he maintains that "this earthly scene contains certain patterns (*exemplaria*) of things heavenly." It is only because the heavenly *exemplaria* are present in earthly things and events that it is possible for us to "mount up" and experience union with God. Repeatedly, therefore, Origen insists that we can contemplate heavenly things *by means of* their "forms and likenesses" as they appear in visible things. It is *by means of* "actual things and copies" (*rebus ipsis et exemplis*) that we can move on to heaven itself.

Origen's metaphysics in no way dichotomizes visible and invisible things. He believes it is possible to move from the letter to the spirit in biblical interpretation precisely because (1) there is a letter from which to ascend, and (2) the letter contains patterns of the spirit, which we can find only by paying careful attention to the letter. The reason we can discover eternal patterns of the spirit in the letter goes back to the Platonic notion of participation (*methexis* or *metousia*). Participation assumes that this-worldly objects are related to eternal forms or ideas, also called universals. Cats, for instance, despite their bewildering variety in terms of size, shape, and color, all share a common essence, an eternal idea that is often called "felinity." This sharing (participating) of numerous cats in a single eternal form means that, *in a real sense*, all cats are related. They don't just happen to look alike (perhaps as the result of some arbitrary divine joke); instead, their similarity is the result of their common participation in an eternal form. Eternal forms, on Plato's understanding, have real existence; in fact, they are more real than the individual cats that we see around us with our physical eyes. It doesn't require a great deal of imagination to realize that the Platonic notion of participation means that visible things (say, individual cats) are closely linked to invisible things (such as the idea of felinity).

Adrian Pabst, in his book *Metaphysics*, argues at length that it is the notion of participation that prevents the kind of dualism with which Platonism is often charged: "The Socratic and Platonist revolution was to discern the presence of perennial structures in ephemeral phenomena and to theorize this presence in terms of the participation of particular things in universal forms."[39] Metaphysical dualism occurs when visible and invisible things are separated. Plato—and on this point, at least, Origen was in wholehearted agreement—used the distinction between visible and invisible things not to separate them but to show that they are joined by means of a participatory link that enables one to move from visible to invisible things. Underlying Origen's exegesis, therefore, is a metaphysic that is profoundly participatory in character. For Origen, just as visible things participate in invisible things, so the letter participates in the spirit. Anagogy or ascent is possible, he believes, precisely because heavenly, invisible realities are *not* separate from earthly, visible things.

The charge of dualism, commonly leveled against patristic metaphysics and exegesis, doesn't stick precisely because of the Platonic notion of participation. It is the modern historical schools of interpretation—Hobbes and his heirs—to which the charge of dualism properly does apply. After all, it is a modern, nominalist metaphysic that truly separates visible from invisible realities (at times by simply denying the latter, resulting in a lapse from dualism into materialist monism).[40]

Even if what I have argued so far is true, some may still object that Origen's approach doesn't yield a very exalted role either for visible things (in metaphysics) or for the letter of the text (in Scripture). After all, even if the *visibilia* are indispensable, our aim is always to move beyond them toward heavenly things. How does such a view allow us to revel in the wonders of the created order and savor the intricacies of the historical narrative of Scripture? There is no denying the anagogical character of Origen's approach: his purpose—in metaphysics and in biblical interpretation—is to ascend. However, just because heavenly things are more glorious than earthly things, that doesn't make the latter lose their splendor; and just because spiritual meaning is of a higher kind than historical meaning, that doesn't leave the latter without significance. Perhaps by valuing visible things less than invisible things, the

39. Pabst, *Metaphysics*, 32.
40. George Steiner, though he focuses on the nineteenth century, refers to this same dichotomy when he speaks of the "broken contract" between word and world. *Real Presences*, 51–134, esp. 93.

church fathers actually accurately captured the significance of both. (While I won't press the point here, I am convinced that it is by denying the presence of *exemplaria* within visible things that we trivialize the latter, since we reduce them to what makes them empirically observable.)[41]

I have made the case for a participatory view of the relationship between nature and the supernatural—or between visible and invisible things—in some of my earlier work.[42] I usually refer to this Christian Platonist understanding of reality as "sacramental ontology," by which I mean that eternal realities are really present in visible things. Since metaphysics and interpretation are two sides of the same coin, I want to explore in this book the way in which we can see this sacramental ontology at work in patristic biblical interpretation. My main argument, therefore, will be that patristic exegesis treated the letter of the Old Testament text (what Origen calls the *manifesta*, and what in sacramental language we may call the *sacramentum*) as containing the treasure of a "hidden" meaning (the *occulta* mentioned above, or the reality or *res* in sacramental discourse), which one can discover in and through God's salvific self-revelation in Jesus Christ.[43]

This book will make clear that the church fathers were convinced of a close (participatory) link between this-worldly sacrament (*sacramentum*) and otherworldly reality (*res*). For the church fathers, the hidden presence of the reality was finally revealed at the fullness of time, in the Christ event—along with everything that this event entails: Christ's own person and work; the church's origin; the believers' new, Spirit-filled lives in Christ; and the eschatological renewal of all things in and through Christ. The church fathers saw this entire new-covenant reality as the hidden treasure already present in the Old Testament. In other words, the reason the church fathers practiced typology, allegory, and so on is that they were convinced that the reality of the Christ event was already present (sacramentally) within the history described within the Old Testament narrative. To speak of a sacramental hermeneutic, therefore, is to allude to the recognition of the real presence of the new Christ-reality hidden within the outward sacrament of the biblical text.

---

41. It seems to me no coincidence, for example, that environmental mismanagement has become such a tremendous problem in the modern world: if the natural order is strictly autonomous and has no link to anything transcendent, we treat it as we see it—a collection of purely quantifiable objects, whose goodness and beauty reach no further than themselves. See H. Boersma, "Reconnecting the Threads," 33.

42. See H. Boersma, *Nouvelle Théologie*, and H. Boersma, *Heavenly Participation*. My recent book on Gregory of Nyssa (*Embodiment and Virtue*) studies his participatory metaphysic, drawing a great deal from his biblical exegesis.

43. See my interaction with N. T. Wright on this point in H. Boersma, "Sacramental Interpretation."

By speaking of a "sacramental hermeneutic," I do not mean to oppose this expression to commonly used terms in connection with patristic exegesis, such as allegory, typology, *theōria*, anagogy, and the like. Each of these terms carries its own particular connotations and functions within a distinct web of meaning with regard to its use (or rejection) both in the early church and in contemporary scholarly discussion. The variation in terminology does have a certain kind of usefulness—though it is notoriously difficult to distinguish the various terms from each other, as is clear, for instance, from contemporary debates with regard to the propriety of distinguishing between typology and allegory.[44] The interconnectedness of these terms stems, in my opinion, from the fact that a sacramental mindset—influenced by Christian Platonist convictions—affected the exegesis of the church fathers.[45] To speak, therefore, of a "sacramental hermeneutic" is not to reject other, perhaps more common labels but rather to allude to the shared metaphysical grounding of these various exegetical approaches.

Irenaeus's Recapitulation as Sacramental Reading

What did the sacramental hermeneutic of the church fathers look like in practice? There is ultimately only one way to find out, and that is by reading them. In this book, therefore, I study the actual exegesis of the fathers to see what it is that they are doing, and to analyze how we can discern the sacramental metaphysics undergirding their exegesis. Each of the chapters zeroes in on a different portion of Scripture and looks at how various church fathers treat the biblical text. By no means do I elide individual particularities or differences between various schools of thought. Throughout this book, I will repeatedly highlight the unique features of the interpreters. It is nonetheless clear to me that we can detect throughout their exegetical corpus a shared sacramental sensibility.

44. Following Jean Daniélou, twentieth-century scholarship often distinguished between typology and allegory by insisting that the former is grounded within history and is biblically based, while the latter is arbitrary and rooted in Philo and in the Platonic tradition. Henri de Lubac convincingly debunked any sharp distinction between the two and demonstrated the christological basis for typological/allegorical exegesis. See H. Boersma, *Nouvelle Théologie*, 180–90. For an excellent recent account of the distinction, see Martens, "Allegory/Typology Distinction." Cf. below in chap. 4, sec. "Melito of Sardis, *On Pascha*."

45. Both typology and allegory move from *manifesta* to *occulta*; both do so on the sacramental understanding that the latter are present in the former; and—most significantly—allegory no less than typology looks for the *occulta* in the divinely revealed reality of Christ and the church. As I will explain below, the reason twentieth-century scholarship commonly (and erroneously) divided the two is that it failed to take seriously the grounding of typology in eternal, divine providence.

Although in this book I do not deal with Saint Irenaeus in any detail, it is nonetheless to this second-century opponent of gnosticism that we need to turn for an understanding of the origin of the sacramental matrix of patristic interpretation. Doing so will also give us a first impression of what the sacramental reading of the church fathers looked like. Irenaeus is known particularly for his understanding of redemption as recapitulation.[46] Thus, we associate the term "recapitulation" with atonement theology and with the doctrine of salvation. Recapitulation means that Christ repeated or retraced the life, death, and resurrection of fallen humanity and, in the process of his faithful and obedient nonidentical repetition, restored and perfected humanity.[47] But recapitulation doesn't only speak of Christ's redemption of humanity; it also implies an approach to interpretation that we may characterize as sacramental in character.

It is of crucial importance, for an understanding both of Irenaeus's approach and of that of the later church fathers, that recapitulation takes its starting point in the climactic salvation-historical events that took place in Jesus Christ—as he was proclaimed by the apostles in accordance with the Scriptures.[48] Irenaeus saw Christ as recapitulating all of human history. He notes that there are four covenants in history: "one, prior to the deluge, under Adam; the second, that after the deluge, under Noah; the third, the giving of the law, under Moses; the fourth, that which renovates man, and sums up (*recapitulat*) all things in itself by means of the Gospel, raising and bearing men upon its wings into the heavenly kingdom."[49] And, just as the Son of God summed up or recapitulated all of history, so he also recapitulated every age level of human beings, from the very young to the very old.[50] Finally, and most importantly, Christ recapitulated Adam's life: "For as by the disobedience of the one man who was originally moulded from virgin soil, the many were made sinners, and forfeited life; so it was necessary that, by the obedience of one man, who was originally born from a virgin, many would be justified and receive salvation."[51] Adam was a "type of the future" (*typus futuri*).[52]

46. See H. Boersma, *Violence, Hospitality, and the Cross*, 121–26.

47. The term "recapitulation" goes back to Eph. 1:10, where we read that God would "unite (*anakephalaiōsasthai*) all things in him, things in heaven and things on earth."

48. This last clause makes clear that Irenaeus (following the New Testament Scriptures) did not understand Christ's recapitulation of history without recourse to the Old Testament. Christ is the one who recapitulated history precisely because the Scriptures proclaimed that this is who he was and what he did.

49. Irenaeus, *Against Heresies* 3.11.8 (*ANF* 1:429).

50. Ibid., 2.22.4 (*ANF* 1:391).

51. Ibid., 3.18.7 (*ANF* 1:448).

52. Nielsen, *Adam and Christ*, 62. Cf. Irenaeus's comment: "For inasmuch as He [i.e., the Son of God] had a pre-existence as a saving Being, it was necessary that what might be saved

Throughout his writings, Irenaeus appeals to Christ as the one who recapitulated what had gone before and as the one who thus brought about salvation.

This principle of recapitulation means that for Irenaeus the proper way to read the Old Testament is with the question in mind: How does this passage speak about Christ? Some Old Testament passages do this, of course, by means of prophetic messianic announcement, so that the reader can discern a prophecy-fulfillment schema. But the Old Testament narratives generally do not have such a plainly intended future reference. Irenaeus nonetheless insists that also seemingly straightforward historical narratives have reference to Christ. For instance, by means of the tenth plague, God "saved the children of Israel, showing forth in a mystery the Passion of Christ, by the immolation of a spotless lamb, and by its blood, given as a guarantee of immunity to be smeared on the houses of the Hebrews."[53] Christ "was sold with Joseph, and He guided Abraham; was bound along with Isaac, and wandered with Jacob; with Moses He was a Leader, and, respecting the people, Legislator. He preached in the prophets."[54] For Irenaeus, the unity of the two Testaments—the result of the identity of the Father of Christ with the God of the Old Testament—demands that we see the presence of Christ in the Old Testament.

When Irenaeus insists on Christ's presence in the Old Testament narratives, he does not mean that there is no difference between the Old and the New Testaments. Quite the contrary! As we shall see momentarily, the salvific events of the new covenant are climactic in the absolute sense of the term. What Irenaeus does by locating Christ in the Old Testament is simply to acknowledge the interpretive significance of Christ for the Old Testament. With the coming of Christ, it is no longer possible to regard the historical events of the Old Testament on the level of visible things only (the *manifesta* of Wis. 7:21). The coming of Christ is the hidden reality (the *occulta*) of the Old Testament narratives, invisible in the text of the Old Testament when it is read all by itself. In other words, Christ has now become the proper interpretive lens for reading the Old Testament.[55]

One of the questions facing typological interpretation is whether or not we should classify it as exegesis. Some will argue that it may be all right to

should also be called into existence, in order that the Being who saves should not exist in vain." Irenaeus, *Against Heresies* 3.22.3 (*ANF* 1:455).

53. Irenaeus, *Proof of the Apostolic Preaching* 25 (ACW 16:64).

54. Irenaeus, *Fragments from the Lost Writings* 54 (*ANF* 1:577).

55. In general terms, when the church fathers borrowed from Platonic metaphysics, we should not read this as an escape from the biblical narrative or as a failure of christological nerve. Throughout this book we will see that the fathers are boldly and robustly Christ centered in their hermeneutic and that it is, in fact, the salvation put into effect by the Christ event that drives their interpretation of the Old Testament.

draw parallels or similarities between aspects of the Old and the New Testaments, but that surely the search for such parallels or similarities should be regarded as a later stage of application to the lives of Christian believers, not actual exegesis or interpretation of the passage itself. In other words, some may allow for typology under the rubric of application rather than regard such typology as a form of legitimate exegesis. David L. Baker, for example, while by no means hostile to typology, insists: "Typology is not exegesis. The biblical text has only one meaning, its literal meaning, and this is to be found by means of grammatical-historical study. If the author intended a typical significance it will be clear in the text. And if we see a typical significance not perceived by the original author it must be consistent with the literal meaning. Typology is not an exegesis or interpretation of a text but the study of relationships between events, persons and institutions recorded in biblical texts."[56] Baker is convinced that typology is not exegesis: a text can only have one (literal) meaning, and this meaning is identical to the authorial intent that we determine by means of grammatical-historical study.

It is certainly true that some interpretations are better than others and that some are flat wrong. But the assumption that the biblical text carries only one meaning, namely, the one intended by the author, seems to me rooted in an approach that models exegesis on the natural sciences[57] and, for all practical purposes, obviates the role of the Holy Spirit within the actual interpretive process. For Irenaeus, the principle of recapitulation implies that such a scientific approach to interpretation fails at a crucial point: it doesn't look for the unity between the two Testaments or for the unity between the God of creation and the God of redemption, and as a result it doesn't begin the interpretive process with Jesus Christ. In other words, for Irenaeus recapitulation is not just a neat, harmless device that people are free to use in order to apply the Old Testament Scriptures to their personal lives. Rather, he regards recapitulation as an essential tool for proper understanding of the Scriptures.

As a result, Irenaeus sharply assails his gnostic opponents for twisting the meaning of Scripture. He discusses in detail their mythological cosmology and their interpretation of Scripture, and he insists that they are "evil interpreters of the good word of revelation."[58] The reason is that by dividing up the Scriptures they fail the ultimate hermeneutical test, that of recapitulation:

> If anyone, therefore, reads the Scriptures with attention, he will find in them an account of Christ, and a foreshadowing of the new calling (*vocationis*). For

56. Baker, "Typology," 149.
57. Cf. chap. 2, sec. "Gregory's Literal Reading as Theological."
58. Irenaeus, *Against Heresies* 1, preface (*ANF* 1:315). Cf. Donovan, *One Right Reading?*, 57.

Christ is the treasure that was hid (*thesaurus absconsus*) in the field [Matt. 13:44], that is, in this world (for "the field is the world"); but the treasure hid in the Scriptures is Christ, since He was pointed out by means of types and parables. . . . When it [i.e., the law] is read by the Christians, it is a treasure, hid indeed in a field, but brought to light by the cross of Christ.[59]

Note that for Irenaeus Christ is already present in the field of the Old Testament and that we simply need to find him there. In other words, Irenaeus's hermeneutic of recapitulation is not something that follows *after* the meaning has already been ascertained, whether by means of a grammatical-historical or a historical-critical method. Rather, his hermeneutic of recapitulation is instrumental in ascertaining the actual, divinely intended meaning. By reducing theological interpretation to an afterthought, we render ourselves subject to Irenaeus's censure by failing to find the treasure hid in the field. For Irenaeus, the field of the Old Testament is a sacramental field, which hides the treasure of Jesus Christ.

Retrieving Sacramental Reading: Meaning, Virtue, Progress, and Providence

It will be clear that this book is not a dispassionate study of early Christian thought. While I have tried to read the primary sources carefully, my aim is to make clear why patristic readings of Scripture continue to be relevant. At the same time, it is not the argument of this book that we should simply copy the church fathers' exegetical choices — though in a number of cases it may be quite warranted to do so. I limit myself to the argument that a sacramental reading of Scripture lies at the heart of patristic interpretation, and it is this common patristic sensibility that I am convinced the church needs to retrieve today. Put differently, the conviction that Christ is the hidden treasure present in the *visibilia* of the Old Testament Scriptures seems to me something that carries over directly from the church fathers (via the Great Tradition of the church) to our situation today.[60] Over against the dualistic metaphysic of modernity, a sacramental reading of Scripture helps us recover an integrated vision of reality, one that is centered on Jesus Christ as the true reality (*res*), in which all created things (*sacramenta*) hold together.

59. Irenaeus, *Against Heresies* 4.26.1 (ANF 1:496). The first set of round brackets is original; I have added the second. For Irenaeus it is when Christ is no longer visible to physical eyes because of his passion that the Scriptures open up for us, that we can finally see Christ again, now in and through the apostolic preaching of the gospel. I owe this insight to Fr. John Behr.

60. I reflect in more detail on the question of nostalgia for an earlier time period in the epilogue of my book of sermons, *Sacramental Preaching*, 197–204.

It may be helpful to highlight some characteristics of this sacramental reading, seeing as they are central to patristic exegesis. I will limit myself to four features, which show the continuing significance of the sacramental character of patristic exegesis.[61] First, "meaning" is something different in the sacramental reading of the church fathers than in most contemporary historical interpretation. Though they are not indifferent to authorial intent, the fathers do not treat the meaning of Scripture as a historic artifact that we recover by means of exegesis. Stephen Fowl makes the observation that attempts to discover the one determinate meaning of the biblical text face a serious problem. This approach, comments Fowl, "must force Christians to view the overwhelming majority of the history of Christian biblical interpretation as a series of errors, of failed attempts to display the meaning of the text."[62] Fowl seems to me exactly right. If throughout history exegetes simply attempted to find the one right meaning, this would imply that up to today, all of these attempts have ended in failure. Meaning, for the church fathers, functions differently: it is centered on Christ and the church. Though meaning is obviously connected to its historical origins, for the church fathers it is more forward looking than backward looking.

As a result, the church fathers show little interest in finding the one true meaning of the text.[63] In the following chapters we will see many examples of the fathers being open to multiple meanings of any given passage of Holy Scripture.[64] Brian Daley, in a wonderful essay on patristic interpretations of the psalms, quotes the following passage from Augustine's *Confessions*: "So when one person has said 'Moses thought what I say,' and another 'No, what I say,' I think it more religious in spirit to say 'Why not rather say both, if both are true?' And if anyone sees a third or fourth and a further truth in these words, why not believe that Moses discerned all these things? For through him the one God has tempered the sacred books to the interpretation of many, who could come to see a diversity of truths."[65] In Augustine's high view of the

---

61. The four points that follow, therefore, do not simply form a general list of characteristics of patristic exegesis that I think are worth recovering. Such a list would surely include a focus on the ecclesial context and the rule of faith (confessional grounding) of our reading of Scripture. I draw attention to these matters in various places throughout this book. Here I am interested in the more restricted question of why it is that the sacramental character of patristic exegesis is worth retrieving.

62. Fowl, *Engaging Scripture*, 36.

63. Hans-Georg Gadamer's hermeneutical concerns are in line with this earlier patristic approach. See chap. 9, sec. "Christological Reading and the *Wirkungsgeschichte* of the Text."

64. See chap. 5, sec. "Scripture as Incarnate Logos," and chap. 10, sec. "Gregory of Nyssa and Multiplicity of Meaning."

65. Augustine, *Confessions* 12.31.42 (Chadwick, 270–71). Cf. Daley, "Patristic Exegesis," 199.

divine origin of Scripture, a single interpretation cannot possibly exhaust the riches inhering in the biblical text.[66] In other words, since the christological reality of the sacrament displays the very character of God, we may expect biblical meaning to be infinite in its possibilities. To retrieve the sacramental exegesis of the church fathers, therefore, is to open ourselves to the infinite mystery of meaning that God invites us to explore in Christ.

Second, the forward-looking element of patristic exegesis implies that the church fathers were interested in how the biblical text can transform its readers. My recent explorations of Gregory of Nyssa (ca. 335–ca. 394) have made me keenly aware how important virtue (*aretē*) was for the fourth-century Cappadocian.[67] He doesn't treat virtue as just part of the application of the text that follows after we've carefully articulated its meaning. Saint Gregory knows of no such gap between exegesis and application. Rather, he regards virtue as (1) a prerequisite for good reading, (2) the proper contents of the biblical text, and (3) the aim of the exegetical process.[68]

How does Gregory see each of these three roles of virtue functioning? Not everyone, avers Gregory, is equally ready to read the Song of Songs and to grasp its intended message in its greatest depth, and so virtue is the skill that makes for better reading. After he has preached his first two homilies on the Song, he makes clear to his listeners that his intent with these first two sermons has been that the "sense contained in the words" might be "washed and scrubbed to remove the filth of the flesh," so that his listeners may now be ready to listen to the bridegroom's own voice in the third homily.[69] In other words, one needs virtue to be able to understand or appropriate the biblical text properly. Furthermore, for Nyssen, the very subject matter of the text is virtue. The ultimate reason for this is that he believes virtue, in its true

66. Commenting on this same passage in Augustine, Martin Irvine observes: "The biblical text is by nature polysemous, and multiple interpretations are, therefore, not a cause for anxiety but a result of the very nature of interpretation." *Making of Textual Culture*, 270. He further suggests that the "supreme Text," Scripture, "can never signify its totality—the sum of its productivity of meaning—in one temporally instantiated act of interpretation, but continuously promises and postpones this totality through dissemination in a limitless chain of interpretations in supplementary texts. This model of textuality implies that a variorum commentary on the Scriptures compiled at the end of the world would still be temporally closed, superseded by a signless, transcendental grammar." Ibid., 271.

67. I have highlighted this throughout my book *Embodiment and Virtue in Gregory of Nyssa*, but particularly in the last chapter (211–46).

68. To be sure, the threat of moralism is a real one at this point. Thanks to his pervasive Christology and his doctrine of participation, Gregory escapes this danger, but history isn't without examples of theologians who use the biblical emphasis on virtue to advocate a self-help religion. See H. Boersma, *Embodiment and Virtue*, 215–21.

69. Gregory of Nyssa, *Homilies on the Song of Songs* 3.71 (WGRW 13:79–81).

sense, should be spelled with a capital V, since God himself is virtue. Gregory explains in his *Homilies on the Beatitudes* that by enabling us to participate in virtue, God allows us to participate in himself.[70] Since the biblical text has God for its true subject matter, it has virtue for its subject matter. And finally, since it is our aim to share more deeply in the life of God, virtue is also the very aim of biblical interpretation. As we will see in a later chapter, Nyssen treats the five books of the Psalter as so many stages of growth in virtue.[71] The very contents of this biblical book are shaped, according to Gregory, by these various steps, and it is the reader's task to detect them and to follow along in this process of ascent, so that he may be transformed by the biblical text. The purpose of the Psalter, claims Gregory, is "not to teach us mere history, but to form our souls in accordance with God through virtue."[72]

This emphasis on virtue keeps us from treating Holy Scripture as if it were merely a book that presents us with fascinating literature from a bygone age or that gives us invaluable information for studying the history of religion. The notion that we ought to read Scripture as one would any other book—a notion that has gained remarkable traction ever since Benjamin Jowett proposed it in his 1860 essay, "On the Interpretation of Scripture"[73]—is problematic not just because it narrows our perspective on what constitutes exegesis but especially because it undermines piety and reverence with regard to Scripture as divine revelation and as a result hinders progress in virtue. Brian Daley makes the observation that early Christian exegetes often defended their exegetical choices by saying such choices are more "reverent" (*eusebēs*) or more "appropriate to God" (*theoprepēs*) than other options. He comments: "It might be possible, in fact, to characterize the dominant procedure of Scriptural interpretation in the early Church as a 'hermeneutic of piety': a sense that the ultimate test for the adequacy of any explanation of a Biblical passage's meaning is the degree to which that explanation fits with Christian 'religion,' with the Church's traditional understanding of the holiness and uniqueness of the God who reveals himself in the Biblical story, and with the holiness to which all the story's hearers are called in response."[74] Daley's point is that a "hermeneutic of piety" has a stance of reverence toward the Scriptures, which serves as a filter for what counts as proper interpretation.

70. See chap. 10, sec. "Gregory of Nyssa and Multiplicity of Meaning."
71. See chap. 6, sec. "Restoring Harmony: Virtue and Emotions in the Psalms."
72. Gregory of Nyssa, *Treatise on the Inscriptions* 2.117 (Heine, 164).
73. Jowett, "Interpretation of Scripture," 330–433. Cf. Moberly, "'Interpret the Bible,'" 91–110.
74. Daley, "Patristic Exegesis," 202. Cf. also Daniel J. Treier, who treats "reading as piety" as one of the three main dimensions of precritical theological interpretation. *Introducing Theological Interpretation*, 41–45.

Third, and closely related to the previous point, different levels of maturity lead to different readings of Scripture. The Bible repeatedly warns its readers that as "infants" (*nēpioi*) or "fleshly people" (*sarkinoi*) they are only able to handle milk and aren't ready yet for the solid food that "spiritual people" (*pneumatikoi*) eat (1 Cor. 3:1–3; Heb. 5:12). Such admonitions imply different levels of maturity among the readers of Scripture, with greater maturity implying better reading skills. This reality is something to which modern readers are often ill-attuned. The reason for this blind spot is the dichotomy to which I alluded earlier: most contemporary interpretation intentionally restricts itself to the natural level of historical cause-and-effect. By contrast, for ancient Christian readers, such passages were crucial inasmuch as they illustrate the principle that greater spiritual maturity implies a better understanding of the sacred text.[75]

Origen, in his book *On First Principles*, famously distinguishes three levels of reading: the first—the literal reading of the "flesh of the scripture"—is for the "simple"; the second—edification in line with the "soul of scripture"—is for people who have made "some progress"; and the third—which gives us the hidden mystery of the "spiritual law"—is for those who have become perfect.[76] "For," writes Origen, "just as man consists of body, soul and spirit, so in the same way does the scripture, which has been prepared by God to be given for man's salvation."[77] Karen Jo Torjesen has argued that Origen describes the three groups as three stages of an "upward trajectory" with "three stages of development."[78] According to Torjesen, we are meant to map these three stages onto Origen's well-known classification of the three books of Solomon—Proverbs, Ecclesiastes, and the Song of Songs—where the first presents us with morals or ethics by way of preliminary instruction, the second teaches us physics or natural knowledge, and the third introduces us to enoptics, "by which we go beyond things seen and contemplate somewhat of things divine and heavenly."[79]

Seeing as these three books progressively lead us into the heavenly reality of union with Christ, the three dimensions of body, soul, and spirit too must be seen as steps in the process of salvation, explains Torjesen.[80] Accordingly, she argues, Origen's distinction between body, soul, and spirit doesn't describe an exegetical procedure or method that we are meant to apply to the biblical

75. See Clark, *Reading Renunciation*, 350–51.
76. Origen, *On First Principles* 4.2.4 (Butterworth, 275–76).
77. Ibid., 4.2.4 (276).
78. Torjesen, "'Body,' 'Soul,' and 'Spirit,'" 20.
79. Origen, *Commentary on the Canticle of Canticles*, prologue (ACW 26:40).
80. Torjesen, "'Body,' 'Soul,' and 'Spirit,'" 21.

passages we're explaining.[81] They are not three distinct senses or meanings as much as three different ways in which the exegete can edify the reader, depending on the spiritual progress the latter has made.[82] Origen is by no means interested in giving his reader a straightforward method for interpreting the Scriptures: "Body, soul, and spirit of Scripture do not designate three levels of meaning in the interpretation of texts but a threefold 'usefulness' of Scripture in ordering the doctrines that correspond pedagogically to the soul's progress."[83] Torjesen thus reminds us that Origen wants to turn his listeners from "fleshly people" into "spiritual people."

Of course, the notion of different levels of interpretation can cause elitism. This happens when we treat the various stages as compartments that are hermetically sealed off from one another, so that the stages no longer allow for the soul to progress from the one stage to the next. A related perennial temptation is for the "perfect" to look down on the "simple." In principle, however, the spiritual interpretation of the church fathers is not an exercise in elitism; there is no elitist hiding of spiritual truths from the majority of the Christian church. The intent is the opposite, namely, that as many as possible may come to recognize invisible things by means of visible things. Origen's *On First Principles* is intended to give pedagogical guidance on how to encourage people in their ascent to greater spiritual maturity and more in-depth reading of the Scriptures. Origen and others therefore preached their allegorical sermons freely to all, in hopes of advancing people's spiritual maturity and virtue as they grew closer to Christ. By contrast, as Harrisville and Sundberg point out, it is actually the principles of historical criticism, first introduced by Baruch Spinoza, that imply elitism inasmuch as only a small, academically trained group of people are properly equipped to do the work of historical exegesis. For Spinoza, "it is only an educated elite that is fit to judge what is and what is not reasonable. The true exposition of the Bible is confined exclusively to the intellectual class in society, not the masses."[84]

The fourth feature of sacramental reading that characterizes patristic exegesis is its grounding in divine providence—God's guidance of his people and of the world to their intended end. This importance of providence for early Christian exegesis stands out most clearly when we compare the allegorizing

81. Ibid., 22.

82. Ibid., 24. See also Byassee, *Praise Seeking Understanding*, 41–42.

83. Torjesen, "'Body,' 'Soul,' and 'Spirit,'" 24. Reno and O'Keefe refer to this pedagogical function as the "disciplining, ascetic logic" of the literal sense. The "literal sense of scripture," they argue, "like the bodily world created and governed by God, has an ascetic economy." *Sanctified Vision*, 135.

84. Harrisville and Sundberg, *Bible in Modern Culture*, 42.

in Hellenistic philosophy with that of Christian theologians. When ancient philosophers allegorized the Homeric myths, they did so in Homer's defense, since his descriptions of the violent passions of the gods appeared offensive when taken literally. R. P. C. Hanson mentions the example of Heraclitus's *Homeric Questions* in the first century AD, whose purpose, explains Hanson, was "to explain away anything that is theologically shocking." By allegorizing, therefore, Heraclitus turned Homer's embarrassing passages "into either psychological or scientific statements."[85] It will be clear that this philosophical practice of allegorizing had no need for divine providence. Divine providence, after all, presupposes a history that God faithfully sustains and governs.

In contrast to Hellenistic interpreters of Homer, the church fathers treated salvation history as indispensable. They recognized God as its author from the fact that he often acts in similar ways throughout history. Divine providence was recognized in the functioning of typology in Scripture.[86] The New Testament often discusses the salvation that God works in Christ through the Spirit in terms that remind one of events, people, or institutions mentioned in the Old Testament.[87] They thus function as types of New Testament realities. The relationship between Old Testament types and New Testament antitypes (or archetypes) is grounded within the biblical text. This recognition of typology within Scripture is by no means a patristic peculiarity. Twentieth-century Old Testament scholar Gerhard von Rad also draws our attention to it: "Not only in Paul and Hebrews, but in the Synoptic Gospels as well, the New Testament saving events are frequently regarded as the antitypes of events and institutions in the Old."[88] Von Rad concludes, therefore, that the Christ event of the New Testament sheds light on the contents of the Old. He comments that "we do not confine ourselves only to the Old Testament's own understanding of the texts, because we see them as part of a logical progression whose end lies in the future."[89] In other words, because within the progression of history we can see similarities between type and antitype, we are justified to recognize Christ within the Old Testament narrative.[90]

---

85. Hanson, *Allegory and Event*, 58.

86. Cf. Kevin J. Vanhoozer's comment: "The canonical connection between various types and antitypes (e.g., persons, things, events) finds its ground and justification in a belief in divine providence, in the continuity of God's plan as it unfolds in the history of redemption." "Providence," 644.

87. I discuss this in connection with the wilderness journey in chap. 4, sec. "Typology in Scripture."

88. Von Rad, *Old Testament Theology*, 2:365.

89. Ibid., 2:371.

90. For a helpful discussion of von Rad's approach to typology, see Nichols, *Lovely, Like Jerusalem*, 168–73.

In at least two ways, however, the church fathers moved beyond the kind of typology that I have just discussed—and the way in which they move beyond it illustrates why we shouldn't make a clear-cut distinction between typology and allegory. In the first place, the fathers did not restrict themselves to discerning typological relationships between the Old and New Testaments. They were convinced that the church is caught up in Christ's redemptive work, so that the archetype isn't just the person of Christ (and what he did) as an isolated figure; rather, the church, as his body, is included within the christological archetype. It is Christ *and* his church that are prefigured by a variety of types in the Old Testament. As twentieth-century patristics scholar Jean Daniélou makes clear, this means that the church's life—and in particular the liturgical practices of baptism and Eucharist—are God's miraculous acts of salvation (*mirabilia dei*) typologically foreshadowed in the Old Testament (and climactically fulfilled in Christ).[91] The church's own life, therefore, is included within the typological unfolding of salvation history.

Second, as mentioned above, the church fathers were convinced that the typological structuring of salvation history is grounded within divine providence. Because they believed both type and archetype to be anchored in eternal providence, there is a sense in which they thought of type and archetype as coinciding. The reason type and antitype (or archetype) look alike is, according to the fathers, that both participate in God's foreknowledge. Matthew Levering therefore speaks of "participatory exegesis" in his excellent book *Participatory Biblical Exegesis*. His main argument, as he writes at the outset of the book, is "that Christian biblical exegesis, in accord with the Christian and biblical understanding of reality, should envision history not only as a linear unfolding of individual moments, but also as an ongoing participation in God's active providence, both metaphysically and Christologically-pneumatologically."[92] Levering rightly argues that the doctrine of participation makes it possible for type and antitype to co-inhere. Using the terminology of this book, we may say that it is the sacramental linking of historical events to divine providence that allows us to recognize Christ (and the church) within the types of the Old Testament. It is the vertical, providential link between heaven and earth that enables us to see that eternal realities are made present—in the sacramental sense of "real presence"—within the historical events of the Old Testament narrative.

On this understanding, although the Christ event as the climactic event of salvation history follows chronologically after the Old Testament types that

---

91. For careful discussion of particular typological links, see Daniélou, *Bible and the Liturgy*, and Daniélou, *From Shadows to Reality*. Cf. the discussion in H. Boersma, *Nouvelle Théologie*, 168–80.

92. Levering, *Participatory Biblical Exegesis*, 1.

foreshadow it, theologically the Christ event is prior to the Old Testament types. As Jesus puts it in John 8:58: "Truly, truly, I say to you, before Abraham was, I am." And because Christ precedes Abraham—and is, we could say, "really present" in Abraham—the patriarch becomes a sacrament, a *sacramentum futuri* as the church fathers would say. It is the christological fulfillment, therefore, that is the prototype or archetype on which the Old Testament types are patterned.[93] Typological exegesis is sacramental in character only when it doesn't just take into account the chronological (horizontal) connection between similar events and people but also takes seriously their theological (vertical) interconnectedness. Christ, the archetype at the climactic point in salvation history, is at the same time the eternal archetype in which God's providential plan of salvation originates. God's providence isn't an abstract, arbitrary determination of history's unfolding made according to unfettered divine power (*potentia absoluta*); rather, it is God's fitting, Christ shaped plan that unfolds in line with God's character, so that throughout history we can say: that's typically the God we know in Jesus Christ. The basic reason typology and allegory cannot be sharply distinguished is that typology, properly understood, is not just a historically unfolding series of events; instead, typology, much like allegory, looks up from the types in history to their eternal archetype, the providential Word who has become incarnate in Christ.[94]

Conclusion

The separation of visible from invisible things in the modern period means that we often fail to recognize how the unfolding of history is anchored in God's providential care. Reformed theologian John Webster alludes to this when he comments that it has become difficult for us to affirm that "texts with a 'natural history' may function within the communicative divine economy."[95] Within the dualism of the modern period, it becomes hard for us to affirm divine providence and, *a fortiori*, to affirm that divine providence has a bearing on how we read the Scriptures. The cultural ethos of the modern period tempts us to deny that God is intimately at work within the "natural history" that we see described on the surface of the biblical text. As Webster puts it: "Part of what lies behind this denial is the complex legacy of dualism and

93. This explains Edward Pusey's predilection for the term "archetype" over "antitype." See chap. 9, sec. "Edward Pusey's Sacramental Typology."
94. Again, it is Origen who clearly perceived that historical events carry a sacramental dimension because of their grounding in divine providence. See chap. 5, sec. "History's Rightful Place."
95. Webster, *Holy Scripture*, 19.

nominalism in Western Christian theology, through which the sensible and intelligible realms, history and eternity, were thrust away from each other, and creaturely forms (language, action, institutions) denied any capacity to indicate the presence and activity of the transcendent God."[96] According to Webster, it is the dualism of the modern period that undermines a robust sense of divine providence.

The implications for biblical interpretation will be obvious. The loss of faith in providence implies a loss of faith in the sacramental typology of the church fathers. John J. O'Keefe and R. R. Reno describe this loss by saying that "we have trouble accepting the crossing of the Red Sea as connected in reality to the death of Jesus and Christian baptism. We regard it as present and real only in the imagination of the interpreter." The reason for this, they rightly suggest, is "our profound lack of confidence in the patristic under-standing of the divine economy"—in other words, our failure of nerve with regard to divine providence.[97] A sacramental understanding of the relationship between *visibilia* and *invisibilia*, between *manifesta* and *occulta*, results from a robust understanding of God's providential guidance in history, which sees in Christ (as well as in the types that adumbrate his coming) the true expres-sion of God's providential plan of salvation.

96. Ibid., 19–20.
97. O'Keefe and Reno, *Sanctified Vision*, 88.

2

LITERAL READING

Gregory of Nyssa and Augustine
on the Creation Accounts of Genesis

Patristic Interest in Reading by the Letter

The patristic proclivity toward spiritual exegesis raises the question of how seriously the church fathers took the literal meaning of the biblical text. One of the most common accusations against the scriptural interpretation of the church fathers is that by allegorizing the biblical text, they failed to take seriously the literal meaning and, along with it, the history it recounts. After all, if we use the elements of the text as occasions to reflect on matters that seem to have little to do with the text—human virtues, events in the life of Christ, prophecies about the church, and the like—then how do we take seriously the literal meaning that the author intended and that the original hearers would have understood?

This chapter deals specifically with the question of what the church fathers—in particular Gregory of Nyssa (ca. 335–ca. 394) and Augustine (354–430)—were doing when they read the creation accounts literally. My intent is not to give a complete overview of the two theologians' readings of the Genesis accounts. My purpose is more focused: through an analysis of their literal reading of the creation accounts, I hope to make clear some of the ways in which their literal readings are rather different from those of most modern readers. Though I will focus on the creation accounts, many other biblical passages would also have provided a suitable lens through which to look at the question of a literal reading of Scripture, and in subsequent chapters I will return to questions related to it (as well as to the place of history).

Nonetheless, the first two chapters of Genesis provide a particularly interesting test case. On the one hand, conservative evangelical readings often attach great importance to the literal and historical character of the creation accounts, and it is therefore of some interest to look at what the church fathers did when they provided a literal reading of these biblical passages. On the other hand, adherents to the Documentary Hypothesis in the tradition of Julius Wellhausen divide the two creation narratives between a Priestly (Gen. 1:1–2:3) and a Yahwist (Gen. 2:4–3:24) account, each with its own theological emphasis. The two interpretive approaches are in some ways each other's mirror opposites, and the history of the fundamentalist-liberal divide through much of the twentieth century witnesses to the sharp divergences between the two in terms of how they deal with the biblical text and with matters of Christian doctrine. Nonetheless, both sides are deeply invested in what lies *behind* the text—which for literalist evangelicals is the straightforward, historical events as recounted in these two chapters and for historical critics is the historical development of Israelite religion.

For many of us, schooled in some version of one of these two approaches (or perhaps a combination thereof), reading the church fathers on Genesis 1 and 2 requires a major adjustment. Their readings don't fit in either the conservative evangelical or the historical-critical camp.[1] The reason is not simply that the fathers' allegorizing of the text rendered them relatively unconcerned with authorial intent and historicity.[2] Something more basic is at stake: for Nyssen as well as for Augustine it was impossible to conceive of a literal meaning of Scripture in isolation from theological or spiritual considerations. My discussion aims to show that Gregory and Augustine's understanding of what it means to read the text literally is rather different from that of most modern exegetes, since they were convinced that only by taking into account the theological subject matter of the text can one do true justice to the literal meaning of the text.

---

1. To be sure, the reverential attitude that both Gregory and Augustine displayed toward the biblical text as divine revelation means that twentieth-century fundamentalism has in some sense a deep kinship with patristic exegetes, whereas this same attitude is missing from much historical-critical scholarship.

2. Augustine had an interest in both, and in particular in authorial intent. See, e.g., Augustine, *De Doctrina Christiana* [*On Christian Teaching*] 1.88 (Green, 27). At the same time, human authorial intent was by no means Augustine's overriding concern. Cf. Toom, "Was Augustine an Intentionalist?," 185–93.

Though it would obviously be erroneous to attribute to the church fathers the kind of historical consciousness that typifies contemporary exegetes, they did pay attention to questions of authorial intent, of the text's literal meaning, and of the historicity of biblical narratives. The great twentieth-century patristics scholar Henri de Lubac observes that Origen—often thought to be excessive in his allegorizing as well as lacking in historical and literal sensibilities—was actually keenly interested in the literal meaning of the text and in the history that it describes.[3] De Lubac notes that, for the church fathers, allegorizing elements of the text typically didn't preclude the acceptance *also* of a literal or historical level of meaning. De Lubac's overall message is that it is simply impossible to charge Origen with ignoring or denying the importance of the historical or literal meaning of the text.

De Lubac goes so far as to suggest that Origen took the historicity of biblical accounts much more seriously than do many contemporary historical critics. Origen, insists de Lubac, took "meticulous care" to justify the literal meaning of the flood (Gen. 6–8), of Lot's wife being turned into a pillar of salt (Gen. 19), of the ten plagues against Egypt (Exod. 7–11), of the Balaam narrative (Num. 22–24), and of the miracle of Joshua stopping the sun (Josh. 10)—the historicity of which is, of course, commonly rejected by modern exegetes.[4] De Lubac represents Origen's viewpoint by commenting: "It is always necessary to know this perceptible, literal, historical aspect. It is appropriate to begin by studying it; it normally serves as the basis for spiritual understanding. Sometimes it will be good to pause there awhile. If necessary, a geographical or topographical consideration will come to establish its basis in fact."[5] As I hope to make clear in chapter 5, de Lubac does exaggerate: Origen wasn't quite as insistent on the historicity of the biblical narratives as de Lubac suggests. Still, de Lubac makes an important point: Origen was not troubled by the miraculous nature of historical narratives in Scripture, and he seems to have accepted the historicity of most of the biblical narratives at face value.

The few exceptions that the Alexandrian theologian posited concerned biblical narratives describing human origins and the eschaton.[6] In other words, Genesis 1–3 was among the very few biblical accounts that Origen did *not* take literally. Indeed, usually the examples of Origen allegedly ignoring history are taken either from Genesis 1 and 2 or from the book of Revelation. De Lubac comments in a fine passage: "Origen reacted against those who,

---

3. The title of his 1950 book on Origen, *History and Spirit*, speaks to de Lubac's conviction that Origen was actually *very* concerned with history and with the historical meaning of the text.

4. De Lubac, *History and Spirit*, 107.

5. Ibid., 108–9.

6. Ibid., 116, 227.

in their interpretation of the eschatological texts, let themselves be deceived by the words and images to the point of concocting 'inept fables and empty fiction'; to the point, for example, 'of going so far as to believe that after the resurrection one would use bodily food and that one would drink wine, not at all from that true Vine destined for eternal existence, but from a material vine.'"[7] Origen appears to have been convinced that both the fall and the second coming put up barriers to our knowledge, such that we must read any descriptions of paradise or of the new Jerusalem allegorically. Peter Bouteneff notes that Origen "saw it as sheer folly to hold that Genesis 2 described a physical garden planted by God, with trees from which one could pluck and eat."[8] Not all his contemporaries were equally impressed with such allegorizing of the creation narratives. But it is important to keep in mind that in most of Origen's biblical exegesis, a literal reading of the text accompanied his allegorical interpretation.

To modern interpreters, Gregory's and Augustine's readings "by the letter" (*ad litteram*) may seem more akin to Origen's allegorizing than to our own literal readings of the text. In some ways, this is hardly surprising, seeing as both theologians were, directly or indirectly, influenced by Origen and his allegorizing approach. The writings of Origen, including their allegorical exegesis, deeply impacted Nyssen, even though he was perhaps careful to shy away from some of the more controversial aspects of Origen's theology. And although Origen had a more indirect influence on the bishop of Hippo (as it was the allegorical preaching of Saint Ambrose in Milan that first allowed Augustine to take the Christian faith seriously), Augustine was also acquainted with at least *some* of Origen's work on Genesis.[9] Thus, Origen's interpretive approach reached both pastor-theologians; allegory was important to both of them, and the duality of history and spirit that we see in Origen's interpretation also stamped the thinking of Gregory and Augustine.

What stands out in both theologians' readings on the creation narrative—and in what follows I will focus mainly, though not exclusively, on Gregory's *On the Making of Man* and on Augustine's *The Literal Meaning of Genesis*—is their concern with the actual words of Scripture and with the meaning of those words. Whatever we may think of their exegetical approaches, it is important to recognize that both were engaged in a literal exegesis of Genesis 1 and 2 that deeply reflects on what the text actually says. So if perhaps we have the impression that the church fathers ignored the literal meaning of the text, we

7. Ibid. De Lubac's quotation is from Origen's prologue to his *Commentary on the Canticle of Canticles*.

8. Bouteneff, *Beginnings*, 118–19.

9. Fiedrowicz, general introduction to *On Genesis*, 18.

must recall that two of the most well-known allegorizers among them took literal interpretation so seriously that they wrote entire books on the literal meaning of Genesis 1 and 2. As this chapter will make clear, theologians such as Saint Gregory and Saint Augustine did not downplay literal reading but opened it up to include the theological factors that they were convinced impinged on its proper handling.

Gregory of Nyssa, *On the Making of Man*

Saint Gregory's *On the Making of Man* is of particular interest because it deals with the intersection of exegesis and the human body and sexuality. Gregory wrote his book in the year 379 as he set out to complete a work that his recently deceased elder brother, Saint Basil of Caesarea (ca. 329–379), had left unfinished. Basil had written a book on the six days of creation, the *Homilies on the Hexaemeron*, but in this work he had not dealt with the creation of humanity.[10] Gregory explains in his introduction that he intends to complete Basil's venture so as to prevent people from blaming his brother for a shortcoming in his work on the six creation days.[11] Gregory was of course aware that Basil's *Homilies on the Hexaemeron* had mostly eschewed deliberate allegorizing and had presented a literal depiction of the creation event. Basil, perhaps taking care to avoid any charges of Origenist allegorizing, had commented in his final sermon:

> I know the laws of allegory, although I did not invent them of myself, but have met them in the works of others. Those who do not admit the common mean-ing of the Scriptures say that water is not water, but some other nature, and they explain a plant and a fish according to their opinion. They describe also the production of reptiles and wild animals, changing it according to their own notions, just like the dream interpreters, who interpret for their own ends the appearances seen in their dreams. When I hear "grass," I think of grass, and in the same manner I understand everything as it is said, a plant, a fish, a wild animal, and an ox. "Indeed, I am not ashamed of the gospel" [Rom. 1:16].[12]

Basil attacks allegorizing rather sharply. As Peter Bouteneff correctly points out, however, we should not read too much into these comments; Basil, after

10. For Basil's *Homilies on the Hexaemeron*, see Basil of Caesarea, *Exegetic Homilies* 1–9 (FC 46:3–150). Some believe that two other sermons, dealing with Gen. 1:26–27 and 2:7, are in fact also Basil's and complete his sermon series on the Hexaemeron. These two disputed sermons can be found in St. Basil the Great, *On the Human Condition*.

11. Gregory of Nyssa, *On the Making of Man*, preface (NPNF[2] 5:387).

12. Basil of Caesarea, *Exegetic Homilies* 9.1 (FC 46:135).

all, was well known for allegorizing Scripture.[13] Nonetheless, it remains true that in these sermons he avoids allegorizing the details of the biblical text of Genesis 1, and Nyssen continues in a similar vein as he exposits the biblical depiction of the origins of human existence in *On the Making of Man*.

One of the main impressions that even a cursory reading of Gregory's book leaves with us is its strong sense of otherworldliness, its contempt for this-worldly realities, including marriage, sexuality, and gender. Gregory's reading of the biblical text fits hand in glove with his ascetic theology, and this asceticism is served by Gregory's argument for a twofold creation of human beings: the creation of the universal "man" or humanity on the one hand and the creation of particular men and women on the other hand. Gregory grounds this separation in the biblical text: he splits Genesis 1:27 ("So God created man in his own image, in the image of God he created him; male and female he created them") into two parts. He makes the first part of the verse refer to the universal "man" or humanity, which God creates as a concept in his own mind—with the intent of eventually bringing it into existence (by means of a historical development that culminates in the eschaton). This universal is like a Platonic form—Gregory calls it the "prototype"—in which all particular or individual human beings participate.[14] So, when the first half of verse 27 says, "So God created man in his own image, in the image of God he created him," Gregory is thinking of the first "creation" in the mind of God of the universal "man," which is neither male nor female. Nyssen reads this first part of verse 27 through the lens of Galatians 3:28, where Saint Paul states that in Christ there is "no male and female." Christ is the universal; he is the prototype; he is the very image of God. And since in Christ there is "no male and female," the conclusion must be that when verse 27 claims that God created man "in the image of God," this universal "man" was not a male or a female figure.[15] The perfect figure of humanity, as it exists in the mind of God and as he will bring it into reality in the eschaton, is without sex or gender. Accordingly, when Jesus speaks of our heavenly future, he makes the point that human beings "neither marry nor are given in marriage," since they will be "equal to angels" (Luke 20:35–36). Saint Gregory concludes from this that if "the life of those restored

---

13. Bouteneff, *Beginnings*, 126–31.

14. I have argued elsewhere that for Gregory the creation of the universal "man" is God's foreknowledge of the "fullness" (*plērōma*) of all human beings at the end of time. H. Boersma, *Embodiment and Virtue*, 104–5. Johannes Zachhuber helpfully puts it as follows: "Without going into all the details of the interpretation of this text it seems evident to me that the creation of 'man' reported here is essentially the creation of that immanent form in its seminal aspect of potential perfection. This seminal form is only 'potentially' complete in its original state and therefore must develop into its actual pleroma." "Once Again," 95.

15. Gregory of Nyssa, *On the Making of Man* 16.7 (NPNF² 5:405).

is closely related to that of the angels, it is clear that the life before the transgression was a kind of angelic life, and hence also our return to the ancient condition of our life is compared to the angels."[16] For Gregory, in important ways, the end is like the beginning; that is to say, it is angelic.

The second part of Genesis 1:27 reads, "Male and female he created them." According to Gregory, this statement about gendered human beings has no reference to the image of God mentioned in the first half of the verse. The gendered character of human beings, along with the passions associated with sexual activity, is, Nyssen figures, excluded from the image of God. After all, he observes, the gendered character of human beings is "a thing which is alien from our conceptions of God."[17] This means, Gregory maintains, that there would have been no sexual activity in paradise. Should there have been procreation in paradise, in line with Luke 20:35–36 it would have been of an angelic kind, entirely different from sexual procreation as we know it today in our postlapsarian state. Gregory comments that "whatever the mode of increase [or procreation] in the angelic nature is (unspeakable and inconceivable by human conjectures, except that it assuredly exists), it would have operated also in the case of men, who were 'made a little lower than the angels' [Ps. 8:6], to increase mankind to the measure determined by its Maker."[18] So while the distinction between male and female was present before the fall (according to the second part of Gen. 1:27), this gendered existence was not part of the image of God (seeing as only the rational soul of the universal "man" was the image of God), and there was no sexual activity prior to the fall. For Gregory, only the human intellect is made in God's image. In contrast, our gendered, bodily existence puts us in touch with the irrational animals. This gendered existence is, after all, something that we have in common only with them.

It may seem odd that God created gendered human beings already in paradise if sexual procreation is strictly associated with the fall and with the passions. Gregory, however, came up with an ingenious solution to this conundrum. The reason God created gendered human beings already before the fall is that he knew that Adam and Eve would misuse their freedom and that the fall would occur:

> But as He perceived in our created nature the bias towards evil, and the fact that after its voluntary fall from equality with the angels it would acquire a fellowship with the lower nature, He mingled, for this reason, with His own image, an element of the irrational (for the distinction of male and female does not

16. Ibid., 17.2 (*NPNF*[2] 5:407).
17. Ibid., 16.8 (*NPNF*[2] 5:405).
18. Ibid., 17.2 (*NPNF*[2] 5:407).

exist in the Divine and blessed nature);—transferring, I say, to man the special attribute of the irrational formation, He bestowed increase upon our race not according to the lofty character of our creation; for it was not when He made that which was in His own image that He bestowed on man the power of increasing and multiplying; but when He divided it by sexual distinctions, then He said, "Increase and multiply, and replenish the earth." For this belongs to the irrational element, as the history indicates when it narrates that these words were first spoken by God in the case of the irrational creatures.[19]

According to Gregory, God anticipated that Adam and Eve would fall, and he accordingly gave them gendered bodies that would eventually, after the fall, allow them to procreate in the same manner as the irrational animals. While Gregory quotes the prelapsarian divine command that human beings increase and multiply (Gen. 1:28), he fails to draw attention to the obvious difficulty that this poses for his exegesis, namely, that the text seems to suggest that the presence of sexual activity is not dependent on the fall into sin. Since for Gregory it was important that sexual differentiation and activity—along with the passions—be treated as extraneous human attributes, merely the result of the fall, he conforms his literal reading of Genesis 1:27–28 to fit this theological anthropology. The exegetical result, however, seems less than satisfying.

To summarize our findings of Gregory's reading of Genesis 1:27–28 thus far, we can say that the Cappadocian father's exegesis is marked by two features. First, it entails a double creation of humanity: the conceptual, universal "man," the eternal prototype, was created in the image of God; God then created particular people, "male and female," based on his foreknowledge of the fall. Second, this twofold creation implies that prior to the fall there was no sexual activity. God created male and female human beings, but their sexuality was, we could say, latent or dormant. It became operative only after the fall. So sexual differentiation was an advance provision from God to enable human beings to flourish outside the garden and to reach the foreordained number of human beings in a fallen world. In short, although sexual activity may be important in today's world, Gregory was convinced it did not exist before the fall, and it also will not be there in the resurrection.[20]

The reading of Gregory as I have just presented it fits largely with the way he speaks about gendered existence and about the passions elsewhere. Throughout his writings—but perhaps most clearly in *On the Soul and the*

19. Ibid., 22.4 (NPNF[2] 5:411–12); see also ibid., 16.14 (NPNF[2] 5:406), 17.4 (NPNF[2] 5:407).
20. Ibid., 17.2 (NPNF[2] 5:407), 22.4–5 (NPNF[2] 5:411–12). John Behr presents a different interpretation of Gregory's *On the Making of Man* in "Rational Animal," 219–47. His reading sees Gregory as taking a positive view of the body and of sexuality, including prior to the fall. Cf. my discussion of Behr's position in *Embodiment and Virtue*, 100–109.

Resurrection and in the *Catechetical Oration* (both dating from roughly the same period as *On the Making of Man*)—Gregory argues that the animal passions, sexual activity, and eating and drinking, along with mortality, first arose in the postlapsarian situation. They are all part of human life in the "tunics of hide" that God provided for Adam and Eve after the fall (Gen. 3:21).[21] Toward the conclusion of *On the Soul and the Resurrection*, Gregory's dying sister Macrina instructs him by contrasting the resurrection body with the current, fallen condition of the human body:

> Since all that was mingled with our human nature from the irrational life was not in us before our humanity fell through vice into passion, then of necessity when we abandon passion, we shall also abandon all that is observed in company with it. No one therefore could reasonably expect in that other life the things that accrue to us through passion. If someone clad in a tattered tunic is stripped of that covering, he would no longer see on himself the unseemliness of what has been discarded. So also with us, when we have put off that dead and repulsive tunic made for us from the skins of irrational animals—for when I hear *skins* (Gen 3.21) I take it to mean the aspect of the irrational nature with which we were clothed when we became habituated to passion. In putting off that tunic then, we shall cast off along with it all that belonged to that skin of the irrational animals that was about us. And what we received from the skin of the irrational animals was sexual intercourse, conception, childbearing, sordidness, breastfeeding, nourishing, excretion, gradual growth to maturity, the prime of life, old age, disease, and death.[22]

The human cycle of life and death, along with everything that is caught up in that cycle, is the result of an embodiment in the form of tunics of hide, with which God clothed human beings after the fall. Saint Gregory was convinced that this mode of human embodiment is strictly limited to our fallen state: both in the original paradise and in our future heavenly bliss, the human body is angelic in character. As Lucas Mateo-Seco puts it: "The fact that the 'tunics of hide' are something added and extraneous to our nature implies that, in

21. There is a tension between Gregory's ideas that gender is prelapsarian according to Genesis 1:27 (in *On the Making of Man*) and that the "tunics of hide" are postlapsarian according to Genesis 3:21 (in *On the Soul and the Resurrection* and elsewhere). Perhaps Gregory means to suggest that the tunics of hide are a development subsequent to gendered existence, but the problems are (1) that all his descriptions of the tunics of hide (bodily life involving the passions, eating and drinking, sexual activity, and mortality) fit with the human division into genders; and (2) that gender distinctions lose their usefulness in the hereafter—as Gregory insists in his dialogue with Macrina. Gregory of Nyssa, *On the Soul and the Resurrection* 59–62 (Silvas, *Macrina the Younger*, 238).

22. Gregory of Nyssa, *On the Soul and the Resurrection* 74–75 (Silvas, *Macrina the Younger*, 239–40).

the resurrection, our bodies will be transformed according to the Scripture (1 Cor. 15.35–58)."[23]

Gregory's exegesis of Genesis 1:27–28 obviously serves his theological and spiritual interest of renunciation. As such, his interpretation fits with the understanding that he has of the garden described in Genesis 2 and 3. In chapter 19 of *On the Making of Man*, Nyssen raises a question about eating and drinking in paradise. He begins by asking whether the absence of food in the hereafter precludes a possible return to a paradisal form of life. After all, in paradise Adam had been allowed to eat of "every tree" in the garden of Eden (with the Hebrew word *'eden* meaning "delight") (Gen. 2:16), something that doesn't seem to fit with an eschaton without food and drink. But Gregory is unconvinced that there was physical food in the Edenic garden. Appealing to various biblical passages that speak of spiritual food and drink (Prov. 9:5; Isa. 12:3; Amos 8:11; John 7:37), he argues that "every tree" in paradise is a reference to "every form of good," where "the whole is one."[24] "Every tree" in verse 16 is identical, therefore, to the "tree of life" in verse 9: "It seems to me that I may take the great David and the wise Solomon as my instructors in the interpretation of this text: for both understand the grace of the permitted delight to be one,—that very actual Good, which in truth is 'every' good;—David, when he says, 'Delight thou in the Lord' [Ps. 37:4], and Solomon, when he names Wisdom herself (which is the Lord) 'a tree of life' [Prov. 3:18]."[25] For Nyssen, since Scripture insists that our Edenic delight must be in the Lord and that Wisdom is a "tree of life," it is evident that the Lord himself constitutes the delightful fruit of paradise. I have argued elsewhere that Gregory, in line with Origen, regarded paradise as an intelligible reality, to which we will be restored after death.[26] Neither in the original garden nor in the future paradise—which are one and the same according to Gregory— are there literal animals, trees, rivers, or luminaries.[27] And so, when in his *Homilies on the Beatitudes* Gregory reflects on the apostle Paul's hunger and thirst for righteousness, he explains that they are a paradisal desire for God himself: "I suppose the great Paul, too, who had tasted of those ineffable fruits from paradise, was at the same time full of what he had tasted and always

---

23. Mateo-Seco, "Tunics of Hide," 770. I cannot discuss in detail how Gregory believed the body can change shape, but the underlying reason is his Platonic, idealist view of matter, in which matter is made up of intelligible properties. Cf. J. Hill, "Gregory of Nyssa," 653–83; Arruzza, "La Matière immatérielle chez Grégoire de Nysse," 215–23.

24. Gregory of Nyssa, *On the Making of Man* 19.3 (NPNF² 5:409).

25. Ibid., 19.4 (NPNF² 5:409).

26. H. Boersma, *Embodiment and Virtue*, 44–50.

27. See Sutcliffe, "St. Gregory of Nyssa and Paradise," 342–44.

hungering for it."[28] We may conclude that Saint Gregory's spiritualized reading of paradise follows his overall ascetic theology.

Gregory's Literal Reading as Theological

Obviously, Nyssen's literal reading of the creation accounts differs markedly from the approach taken by almost every modern commentary. This has to do with the way his metaphysical convictions intersect with his exegesis. As I have already made clear, every interpretation of the text is shaped by the reader's metaphysical presuppositions. Usually these operate at a subconscious level, and therefore we sometimes think that we can read the Bible on its "own" terms, without metaphysical presuppositions. I don't think that works; everyone, it seems to me, does metaphysics.[29] Not every metaphysical approach, however, is equally suitable to the Scriptures, since metaphysical presuppositions come to the fore also in the biblical witness. Many of the church fathers, Saint Gregory included, were convinced that a Platonic metaphysic is remarkably—though by no means across the board—compatible with the biblical outlook. The overall argument of this book suggests they were right, and it is their Christian Platonism that allowed them to read the Scriptures in the way that they did.[30]

By dividing Genesis 1:27 in half—with the first half referencing the universal genderless humanity in the mind of God and the second half the actual, gendered human beings in paradise—Gregory may not directly be importing the Platonic metaphysical distinction between forms and their instantiations, but it's nonetheless clear that without a Platonic background such a distinction would make little sense. It is Nyssen's metaphysic that allows him to distinguish sharply between the first and the second half of verse 27—although, to be sure, Gregory would likely want to add that this metaphysic is christologically conceived, since it is Christ who is the genderless new humanity of Galatians 3:28, and all human beings find their ultimate eschatological reality in him. I think Gregory's reading of Genesis 1:27 is hard to defend: the division of this verse into two distinct parts doesn't do justice to the inner coherence of the verse and of the narrative as a whole. But his underlying distinction between a universal humanity and the creation of individual human beings is one that

28. Gregory of Nyssa, *Beatitudes*, Sermon 4 (ACW 18:129).
29. Tyson, *Returning to Reality*, 1.
30. Old Testament scholar Robin A. Parry argues at length that the participatory, sacramental approach of Christian Platonism is foreshadowed in the biblical canon. See his *Biblical Cosmos*, 168–79.

would have appealed to many in the premodern era, and—depending on one's metaphysical assumptions—there is no reason the distinction shouldn't be allowed to intrude upon one's interpretation of the text.

We see Gregory's theological considerations—shaped in part by his Platonic philosophical assumptions—come to the fore in his reading of the text in many ways. One interesting example is his appeal to divine foreknowledge in explaining why God created gendered human beings. Again, my point is not to defend this particular appeal to foreknowledge. But I do believe that Gregory is fundamentally right to allow theological categories to impinge on his interpretation of the biblical text—including its literal meaning. His theological approach to the text pays off particularly as he deals with the question of the functioning of the passions and of sexual intercourse in paradise. As we have seen, Gregory takes his starting point here in the eschatological future, which he believes to be without sexual activity (cf. Luke 20:35–36). Gregory's conviction that the eschatological paradise is basically the same as the garden of Eden (though only the former contains the realized perfection of all humanity in Christ) means that he cannot accept the notion of sexual activity in paradise—which in turn leads to his exegetically forced reading of Genesis 1:27. Needless to say, a world of theological considerations and assumptions enters into Gregory's reading at this point. Gregory's ascetic mindset, his Platonically colored view that the end is much like the beginning, his christological convictions (Christ as the one, universal, new human being), and his universalist eschatology (the notion that all human beings find their destiny in Christ as the new humanity) all shape his literal reading of the creation narratives.

It may seem as though Gregory's literal reading of Genesis 1–3 has turned out to be remarkably nonliteral. And in some ways that is true. Gregory spiritualizes or allegorizes many elements of the biblical text—the "man" of Genesis 1:27, as well as the food, the trees, and other created objects mentioned in the Bible's first couple of chapters—so as to preclude any hint that they refer to this-worldly, physical realities. It would not be out of place, however, to suggest that for Gregory the spiritual meaning is actually in some way *identical* to the literal meaning (or, as he would put it, the "surface level"—*to procheiron*—of the text). That is to say, Gregory would consider it inappropriate to read the creation narratives as if we were supposed to take them at face value, as though they described a literal unfolding of events in time and space. For Nyssen, there simply *is* no historical or literal meaning underlying the spiritual reading of the creation accounts. His theological and ascetical concerns render pointless the distinction between a literal and a spiritual reading of the creation narratives.

Another significant feature of Gregory's interpretation is the way in which he links passages from elsewhere in Scripture with a particular text that he is trying to understand. We already saw that in arguing that "every tree" (Gen. 2:16) and the "tree of life" (Gen. 2:9) are one and the same, both referring to the Lord himself, Nyssen has recourse first to various biblical passages that speak of the Lord as our food and drink—which, for Gregory, makes it at least plausible that we should regard the Lord himself as the fruit of the trees in paradise—and then to several biblical texts where the very terms used in Genesis 2 ("delight" in Ps. 36 [37]:4 and "tree of life" in Prov. 3:18) are linked to the Lord himself.[31] O'Keefe and Reno refer to this use of the biblical text— which we will encounter repeatedly throughout this book—as "associative" reading.[32] Ancient readers, they explain, relished verbal associations between different passages, which allowed them to leap from one passage to the next. O'Keefe and Reno see this approach as increasing both the breadth and the depth of interpretation.[33]

What is it that allowed Gregory—as well as other patristic exegetes—to make such verbal associations? It seems to me a combination of three factors is at work, namely, the unity of Scripture, the theological subject matter of the text, and the spiritual aim of all biblical interpretation. First, the unity of the Scriptures was a key assumption for all patristic exegetes. Gregory was not interested primarily in the history that lies behind a particular biblical text—either the history described in a narrative account or the developmental history of the text itself. Nor was he particularly keen on establishing the "biblical theology" of individual biblical books, an approach that generally takes the intent of the biblical author as its starting point and goal.[34] Instead, Gregory assumed that we have received the canonical Scriptures—Old and

31. Of course, the christological reading of "wisdom" and hence of the "tree of life" in Prov. 3.18 is itself grounded in passages such as 1 Cor. 1:24 and Col. 2:3, where Christ is identified as wisdom. Contemporary historical exegetes are divided on the legitimacy of reading Saint Paul's reference to Christ as our wisdom against the background of the book of Proverbs. See ch7n4 below. Gregory would likely have argued, rightly I think, that regardless of Paul's authorial intent, our understanding of the meaning of Scripture is determined by the theology that we derive from the canonical Scriptures as a whole.

32. O'Keefe and Reno, *Sanctified Vision*, 63–68. Frances Young refers to this same practice as "intertextuality." She comments, "It was natural, given the acceptance of intertextuality in the ancient world, to suppose that coincidence of word or phrase was significant." *Biblical Exegesis*, 133.

33. O'Keefe and Reno, *Sanctified Vision*, 66. In an insightful article, Randall S. Rosenberg reflects on the similarities between patristic interpretation and art (as understood by Bernard Lonergan); Rosenberg argues that Origen's "manner of proceeding resembles a kind of artistic improvisation." "Drama of Scripture," 138.

34. See the illuminating discussion of biblical theology in Treier, *Introducing Theological Interpretation*, 104–10.

New Testaments—as one unified whole and that the divine origin of this canonical unity informs our reading of the text.

Thanks to the theological exegesis advocated among the Yale school, some recent biblical interpretation has regained a sense of the theological significance of Scripture's unity. Brevard Childs, for instance, comments on the importance of "the Christian affirmation that the church's Bible comprises a theological unity," and he adds: "A level of theological construction is brought together in rigorous reflection in which the full reality of the subject matter of Scripture, gained from a close hearing of each separate Testament, is explored."[35] As part of this process, according to Childs, the interpreter "moves from the reality itself back to the textual witness."[36] The result is that, in light of the newness of Jesus Christ, both Old and New Testaments "take on fresh life."[37] By way of example, Childs comments: "As a result, in spite of generations of scholarly denial, few Christians can read Isaiah 53 without sensing the amazing morphological fit with the passion of Jesus Christ."[38] This unity of the Scriptures, centered on Christ, affects the way we read the Bible: "Our modern critical understanding of the task of exegesis, whether on the left or right of the current theological spectrum, needs major overhauling. . . . At a very minimum it implies that biblical interpretation cannot continue in its present isolation, cut off from the essential aid of church history, patristics, and dogmatics, but must strive to combine its discipline within the widest possible context of rigorous theological training in the service of church and world."[39] Childs' point that the unity of Scripture affects the way we read the Bible means in turn that we allow the tradition's theological witness to the unified meaning of the Bible to influence the way we read it.[40] Gregory's verbal associations are possible only because he believes that he is justified in reaching across the boundaries of individual biblical books (and their historical backdrop) in trying to determine their meaning for the church today.

Childs, in the comments I just quoted, focuses on the theological subject matter of the text. This brings us to the second central feature of Gregory's associative reading. Clearly, we cannot adequately explain the unity of the canonical Scriptures by appealing to the intent of the biblical writers. After

35. Childs, "Toward Recovering Theological Exegesis," 23.
36. Ibid., 24.
37. Ibid.
38. Ibid.
39. Ibid., 25.
40. Despite the influence of Childs' approach, not all biblical scholars are convinced by it, and many have criticized it. See, for instance, Barr, "Childs' Introduction," 12–23; Barr, *Holy Scripture*, 130–71; Collins, *Bible after Babel*, 140–42. For an insightful discussion, see Provan, "Canons to the Left of Him," 1–38.

all, their purposes in writing, though at some fundamental level unified, were varied. Gregory would insist that to explain the Scriptures properly we must have recourse to their shared subject matter, which is God in Christ—the one whom the church worships and confesses in her faith. Kevin Vanhoozer observes that "biblical scholars must have recourse to theology in order to make sense of the Bible's main subject matter, God," and he adds that only theological interpretation "ultimately does justice to the subject matter of the text itself."[41] Appealing to Werner Jeanrond, Vanhoozer insists, "Because biblical texts are ultimately concerned with the reality of God, readers must have a similar theological interest."[42] O'Keefe and Reno, similarly objecting to the notion that the subject matter of the text would be some historical event of the past that we can establish through source criticism or redaction criticism, maintain that the subject matter is the text itself.[43] I am not quite convinced by this description, since the text refers *beyond* itself to the God who reveals himself in and through the biblical text. But O'Keefe and Reno are surely right that the church fathers were textual people; they believed that it is through the very words of the Scriptures that God reveals himself, so that the words themselves—the *ipsissima verba*—matter.

For Gregory and other church fathers, therefore, the literal sense is not what we arrive at through some universally accessible scientific method. Such an approach mistakenly reduces exegesis to a purely historical discipline, ignoring the very subject matter that exegesis is meant to bring to the fore. Exegesis is in the first place a theological discipline: it aims to place before us the God we know in Jesus Christ. Historical investigation simply is not suitable for that task. Such scientific exegesis also falls prey to what Andrew Louth (following George Steiner) has termed the "fallacy of imitative form," by which the social sciences—including biblical exegesis—adopt a scientific "method" in imitation of the experimental hard sciences. This approach ignores that the humanities, which are historical in character, study human beings in particular temporal circumstances and cannot conduct verifiable experiments.[44] In other words, even if exegesis were a purely historical discipline, then still it would be erroneous to assume that some kind of objective method could lay bare for us the history behind the text. So, when theologians such as Basil and Gregory set out to investigate the literal (or "surface") meaning of the text, they looked to see what the words on the page, taken in their canonical context, say about their proper subject matter.

41. Vanhoozer, "Introduction," 20.
42. Ibid., 22–23.
43. O'Keefe and Reno, *Sanctified Vision*, 13, 116.
44. Louth, *Discerning the Mystery*, 10–11.

Finally, readers such as Nyssen combined their assumption of the unity of the Scriptures and their focus on the subject matter of the Scriptures with the recognition that the aim of exegesis is a spiritual one. Lewis Ayres and Stephen Fowl comment that we should "attend to those methods for the reading of Scripture that are most helpful for building up the Christian community in faith and appropriate practice."[45] Saint Gregory would certainly have echoed this comment. For him, the overriding aim of biblical interpretation is the growth of virtue, through which we come to participate more deeply in the life of God. In a number of his works, Gregory focuses on virtue as the aim of interpretation.[46] *On the Making of Man* is no exception in this regard.[47] A literal or surface reading of the text always already asks for the spiritual payoff. Stephen Fowl rightly speaks of a cyclical relationship between virtue and interpretation. On the one hand, theological interpretation helps us cultivate virtue; Fowl refers to this as "virtue-through-interpretation." On the other hand, being virtuous also helps us in our interpretation of Scripture; Fowl calls this "virtue-in-interpretation."[48] Verbal association was legitimate for readers such as Gregory inasmuch as it assists in the spiritual journey of the virtuous reader of Holy Scripture.

Some may want to argue that each of these three elements—the unity of Scripture, its subject matter, and its aim—takes us beyond biblical exegesis, and certainly beyond a literal reading of the Bible. Such an objection is entirely understandable. After all, for several centuries now, exegesis has been regarded as an (objective) historical discipline. But for Gregory it was not. Gregory, and with him the entire premodern Christian tradition, regarded the biblical text as a sacred text, which meant that it placed its own peculiar demands on the reader. The result is that for Gregory there was no such thing as a discrete, separate "literal" reading of the Bible, which we can juxtapose over against a subsequent "spiritual" or allegorical reading.[49]

45. Ayres and Fowl, "(Mis)reading the Face of God," 528.

46. I have summarized the place of virtue across Gregory's oeuvre in *Embodiment and Virtue*, 211–14.

47. Gregory begins the preface with a word of praise regarding the virtue of his brother Peter: "If we had to honour with rewards of money those who excel in virtue, the whole world of money, as Solomon says, would seem but small." *On the Making of Man*, preface (NPNF[2] 5:387). Gregory describes virtue as akin to a royal robe, allowing us to have dominion in paradise (ibid., 4.1 [NPNF[2] 5:391]), and he insists that we resemble divine beauty by means of our many divine virtues (mind, word, love, sight, hearing, understanding) (ibid., 5.2 [NPNF[2] 5:391]). Later in the same book, he insists that virtue arises when reason holds sway over the emotions (ibid., 18.5 [NPNF[2] 5:408]).

48. Fowl, "Virtue," 837–39.

49. This is clear, for example, from Gregory's division of *The Life of Moses* into a *historia* section and a *theōria* section. Gregory does nothing to hide his theological commitments and

Now, of course, a distinction can be made, and throughout the history of biblical interpretation it has often been made. But just as nature and the supernatural cannot be separated, so too literal and spiritual readings of Scripture cannot be separated. The reason is that just as, from the outset, nature is geared toward a supernatural end, so too, from the beginning, the church fathers' "surface" readings of the text aim for a spiritual goal.[50] In fact, the supernatural end of the Christian life is one and the same as the spiritual goal of interpretation. The purpose in both cases is the vision of God in eternal fellowship with him. One of the reasons the playfulness of patristic exegesis often frustrates modern readers is that the church fathers refused to treat the literal or historical level of meaning as a strictly independent endeavor, entirely separate from the supernatural end of their encounter with the sacred text. The fathers refused to separate the supernatural end of the beatific vision from the natural desire that leads up to it. They were persuaded that only a participatory, holistic approach takes seriously that, from the very outset of our earthly pilgrimage, the supernatural end of the beatific vision is our ultimate fulfillment.

Augustine's Turn to Literal Exegesis

Saint Augustine busied himself with the biblical creation accounts throughout his career. He was initially forced to do so by the threat of Manicheism.[51] Two of the main characteristics of this tremendously influential Persian religion were its metaphysical dualism and its literal interpretation of the Old Testament. With regard to the former, at the heart of the Manichean religion was a dualism between light and darkness, between goodness and evil, between the spiritual and the material. This overall dualism manifested itself in the notion of an eternal struggle between these two metaphysical principles. As a result, the Manicheans staunchly opposed Jewish and Christian monotheism, which entailed the idea of one good God as creator and redeemer. One of the Manicheans' trump cards was that their dualism allowed them to explain the existence of evil. Evil was not a difficult problem or a mysterious reality. Evil was a problem only for those—Jews and Christians—who believed in the existence of a single, good creator God.

---

repeatedly acknowledges divine providential governance (through miracles and otherwise) in the historical part of the commentary.

50. Henri de Lubac, in particular, has drawn attention to the link between a sacramental understanding of the nature-supernatural relationship and a sacramental approach to biblical interpretation. I discuss his approach in H. Boersma, *Heavenly Participation*, 144–53.

51. For a helpful discussion of Manicheism, see Coyle, "Mani, Manicheism," 520–25.

The Manicheans also insisted on reading the Old Testament narratives as literal accounts. As literal accounts, they were, so it seemed to the Manicheans, filled with ridiculous notions. For instance, the God of the Old Testament looked more like a human being than a god, and even as a human being he often came across as a rather immoral figure. The creation accounts in Genesis 1 and 2, in particular, were so obviously absurd that one could not possibly worship the creator God who appeared in them. These chapters' human ways of speaking about God, along with the divine activities described therein, seemed bizarre to Manicheans.[52]

The young Augustine himself was, for a time at least, impressed by the Manichean objections to the Genesis narratives. When, as a nineteen-year-old, he picked up a Bible, it seemed to him "unworthy in comparison with the dignity of Cicero."[53] In fact, Augustine was so taken by the overall Manichean position that he joined the sect for several years before he became a Christian, even though he apparently never made it beyond the outward group of "hearers" to the "elect" initiates of the sect. When, as an instructor in rhetoric, Augustine came to Milan and there listened to the sermons of Saint Ambrose, he was struck not just by the preacher's rhetorical skills—which is why Augustine had come to listen to him in the first place—but also by Ambrose's interpretation of the Scriptures. The bishop of Milan, so it appeared, had a way of dealing with the interpretive obstacles for which the Manicheans ridiculed the creation narratives. Saint Augustine relates in his *Confessions* the impression that Ambrose's preaching made on him:

> More and more my conviction grew that all the knotty problems and clever calumnies which those deceivers of ours [the Manicheans] had devised against the divine books could be dissolved. I also learnt that your sons, whom you have regenerated by grace through their mother the Catholic Church, understood the text concerning man being made by you in your image (Gen 1:26) not to mean that they believed and thought you to be bounded by the form of a human body. . . .
>
> And I was delighted to hear Ambrose in his sermons to the people saying, as if he were most carefully enunciating a principle of exegesis: "The letter kills, the spirit gives life" (2 Cor 3:6). Those texts which, taken literally, seemed to contain perverse teaching he would expound spiritually, removing the mystical veil.[54]

Ambrose's preaching made clear to Augustine that the creation of human beings in the image of God doesn't necessarily mean that the human body

52. Cf. Fiedrowicz, introduction to *On Genesis*, 25–38.
53. Augustine, *Confessions* 3.5.9 (Chadwick, 40).
54. Ibid., 6.3.4, 6.4.6 (Chadwick, 93–94).

is created in God's image—which had been one of the main Manichean occasions for ridiculing the God of the Old Testament. On that reading, the
implication appeared to be that God himself has a body. Ambrose alluded to
another option: it is reason, the human intellect, that constitutes the image
of God. Both here and in dealing with other biblical passages, Ambrose's
preaching, influenced by Origen, seemed to Augustine to provide a helpful
way of interpreting passages that attribute human characteristics to God.
Over against literalistic readings of such texts, Ambrose posited 2 Corinthians
3:6—"the letter kills, but the Spirit gives life." This Pauline interpretive principle required, according to Ambrose at least, an allegorical reading of those
passages that, taken literally, would yield implications that are not worthy of
God (*theoprepēs*, or *dignum deo* in Latin).

As a result, one of the first things Augustine did when he came back to
North Africa was to write a commentary on Genesis against the Manichele-
ans: *On Genesis: A Refutation of the Manichees* (388/389).[55] It is very much
an allegorical commentary on the text, heavily influenced by Ambrose's
Hexaemeron—his commentary on the six creation days. Later, when Augustine looked back on his first commentary on Genesis, he was no longer
so convinced of its strident, allegorical approach. Augustine reflected on his
youthful commentary by acknowledging:

> My aim was to confute their [i.e., the Manicheans'] ravings as quickly as pos-
> sible, and also to prod them into looking for the Christian and evangelical faith
> in the writings which they hate. Now at that time it had not yet dawned on me
> how everything in them could be taken in its proper literal sense; it seemed to
> me rather that this was scarcely possible, if at all, and anyhow extremely diffi-
> cult. So in order not to be held back, I explained with what brevity and clarity
> I could muster what those things, for which I was not able to find a suitable
> literal meaning, stood for in a figurative sense; I did not want them to be put
> off by being faced with reams of obscure discussion, and so be reluctant to take
> these volumes in their hands.[56]

Here Augustine makes clear that, for the sake of brevity and clarity, he had jumped
straight to allegorical interpretation in his early Genesis commentary against the
Manicheans. It would have taken too much, according to the young Augustine,
to explain the intricacies of the various possible literal meanings of Genesis 1–3.

The result, of course, was a rather polemical, and perhaps one-sided, piece
of work: over against the Manicheans' literal reading of Genesis, Augustine

---

55. Cf. the introduction to "Augustine on Genesis," in Nichols, *Lovely, Like Jerusalem*, 201–20.
56. Augustine, *Literal Meaning of Genesis* 8.2.5 (WSA I/13:348–49).

presented a straightforwardly allegorical account of these chapters. At the early Augustine's hand, the six creation days became six ages of the world.[57] Moreover, Augustine averred, people also had six days in their personal lives. And after working for those six days, doing "works that are very good, we should be hoping for everlasting rest."[58] The tree of life in the middle of paradise signified "the wisdom by which the soul is made to understand that it has been set at a kind of mid-point in the whole order of things, so that although it has every material, bodily nature subject to it, it has to realize that the nature of God is still above itself."[59] The four rivers in paradise stood for the four cardinal virtues: prudence, fortitude, temperance, and justice.[60] When the first human pair made themselves aprons of fig leaves, God clothed them with tunics of hide, which indicates that while Adam and Eve "set their hearts on the pleasures of lying after turning their backs on the face of Truth," "God changed their bodies into this mortal flesh, in which lying hearts are concealed."[61] So, like Gregory of Nyssa, Augustine interpreted the tunics of hide as the "mortal condition of this life."[62]

Much in this approach to the biblical text changed when Augustine grew older. He was not necessarily repudiating the allegorizing of his earlier years, but he did take the literal meaning of the creation accounts more seriously. With his Manichean phase in the more distant past, there was less of an immediate need to counter Manichean teachings by means of allegorical exegesis. Perhaps, also, he came to the realization that if he were to battle the Manicheans on their own turf, that of literal exegesis, this might result in a particularly powerful rebuttal of their teaching.[63] So, about five years after his initial refutation of the Manicheans, he wrote a second commentary, this time a literal one. Feeling inadequate to the job, however, he never finished it, so that this unfinished work has come to us under the title *Unfinished Literal Commentary on Genesis* (ca. 393–395). Augustine continued working on the first chapter of Genesis in the concluding three books of his *Confessions* (ca. 397–401), and he finally wrote his masterful tome on the interpretation of Genesis 1–3 between the years 401 and 416. Containing twelve elaborate chapters, the book was entitled *The Literal Meaning of Genesis*.

57. Augustine, *On Genesis* 1.23.35–41 (WSA I/13:62–67).
58. Ibid., 1.25.43 (WSA I/13:67–68).
59. Ibid., 2.9.12 (WSA I/13:79).
60. Ibid., 2.10.13 (WSA I/13:80–81).
61. Ibid., 2.21.31 (WSA I/13:92–93).
62. Ibid.
63. K. E. Greene-McCreight suggests that Augustine "realizes that allegorical interpretation alone is not sufficient to win the Manichees to the 'orthodox' faith." *Ad Litteram*, 33.

Theological Literalism in Saint Augustine

Augustine's mature commentary, *The Literal Meaning of Genesis*, is marked by a deep sense of exegetical humility. It is not a pseudo-humility that stems from a skeptical approach to the biblical text or from lack of confidence in the teaching of the church. Augustine does not turn to the Manicheans or to other heretics in order to find out whether perhaps he has been wrong in his approach to the biblical text; and when it comes to the church's teaching, Saint Augustine is quite clear on what he believes. The humility of the bishop of Hippo stems instead from his recognition that not all exegetical choices directly affect the teaching of the church or vice versa and that he is only one reader of Scripture, contributing together with many others to the church's insights into the riches of the biblical text. As a result, Augustine wears his exegetical prowess lightly, and he is often quite willing to allow for readings different from his own, as long as they fall within certain theological parameters.

Augustine displays in this commentary a fondness for approaching the biblical text by confronting it with a host of questions. We could even say that the standard way for Augustine to introduce the exegesis of a particular passage is not by stating what he thinks it means but by asking questions: Could it be that such and such, or could it be thus and so?[64] Often Augustine openly admits that the meaning is not quite clear to him, and he fails to make a choice among the various options that he has presented. He readily acknowledges at one point that "we in our ignorance have to fill in by conjecture the gaps which he [the Spirit] by no means out of ignorance left in the picture."[65] And even when in the end he does make an exegetical choice, Augustine will nonetheless often acknowledge the reader's privilege to opt for a different interpretation. At the beginning of book 9, when discussing why Genesis 2:19 states (in Augustine's Old Latin translation of the Greek text) that "God *still* fashioned from the earth all the beasts of the field," Augustine gives his own opinion and then comments: "And should you think that this knotty problem ought to be disentangled in a different way, you must pay as careful attention as I paid to all those details in order to reach my conclusion;

64. For a few examples, see Augustine, *Literal Meaning of Genesis* 3.24.36 (WSA I/13:239), 5.7.21–5.10.6 (WSA I/13:286–89), 9.2.3 (WSA I/13:377–78). Augustine argues in *Unfinished Literal Commentary on Genesis* 1.1 (WSA I/13:114) that a questioning approach is appropriate. In his later *Retractations* he comments: "In this work [i.e., *The Literal Meaning of Genesis*], many questions have been asked rather than solved, and of those which have been solved, fewer have been answered conclusively. Moreover, others have been proposed in such a way as to require further investigation." *Retractations* 2.50 (FC 60:169).

65. Augustine, *Literal Meaning of Genesis* 5.8.23 (WSA I/13:287).

and then if you can wrinkle out from them all a more likely conclusion, not only must I not oppose you, I will also be obliged to congratulate you."[66] For Augustine, few things are as brazen as an exegete making the claim that he is the first one finally to have got the text right. Indeed, the bishop comments that "the rash assertion of one's uncertain and dubious opinions in dealing with them [i.e., the Scriptures] can scarcely avoid the charge of sacrilege."[67] Augustine's insistence that the individual interpreter exhibit proper humility is due to the broad parameters of the confession of the church. Within its bounds, individual interpreters can roam with relative freedom, without sensing the need to impose their own understandings of the text on others. For Augustine, the virtue of humility is necessary to arrive at an appropriate literal reading of the biblical text.

It is evident, then, that Augustine, much like Gregory, took the literal meaning or the plain sense to be something rather different from what we today often understand by it. To be sure, Augustine—perhaps more so than Nyssen—did have an eye for authorial intent. Kathryn Greene-McCreight, who in 1999 wrote an excellent book on the way in which Augustine, Calvin, and Barth understood the "plain sense" of Genesis 1–3, rightly comments that "assessing the author's intention is indeed an important factor in plain sense reading for Augustine in *De Genesi ad litteram*."[68] But this concern for authorial intent is only one aspect of a much broader approach to the literal sense. At the very end of book 1, Saint Augustine explains with some care what he tries to do in ascertaining the literal sense:

> And when we read in the divine books such a vast array of true meanings, which can be extracted from a few words, and which are backed by sound Catholic faith, we should pick above all the one which can certainly be shown to have been held by the author we are reading; while if this is hidden from us, then surely one which the scriptural context does not rule out and which is agreeable to sound faith; but if even the scriptural context cannot be worked out and assessed, then at least only one which sound faith prescribes. It is one thing, after all, not to be able to work out what the writer is most likely to have meant, quite another to stray from the road sign-posted by godliness. Should each defect be avoided, the reader's work has won its complete reward, while if each cannot be avoided, even though the writer's intention should remain

66. Ibid., 9.1.1 (WSA I/13:376); see also ibid., 4.28.45 (WSA I/13:269), 5.1.1 (WSA I/13:276). We already saw that Augustine similarly shares his disdain in the *Confessions* for those who claim to know better than others what was in Moses' mind (see chap. 1, sec. "Retrieving Sacramental Reading: Meaning, Virtue, Progress, and Providence").

67. Augustine, *Unfinished Literal Commentary on Genesis* 1.1 (WSA I/13:114).

68. Greene-McCreight, *Ad Litteram*, 70.

in doubt, it will not be without value to have extracted a sense that accords
with sound faith.[69]

After insisting that there is a plurality of literal meanings, Augustine highlights
here three elements. The first is authorial intent, the second scriptural context,
and the third sound faith. So, as far as the literal meaning goes, Augustine
is indeed interested in arriving at the meaning that the human author had
in mind. Recognizing, however, the difficulties that often come up in trying
to grasp the author's intent, Augustine then turns to scriptural context, and
he argues that we may come up with a literal meaning based on contextual
factors, as long as our findings are in agreement with what he calls "sound
faith." And when also the context doesn't offer us help in establishing the
literal meaning, we may then simply turn to "sound faith" itself and give a
meaning to the text that is in line with this sound faith.

As modern readers, we are likely drawn to Augustine's interest in authorial
intent. And it is indeed the first element he mentions here. But we do need to
note that for Augustine "sound faith" also impinges on the literal meaning of
the text. Convinced as he is that the words of Scripture are given by God, he
also believes that Scripture doesn't contradict itself and, what is more, that
even the literal meaning of the text cannot possibly go against the church's
teaching, against "sound faith."

Greene-McCreight makes the point that for Augustine both the rule of
faith and the rule of charity determine, at least in part, the literal meaning
of the text. The so-called rule of faith, which is the basic trinitarian and
christological confession of the church, allows one to determine which readings of the text are plausible and which ones are not.[70] Greene-McCreight
points to an example where Saint Augustine discusses Genesis 2:7, about
God blowing into Adam's nostrils the "breath of life." Augustine rejects
the Manicheist notion, drawn from this verse, that the soul is of the same
substance as God. He comments:

> But we should really be advised by this very word to repudiate such an idea
> as dead against Catholic faith. We, after all, believe that the nature and sub-
> stance of God, which is believed by many, understood by few, to consist in
> the Trinity of persons, is altogether unchangeable, while as for the nature of
> the soul, who can doubt that it can change, whether for better or for worse?
> And accordingly the opinion that the soul and God are of one substance is

69. Augustine, *Literal Meaning of Genesis* 1.21.41 (WSA I/13:188–89).
70. For a helpful overview of patristic understandings of the rule of faith, see Williams,
Tradition, Scripture, and Interpretation, 67–79.

simply sacrilegious; for what else does it mean but that he too is assumed to be changeable?[71]

Note that Augustine rejects an exegetical interpretation on the basis of the church's teaching. The Manicheist literal reading of Genesis 2:7, he claims, cannot be correct because it goes against the Catholic faith. The plain sense, for Augustine, is not identical to an objective or neutral sense, to which everyone has equal access. The rule of faith sets limits on the exegetical options of the biblical reader.

In addition to the rule of faith, the rule of charity also comes into play in determining the literal meaning of the text. This is something on which Augustine especially reflected in *On Christian Teaching*, which he mostly wrote in 397. Here he comments—in line with Gregory of Nyssa, though the latter mostly uses the language of "virtue"—that the purpose of the Scriptures is "to love the thing which must be enjoyed," that is to say, to love God.[72] Augustine then adds that, although the purpose of charity doesn't undermine authorial intent, it does put it in its proper place:

> Anyone with an interpretation of the scriptures that differs from that of the writer is misled, but not because the scriptures are lying. If, as I began by saying, he is misled by an idea of the kind that builds up love, which is the end of the commandment, he is misled in the same way as a walker who leaves his path by mistake but reaches the destination to which the path leads by going through a field. But he must be put right and shown how it is more useful not to leave the path, in case the habit of deviating should force him to go astray or even adrift.[73]

For Augustine, as long as the aim of love guides biblical interpretation, we will reach our destination, simply because love itself *is* the destination. Authorial intent is by no means unimportant, but one may usefully read and interpret Scripture even if he misses the intent of the human author. At all times, the rule of charity ought to guide our interpretation. For Augustine, this gives the reader great "confidence," as he puts it, in reading the Bible.[74] After all, inasmuch as we keep the enjoyment of God—the rule of charity—first and foremost in mind, we cannot really go wrong in our exegesis.

In fact, the paradoxical conclusion that Augustine draws from his discussion is that perfect lovers of God do not need the Scriptures. The reason is

---

71. Augustine, *Literal Meaning of Genesis* 7.2.3 (WSA I/13:325). Cf. Greene-McCreight, *Ad Litteram*, 50–51.

72. Augustine, *De Doctrina Christiana* 1.84 (Green, 27).

73. Ibid., 1.88 (Green, 27).

74. Ibid., 1.95 (Green, 29).

that they have already reached the Bible's very aim. "Therefore," he says, "a person strengthened by faith, hope, and love, and who steadfastly holds on to them, has no need of the scriptures except to instruct others."[75] In short, for Augustine, the rule of faith and the rule of charity—the church's doctrine and morality—ought to affect our understanding of the literal reading of the text. The literal meaning is not something determined in a strictly "scientific" fashion apart from any considerations of the faith.

It may be helpful at this point to consider in greater detail how, concretely, theological considerations informed Augustine's literal exegesis. In the opening paragraph of book 1 of *The Literal Meaning of Genesis*, Augustine distinguishes literal from allegorical readings. He comments that all the divine Scriptures are twofold, so that "in accounts of things done, what one asks is whether they are all to be taken as only having a figurative meaning, or whether they are also to be asserted and defended as a faithful account of what actually happened."[76] Augustine makes clear that the rationale for figurative or allegorical exegesis is that a sacramental relationship is at work. "No Christian," he boldly insists, "will have the nerve to say that they [i.e., the biblical accounts] should not be taken in a figurative sense, if he pays attention to what the apostle says: 'All these things, however, happened among them in figure' (1 Cor 10:11), and to his commending what is written in Genesis, 'And they shall be two in one flesh' (Gen 2:24), as 'a great sacrament in Christ and in the Church' (Eph 5:32)."[77] For Augustine, Paul himself establishes that the Old Testament must be taken in a figurative (or sacramental) sense. The apostle treats the Old Testament as containing figures or sacraments of New Testament realities. Marriage, for example, is a sacrament that prefigures the relationship between Christ and the church. Despite this close, even sacramental link between the literal and the figural, however, *The Literal Meaning of Genesis* represents an attempt to separate and set aside the literal from the allegorical meaning. The bishop of Hippo queries, therefore: "So if that

---

75. Ibid., 1.93 (Green, 28). Cf. Greene-McCreight, *Ad Litteram*, 36, 51–52.

76. Augustine, *Literal Meaning of Genesis* 1.1.1 (WSA I/13:168). Similarly, in his *Unfinished Literal Commentary on Genesis*, before expounding the various historical ways of interpreting Genesis 1:1, Augustine clarifies that there are four ways of explaining the law: historically, allegorically, analogically, and aetiologically: "History is when things done by God or man are recounted; allegory when they are understood as being said figuratively; analogy, when the harmony of the old and new covenants is being demonstrated; aetiology when the causes of the things that have been said and done are presented." Augustine, *Unfinished Literal Commentary on Genesis* 2.5 (WSA I/13:116).

77. Augustine, *Literal Meaning of Genesis* 1.1.1 (WSA I/13:168). Here and elsewhere I have replaced Fiedrowicz's use of italics in rendering Augustine's biblical quotations with quotation marks.

text has to be treated in both ways, what is meant, apart from its allegorical significance, by 'In the beginning God made heaven and earth' (Gen. 1:1)?"[78] Augustine is going to focus on the literal meaning of this verse in isolation from its possible allegorical meanings.

This exposition of the literal meaning of the text remains, however, very much a theological one. As we have already seen, Augustine approaches the text with numerous questions. These questions don't concern either ancient Near Eastern historical background or the formation and development of the biblical text. Rather, Augustine is interested in what it is that individual words refer to, which doctrinal truths he can link to the biblical text, and what the theological implications are of our exegetical choices. So, when he reflects on the first words of Scripture, "In the beginning God made heaven and earth," Augustine asks about the phrase "in the beginning" the following questions: "Does it mean in the beginning of time, or because it was the first of all things, or in the beginning, which is the Word of God, the only begotten Son? And how could it be shown that God produced changeable and time-bound works without any change in himself?"[79] After raising a host of additional questions—none of which modern exegetes would typically ask of the text—Augustine finally indicates that it is the eternal Son of God who is the "beginning" to which the text refers (cf. John 1:1). In fact, Augustine makes a distinction between the first stage of creation by the Son of God in its yet formless imperfection (as "heaven and earth" in Gen. 1:1) in eternity and the subsequent conferral of perfection on this creation in the six days through the Word of God. This six-day creation, according to Augustine, took place in a single moment in eternity, as at that point God created the "seminal principles" (*rationes seminales*) of the tangible objects that he would later put into actual existence.[80]

Once he has arrived at this point, Saint Augustine is ready to relate his trinitarian convictions to the first verses of the text. The Son speaking implies the Father himself speaking as well, since God utters "in an eternal manner, if 'manner' it can be called, a co-eternal Word."[81] This in turn is the reason for the mentioning of the Spirit in Genesis 1:2, since the Spirit's hovering over the water indicates God's approval of the still-imperfect creation to which God was about to give form and perfection.[82] In a similar way, the various

78. Ibid., 1.1.2 (WSA I/13:168).
79. Ibid.
80. Ibid., 1.4.9 (WSA I/13:171–72). Augustine understands the six days (Gen. 1:3–31) as God simultaneously creating the intellectual seminal principles of creation, which is followed by the actual creation of human beings in time (Gen. 2:4b–25).
81. Ibid., 1.5.11 (WSA I/13:172).
82. Ibid., 1.5.11 (WSA I/13:172–73).

creation days indicate the doctrine of the Trinity. On each of the days, God (the Father who begets the Word) speaks (the Word of God), which in turn results in divine approval when God sees that his creation is good (the Spirit). Not only are each of the three divine persons involved in the creation of the world, but this creation—in its eternal point of origin as described in Genesis 1—is also tied to the immanent Trinity itself. The intellectual preparation of creation in eternity is directly bound up with the trinitarian relations of the begetting and procession of the divine persons.

Augustine engages in this kind of exegesis throughout *The Literal Meaning of Genesis*. His literal interpretation typically takes into account the theological subject matter of the text. He continually questions the text from the standpoint of Christian doctrine. Literal exegesis, for Augustine, is in no way separate from the theological teaching of the church. Particularly in depicting the creation of the world, God accommodated himself to human modes of thought, so that, as Michael Cameron puts it, "spiritual understanding was necessary even to recognize the literal sense."[83] Augustine understands this type of theological exegesis as "literal" in character; typology and allegory do not directly intrude upon his exegesis. Nonetheless, the literal exegesis that we find in *The Literal Meaning of Genesis* reflects on the words on the page in the light of the confession of the church.

Conclusion

This book makes the argument that the biblical interpretation of the church fathers is sacramental in character. This is particularly evident, as we will see in the chapters that follow, from the way in which the fathers relate the literal meaning of the text as the external, temporal sacrament (*sacramentum*) to the internal, eternal reality (*res*) revealed in Jesus Christ. For the church fathers, the biblical texts—and in particular the Old Testament narratives—find their fullest meaning in the reality of the mystery (*mysterium*) of Jesus Christ. In other words, the deepest theological reality of the Christian faith, God's self-revelation in Christ, forms the true subject matter of the biblical text.

In this chapter, by contrast, we have not made the sacramental move from literal to spiritual meaning. Instead, we have dwelled with the literal meaning itself, since both Gregory and Augustine wrote commentaries that focused on this literal meaning. The most startling finding with regard to their literal interpretation of the Genesis accounts, however, is that the literal meaning is

---

83. Cameron, *Christ Meets Me Everywhere*, 65.

hardly literal by contemporary standards. Both theologians were convinced that theological factors—the divine subject matter of the text, or the church's confession of faith—properly inform our understanding of the literal meaning of the text. Although they considered it quite appropriate to write a literal commentary (as opposed to a spiritual or allegorical one), they did *not* thereby separate the literal meaning of the Scriptures from their theological beliefs. That is to say, though Gregory and Augustine did not explicitly refer to their literal exegesis as sacramental in character, nonetheless, in some sense, that is what it is. For both theologians, already with a literal interpretation we can read in the creation accounts of angelic procreation, of Christ as the "tree of life," and of the triune character of God himself.

The reason Gregory and Augustine could read the creation accounts sacramentally—all the while convinced they were remaining on the surface level of the text—is that they were convinced that creation is always already theologically (and christologically) shaped. Jason Byassee, in his reflections on Saint Augustine's interpretation of the psalms, makes the point that when Augustine engages in a christological reading of the psalms, often he didn't think he was thereby leaving behind the literal meaning of the text. Rather, Augustine often regarded the christological meaning *as* the literal meaning. Byassee goes so far as to speak of a practice of "Christological literalism" in Augustine's exegesis.[84] "In many cases," writes Byassee, "the letter of scripture is already christological for Augustine, a procedure already announced in the *De doctrina christiana*. He is cued by a New Testament word or motif to a verbal or narratival link in the psalm to read the words there according to a particularly Christian grammar."[85] According to Byassee, Augustine regarded the literal meaning of the biblical text as already referring to Christ as its subject matter.

We have seen something similar in our reflections on Nyssen's and Augustine's expositions of the creation accounts in Genesis. For both exegetes, the line between literal and spiritual interpretations was blurry from the outset. Both interpreters refused to grant full autonomy to a putative realm of pure nature. There isn't any nontheological, independent, purely secular realm, fully shielded from the truths of the Christian faith. From the beginning, therefore—or, as Augustine would put it, from the eternal Wisdom of the Son of God—the biblical text always already bespeaks the realities of the Christian faith. From a modern perspective, it may seem as though Gregory and Augustine undermined the literal meaning of the text through the intrusion of

84. Byassee, *Praise Seeking Understanding*, 215.
85. Ibid., 219.

theological insights. The church fathers themselves, however, were convinced that they were in no way downplaying the literal meaning of the text. To the contrary, they believed—and rightly so, it would seem—that it is only by taking into account the theological subject matter of the text itself, understood according to the true faith of the Christian tradition, that one can do justice to the broad scope of the literal meaning of the text.

3

HOSPITABLE READING

Origen and Chrysostom on the Theophany of Genesis 18

Interpretation as Hospitality

Reading Scripture is like hosting a divine visitor. Patristic reflections on Abraham's welcome of the three visitors by the oak of Mamre remind us that when we interpret the Scriptures, we are in the position of Abraham: we are called to show hospitality to God as he graciously comes to us through the pages of the Bible. Hospitality, offered first by Abraham to the three strangers and then in the next chapter by Lot to the two angels when they require accommodation for the night, is central to the narrative. By looking at patristic treatments of it—particularly those of Origen (ca. 185–ca. 254) and John Chrysostom (ca. 349–407)—we will investigate what they have to say about the hospitality offered by Abraham as well as by Lot. We will also see what this hospitable response to God's appearing by the oak of Mamre has to teach us about how we may appropriately respond to God when he appears to us today in the Scriptures. That is to say, we will look at how Abraham's and Lot's hospitality connects with ours in biblical interpretation as we respond to God's visitation to us in divine revelation.

Human hospitality intertwines with divine hospitality.[1] Abraham's and Lot's actions are predicated on God first appearing to both of them. Genesis

1. I explore hospitality as a metaphor for divine grace in detail in *Violence, Hospitality, and the Cross*.

18 begins with the statement "God was seen by him [i.e., Abraham] near the oak of Mamre while he was sitting at the door of his tent during midday."[2] Similarly, the next chapter starts off with the words "The two angels came to Sodom at evening. Lot was seated beside the gate of Sodom." The famous theophany—the "appearing of God," literally—near the oak of Mamre makes clear that human hospitality is based on divine initiative. When God manifests himself—or, as Genesis 18.1 puts it, when he "is seen" (ōphthē)—he comes in the form of strangers visiting ("three men [*treis andres*] had come and stood above him," the text tells us); the biblical author tells of his coming in the form of words derived from human experience, words that we recognize because we use them in the humdrum of our everyday lives: "Let water now be taken, and wash your feet, and rest under the tree. And I will take bread, and you will eat" (18:4–5). Perhaps most striking about the event is the ordinariness of it all—human form and human words, to whom and to which it is easy to relate.

The paradox strikes us with the first verse of the passage: "God was seen by him near the oak of Mamre while he was sitting at the door of his tent during midday." We are taken aback by the theophany—precisely because it happens in the only way that God can be seen by human beings, namely, in the particularity of time ("during midday") and place ("near the oak of Mamre while he was sitting at the door of his tent"). Saint Thomas Aquinas insists on this particularity in the *Summa Theologiae*: "But the thing known is in the knower according to the mode of the knower."[3] Eugene Peterson does so as well, paraphrasing in *The Message*: "The Word became flesh and blood, and moved into the neighborhood" (John 1:14). With these last words, of course, we have moved from theophany to incarnation, and we should perhaps remind ourselves that the two are by no means to be treated as equivocal, as Saint Augustine reminds us in *On the Trinity*: "The Word in flesh is one thing, the Word being flesh is another; which means the Word in a man is one thing, the Word being man another."[4] All the same, whether God appears in the form of a theophany at Mamre, in the form of a servant in the incarnation, or in the form of words and sentences in Scripture, in each case he graciously condescends to us, extending his hospitality to us in the only way possible,

---

2. Throughout this chapter I will quote the Greek translation (the Septuagint) from Brannan, *Lexham English Septuagint*.

3. Thomas Aquinas, *Summa Theologica*, I, q.12, a.4 ("Cognitum autem est in cognoscente secundum modum cognoscentis"). See also ibid., I, q.75, a.5: "For it is clear that whatever is received into something is received according to the condition of the recipient" ("Manifestum est enim quod omne quod recipitur in aliquo, recipitur in eo per modum recipientis").

4. Augustine, *On the Trinity* 2.2.11 (WSA I/5:107).

namely, by stooping down to our creaturely realities of time and place. Human hospitality is grounded in divine hospitality. Or, as Saint John puts it, "We love because he first loved us" (1 John 4:19).

It is only in an analogous fashion that we can speak of divine hospitality as "hospitality." God's hospitality is rather unlike human hospitality. The Greek fathers marked this infinite difference between our hospitality to God and his hospitality to us by means of the distinction between *philoxenia* (hospitality) and *synkatabasis* (condescension). The term *philoxenia*—a word that is derived from *philos* (friend) and *xenos* (stranger)—describes the stranger turning into a friend. As the opposite of xenophobia (fear of foreigners), *philoxenia* is a virtue that counters our isolationist inclinations, which regularly coincide with nationalistic chauvinism and racial bigotry and feed into a hoarding mentality that neglects the poor and disadvantaged and so undermines the social fabric of society. *Philoxenia* enables us to open up our space to those who are different from ourselves so we can taste each other's foods, learn each other's languages, get to know each other's histories, and come to appreciate each other's customs. At a fairly obvious level, *philoxenia*, turning strangers into friends, is what we see described in the narratives of Genesis 18 and 19. Abraham extends hospitality to three men visiting him by the oak of Mamre; by means of a shared meal, he turns these strangers into friends. His nephew, Lot, extends hospitality to two angels (*angeloi* in 19:1) alone in dangerous city streets, thereby turning strangers into friends.

As we will see, both Origen and Chrysostom have a great deal to say about *philoxenia*; but they also use the term *synkatabasis*, which is a conglomeration of the elements *syn* (together), *kata* (down), and *basis* (going). *Synkatabasis*, then, literally means a "going down together"—or, to put it in the Latinized word we have already met, "condescension."[5] Contemporary patristics scholarship commonly objects to translating *synkatabasis* as "condescension," on the grounds that to call someone "condescending" is not exactly a compliment. To be condescending is the same as being patronizing, snobbish, or pretentious. Some therefore prefer to render *synkatabasis* instead as "accommodation,"[6] "considerateness,"[7] or "adaptation."[8] I want to go to bat, however, for the old word "condescension," taking my cue from

5. For a helpful overview of the use of *synkatabasis*, see Dreyfus, "Divine Condescendence," 74–86.

6. According to Arnold Huijgen, Calvin's pervasive use of the term *accommodatio* is the result of his borrowing from Chrysostom, the Genevan Reformer's favorite church father, though Calvin does so indirectly, via Erasmus. "Divine Accommodation in Calvin," 252–53.

7. R. Hill, introduction to *Homilies on Genesis 1–17*, 17–18. See also R. Hill, "On Looking Again at *Sunkatabasis*," 3–11; and Sheridan, *Language for God*, 41.

8. Rylaarsdam, *John Chrysostom*, 29–30.

Isaac Watts's early eighteenth-century hymn "Christ's Dying Love; Or, Our Pardon Bought at a Dear Price":

> How condescending and how kind
> Was God's eternal Son!
> Our misery reach'd his heavenly mind,
> And pity brought him down.

"Condescension" is a helpful term not only because it quite straightforwardly renders the Greek *synkatabasis* into English but also because, unlike any of its alternatives, it retains the notion of divine descent, a spatial metaphor that reminds us that God voluntarily and graciously stoops down from his divine position to accept the limitations and weaknesses of human frailty and sin.[9] No alternative to "condescension" does quite the same thing.[10]

It's understandable, then, that *synkatabasis* should become the object of patristic praise. *Synkatabasis*, for Origen, Saint John Chrysostom, and other early fathers, is not just a matter of ordinary *philoxenia*, as though we would know precisely what God's hospitality is like by comparing his to ours. We could say that *synkatabasis* is the principle by which God reaches out and adapts to human creatureliness and weakness; it is the way in which divine transcendence relates to the limitations of human existence and to the weaknesses of human sin. This means that our hospitality toward God (*philoxenia*) is predicated on his *synkatabasis*—his condescension—to us. The notion of *synkatabasis* is key to understanding the patristic approach to the divine-human relationship. *Synkatabasis*, writes David Rylaarsdam, "is central to Chrysostom's theological understanding of the way in which the incomprehensible God relates to humanity, whether in theophanies, Scripture, Christ, or the process of salvation."[11]

In what follows, then, I will deal with the theophany by the oak of Mamre as it is discussed by the third-century theologian Origen and by the fourth century preacher John Chrysostom. Both recognized the importance of divine

9. See "condescend, v.," OED Online, June 2015, http://www.oed.com/view/Entry/38511.

10. The above discussion should make clear that I believe the metaphor of hospitality (as depicting divine grace) is not without risks and has only limited, heuristic value. We can speak of divine hospitality only by way of analogy to human hospitality, which implies obvious limitations in terms of our understanding of God. Divine grace is by no means fully "captured" by the term "hospitality," and my distinction between *synkatabasis* and *philoxenia* is one way of alluding to the infinite difference between God's grace and the human response of faith and love.

11. Rylaarsdam, *John Chrysostom*, 30. Cf. R. Hill's comment that for Chrysostom *synkatabasis* "is an extremely rich notion, with a dozen or so distinct notes requiring explication." "St. John Chrysostom," 36.

condescension in trying to grasp something of the mystery of the Mamre theophany. This is not to ignore the obvious differences between the two theologians' approaches to the biblical text: they take note of different aspects of the narrative, and there are striking disparities between their respective treatments of the text. Much of this has to do with differences between the two interpretive traditions that they represent: although we cannot neatly categorize them into two separate schools of thought, there are undeniable differences between Alexandrian and Antiochene modes of interpretation.

An important lesson to draw from our comparison of Origen and Chrysostom is that the divine condescension at work in God's visit to Abraham, in the inspiration of Holy Scripture, and ultimately in the incarnation itself gives rise to a variety of approaches with regard to how we interpret the Scriptures. That is to say, when God steps down into the lives of human beings, drawing on their differing gifts, experiences, cultural circumstances, and ecclesial contexts, the particularity of the interpreters' situations contributes to the way in which they welcome God's grace into their lives. Saint Thomas's insight that "the thing known is in the knower according to the mode of the knower" has something to say about the way we treat the art of biblical interpretation. By no means am I suggesting that we reduce biblical interpretation to the subjectivity of the reader's response, and it is important to safeguard against a free-for-all interpretive pluralism. Still, if it is true that God condescends to us in the Scriptures much like he did in the Mamre theophany, then we may expect our responses to be varied—though a fitting response to divine *synkatabasis* will invariably take the shape of appropriate hospitality. A congruous, Abrahamic approach to interpretation bakes the mystical bread and prepares the good and tender calf in such a way that it does justice to the gracious character of the ultimate divine descent in Jesus Christ.[12]

Origen and Chrysostom emphasized different aspects of the paradox of divine descent, and we will see that their divergent approaches resulted in two rather different understandings of what the human response of hospitality should look like: Origen's vertical approach to hospitality goes hand in hand with allegorical interpretation, while Chrysostom's horizontal view of hospitality corresponds to greater interest in a literal reading of the text. Origen wants us to recognize that the condescension of the transcendent God enables us to see him; Chrysostom draws our attention to the fact that God's condescension renders him immanent to the interpersonal relationships

---

12. Throughout this book, we will come across ways in which the church fathers guarded against subjectivism in interpretation and tried to channel a fitting interpretive response to the biblical text.

where we can meet him. I will argue that the two approaches are not mutually exclusive but that instead a sacramental approach to interpretation recognizes the validity of both. Origen's focus on the reality (*res*) of the sacrament means that he discerns in Abraham's hospitality to God a face-to-face encounter with the transcendent Lord; Chrysostom's attention to the outward sacrament (*sacramentum*) means that he observes in Abraham's hospitality to the stranger a generosity rendered to the God who becomes immanent in time and space. Both approaches give expression to a basic truth of the incarnation: Origen bowing to the divinity of our Lord, Chrysostom praising his humanity; the two are complementary expressions of the mystery of God's ultimate *synkatabasis* in Jesus Christ.

Reading Scripture, then, is like hosting a divine visitor; it is a practice in which we engage in the art of hospitality, responding to God's hospitable condescension (*synkatabasis*) to us in the divine Scriptures. Despite the many exegetical differences between Origen and Chrysostom—and between the Alexandrian and Antiochene traditions more broadly—the two theologians are united in their conviction that the interpretation of Scripture is a hospitable response to the theophanic appearance of God in Christ, which takes place under the oak of Mamre.

Origen: The Son of God at Mamre

Origen, the early third-century theologian from Alexandria, devotes two homilies to the passage in question: *Homilies* 4 and 5 of his *Homilies on Genesis*. Origen doesn't reflect at length on who the three visitors are. The preacher from Alexandria more or less seems to take for granted that one of the three men is the pre-incarnate Son of God—the "Lord," Origen simply calls him—who along with two of his angels stands before Abraham. While the two angels will later depart by themselves in the direction of Sodom in order to destroy the city, Abraham, explains Origen, "received both him who saves and those who destroy," that is to say, both the Lord and his two angels.[13] In line with this identification of the three visitors, Origen observes that although Abraham ran up to all three men to welcome them (Gen. 18:2), "he adores one, and speaks to the one saying 'Turn aside to your servant and refresh yourself under the tree.'"[14]

As he discusses the end of the visit, with the Lord commenting on the pending doom for Sodom and Gomorrah—"After going down, therefore, I will see

13. Origen, *Homilies on Genesis* 4.1 (FC 71:104).
14. Ibid., 4.2 (FC 71:105).

if they are perpetrating according to their crying that is coming to me" (Gen. 18:21)—Origen notes the difference between the verbs of verses 2 and 21. At the outset of the narrative, when the three men visit "righteous Abraham," the text says that they "stood" (*heistēkeisan*) before him; but when the Lord is about to visit the evil cities of Sodom and Gomorrah, he comments that he is "going down" or "descending" (*katabas*) to them. Origen warns his hearers against taking the spatial metaphors literally. The reason Scripture depicts the Lord as "descending" to Sodom and Gomorrah is that he is going to visit them in response to human sin—something that, in Origen's view, obviously does not apply to Abraham, whom he repeatedly calls "the wise man." Origen takes the opportunity to reflect on the Lord "going down" in the incarnation:

> Therefore, God is said to descend (*descendere*) when he deigns to have concern for human frailty. This should be discerned especially of our Lord and savior who "thought it not robbery to be equal with God, but emptied himself, taking the form of a servant" [Phil. 2:6–7]. Therefore he descended (*descendit*). For, "No other has ascended (*ascendit*) into heaven, but he that descended (*descendit*) from heaven, the Son of man who is in heaven" [John 3:13]. For the Lord descended (*descendit*) not only to care for us, but also to bear what things are ours. "For he took the form of a servant," and although he himself is invisible in nature, inasmuch as he is equal to the Father, nevertheless he took a visible appearance, "and was found in appearance as a man" [Phil. 2:7].[15]

Origen does not simply equate the Lord "descending" to Sodom and Gomorrah with his later descent in the incarnation for the sins of humanity: the Alexandrian preacher distinguishes the two events, treating the former as a prefiguration of the latter. Nonetheless, in both events the same divine subject (God or the Lord) "descends," and in both events the Lord takes on human form. Origen's appeal to the famous Philippian hymn draws attention to God's *synkatabasis*, his condescension, which is necessary for him to be able to appear to sinful human beings. Descent, or *katabasis*, implies God taking on a "visible appearance," the form of a servant.

The sermon contrasts this "visible appearance" of the form of a servant with the Lord being "invisible in nature, inasmuch as he is equal to the Father." Though we can't be sure, it is quite possible that we're dealing here with an editorial gloss from Origen's fourth-century Latin translator, Rufinus of Aquileia.[16] The statement touches on a controversial point: Origen (or

---

15. Ibid., 4.5 (FC 71:108).
16. Cf. Ronald E. Heine's comment that "on the whole, the substance can be regarded as representing Origen's thought. The major exception to this statement is theological statements regarding the Trinity and the resurrection of the body. Whenever statements on these subjects

Rufinus) states explicitly that in his divine nature the Son is invisible, which makes him equal to the Father. The *synkatabasis* of the Son of God therefore implies that the eternal Logos *becomes* visible in the incarnation, whereas he is not so in his own nature.

The notion that the Son is "equal to the Father" and as such invisible in his own nature is significant inasmuch as it modifies the earlier theophany tradition. Around the middle of the second century, Justin Martyr had engaged in vigorous debate with his Jewish interlocutor, Trypho, over exactly this same passage.[17] The debate had centered on the divine Son of God, who according to Justin had to be distinguished from the Father and had become incarnate in Jesus Christ.[18] Trypho had maintained that there were actually *two* theophanies in the first two verses of Genesis 18: in the first one God himself appeared ("God was seen by him near the oak of Mamre" [18:1]); while in the second, three angels visited Abraham ("three men had come and stood above him" [18:2]). On Trypho's understanding, it was not God himself, therefore, but one of the three angels who told Sarah the good news that within a year she would have a son (18:14) and who then left, while the other two angels went on to visit Sodom (19:1).[19]

Justin had disagreed. He maintained that there is only one theophany in chapter 18 and that the "God" of verse 1 is one of the "three men" of verse 2: the same one whom Abraham straightaway addresses as "Lord" in verse 3 and who promises Sarah a son in verse 14. Justin pointed out to Trypho that this "Lord" is referred to as "God" three chapters later, when Sarah gives birth to her son (21:2).[20] Justin also explained that when the destruction of Sodom and Gomorrah is recounted, Scripture uses the term "Lord" twice in one sentence. Genesis 19:24 states that "the Lord rained on Sodom and

---

agree with the doctrines of the fourth-century Church they should be regarded with suspicion." Introduction to *Homilies on Genesis*, 38.

17. Thomas B. Falls suggests that the debate took place in Ephesus shortly after the Bar Kokhba revolt (AD 135) and that Justin Martyr wrote up the proceedings in Rome between the years 155 and 161. Falls, introduction to *The First Apology*, 139. Cf. the more technical discussion of Justin's exposition in Trakatellis, *Pre-Existence of Christ*, 60–68.

18. Kari Kloos argues that the Jewish context obscures Justin's real target: Marcionites rejecting a connection between Jesus and the Old Testament or adoptionists insisting that Jesus was merely human. *Christ, Creation, and the Vision of God*, 32.

19. Justin Martyr, *Dialogue with Trypho* 56 (FC 6:232). It appears that Trypho follows an established rabbinic line of exegesis, which included fascinating speculation on the identity and varying missions of the three angels. See Grypeou and Spurling, "Abraham's Angels," 181–203. Philo thought of the three visitors as the living God and Father along with both his creative power, called "God" (by which the living God created the universe), and his royal power, called "Lord" (by which he sustains the universe). *On Abraham* 24.120 (Yonge, 421). Cf. Lavery, "Abraham's Dialogue," 64–65.

20. Justin, *Dialogue* 56 (FC 6:232).

Gomorrah sulfur and fire from the Lord out of heaven."[21] The twofold use of the word *kyrios* (Lord) makes clear, insisted Justin, that we must distinguish between the creator as "Lord" (who *orders* the judgment) and another God, who is also called "Lord" (who *executes* the judgment).[22] According to Justin, therefore, one of the three figures appearing to Abraham is not an angel but the pre-incarnate Logos, here appearing in human form.[23] This Lord is "another God," a subordinate God, who is commissioned by the Father, the creator God, to punish Sodom.[24] So the Father remains invisible; he "has never been seen by any man."[25] By contrast, the figure appearing in the Mamre theophany is "another God and Lord under the Creator of all things."[26] Maria Doerfler summarizes Justin's position by explaining that the duality of lordship "reflects the existence of two gods. . . . One of these, the Father and Maker of all things, remains in heaven invisible and thus inaccessible to creation. The other, identified by Justin as Son and Logos, ministers to the Father in all things as his earthly representative."[27]

The sharp distinction between the invisible creator God and the visible God who appears in the Mamre theophany allows Justin to read the text christologically—though of course it is hard to avoid the impression that he sees the pre-incarnate Lord as occupying a lower rank than the creator God himself. Not surprisingly, this would become a bone of contention in the Arian controversies. Pro-Nicene theologians increasingly abandoned the christological reading of the Mamre theophany out of fear that it might support the Arian cause, substituting for it a trinitarian reading, with Augustine famously arguing for a trinitarian identification of the three visitors.[28]

21. Throughout the pre-Nicene period, Genesis 19:24 functioned as proof that the "Lord" who rained sulfur and fire on Sodom and Gomorrah was the pre-incarnate Christ, to be distinguished from the second "Lord" mentioned in this verse. See, for instance, Irenaeus, *Proof of the Apostolic Preaching* 44; Novatian, *On the Trinity* 18.16; Eusebius, *Book of the Gospel* 5.8 and *Ecclesiastical History* 1.2; Hilary of Poitiers, *On the Trinity* 4.29.

22. Justin points to the parallels of Ps. 109 (110):1 ("The Lord spoke to my Lord") and Ps. 44:7–8 (45:6–7) ("Your throne, O God, is forever and ever. . . . On account of this, God, your God, anointed you").

23. Bogdan G. Bucur, appealing to Larry Hurtado, argues that Justin's christological reading of Old Testament theophanies goes back to the New Testament itself. "Justin Martyr's Exegesis," 44–47.

24. Justin Martyr, *Dialogue with Trypho* 56 (FC 6:237).

25. Ibid., 56 (FC 6:231).

26. Ibid., 56 (FC 6:232).

27. Doerfler, "Entertaining the Trinity Unawares," 488.

28. Ambrose's *On Abraham* anticipates Augustine's trinitarian reading, though Ambrose (1) doesn't polemicize against the Arian cause, (2) follows Origen's allegorizing in several instances, and (3) urges the importance of hospitality toward other people. *On Abraham* 1.32–58 (Tomkinson, 19–29). Cf. the discussion in Mattox, "*Sancta Domina*," 112–17, 128–29. For

Origen makes several comments on the identity of the three visitors that indicate that he follows the interpretive tradition of Justin Martyr—one that was widely accepted also by others in the pre-Nicene Christian tradition.[29] Origen's homily differs from Justin's approach, however, in the comment that although the Lord "himself is invisible in nature, inasmuch as he is equal to the Father, nevertheless he took a visible appearance."[30] Origen (or his translator) is keen to point out the equality of the Father and the Son, something that fits with various other allusions to the Trinity in the homily.[31] So while Origen's homily retains the christological reading of the received tradition, the sermon clarifies the Father-Son relationship by insisting that by nature the Son is invisible just as the Father is invisible. In other words, Origen's sermon aims to prevent people from drawing subordinationist conclusions from seeing Christ in the Mamre theophany, and so Origen (or Rufinus) explains that the *synkatabasis* of the Word in the incarnation is genuinely a descent, one that renders the invisible visible.

Origen: Hospitality as Allegory

I have devoted a fair bit of space to Origen's christological reading of the passage. However, Origen himself doesn't dwell at any length on the identity of the visitors. It is Abraham's hospitality that is central to Origen's overall approach to the passage. The Alexandrian interpreter bookends the two homilies—the beginning of *Homily 4* and the end of *Homily 5*—by drawing attention to Abraham's superior hospitality in comparison with that of Lot.

Augustine's interpretation of the Mamre theophany, see *The City of God* 16.29 and *On the Trinity* 2.4. For insightful discussion on these developments, see Barnes, "Visible Christ," 329–55; Bucur, "Theophanies," 67–93; and Kloos, *Christ, Creation, and the Vision of God*.

29. Justin's christological exegesis of Gen. 18 is followed by Irenaeus, *Proof of the Apostolic Preaching* 43–46; Tertullian, *Against Marcion* 3.9; Novatian, *On the Trinity* 18; Eusebius, *The Book of the Gospel* 5.8–9; *Ecclesiastical History* 1.2; *Ecclesiastical Theology* 2.21; and Hilary of Poitiers, *On the Trinity* 4.24–31. Although all of these authors regard one of the three visitors in some way as the pre-incarnate Lord, they widely differ in how they understand the relationship between the Logos and the Father.

30. Origen, *Homilies on Genesis* 4.5 (FC 71:108).

31. Because the three men—or God—are said to stand "before him," Abraham mixes the bread "with three measures of fine wheat flour," at which point Origen comments: "Everything he does is mystical, everything is filled with mystery." Ibid., 4.2 (FC 71:105). And at the end of the homily, Origen comments: "But let us give attention to make our acts such, our manner of life such, that we may be held worthy of knowledge of God, that he may see fit to know us, that we may be held worthy of knowledge of his son Jesus Christ and knowledge of the Holy Spirit, that we, known by the Trinity, might also deserve to know the mystery of the Trinity fully, completely, and perfectly, the Lord Jesus Christ revealing it to us." Ibid., 4.6 (FC 71:111). Cf. Doerfler, "Entertaining the Trinity Unawares," 499–500.

Numerous elements in the biblical text make clear that Lot was "far inferior"[32] to Abraham. Whereas three men visit Abraham, only two come to see Lot. The visitors stand "before" Abraham (Gen. 18:2), but Lot meets them "in the street" (19:1). The visitors arrive at Abraham's tent at midday (18:1), whereas they come to Lot's place in the evening (19:1). ("Lot could not receive the magnitude of midday light; but Abraham was capable of receiving the full brightness of the light."[33]) The patriarch's eagerness to entertain his guests is clear from the great haste that he and his household demonstrate in preparing for their guests (18:2, 6–7). ("He himself runs, his wife hastens, the servant makes haste. No one is slow in the house of a wise man."[34]) Abraham serves bread made from fine wheat flour, as well as a good and tender calf (18:6–7), whereas Lot merely serves "ground corn" (19:3).[35]

This is not to say that Lot is altogether lacking in hospitality. Origen makes clear that Abraham's nephew escapes Sodom's conflagration because of the hospitality he shows to the angels: "Angels entered the hospitable house; fire entered the houses closed to strangers."[36] Nonetheless, when the angels tell him to escape from the valley of Sodom and run up the mountain (19:17), Lot is unable to do this: "For it belongs to the perfect to say: 'I have lifted up my eyes to the mountains, whence help shall come to me' [Ps. 120 (121):1]. He [i.e., Lot], therefore, was neither such that he should perish among the inhabitants of Sodom, nor was he so great that he could dwell with Abraham in the heights."[37] It is only after having lived in Zoar for some time that Lot gains enough strength to ascend the mountain and live there (19:30).[38] By contrast, Abraham has dwelled all along "in the heights" by the oak of Mamre, a name that Origen, following Philo, deciphers etymologically as meaning "vision" or "sharpness of sight."[39] "Do you see what kind of place it is where the Lord can have a meal?" exclaims Origen. "Abraham's vision and sharpness of sight pleased him. For he was pure in heart so that he could see God" (cf. Matt. 5:8).[40] Abraham's hospitality is such that he is pure of heart, which gives him the ability to see God in the Mamre theophany.

32. Origen, *Homilies on Genesis* 4.1 (FC 71:103).
33. Ibid.
34. Ibid., 4.1 (FC 71:104).
35. Ibid., 4.1 (FC 71:104–5).
36. Ibid., 5.1 (FC 71:112).
37. Ibid.
38. Ibid., 5.2 (FC 71:114).
39. Ibid., 4.3 (FC 71:106). Philo maintains that Mamre is a combination of *min* (from) and *ra'ah* (to see). Philo, *Supplement I*, sec. 4.1, p. 266. Either Origen has in mind the same etymology, or his language of "sharpness of sight" (*perspicacia*) is linked with the Hebrew *mar'eh* (sight, vision). See Heine, "Appendix," 390–91.
40. Origen, *Homilies on Genesis* 4.3 (FC 71:106).

Origen's exegesis focuses on Abraham's hospitality, and one might think that, in line with this, he would turn Abraham into a model for how to care for strangers and the poor. But Origen consistently declines to do so. Despite his emphasis on hospitality, nowhere does he allude to Hebrews 13:2 ("Do not neglect to show hospitality to strangers, for thereby some have entertained angels unawares"). Terms such as "example," "imitation," and the like are almost entirely absent from both homilies.[41] To be sure, in some sense Abraham does function as an example: it is hard to listen to the two sermons and not be awed by the stellar attitude of this perfectly wise character. Abraham's perfection is such that the Lord doesn't need to "descend" to come and visit him. The three men simply "stand" in front of him. After all, it is sin that would make one dwell in the valley and that would necessitate the Lord's *synkatabasis*. Abraham is a mountain dweller; he lives "in the heights."[42] As such, he is a model for a life lived "in the heights," in the presence of God. But Origen does not use the perfection of Abraham's hospitality to encourage his listeners to reach out to others around them.

This raises the question of what kind of hospitality it is that Origen discerns in Abraham in the Mamre theophany. A look back to the previous homily, on Genesis 17, may help us here. This homily makes clear that Abraham was not always as perfect as he appears in chapter 18. On Origen's understanding, Abraham was the recipient of God's gracious condescension or *synkatabasis* in chapter 17, where he receives the name change from Abram to Abraham and also undergoes circumcision.[43] Origen explains in *Homily 3* how Abraham along with others in his household was circumcised, describing in turn his circumcision of the ears, of the lips, of the flesh, and of the heart. Origen treats each of these expressions as allegorical descriptions of people who live pure lives. Regarding circumcision of the heart, Origen comments that it describes someone "who guards the pure faith in sincerity of conscience, about whom it can be said, 'Blessed are the pure in heart, for they shall see God'" (Matt. 5:8).[44] So Abraham encountered God's gracious *synkatabasis* back in chapter 17. By the time we arrive at the Mamre theophany, Abraham has reached such perfection that he is now able to see God: "God was seen by him near the oak of Mamre while he was sitting at the door of his tent during midday" (Gen. 18:1). In Origen's telling of the story, Abraham's vision of God

41. To be sure, at one point Origen comments: "Abraham, the father and teacher of nations, is, indeed, teaching you by these things how you ought to receive guests and that you should wash the feet of guests. Nevertheless, even this is said mysteriously." Ibid., 4.2 (FC 71:105).

42. Ibid., 5.1 (FC 71:112).

43. Ibid., 3.3 (FC 71:91–93).

44. Ibid., 3.6 (FC 71:98).

is the outcome of divine *synkatabasis*, which was accompanied by a name change and circumcision. Abraham's act of hospitality at the oak of Mamre, therefore, is hospitality extended to God as a fitting response to God's gracious condescension in entering into a covenant relationship with Abraham in the previous chapter. None of this has anything to do with caring for the poor.

In this light, it is hardly surprising that Abraham is fully aware of his visitors' identity from the start: "The wise man is not ignorant of whom he has received. He runs to three men and adores one, and speaks to the one saying 'Turn aside to your servant and refresh yourself under the tree.'"[45] Abraham deliberately adores only one of the three visitors; there is no entertaining of angels unawares. Origen sees the divine-human interplay of God's *synkatabasis* and Abraham's hospitality at work in the text; horizontal, interpersonal practices of hospitality are out of the picture. We should, therefore, not mistake Origen's encomium on hospitality as a moral admonition to reach out to strangers. The two sermons are mystical reflections on the intimate engagement between Abraham and the Lord. Living in the heights, near the oak of Mamre, pure of heart—Abraham sees God. This is human hospitality of so exalted a character that divine condescension has become an outmoded style of interaction, something restricted to an earlier, inferior phase in the divine-human relationship. Origen, in effect, has allegorized Abraham's hospitality: it no longer speaks of welcome at a horizontal level from one person to another; instead, it refers to one's openness to and readiness for a face-to-face relationship with God.

Within this overall context of allegorized hospitality, Origen also feels at liberty to allegorize the details of the narrative. "Everything [Abraham] does is mystical, everything is filled with mystery," claims Origen.[46] The bread that Abraham asks Sarah to bake (18:6) is called *enkryphias*, which, Origen explains, refers to secret, hidden, or mystical bread—seeing as it is derived from the Greek verb *enkryptō* (to hide or conceal).[47] Although Origen reads the theophany as the Lord appearing to Abraham accompanied by two angels, he nonetheless also sees a mystical allusion to the Trinity: because the three men—or God—are said to stand "before him," Abraham mixes the bread "with three measures of fine wheat flour"—a "mystical" reference, according to Origen.[48] The "good and tender" calf must be a reference to

45. Ibid., 4.2 (FC 71:105).
46. Ibid.
47. Ibid., 4.2 (FC 71:104–5). An *enkryphias* is a cake baked hidden in ashes.
48. Ibid., 4.2 (FC 71:105). This trinitarian reference may well be Rufinus's editorial gloss, since this vague identification of the three visitors with the three persons of the Trinity seems to contradict the overall christological reading of the theophany.

the incarnation: "What is so tender, what so good as that one who 'humbled himself' for us 'to death' and 'laid down his life' 'for his friends'? He is the 'fatted calf' which the father slaughtered to receive his repentant son."[49] The washing of the Lord's feet (18:4) was necessary because Abraham knew that the "mysteries of the Lord" would involve Christ washing his disciples' feet (John 13:5).[50] Furthermore, Sarah's presence behind the door of her tent (Gen. 18:9 10) can be read at three different levels: it is an example for wives to follow their husbands, it tells us that the flesh should follow the rational sense, and it teaches "something mystical" since in the exodus the Israelites followed God in the pillar of fire and the pillar of cloud (Exod. 13:21).[51] Finally, Origen allegorizes the Lord's apparent lack of knowledge of Sodom's sin (Gen. 18:21) by explaining that the Lord knows those who are his (2 Tim. 2:19) but not the wicked and the impious, saying to them that he doesn't know them (Matt. 7:23; 1 Cor. 14:38).[52]

Chrysostom: Divine Condescension at Mamre and in Scripture

With Saint John Chrysostom's *Homilies on Genesis*, we enter a rather different exegetical world from that of Origen. Chrysostom had grown up in Antioch, where he had studied under the famous pagan rhetorician Libanius, as well as under Diodore of Tarsus, the founder of a catechetical school near Antioch. It is probably while still serving as a deacon in Antioch that Saint John preached his sixty-seven homilies on Genesis, the first half before and during Lent and the rest after Pentecost, of the year 385, the year before he was ordained as a priest.[53] Chrysostom would go on to become the bishop of Constantinople (398), where his straightforward preaching against wealth and extravagance drew the ire of Empress Eudoxia, who saw her luxurious ways targeted by John's preaching.[54] The political intrigue that followed led to his condemnation by the Synod of the Oak (403) and to repeated exiles from that time onward until his death four years later. John's forceful and eloquent sermons earned him the moniker Chrysostom, meaning "Golden

49. Ibid. The biblical quotations are from Phil. 2:6; 1 John 3:16; John 15:13; and Luke 15:23.

50. Ibid. On a more immediate and practical level, Origen suggests that Abraham, by washing the Lord's feet, protected himself against divine judgment: dusty feet might be shaken off as a testimony against a deficient host, and in that case Abraham's punishment would be worse than the judgment the Sodomites were about to undergo (Matt. 10:15; Mark 6:11). Ibid., 4.2 (FC 71:105–6).

51. Ibid., 4.4 (FC 71:107).

52. Ibid., 4.6 (FC 71:109–10).

53. R. Hill, introduction to *Homilies on Genesis 1–17*, 5–6.

54. Kelly, *Golden Mouth*, 211.

Mouth," and the *Homilies on Genesis* that deal with the Mamre theophany and the destruction of Sodom and Gomorrah (*Homilies 41–43*) make clear that the nickname was well deserved.

Chrysostom, as a student of Diodore of Tarsus, was perhaps the most famous preacher that the Antiochene exegetical tradition produced, while the Alexandrian exegetes typically looked to Origen as their main source of inspiration. John's preaching avoided allegorizing and was down to earth, often focusing on themes of poverty and stewardship, and it tended to use straightforward exposition, with careful attention to details. This is not to suggest that Origen failed to pay attention to the details of the text: as we have seen, he loved analyzing the linguistic particularities of the text. But Origen was happy to move quickly from the surface meaning of the text to its higher, allegorical meaning. By contrast, Chrysostom warned against excessive allegorizing, which he believed ran the danger of imposing the reader's own notions onto the biblical text.[55] John followed his teacher, Diodore, who had tried to steer a middle path between what he regarded as unwarranted literalism and radical allegorizing: "This method neither sets aside history nor repudiates *theōria*. Rather, as a realistic, middle-of-the-road approach which takes into account both history and *theōria*, it frees us, on the one hand, from a Hellenism which says one thing for another and introduces foreign subject matter; on the other hand, it does not yield to Judaism and choke us by forcing us to treat the literal reading of the text as the only one worthy of attention and honor, while not allowing the exploration of a higher sense beyond the letter also."[56] John's Antiochene exegesis took seriously the divine *synkatabasis* into the vagaries of human history, and for Chrysostom this meant treating the human form (as well as the historical meaning) of the biblical text with due care and attention.

"Let us examine each of the words with precision," John suggests as he begins his exposition in *Homily 41*, "open up the treasure and disclose all the wealth concealed there."[57] The exegete's "precision"—*akribeia* in Greek—was for Saint John the corollary of the "precision" that characterized the biblical text itself, in which every word was a treasure that had to be dug up. As Robert Hill puts it: "For [Chrysostom] precision marks the narrative and description to be found in the Scriptures, demanding a like precision or care on our part by way of appropriate response to God speaking."[58] Following

---

55. Rylaarsdam, *John Chrysostom*, 127.

56. Diodore of Tarsus, prologue to the *Commentary on the Psalms*, as quoted in Froehlich, *Biblical Interpretation*, 86. Cf. Rylaarsdam, *John Chrysostom*, 128.

57. John Chrysostom, *Homilies on Genesis 18–45*, 41.7 (FC 82:405).

58. R. Hill, "*Akribeia*," 32. See also R. Hill, introduction to *Homilies on Genesis 1–17*, 18; Naidu, *Transformed in Christ*, 70–71.

with precision the details of the biblical text was, for Chrysostom, a matter of proper responsibility on the part of the exegete.[59]

In one of his later sermons on Genesis, as he deals with Jacob's wrestling with God at the Jabbok River (Gen. 32:22–32), the Antiochene preacher returns briefly to the Mamre theophany and links it explicitly with God's gracious condescension to human weakness:

> Don't be surprised, dearly beloved, at the extent of his considerateness (*synkatabaseōs*); rather, remember that with the patriarch as well, when he was sitting by the oak tree, he came in human form (*anthrōpou schēmati*) as the good man's guest in the company of the angels, giving us a premonition from on high at the beginning that he would one day take human form to liberate all human nature (*anthrōpinēn morphēn*) by this means from the tyranny of the devil and lead us to salvation. At that time, however, since it was the very early stages, he appeared to each of them in the guise of an apparition (*schēmati phantasias*), as he says himself through the inspired author, "I multiplied visions and took various likenesses in the works of the inspired authors" [Hosea 12:10]. But when he deigned to take on the form of a slave (*tēn tou doulou morphēn*) and receive our first fruits, he donned our flesh, not in appearance (*phantasia*) or in seeming, but in reality (*alētheia*).[60]

God's appearance to Abraham was condescension (*synkatabasis*) to the weakness of the patriarch's human condition.[61] This divine condescension means that God took the form (*schēma*) of Abraham's humanity, albeit in a vision (*phantasia*). On John's understanding, this shows God's care, as he slowly but surely prepared humanity for the incarnation itself, when he would appear not in the form of a vision but in reality (*alētheia*). In short, for Chrysostom, God's gracious condescension or *synkatabasis* takes into account human weakness (*astheneia*) as he steps down to the limitations of human beings—at first in the human form of the Mamre theophany, and then climactically in the incarnation itself.

What is more, for Chrysostom the biblical narrative, as it takes the form of human words, participates in this same *synkatabasis* of God. Ashish Naidu draws attention to this analogy between incarnation and inscripturation in Chrysostom's thought: "As in the incarnation of the Word, so in the Bible the glory of God is veiled in the flesh of the text—human language and thought. It is by the careful reading and study of the Scriptures that one encounters its true Subject: Jesus Christ. The historical incarnation therefore is viewed as a paradigm for the nature of the Scriptures: God's message is inextricably

---

59. Mitchell, "John Chrysostom (c. 347–407)," 574.
60. John Chrysostom, *Homilies on Genesis 46–67*, 58.12–13 (FC 87:159–60).
61. Cf. the discussion of this passage in Rylaarsdam, *John Chrysostom*, 91, 105.

fused in the human message of the text. God accommodates himself to the reader in the interpretive encounter, thus providing a divine pedagogy for the reader's edification and spiritual life."[62] Divine *synkatabasis* characterizes all of God's dealings with humanity, according to Chrysostom. The result is a profound sense that the human form matters, whenever and wherever God meets up with human beings.

This divine condescension, both to Abraham and to the reader of Scripture, comes to the fore particularly, according to Chrysostom, when Abraham leads the Lord and the two angels away from the oak of Mamre toward the city of Sodom and pleads with the Lord to spare the city. Chrysostom uses the noun *synkatabasis* no fewer than six times in *Homily 42*. "Wonderful is God's considerateness (*synkatabasis*) and his regard for the good man surpassing all reckoning," writes Chrysostom. "I mean, see how he converses with him, man to man, so to say, showing us how much regard the virtuous are accorded by God."[63] God's condescension to Abraham is clear from the back-and-forth dialogue between the two.

God shows a similar kind of condescension also to the biblical reader, when he says that he is "going down to see if their deeds correspond to the outcry reaching me, so as to know if it is true or not" (Gen. 18:21).[64] Chrysostom writes: "What is meant by the considerateness (*synkatabasis*) of the expression, 'I am going down to see'? I mean, does the God of all move from place to place? No indeed! It doesn't mean this; instead, as I have often remarked, he wants to teach (*paideusai*) us by the concreteness of the expression that there is need to apply precision (*akribeia*), and that sinners are not condemned on hearsay nor is sentence pronounced without proof."[65] Divine pedagogy, Chrysostom intimates, means that God graciously comes down to our level in the process of *synkatabasis*. The reader, in turn, must treat the text with precision (*akribeia*), so as to discern properly what it is that God conveys by means of this condescension. In this case, the point behind the concrete expression of God "going down" to find out the true state of affairs in Sodom is to make clear that sin is not condemned on the basis of hearsay.[66]

62. Naidu, *Transformed in Christ*, 82.

63. John Chrysostom, *Homilies on Genesis 18–45*, 42.7 (FC 82:421–22). Earlier, Chrysostom had introduced the notion of *synkatabasis* into the homily with the comment: "See the Lord's loving kindness in employing so much considerateness (*synkatabasei*) by showing regard for the good man and wishing at the same time to reveal the virtue that was concealed in his soul." Ibid., 42.6 (FC 82:421).

64. Ibid., 42.12 (FC 82:424).

65. Ibid., 42.12 (FC 82:424–25) (slightly altered for clarity).

66. Chrysostom seems to struggle somewhat at this point in the sermon. Immediately after this statement, he presents a lengthy digression on how it is *we* who must not pass judgment

Chrysostom sees God's *synkatabasis* coming to the fore particularly when Abraham begins to negotiate with God, gradually lowering his estimate of the number of righteous people in Sodom from fifty to forty-five, to forty, to thirty, to twenty, and finally to merely ten: "I mean, which of us living in the midst of countless evils could ever choose to exercise such wonderful considerateness (*synkatabasei*) and loving kindness in executing a sentence against our peers?"[67] For Chrysostom, God's condescension consists not just in his accommodation to the *feebleness* of human existence but also, and particularly, in his long-suffering, gracious attitude toward the *sinfulness* of human beings, as he is willing to spare the city even in the face of the inhabitants' overwhelming collusion with evil.

Chrysostom: Hospitality as Interpersonal Moral Virtue

John Chrysostom, much like Origen, places Abraham's hospitality at the center of his homilies on Genesis 18 and 19. It is Abraham's virtuous behavior that induces the Lord to appear to him by the oak of Mamre. This is clear from the patriarch's exemplary attitude in the previous chapter, when the Lord first appeared to him (17:1) and gave him the command of circumcision. Abraham—the "just man" (*ho dikaios*), as Chrysostom customarily calls him—obeyed God "without hesitating in the slightest."[68] This ready obedience is the reason God again appears to him in the Mamre theophany: "This, you see, is what our Lord is like: when he sees people grateful in the first instance, he lavishes further kindnesses on them and never desists from rewarding the gratitude of those obedient to him."[69] For Chrysostom, there is a harmonious interplay between divine *synkatabasis* and human hospitality: Abraham responds to the divine appearance of Genesis 17:1 with obedience, which in turn triggers the Mamre theophany of the next chapter, which then again moves Abraham to extend hospitality to God.

---

on our neighbor. Ibid., 42.13–14 (FC 82:425–26). He then suggests that God feigns ignorance of the situation in Sodom either so as to forestall any objections that he hasn't shown sufficient long-suffering or to convey to Abraham his compassionate and affectionate attitude. Ibid., 42.15 (FC 82:426).

67. Ibid., 42.19 (FC 82:428). Cf. Chrysostom's earlier exclamation in the same paragraph: "Who could worthily praise the God of all for his marvelous longsuffering and considerateness (*synkatabaseōs*), or congratulate the good man for enjoying such great confidence?" Ibid. And again a little later: "Do you see the Lord's considerateness (*synkatabasin*)? Do you see the good man's affection? Did you gain an insight into the great power of those who practice virtue?" Ibid., 42.21 (FC 82:429).

68. Ibid., 41.7 (FC 82:405–6).

69. Ibid., 41.7 (FC 82:406).

Abraham, then, is emphatically a "just man" for Chrysostom. But Chrysostom does not link this justice with any kind of intimate, mystical relationship between Abraham and the Lord. For Chrysostom, it is not the vertical relationship with God that is central, and it is not the visitor's divine identity that turns Abraham's act of hospitality into a just act. To be sure, like Origen, Chrysostom assumes that the identity of the three visitors is that of "the Lord of all with his angels."[70] The Antiochene preacher takes his cue from what he regards as allusions to the Mamre theophany in the Letter to the Hebrews and the Gospel of Matthew: "Hence Paul too said, 'Do not neglect hospitality, for through it some people have entertained angels all unawares' [Heb. 13:2], referring precisely to the patriarch. Hence Christ too said, 'Whoever receives one of the least of these in my name, receives me' [Matt. 18:5; 25:40, 45]."[71] So, like Origen, Chrysostom follows the well-trodden pre-Nicene path of a christological reading of the Mamre theophany.

But it is not the identity of his visitor as the pre-incarnate Christ that turns Abraham into a "just man." Unlike Origen, Chrysostom is of the opinion that Abraham does *not* know who his visitors are, and it is precisely this lack of knowledge that makes his virtue stand out.[72] Abraham, explains Chrysostom, simply "realized that people obliged to travel are in need of much service at that time particularly."[73] So when Chrysostom (and here he is no different from Origen) highlights how "the old man runs and flies," having "espied his prey,"[74] the patriarch's hurry is commendable not because he recognizes the Lord but precisely because he does *not* recognize him; Abraham assists someone he believes to be a needy stranger. In other words, Abraham's hospitality functions not at the vertical level, as something offered to God—though that is the serendipitous side effect—but it functions first and foremost at the horizontal level: it is rendered to unknown, needy strangers. In Chrysostom's theology, God condescends to the level of ordinary human relationships; it is at that level, therefore, that the An-

70. Ibid., 41.9 (FC 82:407). How such a theophanic appearance of the pre-incarnate Lord is possible, Chrysostom doesn't claim to understand, apart from simply observing that God condescends to human beings. Rylaarsdam, *John Chrysostom*, 105.

71. John Chrysostom, *Homilies on Genesis 18–45*, 41.7 (FC 82:405). Chrysostom again refers to these passages in the conclusion of *Homily 43* (43.32 [FC 82:453]).

72. Ibid., 41.10 (FC 82:407); 41.11 (FC 82:408). Similarly, Saint John claims that Lot was unaware that his two visitors were angels. Ibid., 43.10 (FC 82:440). He believes that the visitor showed his divine identity to Abraham when he exclaimed, "Nothing is impossible for God, is it?" (Gen. 18:14). Ibid., 41.24 (FC 82:415).

73. Ibid., 41.9 (FC 82:406).

74. Ibid., 41.11 (FC 82:407–8). Lot, according to Chrysostom, had a similar zeal; he "well nigh jumped for joy on seeing them, as though falling upon his prey and not missing the object of his desire." Ibid., 43.9 (FC 82:440).

tiochene preacher believes human hospitality ought to be practiced in the first place.

This emphasis on the moral virtue of interpersonal hospitality means that Chrysostom looks for additional biblical examples showing us how we can offer hospitality and generosity. He digresses, for example, on the hospitality that the widow of Zarephath offered to Elijah (1 Kings 17:8–16)—who, in contrast to King Ahab's purple clothing, wore "only a sheepskin."[75] The widow, despite her extreme poverty, welcomed the prophet by offering him her last meal. The sermon turns from the widow of Zarephath to the poor widow who placed the only two small coins she had in the temple treasury (Luke 21:1–4). Chrysostom's point throughout—quite in contrast to Origen's—is that we ought to "imitate" or "emulate" Abraham, the widow of Zarephath, the poor widow of Luke's Gospel, and Lot, by living hospitable lives: "Since this just man's [i.e., Abraham's] virtue (*aretē*) is so wonderful, therefore, let us bestir ourselves to imitation (*zēlon*) of him, and at least at this late stage let us acknowledge our own nobility, emulate (*mimēsōmetha*) the patriarch."[76] Hospitality demands that, regardless of the status of the person we encounter or of our own material condition, we freely share our possessions and extend liberal care toward the poor.

In line with this moral turn of the hospitality theme, Chrysostom sees the virtue of hospitality as intimately linked to other virtues. Sermons 41–43 constitute a lengthy exposition on the importance of virtue (*aretē*). Saint John makes the point at the beginning of *Homily 42* that Abraham not only was hospitable but also displayed care and compassion. Abraham is also a model of endurance, humility, and faith.[77] The inevitable upshot of this focus on virtue is a sharp challenge to the congregation: "So what excuse remains for us, when, despite the example of one human being adorned with every virtue, we prove to be so bereft as to have no intention to practice any virtue?"[78]

Lot too gets drafted into the service of modeling virtue; Chrysostom doesn't evaluate him nearly as negatively as Origen does. The virtue of Abraham's nephew is the topic of *Homily 43*: his association with Abraham "led him to the very pinnacle of virtue," claims Chrysostom.[79] Living in Sodom rather than in the mountains was by no means an obstacle to Lot; one need not be a desert monk to live a virtuous life. Saint John exclaims: "Where now are those who say that it is not possible for someone growing up in the environment

75. Ibid., 42.26 (FC 82:431).
76. Ibid., 42.5 (FC 82:420).
77. Ibid., 42.1 (FC 82:418).
78. Ibid.
79. Ibid., 43.2 (FC 82:436).

of the city to keep one's virtue, but for this is required retreat and a life in the mountains, and that it is not possible for the man of the house, with a wife and with children and servants to look after, to be virtuous?"[80] Whereas Origen contrasted the valley of Sodom (a hindrance to virtue) with mountainous territory (nearness to God), Chrysostom points out that virtue can flourish in either setting.

Though amelioration of the hardship of strangers and of the poor is important to Chrysostom, this is not the only aim of the virtue of hospitality. The preacher does not hesitate to point out that hospitality has payoffs also for the benefactor. Throughout his life, Abraham "exerted every effort of his own,"[81] as a result of which he was judged "worthy" (*ēxiouto*) of God's help.[82] We ought to follow Abraham in his virtue in "consideration of our salvation,"[83] to "gain a reward for it in the age that never ends,"[84] "taking great care of our salvation."[85] Appealing directly to his listeners' hope to be rewarded with eternal life, the Antiochene preacher intones:

> Let us all imitate this and display much zeal in practicing hospitality, not merely to receive some recompense for these perishable and corruptible things but to lay up for ourselves as well the enjoyment of immortal blessings. You see, if we practice hospitality, we shall welcome Christ here and he will, in turn, welcome us in those mansions prepared for those who love him, and we shall hear from him, "Come my Father's blessed ones, take possession of the kingdom prepared for you from the foundation of the world" [Matt. 25:34]. Why so? "For I was hungry, and you gave me something to eat; I was thirsty, and you gave me something to drink; I was a stranger and you made me welcome; I was in custody and you came to see me" [Matt. 25:35].[86]

Chrysostom's preaching is perhaps characterized by a somewhat one-sided focus on moral demands—along with the prospect of reward. To be sure, the three sermons do have an obvious christological center: the theophany is that of Christ appearing as one of the three visitors, and God's gracious condescension in the theophany is part of a divine pedagogy that foreshadows his *synkatabasis* in the incarnation itself.[87] At the same time, however, the incentive

---

80. Ibid., 43.4 (FC 82:437).
81. Ibid., 42.3 (FC 82:419).
82. Ibid., 42.2 (FC 82:419).
83. Ibid., 42.5 (FC 82:420).
84. Ibid., 43.8 (FC 82:439).
85. Ibid., 43.32 (FC 82:453).
86. Ibid., 41.25 (FC 82:416).
87. Christology also comes to the fore in Chrysostom's insistence that by showing hospitality to strangers we may welcome Christ himself. Rylaarsdam carefully points out the importance

for Christian living stems at least as much from the Abrahamic example as from God's *synkatabasis* in the pre-incarnate Christ. For Chrysostom, the life of virtue leads invariably to its fitting, eternal reward, and he regards it as his task, as a preacher, to lead his listeners toward that end.

Conclusion

We should not exaggerate the differences either between Origen and Chrysostom or between the Antiochene and the Alexandrian interpretive approaches. At several points in this book, we will see that the Alexandrian tradition was not indifferent to the historical or literal meaning of the text; and it is also true that theologians in the Antiochene school were keenly interested in exploring deeper levels of meaning in the biblical text.[88] Diodore of Tarsus, Chrysostom's erstwhile teacher, writes in the prologue to his *Commentary on the Psalms* that "we will not disparage anagogy and the higher *theōria*. For history is not opposed to *theōria*. On the contrary, it proves to be the foundation and the basis of the higher senses." Diodore did add a word of caution: "One thing is to be watched, however: *theoria* must never be understood as doing away with the underlying sense; it would then be no longer *theōria* but allegory. For wherever anything is said apart from the foundational sense, we have not *theōria* but allegory."[89] While Diodore obviously disliked allegory, neither he nor the Antiochene tradition as a whole restricted its exegesis to the literal sense. As Frances Young rightly observes in her book *Biblical Exegesis and the Formation of Christian Culture*: "The traditional categories of 'literal,' 'typological' and 'allegorical' are quite simply inadequate as descriptive tools, let alone analytical tools. Nor is the Antiochene reaction against Alexandrian allegory correctly described as an appeal to the 'literal' or 'historical' meaning."[90]

Young's observation holds true particularly for Saint John Chrysostom: he was perhaps even more interested in spiritual exegesis than were some of his Antiochene predecessors. Chrysostom often employed typology in his

---

(even priority) of divine grace in Chrysostom's synergistic understanding of salvation. *John Chrysostom*, 144–51. Still, these sermons on hospitality do not focus on the participatory union of the believer with Christ: the burden of virtue rests squarely on the listeners, who are told that Abraham's "own goodwill" (*Homilies on Genesis 18–45*, 42.2 [FC 82:419]) and the "effort of his own" (ibid., 42.3 [FC 82:419]) render him worthy of divine help.

88. Naidu, *Transformed in Christ*, 28, 47–51.

89. Diodore, prologue to the *Commentary on the Psalms*, as quoted in Froehlich, *Biblical Interpretation*, 85. Cf. Naidu, *Transformed in Christ*, 52–53.

90. Young, *Biblical Exegesis*, 2.

interpretation of Scripture, something of which Diodore had been rather wary.[91] Chrysostom, comments Ashish Naidu, "reflects a modification of the Antiochene hermeneutical tendencies in a direction which is broadly consonant with the Alexandrian tradition."[92] Origen and Chrysostom are not nearly as far apart as unwarranted caricatures may make us believe.

It is also evident that both preachers take seriously God's *synkatabasis* in relating to human beings. Both use the term—though Chrysostom does so much more pervasively than Origen, and Origen doesn't use the term in his sermons on the Mamre theophany. Both see God's self-revelation—in theophany, in the incarnation, and in the biblical text—as involving divine condescension. Both wish to do justice to the divine transcendence as well as to the divine immanence implied in the theophany. *Synkatabasis*, David Rylaarsdam points out, both reveals and conceals God:

> On the one hand, adapted revelation overcomes the dissimilarity between God and humans by forming a symbolic bridge between the two. Since a corporeal symbol has similarities to the spiritual reality it represents, some knowledge is possible. Yet, on the other hand, Chrysostom's understanding of the symbolic character of revelation does not compromise the incomprehensibility of God. For a symbol and the reality it signifies are not only similar but also different. God is always higher than the reach of any symbolic bridge. In revealing himself, he appears not as he is. Symbols are a limited means of communication, but adequate to lead humans to faith in God's plan of redemption and to a heavenly way of life.[93]

Rylaarsdam's comments hold true not only for Chrysostom but also for Origen. Both preachers believed that God's *synkatabasis* at Mamre reveals and conceals at the same time; similarly, both were convinced that also the incarnation and the inspired Scripture reveal and conceal at the same time.

Yet it is not overly difficult to enumerate the differences between Origen's and Chrysostom's approaches. They each have their own distinct reading strategies and their own styles of preaching. These differences have to do with the fact that the two authors do represent two fairly distinct theological and interpretive traditions. The Alexandrian tradition of Origen treated the allegorizing of the Jewish philosopher and exegete Philo as something that, to a large extent, was transferable to the Christian tradition. The reason for this is that Origen and other Alexandrian exegetes believed that the apostle

91. Naidu, *Transformed in Christ*, 72–75.
92. Ibid., 19.
93. Rylaarsdam, *John Chrysostom*, 103.

Paul himself had allegorized the biblical text. Origen was convinced, therefore, that one couldn't possibly avoid allegorizing if one wished to do justice to the newness of the Christ event.[94] The Antiochene tradition of Diodore of Tarsus and Saint John Chrysostom was much more reticent in the use of allegory: both exegetes were distrustful of the speculative turn that the practice of allegorizing might take, preferring the term *theōria* (contemplation) instead.

The differences in nuance between the Alexandrian and Antiochene traditions are reflected in the exegetical and homiletical choices that Origen and Chrysostom make. The object of Abraham's hospitality is, for Origen, the Lord himself; for Chrysostom, this is true only indirectly: Abraham in the first instance reaches out to a fellow human being in need of food and drink. As a result, Origen's sermon has a more mystical feel. He wants to explore how the biblical text describes the soul's growth in perfection in relationship with God; Chrysostom, by contrast, is interested in fostering particular embodied practices in his listeners. He wants their behavior to be like that of the "just man." Although both exegetes pay detailed attention to the particulars of the text, Origen often does this so that he can determine the allegorical meaning of various textual details, while Chrysostom does it mostly to explore the numerous ways in which Scripture brings to the fore the moral virtues of the main characters of the narrative. Perhaps the difference between the two preachers can best be expressed by noting that for Origen divine theophany is inextricably bound up with transformed *vision* ("sharpness of sight"), whereas Chrysostom connects it with transformed *virtue* (reaching out with compassion). Origen is more vertical whereas Chrysostom is more horizontal in his reading of the Mamre theophany.

Finally, we can put the difference between the two approaches in sacramental terms. Origen is typically intrigued with the transcendent, hidden truth of the theophany, of the incarnation, and of the Scriptures: Abraham's spiritual vision at Mamre gives him access to the inner reality (*res*) of the sacrament. Chrysostom is much more at home with the immanent, revealed symbol of the theophany, of the incarnation, and of the Scriptures: Abraham's hospitality to strangers indicates that there is no way of bypassing the outward symbol of the sacrament (*sacramentum*). Both approaches have their strengths: Origen beautifully highlights the importance of the contemplative life, of the vision of God as the sacramental aim of Abraham's hospitality, and Chrysostom rightly emphasizes that we dare not circumvent the embodied, sacramental grounding of the active life. Both approaches also have their weaknesses: Origen can come across as ignoring the significance of the human form in

94. See de Lubac, "Hellenistic Allegory," 165–96.

which God reveals himself in history; Chrysostom may seem to be courting a moralism that reduces salvation to the emulation of human examples.

We need the complementarity of the two approaches. Both, after all, are sacramental in character, even if the one tends to emphasize the inward reality and the other the outward sacrament. The tension between the two exegetes is one that we should be hesitant to relinquish, because it is only by retaining the tension that we can give expression to the paradox of the incarnation. When in the incarnation God stoops down in gracious love, he invites us to enter into Christ and so to join the very life of God himself. This divine grace is the ultimate form of hospitality, of which human hospitality is a mere shadow. Or, to put it theologically, ordinary human hospitality (*philoxenia*) is merely an analogous participation in God's gracious condescension (*synkatabasis*) in Jesus Christ.

In the incarnation, we witness the paradox of God himself appearing in human form. This preeminent act of *synkatabasis* cannot be explained either by an extreme Alexandrian focus on the divinity of Christ or by a radical Antiochene insistence on his humanity. It is in the paradoxical tension between the two that the truth of God's condescension in Christ is to be found. When it comes to biblical interpretation, perhaps we retain this tension best by acknowledging that Origen's allegorizing of hospitality and Chrysostom's injunction of caring for the poor each give expression to an indispensable aspect of what hospitable reading looks like in response to theophanic revelation.

4

OTHER READING

Melito of Sardis and Origen
on the Passover of Exodus 12

The Exodus: Allegory as Arbitrary Reading?

Can patristic allegorical interpretation still be of use to us today? This is
a weighty question, since by definition "allegorizing" may seem to imply
misinterpretation of the biblical text. The etymology of the term "allegory"
speaks for itself: *allos* (other) and *agoreuein* (to speak); hence, "to speak
other"—other, that is, than what the words themselves appear to say. By what
right would one "speak other" than what the words themselves convey? And
how does such a practice of allegorizing not turn into an arbitrary imposition
of our own preconceived notions onto the biblical text? By way of response
to these questions I will turn to the exodus from Egypt, in particular the
institution of the Passover at the beginning of the exodus narrative in Exodus
12. I will take for my guides in the reading of this segment of Scripture two
early Christian interpreters of the passage, Melito of Sardis (died ca. 180)
and Origen of Alexandria (ca. 185–ca. 254). In their readings of Exodus 12
we come face-to-face with questions regarding the validity of allegorical
exegesis.

A full response to the questions just mentioned would bring in numerous aspects of patristic exegesis that I cannot properly deal with in this

chapter.[1] What I can do, however, is give the reader a taste of what the church fathers were doing when they read the biblical text and also provide some insight into what I believe to be the key element that motivated and determined the kind of exegesis that we witness in their writings. This chapter is divided into two segments. In the first, I want to explain why it is that the fathers thought that in their exegesis they were simply following the Bible's own approach to interpretation. The kind of typological or allegorical reading that we find in the fathers is one that they saw present within the Scriptures themselves. They read Scripture in light of the new realities of Christ and of the church, an exegetical approach fundamentally rooted within Scripture itself—or, at least, so they were convinced. In the second part, I will turn to a specific example, namely, the exegesis of the Passover in two identically named works—both called *Peri Pascha* (About the Passover)—written by Melito of Sardis and Origen. Throughout, I will make the argument that what stands out in the typological or allegorical interpretation of both works is the unabashedly christological reading of the text. In fact, Christology is so central to both writers that they were convinced that Christ (and, by implication, the church) is already present within the history described in Exodus 12. That is to say, Christ and the church constitute the New Testament mystery that is sacramentally already present within the Old Testament text.

As modern readers we tend to be anxious about exegesis becoming a free-floating, arbitrary endeavor—free from boundaries, guidelines, and the possibility of verification. This is the concern regarding patristic interpretation that I encounter most frequently: its apparently arbitrary character. Interestingly, within the early church this objection was never voiced—not even by those most staunchly opposed to the allegedly nonhistorical approaches of Origen and others from what is sometimes called the Alexandrian school of interpretation.[2] I suspect that the main reason no one in the early church

1. A full response to the objection of arbitrariness would have to include discussion of the following elements: (1) the wide variety of results yielded by historical exegesis, which exposes it, no less than the church fathers, to the charge of arbitrariness; (2) the often remarkable similarities in approach and actual exegetical outcome among a broad range of premodern interpreters; (3) the church's liturgy and "rule of faith" as setting boundaries for what constitutes proper interpretation; (4) the Spirit's guidance of the faithful in the church in adhering faithfully to the divine intentions of the church's book; (5) the function of spiritual benefit or usefulness (*ōpheleia*) as simply being more important to the believer than arriving at the exact authorial intent; and (6) many premodern interpreters' openness to multiple interpretations of one particular text.

2. To be sure, as we have already seen (chap. 3, sec. "Chrysostom: Divine Condescension at Mamre and in Scripture"), Antiochene interpreters such as Diodore and Chrysostom did object to Alexandrian exegetes imposing an "other" meaning on the text that they regarded as

worried about arbitrariness in typological or allegorical exegesis is that they regarded the Bible as the book of the church. That is to say, the Scriptures were linked to the liturgy and the faith of the church. We often think of biblical exegesis as lying within the purview of the academy and of liturgy as the domain of the church; not so the church fathers. For them, the way we read the Bible has everything to do with how it functions in the church. Exodus 12, for Melito and Origen, speaks not just of historical realities of long ago; it speaks of the liturgical gathering of the church as well as of the confession that the church holds dear. *Lex orandi, lex credendi* is the catchphrase expressing this conviction: the rule of prayer (the liturgy) is closely linked to the rule of faith (what we believe). Our interpretation of the Bible (and our doctrine) is intimately tied up with our worship practices. I believe that this holds true whether or not we acknowledge the validity of the connection—that is to say, it operates within ecclesial contexts of all different traditions—but the early church's preachers and theologians were keenly aware of this close link.[3] It means that the exegesis of Scripture did have concrete boundaries, guidelines, and points of verification, and these were given by the church's liturgy and confession. It is because exegesis wasn't a self-governing endeavor but instead functioned within an ecclesial setting that no one expressed the fear that typology and allegorizing might run amok.[4]

Typology in Scripture

The church fathers were convinced that the Bible itself anticipated their ecclesial, theological readings. For them, what justified their interpretation of the Scriptures was the way in which the New Testament authors had approached the Old Testament, and before that, the way in which, within the Old Testament, earlier passages had been read by later authors. This comes to the fore with particular clarity in the way in which the Passover account of Exodus 12 (along with the rest of the narrative of the exodus from Egypt) functions within the later biblical witness. Before we turn to Melito and Origen, therefore, I want to look at how the Passover narrative functions

---

foreign to it. But the Antiochenes recognized that this imposition wasn't a matter of personal whim, something random or arbitrary.

3. For a fine recent discussion of the link between exegesis and the church's faith, see Hall, "Creedal Hermeneutics," 109–26.

4. As we will see, a shared ecclesial context doesn't preclude exegetical disagreement. Melito and Origen take different approaches to Exod. 12, but the disagreement falls within the church's confessional "rule of faith," which ensures that both theologians approach the text christologically and sacramentally.

in the Bible itself. I am taking my cue from Jean Daniélou's excellent 1950 publication, *From Shadows to Reality: Studies in the Biblical Typology of the Fathers*.[5] Daniélou's basic argument is that we can properly understand the fathers only by regarding their interpretation as an extension of the typology that the Scriptures themselves employ. Daniélou puts it as follows: "The Fathers have rightly insisted at all times that the types of the Exodus are fulfilled in the life of Christ and the Church, and in this they have but followed the teaching of the New Testament, which shows that these types are fulfilled in Christ."[6] So the typological lines, according to Daniélou, run from Exodus, via the Prophets, to Christ and the church; and this typological development, he argues, is anchored in the Bible itself.

How is this the case? Daniélou shows how already the Prophets announce a new, future exodus, one that has each of the main features of the first exodus: a crossing of the sea, a desert journey, living water pouring from rocks, a cloud, and a new covenant.[7] Daniélou turns to Hosea 2:14–15:

> Therefore, behold, I will allure her,
>   and bring her into the wilderness,
>   and speak tenderly to her.
> . . . .
> And there she shall answer as in the days of her youth,
>   as at the time when she came out of the land of Egypt.

Later, in chapter 12, Hosea promises that Israel will again live in tabernacles:

> I will again make you dwell in tents,
>   as in the days of the appointed feast. (Hos. 12:9)

For Hosea, Israel's original exodus serves as a type that corresponds to the antitype of her anticipated restoration. Isaiah does much the same thing, as Daniélou explains with reference to Isaiah 11:15–16:

> And the Lord will utterly destroy
>   the tongue of the Sea of Egypt,
> and will wave his hand over the River
>   with his scorching breath,

---

5. Daniélou, *From Shadows to Reality*. This book was first published in French under the title *Sacramentum futuri: Études sur les origines de la typologie biblique*, Études de théologie historique (Paris: Beauchesne, 1950).

6. Daniélou, *From Shadows to Reality*, 153.

7. Ibid., 155–57.

. . . .
And there will be a highway from Assyria
    for the remnant that remains of his people,
as there was for Israel
    when they came up from the land of Egypt. (cf. Isa. 10:26)

The exodus theme is unmistakable. According to Isaiah 4:5, on the day of Israel's redemption, "the LORD will create over the whole site of Mount Zion and over her assemblies a cloud by day, and smoke and the shining of a flaming fire by night." Again, the fire and the cloud are reminiscent of the exodus (Exod. 13:21; Ps. 77 [78]:14). Finally, according to Isaiah 10:26, God will wield against his enemies "a whip, as when he struck Midian at the rock of Oreb. And his staff will be over the sea, and he will lift it as he did in Egypt." These early chapters of Isaiah consistently anticipate a redemption that will be in line with the exodus from Egypt.

The later chapters of Isaiah seem to Daniélou to be even more insistent in the way they recall the exodus from Egypt. Isaiah 43:16–19 exclaims:

Thus says the LORD,
    who makes a way in the sea,
    a path in the mighty waters.
. . . .
"Remember not the former things,
    nor consider the things of old.
Behold, I am doing a new thing;
. . . .
I will make a way in the wilderness
    and rivers in the desert."

There will be a pillar of fire and a cloud as in the exodus; water will again come from the rock (Isa. 48:21); and, unlike the first exodus, this new one will not be a hasty flight but will take the form of a triumphal march:

For you shall not go out in haste,
    and you shall not go in flight,
for the LORD will go before you,
    and the God of Israel will be your rear guard. (Isa. 52:12)

According to Jeremiah, the grandeur of the new exodus will far outshine the old: "Therefore, behold, the days are coming, declares the LORD, when they shall no longer say, 'As the LORD lives who brought up the people of

Israel out of the land of Egypt,' but 'As the LORD lives who brought up and led the offspring of the house of Israel out of the north country and out of all the countries where he had driven them.' Then they shall dwell in their own land" (Jer. 23:7–8). In the same way, the new covenant will be greater than the old, according to the famed prophecy of Jeremiah 31 (which states that the new covenant will not be "like the covenant that I made with their fathers on the day when I took them by the hand to bring them out of the land of Egypt" [Jer. 31:32]). Thus, while typology is based on similarities between the original type and the later antitype, there are also significant differences: the glory of the new exodus will be much greater than that of the initial one.

The New Testament, the Gospel of Matthew in particular, picks up on this exodus theme of the Prophets and—as Daniélou makes clear—shows it as being fulfilled in Christ.[8] Jesus Christ, returning from Egypt after Herod's death, fulfills the prophecy of Hosea, "Out of Egypt I called my son" (Hos. 11:1; cf. Matt. 2:15). John the Baptist serves as the "voice of one crying in the wilderness: 'Prepare the way of the Lord'" (Matt. 3:3; cf. Isa. 40:3). After his baptism, which functions as his own Red Sea crossing, Jesus, much like Israel, is "led up by the Spirit into the wilderness" (Matt. 4:1). There he fasts for forty days and forty nights (Matt. 4:2), a number corresponding to the forty years of the wilderness journey and the forty days of Moses' fast. The three temptations in the desert echo the temptations of Israel in the wilderness.[9] The evangelist presents Jesus as the new Moses, with his Sermon on the Mount serving as the new law.[10] Jesus distributes bread as Moses distributed manna (Matt. 14:19); and Jesus sends out seventy disciples much as Moses chose seventy elders (Luke 10:1; Num. 11:16).

Something similar, Daniélou explains, takes place in John's Gospel, which he argues functions "as a kind of Paschal catechetical instruction, to show

8. Daniélou, *From Shadows to Reality*, 157–60.

9. Matthew gives ample evidence of such echoes: just as Jesus is "led up" (*anēchthē*) by the Spirit into the wilderness (Matt. 4:1) for a forty-day fast (Matt. 4:2), so God "led Israel" (*ēgagen* in the Septuagint) in the wilderness (Deut. 8:2), letting them hunger for forty years (Deut. 8:3). In response to the first temptation—Satan's suggestion that Jesus command stones to become loaves of bread—Jesus quotes Deut. 8:3 ("man does not live by bread alone, but man lives by every word that comes from the LORD"; cf. Matt. 4:4). In response to the second temptation—that Jesus throw himself down from the pinnacle of the temple—Jesus quotes Deut. 6:16 ("You shall not put the LORD your God to the test, as you tested him at Massah," a reference to the wilderness event described in Exod. 17:1–7; cf. Matt. 4:7). When in the third temptation Satan tells Jesus to worship him (Matt. 4:9), Jesus appeals to Deut. 6:13, a warning to Israel to worship only the Lord (Matt. 4:10).

10. Interestingly, in the fifth century Pope Leo the Great saw Moses as a type of the apostles in the Sermon on the Mount, since both Moses and the apostles were the recipients of divine instruction on a mountain. See chap. 10, sec. "Interpreting between Cave and Mountain."

to those baptized on the night of Holy Saturday that the Sacraments they then received were divine interventions which continued the great acts (the *magnalia*) of Yahweh at the time of the exodus and also at the time of the Passion and resurrection of Christ."[11] In other words, Daniélou sees the setting of Saint John's Gospel as a liturgical one—connected to the baptism of catechumens—and he argues that John locates the catechumens typologically in line with the exodus and with the suffering and resurrection of Christ. Daniélou points to the Word appearing in various forms in John's Gospel: as the Shekinah, the glory of God (John 1:14); as the bronze snake lifted up in the desert (3:14); as the manna coming down from heaven (6:31–51); as the water gushing from the rock (7:37–38); as the pillar of fire (8:12); and as the Passover lamb whose blood washes away the sins of the world (1:29; 19:36).[12] In each of these cases, the Gospel writer presents Jesus as the reality foreshadowed in the Old Testament exodus narrative.

Daniélou elaborates on the Old Testament backdrop of other New Testament books in similar fashion,[13] and he concludes with the comment:

> A deep impression forms itself on our mind after reading these many texts. It was the clear intention of the New Testament writers to show the mystery of Christ as at once continuing and surpassing the outstanding events in the story of Israel at the time of Moses. God had revealed his might in redeeming the chosen people. But the human race remained subject to another captivity more exacting and spiritual in nature. The Prophets had foretold that the might of God would be seen in a new redemption, on a far greater scale, which would inaugurate the New Covenant. The burden of the New Testament writers is to show that all this has been fulfilled in Jesus Christ.[14]

In biblical typology, the exodus plays a major role, and the linear pattern that emerges runs from the historical exodus itself, via the Prophets—who announce a new exodus—to Christ and the church.

The way in which the exodus theme is developed throughout Scripture can serve as a paradigm for patristic spiritual interpretation and explains why it is that the church fathers allegorized without worrying that their exegesis might turn arbitrary. Take the well-known example of the narrative of the bronze snake in Numbers 21. The people complain to Moses about the lack of food and drink (21:5), and in response the Lord sends venomous

11. Daniélou, *From Shadows to Reality*, 161.
12. Ibid.
13. Ibid., 163–65.
14. Ibid., 165.

snakes (21:6). So the people repent, and Moses prays for them (21:7–8). We then read: "The LORD said to Moses, 'Make a fiery serpent and set it on a pole, and everyone who is bitten, when he sees it, shall live.' So Moses made a bronze serpent and set it on a pole. And if a serpent bit anyone, he would look at the bronze serpent and live" (21:8–9). Most of us know the Gospel of John quite well, and it doesn't strike us as odd or arbitrary to find here a christological reference: "As Moses lifted up the serpent in the wilderness, so must the Son of Man be lifted up, that whoever believes in him may have eternal life" (John 3:14–15). The fathers—and Daniélou shows this with references to Tertullian, Cyril of Jerusalem, and Gregory of Nyssa—eagerly appropriated this connection between Numbers 21 and John 3.[15] Neither John the Evangelist nor the church fathers appear to have had the kind of historical consciousness that made them shrink back from a christological reading of Numbers 21. Surely, though, John's use of the story of the bronze snake must raise some historical-exegetical eyebrows. It can hardly have been the historically intended meaning of the book of Numbers to make a prophetic announcement about the coming Messiah. Clearly, Saint John moves well beyond authorial intent in his treatment of this passage.

Assuming that John's Gospel and the church fathers were right about seeing the bronze snake as a type of Christ—or, we might say, if John read Numbers 21 allegorically[16]—this raises an important question: Could we perhaps do something similar with other elements in the exodus narrative?[17] The fathers thought they could and should. Moses praying with his arms outstretched (Exod. 17:11–13) was, many of the fathers maintained, a type of Christ.[18] Joshua leading the people into the promised land became a type of Christ's

15. Ibid., 167–68.

16. I am deliberately intermingling the categories of typology and allegory. Whatever distinctions we may impose, the church fathers did not differentiate between the two. I discuss the distinction in further detail below.

17. Richard Longenecker argues that we should not replicate the New Testament authors' allegorizing because, unlike the biblical authors, we are not inspired by the Holy Spirit. *Biblical Exegesis*, 193–98. This argument seems to me unpersuasive. It supposes that, thanks to the Spirit's leading, the biblical authors in their teaching were kept from error despite their odd interpretive method. This raises several questions: (1) Is it possible thus to separate doctrine and interpretation, seeing as the former results from the latter? (2) On what grounds did the biblical authors believe they could use allegorical exegesis? (3) If the New Testament authors won't teach us how properly to read Scripture, who will? The Scriptures themselves nowhere suggest that we should not follow their approach to interpretation, and it seems to show greater fidelity to Scripture to follow its modes of interpretation than to argue for their unrepeatability. Peter J. Leithart discusses (and critiques) Longenecker's position in *Deep Exegesis*, 32–34, 36–37. Leithart concludes his discussion by explaining that typological reading "is simply reading of earlier texts in the light of later texts and events." Ibid., 74.

18. Daniélou, *From Shadows to Reality*, 168–69.

redemption. The wood that Moses threw into the bitter water so that it became sweet (Exod. 15:25) turned into a type of the cross, which transforms the waters of baptism.[19] And the twelve springs and seventy palm trees at Elim (Exod. 15:27) stood for the twelve apostles and the seventy disciples (Luke 10:1). What is it that convinced the early church's interpreters to do all this? At bottom, this exegesis is grounded in one underlying conviction: as God's people we are implicated directly in the exodus that takes place in Christ. We ourselves are taking the exodus journey. Since, according to the Prophets, the new exodus would be similar in character to the first, the church fathers felt compelled to look for similarities between the old exodus and the new.[20]

Thus, speaking of the twelve springs and seventy palm trees, Daniélou perceptively observes:

> This numerical correspondence will probably strike us at first sight as rather artificial. But can we be quite sure of this? We are not to expect in "twelve fountains" a hydrographical exactitude. We can consider what light Jewish tradition will afford. From this we learn that the Red Sea opened in twelve divisions to allow the twelve tribes to pass (Ps. 136:13). The Koran shows us another tradition, that Moses caused twelve springs to gush forth from the rock (*Koran*, VII, 160). It seems that we must emphasize the connection of the twelve springs with the twelve tribes, as did the Rabbis, who saw in the twelve springs a type of the twelve tribes. . . . And as we said above, it seems quite clear that the choice of the twelve Apostles by Christ had its relation to the twelve tribes.[21]

Far from being arbitrary, each of these exegetical choices—perceiving the cross in Moses' outstretched arms as well as in the wood that sweetened the waters, discerning Jesus in Joshua, recognizing the apostles and disciples in the twelve springs and the seventy palm trees —result from the church fathers' conviction that in Christ they had embarked on a new exodus. It is Christology, therefore (or, to put it differently, it is the new exodus), that shaped their readings and kept these from turning into random allegorical impositions. The fathers' readings of Moses' outstretched arms, of the wood sweetening the waters, of Joshua conquering Canaan, and of the waters and trees of Elim

19. Ibid., 171–72.

20. Henri de Lubac points out that medieval theologians often distinguished between "allegory of deed" (*allegoria facti*) and "allegory of word" (*allegoria dicti*). *Medieval Exegesis*, 87–88. What makes Scripture's allegorizing different from Hellenistic allegorizing, according to de Lubac, is the fact that it is grounded not only in words but also in the underlying historical events themselves. Scripture, de Lubac points out, is in some sense "doubly" the Word of God: "God speaks to us in it with words about what he has spoken to us in deeds." Ibid., 88.

21. Daniélou, *From Shadows to Reality*, 173.

were in no way different from John's reading of the narrative of the bronze snake. Their allegorical exegesis simply followed the biblical example of trying to locate Christ's redemption in the Old Testament texts.

The fathers based their exegesis on the way in which the Prophets and the New Testament speak of God initiating a new exodus. The implication is that the early church's preachers believed that a new exodus was taking place in Christ and in the liturgical life of the church. This may be a novel claim to some of us, especially those of us who worship in a nonsacramental (or nonliturgical) context. But we cannot avoid this link between the exodus and the liturgy when we take the church's early exegesis seriously. As we will see, both Melito and Origen were convinced that it is through the liturgy that God allows us to join in the new exodus, which is the great archetype anticipated by Israel's rescue in the book of Exodus.

If the liturgy genuinely makes us join the exodus journey, then this fills the liturgy with tremendous significance. We see this liturgical prominence reflected in the patristic exegesis of the Red Sea crossing and of the eating of the manna: they are types of the sacraments of baptism and Eucharist. Initiation of new believers into the church was centered on these two sacramental acts. In light of the famous passage of 1 Corinthians 10—"All were baptized into Moses in the cloud and in the sea, and all ate the same spiritual food, and all drank the same spiritual drink. For they drank from the spiritual Rock that followed them, and the Rock was Christ" (10:2–4)—the fathers saw in the exodus event the sacramental initiation of new believers into the church.[22]

It would take us too far afield to go through each of the individual church fathers, but Daniélou shows that this exegetical approach was a common feature of the patristic tradition. Numerous church fathers saw references to baptism and Eucharist in the exodus narrative.[23] The overall picture that emerges from reading these early interpreters is the following: baptism, which took place on the night of Holy Saturday, recalled the departure from Egypt and from the realm of sin; in the rite of initiation, the proselyte passed through each of the stages that the Israelites had also gone through. The Pauline passage of 1 Corinthians 10 provided a basis for this link between the baptizand and the Israelites.[24] As a result, a broad-ranging allegorical network emerged: Egypt became the world of the human passions; the waters of the Red Sea

22. Ibid., 176.
23. Daniélou refers to Tertullian, Didymus the Blind, Zeno of Verona, Ambrose, Cyril of Jerusalem, Aphraates, Origen, Gregory of Nyssa, Basil of Caesarea, Hilary of Poitiers, John Chrysostom, Theodoret, Cyprian, Gregory of Elvira, Eusebius of Caesarea, and Augustine. Ibid., 177–201.
24. Ibid., 176.

were seen as the means of salvation; Pharaoh and his soldiers were interpreted as the devil and his companions; the pillar of light became Christ, and the pillar of cloud the Holy Spirit; the blood of the lamb was identified with the blood of Christ that put the demons to flight; the three-day journey into the wilderness turned into the Paschal triduum (Good Friday, Holy Saturday, and Resurrection Sunday); the manna was the Eucharist; and the water from the rock was understood either as the cup of salvation in line with 1 Corinthians 10 or as baptism, following John 7:37.[25]

One specific example may be worth highlighting, that of Theodoret of Cyrus (ca. 393–ca. 458/466), an Antiochene interpreter often regarded as fairly open to nonhistorical modes of interpretation. His exegesis serves as a word of caution against distinguishing too sharply between Antiochenes and Alexandrians, as if the former sharply rejected allegorizing while the latter advocated for it. Theodoret's interpretation shows little hesitance in making use of what we may term "christological/ecclesial allegorizing."[26] The Red Sea, Theodoret explains, "is the type of the baptismal font, the cloud of the Holy Spirit, and Moses of Christ our Saviour; the staff is a type of the Cross; Pharaoh of the devil and the Egyptians of the fallen angels; manna of the divine food and the water from the rock of the Saviour's Blood. Just as they enjoyed a wonderful refreshment coming from a miraculous source, after they had passed through the Red Sea, so we, after the saving waters of Baptism, share in the divine mysteries."[27] Theodoret reads the exodus allegorically as referring to the church and her sacraments. Daniélou rightly comments: "This passage brings out better than any other the value of the liturgical comparison."[28] The church fathers were convinced that in the liturgy—in baptism and Eucharist—they were taken up into the sacramental mystery of Christ himself. By implication, they were also taken up into the new exodus. Thus, there was nothing arbitrary about scrutinizing the exodus narrative for christological and ecclesiological references. The typological or

25. Ibid., 177–201.
26. Richard J. Perhai, in his recent book *Antiochene* Theōria *in the Writings of Theodore of Mopsuestia and Theodoret of Cyrus*, shows that Theodoret loved to speak about his exegetical approach as an exercise in *theōria*—which Perhai refers to as "a spectacle, visual observation, mental discernment, contemplation, and spiritual or prophetic perception (usually of a vision or some other revelation)" (70). At the same time, Theodoret wasn't shy to "promote figurative (τροπικῶς) and at times allegorical (ἀλληγορικόν) interpretation—seen most acutely in his *Commentary on the Song of Songs*." Ibid. Perhai offers the following explanation: "Perhaps the echoes of anathemas from the Council of Ephesus (431) along with his ascetic sensibilities overcame his Antiochene historicism—leading to his most allegorical exegesis." Ibid., 62.
27. As quoted in Daniélou, *From Shadows to Reality*, 194.
28. Ibid.

allegorical reading of the exodus passages was rooted in biblical precedent and in liturgical celebration.

Melito of Sardis, *On Pascha*

So far I have used Daniélou's broad treatment of the church fathers to illustrate that Christology governed their typological exegesis. Christ was the great archetype, and as such his person, his words, and his deeds determined the search for Old Testament types that might correspond in some way to the marvelous newness of the Christ event. Needless to say, this approach assumes great confidence in God's providential guidance of the events of history.[29] The early church discerned similarities between type and antitype because of the conviction that at different points throughout salvation history the character of God comes to expression in similar ways. On this understanding, God's action in and through Christ determines the way in which we interpret his earlier dealings with humanity as well. In the light of Christ, it is no longer possible to read the Old Testament in the same way as before. This conviction, more than anything else, determined the church fathers' reading of the Old Testament. They were persuaded, rightly I believe, that they simply followed the Bible's own understanding of God's dealings with his people.

With this background, I will now turn to the Passover celebration and to the church's appropriation of the Exodus 12 narrative. The liturgical setting of the interpretation of Scripture is particularly clear in Melito of Sardis's homily *On Pascha*. Melito likely preached the sermon, which dates from about AD 160 to 170, as a means of introducing the eucharistic celebration. It was in the celebration of the Eucharist that the Scriptures came to their fulfillment, according to Melito. This notion—that the reality of the Scriptures was present here, in the liturgy—means that each of the elements of the liturgy took on great significance. For example, many regarded the very time slot of the Easter celebration as a matter of crucial importance. Since Easter was the Christian celebration of the Passover, Melito argued that it had to be celebrated on the same day that the Jewish Passover was celebrated: the evening of the fourteenth day of the first month (Nisan).[30] As a result, Melito and other Asian Christians who celebrated Easter on this precise date became

29. Matthew Levering highlights God's providential guidance as the key to participatory exegesis in his superb book *Participatory Biblical Exegesis*. Cf. chap. 1, sec. "Retrieving Sacramental Reading: Meaning, Virtue, Progress, and Providence."

30. This is in line with the instruction of Exod. 12:2–3. I have published a sermon on this passage in *Sacramental Preaching*, 15–26.

known as "Quartodecimans," or "Fourteeners."[31] Other churches, including the church of Rome, celebrated Easter on the Sunday following the Passover celebration, which meant a break with the precise regulation of Exodus 12 as well as with Jewish tradition.

This disagreement turned into a high-stakes controversy in the late second century. Saint Irenaeus, the bishop of Lyons in central France, wrote a letter to Pope Victor in Rome to try to convince him to allow the Asian churches freedom in what he considered a nonessential liturgical matter. We may find it difficult to appreciate that this issue led to such a sharp, protracted controversy. But we need to recognize that at stake was the church's ability to say that the exodus from Egypt was the *church's* exodus—that we ourselves are the ones making the exodus journey. The celebration on the fourteenth of Nisan, for Melito and other Asian Christians, gave expression to the typological reading of the exodus event. Melito, in *On Pascha*, places himself squarely in the tradition of the Quartodecimans, and so his typology moves from the church's liturgy back to the Jewish Passover in order to appropriate for the church the Passover celebration of Exodus 12.

Melito speaks of the historical Passover celebration of Exodus 12 as "type" (*typos*) and of the fulfillment in Christ as "reality" or "truth" (*alētheia*). "For there was once a type, but now the reality has appeared."[32] Melito also uses the terminology of "mystery" (*mystērion*). He begins by saying, "The Scripture of the exodus of the Hebrews has been read, and the words of the mystery have been declared."[33] Repeatedly, he speaks of the "mystery" of the Pascha.[34] The term "mystery" would become quite prominent in the later Christian tradition. It has its roots in Scripture itself, especially the Pauline Letters. In Ephesians 5, Saint Paul speaks of the bodily union between husband and wife and then comments, "This is a profound mystery" (*mystērion*), adding that he is "saying that it refers to Christ and the church" (Eph. 5:32). The Latin text of the Vulgate renders the word *mystērion* as *sacramentum*. Indeed, throughout the subsequent tradition, the term "mystery" has held sacramental significance.

---

31. See Stewart-Sykes, introduction to *On Pascha*, 1–2. The Quartodecimans defended their liturgical practice by adopting the synoptic chronology, according to which Jesus celebrated the Last Supper on the fourteenth of Nisan, with the crucifixion taking place the next day. The alternative practice followed the Johannine chronology, according to which Jesus celebrated the Last Supper on the day *before* the fourteenth of Nisan, thus arguably setting precedent for a different ecclesial practice. Daly, introduction to "Treatise on the Passover," 7–8.

32. Melito, *On Pascha* 4 (Stewart-Sykes, 38). Throughout, I use Stewart-Sykes' translation. For the Greek text, see Melito of Sardis, *On Pascha and Fragments*.

33. Melito, *On Pascha* 1 (p. 37).

34. Ibid., 2 (p. 37), 15 (p. 40), 31 (p. 45), 33 (p. 45), 34 (p. 45), 46 (p. 48), 58 (p. 52), 59 (p. 52), 61 (p. 53), 65 (p. 54). Cf. Hainsworth, "Force of the Mystery," 107–46.

The word didn't have quite the same connotations that it has for us today. Certainly, it did not refer to a puzzle of sorts, whose secret we can uncover by means of clever investigation, a connotation that comes through when we talk about mystery novels, for example. For the patristic and medieval mindset, the word meant something slightly—but significantly—different. "Mystery" referred to realities behind the appearances observable by the senses. That is to say, although our hands, eyes, ears, nose, and tongue are able to access reality, they cannot *fully* grasp it. They cannot *comprehend* it. Twentieth-century patristics scholar Henri de Lubac explains: "In Latin *mysterium* serves as the double for *sacramentum*. For Saint Augustine, the Bible is essentially the 'writing of the mysteries,' and its books are the 'books of the divine sacraments.' The two words are often simply synonyms."[35]

Further, de Lubac argues that when at times medieval theologians did distinguish between *sacramentum* and *mysterium*, they typically saw the former as the sacramental sign and the latter as the spiritual reality:

> They are sometimes distinguished as the two terms of a relation or as the two poles of an alternating movement. Then *sacramentum* designates rather the exterior component, the "envelope," as Saint Augustine says: "Christ has been preached by the prophets almost everywhere with a wrapping of sacrament." This is the sign or the letter as bearer of the sign: "the signs of things are in the sacraments." Whether thing or person, fact or rite, it is the "type," the correlative of the mystery, just as the "figure" or "image" is the correlative of the "truth": "the sacrament comes before the truth of the thing." It is the *sacrum* [sacred thing] rather than the *arcanum* [hidden thing]. The mystery is this *arcanum* itself. It is the interior component, the reality hidden under the letter and signified by the sign, the truth that the figure indicates; in other words, the object of faith itself.[36]

This quotation may be somewhat lengthy and dense, but it captures exactly how, for the church fathers, exegesis was sacramental. The "exterior" of the letter, while indispensable, had a purpose that lay beyond itself. Its purpose was the "interior" of the Spirit. The type or figure of the Old Testament had as its *telos* the hidden reality of Christ, revealed in the New Testament.

The sacramental character implied in the notion of mystery comes through already in Melito's use of the term. When in the above discussion I mentioned the biblical origins of typology, we saw that it was based on the similarities

35. De Lubac, *Medieval Exegesis*, 20. Jason Byassee also makes the point that for Augustine interpretation was sacramental in character. *Praise Seeking Understanding*, 233–39.
36. De Lubac, *Medieval Exegesis*, 21.

of divine action across history. Typology identifies a historical progression from the exodus, via the Prophets, to the christological reality in the New Testament. Daniélou accentuates this horizontal, historical, forward-looking character of typology, and he is certainly right to do so. But he overemphasizes it.[37] This comes to the fore in Daniélou's popularizing of the distinction between allegory and typology. On his understanding of patristic exegesis, it is the Alexandrians (followers of Origen) who especially used allegory. Allegory was derived from Philo; it was moralizing; it looked for eternal realities; it was upward looking; it ignored history; and as a result it was arbitrary in its interpretation of the Bible. By contrast, the Antiochene typological approach, according to Daniélou and others, was biblical rather than pagan in origin; it was christological rather than moralistic; it was forward looking; it looked for historical progression rather than for links with eternal realities; and as a result it avoided arbitrariness.

De Lubac, Daniélou's own teacher, demonstrated decisively that his student's opposition between allegory and typology was alien to the church fathers.[38] Most patristics scholarship today has abandoned any sharp distinction between allegory and typology, and I am largely sympathetic to this new consensus.[39] And we see evidence for it in Melito. Without doubt, Melito's typology is historical, in that it moves from the Passover of Exodus 12 to the suffering of Christ. But the typology involves more than *just* a historical or chronological move. The forward move from type to antitype or from shadow to reality is for Melito at the same time an upward move, from temporal, earthly types to eternal, heavenly realities.[40]

Paragraph 2 of *On Pascha* may serve to illustrate this. Here Melito comments: "Therefore, well-beloved, understand, how the mystery (*mystērion*)

37. See H. Boersma, *Nouvelle Théologie*, 168–80.
38. De Lubac, "Typology and Allegorization," 129–64.
39. See, for example, Saint Gregory of Nyssa's comment about biblical passages that speak "in a concealed manner by way of enigmas and below-the-surface meanings": "One may wish to refer to the anagogical interpretation of such sayings as 'tropology' or 'allegory' or by some other name. We shall not quarrel about the name as long as a firm grasp is kept on thoughts that edify." *Homilies on the Song of Songs*, preface, 5.23, 5.27–5.2 (WGRW 13:3, 5). As we have already seen, Theodoret of Cyrus (as well as others) speaks of types where modern scholars would typically speak of allegories (see above, note 26). See also the discussion in Martens, "Allegory/Typology Distinction."
40. Henry M. Knapp helpfully notes that "Melito's typological hermeneutics enable him to draw out the correspondence between the past and Christ by stressing three elements of the type/reality: (1) the precious value of the type in its time, (2) the escalated nature of the fulfillment of the type, and (3) the surpassing greatness of the reality which effectively negates any on-going worth of the type." "Melito's Use of Scripture," 374. Unfortunately, Knapp continues to build on Daniélou's outmoded distinction between typology and allegory.

of the Pascha is both new and old, eternal and provisional, perishable and imperishable, mortal and immortal." Notice that Melito is able to shift effortlessly from horizontal language ("new and old") to vertical language ("eternal and provisional, perishable and imperishable, mortal and immortal"). And he keeps up this vertical language throughout. The reason is that we have in Melito not just a (nominalist) succession of unrelated, fragmented historical incidents.[41] The progression from the Passover to the suffering of Christ and so to the eucharistic celebration is not just a historical progression of separate moments in time. Rather, these events have an *internal* relationship to each other. And it is this internal relationship to later events that turns the Passover of Exodus 12 into a "mystery."

Melito makes this particularly clear at the height of his exposition, immediately prior to his explanation of typology. Addressing the angel of death directly, in paragraph 32 he asks: "Tell me angel, what turned you away? The slaughter of the sheep or the life of the Lord? The death of the sheep or the type of the Lord? The blood of the sheep or the spirit of the Lord?" Notice how he pulls type and antitype apart here, as he asks the central question: What was the origin of the salvation of the Hebrews? Was it the blood of the sheep or that of Christ? His answer is unequivocal: "It is clear that you turned away seeing the mystery (*mystērion*) of the Lord in the sheep and the life of the Lord in the slaughter of the sheep and the type of the Lord in the death of the sheep. Therefore you struck not Israel down, but made Egypt alone childless."[42] The reality of Christ—the historically later event—was mystically or sacramentally present already in the Passover celebration of the Hebrews. The two historical events slide inside one another; and it is the eternal, immortal character of the christological archetype that infuses the temporal and provisional Passover of Exodus 12 with its saving power. Paragraph 69 is equally explicit. Speaking of Christ, Melito comments: "This is the Pascha of our salvation: this is the one who in many people endured many things. This is the one who was murdered in Abel, tied up in Isaac, exiled in Jacob, sold in Joseph, exposed in Moses, slaughtered in the lamb, hunted down in David, dishonored in the prophets."[43] The sufferings of each of these Old

---

41. Nominalism (from the Latin *nomen*, meaning "name") holds that sensible objects (such as dogs) do not participate in intelligible universals (such as the canine species); we simply assign "names" to individual objects on the basis of their apparent similarities. Realism, by contrast, insists that the similarities arise from the objects' participation in eternal forms or universals. Nominalism became popular in modernity especially through the influence of William of Ockham (ca. 1287–1347). See H. Boersma, *Heavenly Participation*, 79–81.

42. Melito, *On Pascha* 33 (p. 45).

43. For a discussion of the Akedah in Melito, see Wilken, "Melito," 53–69. Melito's language here is reminiscent of a statement from Irenaeus that I quoted earlier (ch1n54).

Testament figures were "mysteries," according to Melito, of the sufferings of Christ. The archetype—Christ himself—suffered *in* the suffering of the earlier types.[44] The Old Testament types contain a mysterious, inner depth that the language of historical progression cannot capture.

Melito clarifies his approach by referring to the "writing of a parable" (*graphē parabolēs*) in language and the use of a "model" or "preliminary sketch" (*typos prokentēmatos*) in sculpting.[45] He compares the law to a parable that alludes to the reality of the gospel narrative, and he likens the Jewish people as a preliminary sketch to the church as the repository of reality.[46] And so he comments: "When the thing comes about of which the sketch was a type, that which was to be, of which the type bore the likeness, then the type is destroyed, it has become useless, it yields up the image to what is truly real. What was once valuable becomes worthless, when what is of true value appears."[47]

As a small but important aside as we transition from Melito to Origen, I should note that Melito employs etymology in defense of his christological reading of the Passover. We see this in paragraph 46: "What is the Pascha? It is called by its name because of what constitutes it."[48] The word "Pascha" (*pascha*), maintains Melito, comes from the word "suffering" (*paschein*). Among the church fathers, etymology was a common strategy in trying to identify the christological or ecclesial meaning of the Old Testament. This approach had already been used by Philo, and the church fathers' love of words and their meaning predisposed them to follow Philo in order to find the spiritual, christological meaning of the text by means of etymology.[49]

Origen, *Treatise on the Passover*

The etymology that Melito assumed—the move from *pascha* to *paschein*—is an interesting one, especially in light of the way in which Origen deals with it in his *Treatise on the Passover*, a book to which we now turn. Origen wrote his *Peri Pascha* around 245, approximately eighty years after Melito's work by the same title. Origen's book is in many ways quite different from that of Melito. The flowery rhetoric of Melito's sermon gives way to a rather straightforward two-part treatise. Origen presents his main argument in the first part:

44. Melito, *On Pascha* 59 (pp. 52–53).
45. Ibid., 35–36 (p. 46), 39–40 (p. 47). I have slightly changed the translation.
46. Ibid., 40 (p. 47).
47. Ibid., 37 (p. 46).
48. Ibid., 46 (p. 49).
49. See Van den Hoek, "Etymologizing in a Christian Context," 122–68.

he wants to correct a misunderstanding of how the typology of the Passover works. In the second part he presents the spiritual interpretation of Exodus 12—although, since he has done a great deal of work in terms of typological interpretation already in part 1, the second part turns out to be rather brief.[50]

In part 1, as he corrects a misunderstanding of the "mechanics" (if we may use that term) of the typology of the Passover, Origen makes a small but, in his eyes, important distinction. He rejects the notion that the Passover was a figure or type of Christ's passion. Now, we just saw that this view, rejected here by Origen, was exactly that of Melito. And Hippolytus of Rome (ca. 170–ca. 236) too had typologically connected the Passover to Christ's passion, and it may well be that Origen wrote directly to counter Hippolytus's view.[51] Origen insists that instead of being a type of Christ's *suffering*, the Passover is a type of Christ *himself* and of his "passing over" to the Father, and that as a result the Passover functions also as a type of *our* "passing over" to the Father. The church, after all, is included in Christ.[52] Careful textual critic that he was, Origen recognized that the interpretation that Melito and others had put forward errs because it fails to take into account the Hebrew original. "Most of the brethren," comments Origen, "indeed perhaps all, think that the Passover (πάσχα; *pascha*) takes its name from the passion (πάθος; *pathos*) of the Savior."[53] He then correctly points out, however, that the Greek *pascha* is simply the Hellenized form of the Hebrew *pesakh*, which means "passage" or "Passover," and which, when translated into Greek, would have to be rendered by the word *diabasis*.[54]

For Origen, this was more than just a lexical matter. He rejected the typological link between the Passover and Christ's suffering in part because he stood in a different tradition than that of Hippolytus, Melito, and the Quartodecimans. Melito's Asian tradition tended to be more literal or historical in its exegesis than the Alexandrian tradition of Origen. We have already seen that we need to be careful about positing absolute contrasts in terms of ancient schools of biblical interpretation. We cannot state simply that the Asian tradition was typological while the Alexandrian tradition was allegorical. Still, it is probably significant that Melito, from within the Asian

---

50. Origen, *Treatise on the Passover* 39.9–50.8 (ACW 54:49–56).

51. Daly, introduction to "Treatise on the Passover," 6. In the late second century, Apollinaris of Hierapolis also made the link between the Passover and the suffering of Christ. See Dawson, *Christian Figural Reading*, 66.

52. Daly, introduction to "Treatise on the Passover," 6–7.

53. Origen, *Treatise on the Passover* 1 (ACW 54:1). Here and in what follows, transliterations from Origen's treatise are mine.

54. Ibid. Cf. Daly, introduction to "Treatise on the Passover," 6; Simonetti, *Biblical Interpretation*, 26–27.

tradition, insisted on the Jewish Passover being the typological counterpart to the passion of Christ. Origen's lineage was a different one and went back, via Clement of Alexandria (ca. 150–ca. 215), to the Jewish Platonic philosopher Philo (ca. 20 BC–ca. AD 50). Origen's predecessor, Clement, had recognized that the term *pascha* has to do not with suffering but with passage. And in this Clement had followed Philo: for Philo the Passover had been an allegory describing the passage of the soul from the material world into the eternal, spiritual world.[55]

As a result, Origen presents several arguments against the Jewish Passover being a type of Christ's suffering. First, he argues that while in the Passover saints used to sacrifice a lamb, Christ instead was sacrificed by "criminals and sinners."[56] This contrast would seem to rule out a direct typological link between the Passover and the suffering of Christ. Second, this means, according to Origen, that it is Christians (the saints) who eat the true Passover lamb when they consume the body of Christ. The Passover typologically foreshadows not the suffering of Christ but the church's eschatological participation in Christ. This participation occurs, John David Dawson points out, in the very practice of one's allegorical reading of the exodus narrative: Origen "identifies the consuming of the lamb with the allegorical reading of Scripture which is contrasted with various deficient modes of reading."[57] In our reading of the Scripture, we eat Christ's flesh and drink his blood (John 6:53).[58] So, according to Origen, the antitype of the Passover is not just Christ's suffering but Christ himself in his act of passing over, along with our participation in this passing over to the heavenly realm as we read the Scriptures in a spiritual rather than a physical manner.[59]

John O'Keefe and R. R. Reno, in their book *Sanctified Vision*, explain how Origen wants us to read the Passover narrative christologically: "Having blocked a false reading of Israel's Passover as verbally connected to Jesus' passion, Origen turns toward what he envisions as a fuller and more fruitful interpretation of the relationship between the Passover and the saving work of Jesus Christ. This fuller reading forces us to connect the narrative moments of dedication, roasting, eating, and celebration to the manner of our

55. Daly, introduction to "Treatise on the Passover," 8.

56. Origen, *Treatise on the Passover* 12 (ACW 54:34).

57. Dawson, *Christian Figural Reading*, 72.

58. Cf. Virginia Burrus's comment on Origen's treatise: "To read is to eat and to be metabolically changed into something other, even as the ingested text itself is also changed." "'Passover Still Takes Place Today,'" 240.

59. Origen, *Treatise on the Passover* 13–14 (ACW 54:34–35). As a third argument, Origen notes that Christ himself makes the bronze snake of Numbers 21—not the Passover—the type of his suffering (John 3:14). Ibid., 14–15 (ACW 54:35–36).

participation in Christ's life, teaching, death, and resurrection."[60] So according to Origen, the antitype of the Passover is not just Christ's suffering but Christ himself in his act of passing over. In particular, as Origen makes clear later on in his treatise, it is the Passover *lamb* that is a type of Christ.[61] The hermeneutical issue for Origen, then, becomes how we relate to Christ as our Passover lamb—and he answers this by suggesting an allegorical interpretation of the exodus narrative.

However one may evaluate Origen's arguments here, it is important to notice that he presents a detailed exegetical argument against the Quartodecimans. He rejects the view of Melito and Hippolytus on exegetical (partially linguistic) grounds, and he attaches significant liturgical and theological consequences to his rejection of the Asian tradition.[62] This is important because it is especially Origen—and the tradition following the Alexandrian theologian—who has been much lampooned for his so-called arbitrary allegorical exegesis.[63] There is nothing arbitrary about what Origen does here. He presents a careful, rational argument for choosing one particular typological reading of the Passover over another. One may well disagree with his particular choice, or even reject his allegorical approach altogether (though obviously I am not inclined to do the latter myself). But any such disagreement cannot take the form of a claim that allegory is an arbitrary de-historicizing of the biblical text.[64] Such a position simply betrays lack of familiarity with Origen's work.

Origen is quite aware that the interpretive move from the historical to the spiritual is a delicate process. The important point in this process, in connection with the Passover, is absolutely evident to him: "That the Passover still takes place today, that the sheep (πρόβατον; *probaton*) is sacrificed and the people come up out of Egypt, this is what the Apostle is teaching when he says: 'For Christ, our paschal lamb, has been sacrificed. Let us, therefore, celebrate the festival, not with the old leaven, the leaven of malice and evil, but with the unleavened bread of sincerity and truth' (1 Cor. 5:7–8). If 'our Passover has been sacrificed,' Jesus Christ, those who sacrifice Christ come up out of Egypt, cross the Red Sea, and will see Pharaoh engulfed."[65] Origen's key argument is that the Old Testament historical events surrounding the exodus

60. O'Keefe and Reno, *Sanctified Vision*, 52.
61. Origen, *Treatise on the Passover* 42 (ACW 54:50–51).
62. Alistair Stewart-Sykes argues that it "is quite possible that Hippolytus's community had a Quartodeciman past." *Lamb's High Feast*, 194.
63. For an excellent corrective, see Martens, *Origen and Scripture*.
64. I am not arguing that Origen doesn't at times downplay the historicity of the text. He does, as I make clear in chap. 5, sec. "History's Rightful Place."
65. Origen, *Treatise on the Passover* 3 (ACW 54:28). Here and elsewhere I have replaced Daly's use of italics in rendering Origen's biblical quotations with quotation marks.

still take place today. They take place in believers' identification with Christ as they recognize him in their spiritual reading of the narrative. This means that despite the particular exegetical disagreement that Origen may have with Melito, the two interpreters agree on the underlying point, namely, that the Old and New Testament events ought to be identified with each other. The Old Testament Passover in some way sacramentally or mystically contains the New Testament reality of the Christ event. The two theologians agree that we ourselves are the ones taking the exodus journey.

Origen makes several fascinating textual observations as he makes his exegetical case that we may rightly perceive today's ecclesial situation *within* the ancient text. He notes, for instance, the distinction between "beginning" and "first" in Exodus 12:1–2: "This month shall be for you the beginning of months; it shall be the first month of the year for you."[66] When we look simply for the historical meaning, we may note that the Passover was celebrated in the first month of the year, the month of Nisan. "As far as the history goes," says Origen, "this month is indeed the 'first month.'"[67] But he then adds (and here he moves to the spiritual meaning) that when Christ came, he showed the true Passover, the true "passage," and to describe *this* spiritual reality the text uses the term "beginning" rather than "first." As Origen explains: "And for the one in the passage, 'the beginning of months' is when the month of passing over out of Egypt comes around, which is also the beginning of another birth for him."[68] Origen argues that this spiritual "beginning" or new birth takes place through the water of baptism. This spiritual meaning of the text—based on the distinction between the words "beginning" and "first"—is relevant, according to Origen, only for the perfect. It is only "for you," the text says; that is to say, it is only for Moses and Aaron.[69]

In similar fashion, when Exodus 12:9 states, "Do not eat any of it raw or boiled in water, but roasted," Origen discerns here three different approaches to the Scriptures. If people simply follow the literal meaning of the Scriptures, it is like eating the flesh of the Savior raw. This is a Jewish, literalist approach to interpretation.[70] Heretics, on the other hand, add water and so boil the flesh with water. It is only Christians who roast the flesh of the Scriptures with fire—the fire of the Holy Spirit.[71] Roasting the flesh of

66. Ibid., 4 (ACW 54:29). I am following the biblical translation used in Origen's *Treatise on the Passover*.

67. Ibid.

68. Ibid.

69. Ibid., 5 (ACW 54:29).

70. Ibid., 28–29 (ACW 54:42).

71. Ibid., 26–27 (ACW 54:41–42). Cf. ACW 54:98n33.

Scripture with the fire of the Spirit, maintains Origen, refers to a spiritual reading of the text.

When he finally devotes a separate section of his book (part 2) to the spiritual meaning of the Passover, Origen begins by speaking of "mystery" (the same language we have already encountered in Melito): "Since the sacred ceremony and sacrifice of the Passover was already carried out in mystery (μυστηριωδῶς; *mystēriōdōs*) in the time of Moses . . . we now raise the question whether . . . it is also carried out in a different manner in our own time, the time of fulfillment—'upon whom the end of the ages has come' (1 Cor. 10:11)."[72] The Passover was not just a historical event; at its heart it already contained the New Testament mystery. And so Origen explicitly distinguishes here between the historical meaning and the ana-gogical (upward-leading) or spiritual meaning of Exodus 12. The former refers simply to the original event; the latter speaks of the "passage" of Christians, mystically present already within the events narrated within the book of Exodus.[73] The result is an exegetical approach that is sacramental in character: the very reading of the Scriptures, in an allegorical mode, is our participation in the Passover event of Exodus 12. As Dawson puts it: "Indeed, Origen will argue that Scripture is itself a sacrament like the Eucharist. Christ the lamb is still the Word, that Word is found in Scripture, and eating the Word refers to the interpretation of Scripture. . . . The ancient Passover continues to be celebrated, then, in the allegorical reading of Scripture, which is not a disembodiment through interpretation but instead a consumption of a body through reading."[74] It is the distinction between historical and spiritual meaning, therefore, that allows Origen to speak of Christ as the true Passover lamb and also to discuss the "passage" of those who are included in Christ.

Conclusion

Melito recognized that the angel of death turned away from the houses of the Hebrews not because of the blood of the sheep but because of the blood of Christ. For Melito, the reality of Christ was really present in the Passover event. Similarly, Origen maintained that "the Passover still takes place today." Apparently, the church's liturgical celebration is for Origen already present in the Passover event and vice versa. Both authors are convinced that the Pass-

72. Ibid., 39 (ACW 54:49).
73. Ibid.
74. Dawson, *Christian Figural Reading*, 71.

over event is something in which we today participate. We ourselves celebrate the Passover, and we ourselves take the journey out of Egypt. The reason for both authors is simply this: the Old Testament history is a mystery, or a sacrament, in which the New Testament realities of Christ and the church are already present. We have a place—a real place rather than one arbitrarily imposed—within the narratives of the Old Testament.

I began this chapter by asking two questions: By what right would one "speak other" than what the words themselves convey? And how does such a practice of allegorizing not turn into an arbitrary imposition of our own preconceived ideas onto the biblical text? It has not been my purpose to provide a full or adequate response to these questions. At the same time, I am hoping that by turning to patristic exegesis of Exodus 12, I have given some insight at least into how these early Christian readers would have responded to our questions.

My hunch is that both Melito and Origen would have responded by saying something like the following:

> We don't care too much what you call the kind of scriptural reading that we are engaged in. You may call it typology, allegory, *theōria*, anagogy, spiritual reading—it really doesn't matter that much. Each of these terms is suitable to express what we're trying to do. Our reading is indeed "other" than what the words themselves convey in the sense that we look to the words on the "surface" of the text as merely sacraments: words that contain in themselves the greater reality of the Christ event. The words are the outward sacrament; Christ is the inward reality of grace. History and spirit, sacrament and reality, are indeed different things. So typology or allegory does look for something "other." But if by "other" you mean something completely different, something unrelated, then, no, we're not "speaking other" than what the words themselves convey. We're simply exposing the deeper, underlying meaning that is inherent in the text itself.
>
> It's hard for us to wrap our minds around the suspicion that we whimsically impose random notions onto the text. Never have we encountered that concern before. If it's true that we simply uncover a hidden meaning that is present already in the text—if there is a *real presence* of Christ and his church in the ancient narratives—then this cannot possibly be an arbitrary thing: we can find only what's already there!
>
> Furthermore, arbitrariness is something that you get by removing the biblical text from its proper surroundings of the believing community, away from its liturgical setting and its confession of faith. The context within which a christological reading of the text makes sense is that of the church. Therefore, the "right" by which we move from history to spirit, from temporal to eternal realities, has everything to do with the Bible being the church's Bible. And

that implies, we believe, that in an important sense the Bible belongs *not* to the academy.

Such, I think, would be the response of Melito and Origen to our modern-day suspicions of allegorical interpretation—a response that I believe makes sufficiently clear why it is that still today they serve as faithful guides in our reading of the biblical text.

5

INCARNATIONAL READING

Origen on the Historical Narrative of Joshua

Allegory and Event

Origen of Alexandria (ca. 185–ca. 254), one of the most influential and most controversial theologians of the ante-Nicene church, continues to inspire discussion and debate. In the previous chapter, we took a first look at his allegorizing of Scripture. I now want to broaden this analysis by investigating in greater depth his approach to biblical interpretation. He famously outlines this approach in *On First Principles*, where he advocates a threefold reading of the biblical text: historical, moral, and spiritual.[1] The objections to this are well known. Origen derives this threefold interpretation from his tripartite anthropology: the literal meaning corresponds to the body, the moral meaning to the soul, and the spiritual meaning to the spirit. In this way, a tripartite, Platonically based anthropology determines Origen's approach to Scripture.[2] Thus, so the charge goes, he relies more on Philo and thus on Platonic philosophical categories than on Scripture itself, which means that

1. Origen, *On First Principles* 4.2.4 (Butterworth, 275–77).
2. Cf. chap. 1, sec. "Retrieving Sacramental Reading: Meaning, Virtue, Progress, and Providence."

in his exegesis the philosophical dross covers the pure gold of Scripture. This Philonic influence can be seen in Origen's allegorical interpretation, which far too often downplays, ignores, or denies the historical meaning of the text. History, according to this objection, disappears as a meaningful category, to be replaced with otherworldly concerns. Briefly put, the vertical displaces the horizontal.

Furthermore, by moving directly from a historical to a moral reading of Scripture, Origen's interpretation is allegedly moralistic in character. He is mainly concerned, so the argument goes, with what the text says about Christians' moral actions; as a result, the historical particularities of the text move into the background. Immediately connected to this is the observation that Origen's allegorizing causes him largely to overlook the literal meaning and to jump straight to the moral and allegorical levels of reading, which—seeing as they are bereft of historical grounding—cannot but lapse into an arbitrary imposition of the reader's own insights onto the biblical text. The historical and the spiritual seem separated in Origen's interpretation, with the former disappearing into oblivion and the latter taking on a capricious character.

These objections have most famously and forcefully been presented by R. P. C. Hanson, in his influential 1959 study, *Allegory and Event*. To be sure, Hanson's position by no means forms the consensus among patristics scholars. Nine years before Hanson's book appeared, Henri de Lubac had published a study of Origen's interpretation of Scripture, entitled *History and Spirit*, in which he presented a vigorous defense of the Alexandrian theologian's approach to Scripture. De Lubac's study has recently been published in English translation.[3] De Lubac's defense of Origen notwithstanding, Hanson's denunciation of the latter's approach has been tremendously influential, not in the least because it fit the more historical mold that dominated biblical exegesis in the twentieth century.

In this chapter I will focus on Origen's homilies on Joshua, and I hope to show from these homilies (as well as from additional reflections on Origen's theology) that, even though he does downplay the historical character of some events described in the book of Joshua, Origen nonetheless values the historical level in a subordinate sense as a result of the sacramental cast of his exegesis. We can appreciate how Origen's exegesis functions only if and when we come to understand the sacramental structure that lies at the basis of his interpretation. What is more, inasmuch as history serves in this sacramental role, the footing of Origen's valuation of history is more secure than that of

3. For a more recent positive evaluation of Origen, see Martens, *Origen and Scripture*.

many contemporary historical exegetes, for whom the category of history has no grounding beyond itself.[4]

Origen's Polemical Context

There is no denying that Origen's interpretation of Scripture is markedly different from nearly all modern and late modern readings. The very strangeness of his exegesis, the mere fact that it is so different from what we are used to, makes it difficult for us to recognize its value. I suspect that in many cases we do not disagree with Origen from the outset. Disagreement, after all, implies understanding. One significant obstacle to our understanding of Origen's reading of Scripture is that we are so conditioned by our modern surroundings that reading Origen leads us into an alien world, a world that, at least initially, we have difficulty comprehending. And without comprehension, we cannot possibly come to agreement or disagreement—which, of course, hinders our enjoyment of Origen's exegetical work. One of our first tasks then, if we are to evaluate his allegorizing of Scripture, is to familiarize ourselves with some of his writings, and for this occasion I have chosen to reflect on Origen's homilies on Joshua. I have purposely chosen this particular Bible book because it is, more than any other, a book of violence. It is a book that offends, a book that not only ancient readers but also contemporary Christians find difficult to appropriate. How is a book such as Joshua—with its stories of conquest, its incitement to genocide, and its distributions of conquered areas—Christian Scripture?

This question was Origen's question no less than it is ours. To be sure, as I indicated, our twenty-first-century context is rather different from Origen's third-century world. Our apprehension of violence is fueled by late modern sensibilities that condition us to be fearful of the role that religion may play in military conflicts, nervous about the imposition of ideological regimes that do not allow for difference or dissent, and concerned about the victims of oppression, abuse, and marginalization. The postmodern celebration of difference goes hand in hand with the rejection of the violent hegemony of sameness that characterized modernity. In such a context, it is difficult to appropriate Old Testament books such as Joshua.

Origen too struggled with the appropriation of Joshua. It was particularly the opposition of two religious groups that made it difficult for Christian theologians such as Origen to refer to the book of Joshua as Christian Scripture.

4. This point is made particularly eloquently by Martens, "Origen against History?," 635–56.

Two alternative interpretations vied for people's allegiance, and both of them rejected a Christian reading of this book. The first was a Jewish reading. Throughout his homilies and commentaries, Origen finds himself at odds with Jewish readings of the text. In particular, he objects to the literalness of Jewish interpretation. Repeatedly, when he makes his case for a spiritual reading of the text, Origen polemically questions the Jewish approach. For instance, when Joshua the son of Nun is told to circumcise the Israelites a second time (Josh. 5:2), Origen immediately comments: "I may wish in this place to inquire of the Jews how anyone is able to be circumcised a second time with the circumcision of the flesh."[5] Origen here makes the simple observation that it is physically not possible to circumcise a person twice. As a result, he puts forward a spiritual reading, according to which the first circumcision is the putting aside of the errors of idolatry in favor of the law of Moses and the second is the acceptance of Christ, the circumcision by means of "the rock, who is Christ."[6] Origen speaks of "those Jewish defenders of the letter who are ignorant of the spirit of the Law."[7] He mentions the person who is "outwardly a Jew" and thinks that "nothing else but wars" constitute the topic of the book of Joshua.[8] As a result, the Jews "become cruel and implacable," maintains Origen.[9] A strictly historical reading, in Origen's context, is the reading advocated by his Jewish opponents.

Our first instinct, perhaps, is to shrink back from such anti-Jewish rhetoric as unseemly, even anti-Semitic.[10] But we need to be careful with such accusations, understandable though they may be, particularly in the light of the horrible history of the twentieth century. Without trying to excuse the excesses of some of Origen's ad hominem statements against the Jews, we need to keep in mind that for Origen anti-Jewish rhetoric is less a matter of anti-Semitism than it is a matter of securing the right to interpret the Scriptures from the perspective of the reality of Christ. We cannot understand any of the fathers' anti-Jewish discourse if we fail to keep in mind the importance of the question "Whose Bible is it?" with regard to the Hebrew Bible or the Old Testament. So in *Homily 17* Origen insists that in the division of the land of Judea related in the book of Joshua, we can see a "copy and shadow" of a heavenly division (cf. Heb. 8:5).[11] Accordingly,

---

5. Origen, *Homilies on Joshua* 5.5 (FC 105:63). See also ibid., 7.5 (FC 105:79).
6. Ibid., 5.5 (FC 105:63). Cf. Josh. 5:2; 1 Cor. 10:4.
7. Origen, *Homilies on Joshua* 9.4 (FC 105:99).
8. Ibid., 13.1 (FC 105:125).
9. Ibid., 15.6 (FC 105:149).
10. This is largely the approach that Jason Byassee takes with regard to Saint Augustine in his otherwise fine study *Praise Seeking Understanding*.
11. Origen, *Homilies on Joshua* 17.1 (FC 105:157).

Origen regards the earthly Jerusalem, its temple and altar, the visible worship with its priests and high priests, as well as the various regions and towns of Judea, as imitations of "heavenly things."[12] He observes that all these "imitations" have disappeared with the incarnation. The reason is that "at the coming of God our Savior, truth descended from heaven."[13] And so Origen appeals to the Jews to turn from the "shadows" and "types" to the "truth" of the reality that has come with Christ: "If therefore, O Jew, coming to the earthly city of Jerusalem, you find it overthrown and reduced to ashes and embers, do not weep as you do now 'as if with the mind of a child' [1 Cor. 14:20]; do not lament; but search for a heavenly city instead of an earthly one. Look above! And there you will discover 'the heavenly Jerusalem that is the mother of all' [Gal. 4:26]."[14] For Origen, as well as for many other church fathers, anti-Jewish rhetoric was in the first place a polemic aimed at securing the Old Testament as Christian Scripture. It had to be read not in a fleshly but in a spiritual fashion. This is not to suggest that anti-Jewish writing never slid into anti-Semitism. On a regular basis it did. But we do need to keep in mind the hermeneutical concern—and, tied in with this, the even more important question of Christian identity—that motivated church fathers such as Origen. With twenty centuries of Christian history behind us, we have a long tradition that recognizes the Old Testament as Christian Scripture, and as a result we simply do not experience the same anxious concern that the church fathers did to secure the Old Testament as the church's book.

The second alternative Old Testament interpretation was that of the gnostics. During much of the second and third centuries, gnostic groups were highly influential in their attempt to supplant mainstream Christianity as the leading religion of the empire. Since gnostics tended to be syncretistic in their approach and were quite willing to adopt elements of the Christian Scriptures that they could fit in with their own theological emphases, gnosticism turned out to be a dangerous alternative to the church.[15] Many gnostic groups aimed at secret knowledge (*gnōsis*), which would allow them to escape this evil, material world. As Walter Wink puts it, "For many Gnostics, Creation was not followed by a Fall, as in Judaism and Christianity; Creation was the Fall. They were a single, tragic event."[16] Valentinian and Basilidian gnostics

12. Ibid. See also ibid., 2.1 (FC 105:37–38).
13. Ibid., 17.1 (FC 105:157).
14. Ibid., 17.1 (FC 105:158).
15. See Lee, *Against the Protestant Gnostics*, 11. For Origen's relationship to gnostic groups, see Brakke, *Gnostics*, 128–32.
16. Wink, *Cracking the Gnostic Code*, 16.

were prominent in Alexandria, while in Caesarea, where Origen spent many of his most productive years, the Marcionites proved to be influential in their rejection of the authority of the Old Testament.[17]

Since for the fathers doctrine was always a matter of scriptural interpretation, it was primarily the reading of Scripture that divided Christians from gnostics. In the late second century, Saint Irenaeus had done battle with the gnostics in his five-book *Against Heresies*, and in the third century, it was up to Origen and others to fight these same heretical groups. Origen repeatedly mentions Valentinus, Basilides, and Marcion in the same breath.[18] Preaching in Caesarea, he was perhaps mostly concerned with Marcion and his disciple Apelles.[19] Marcion discarded the Old Testament as unworthy of the God of the New Testament. The human ways in which the Old Testament describes God (its anthropomorphisms), the violence that this God and his people embraced, and the many immoralities depicted in the Old Testament Scriptures led Marcion to reject the Old Testament altogether and to posit the existence of two gods: a god of the Old Testament and a god of the New Testament. As a result, when Origen did battle with the gnostics, this was a struggle against a literalist reading of the Old Testament, much like his fight against Jewish interpretations.

Thus, when Joshua enlisted the Gibeonites as "cutters of wood" and "drawers of water" in the service of the Israelites (Josh. 9:21), the Marcionites objected to such inconsiderate, perhaps even immoral, behavior on the part of Joshua. "Of course," comments Origen in *Homily 10*, "it must be observed that the heretics reading this passage, those who do not accept the Old Testament, are accustomed to make a malicious charge and say, 'See how Jesus the son of Nun showed no human kindness, so that, although permitting salvation, he inflicted a mark of infamy and a yoke of servitude upon those men who had come to him in supplication.'"[20] Origen proceeds to defend Joshua's actions by contrasting the unworthy attitudes of the Gibeonites to the exemplary behavior of Rahab. He then provides a spiritual interpretation of the Gibeonites' identity as people who go through all the right motions in church while making no effort to restrain their vices and to cultivate virtuous habits: "Let them know they will be assigned a part and lot with the Gibeonites by the Lord Jesus."[21] Origen defends Old Testament Scripture against the

---

17. De Lubac, *History and Spirit*, 56.

18. Ibid., 54. See also Origen, *Homilies on Joshua* 7.7 (FC 105:83), 12.3 (FC 105:123).

19. De Lubac, *History and Spirit*, 57.

20. Origen, *Homilies on Joshua* 10.2 (FC 105:111). The Septuagint renders Joshua's name as "Jesus," which is the Greek name that Origen uses here and elsewhere.

21. Ibid., 10.3 (FC 105:112).

gnostic accusation of cruelty by insisting on an allegorical interpretation of the text of Joshua.

Our historical and cultural context is in many ways different from that of Origen. But this doesn't render his exegesis any less timely. Origen aims his polemics against Jewish and gnostic interpretations of Scripture. Over against the Jews, he insists that their exegesis cannot circumvent the accusation that the biblical text, with its violence and immorality, is unworthy of God. They need spiritual exegesis to overcome this difficulty. While the gnostics' exegesis does not face the same difficulties with regard to religious violence, they only avoid this problem by rejecting the book of Joshua altogether. Both groups, however, make the same basic mistake, according to Origen: they read the text on a literal level only and by doing so fall into the trap of a carnal reading of the Old Testament Scriptures.[22] Both problems with which Origen struggles— that of an overly literal reading of the text and that of religious violence—are issues we face today as well. Historical readings of Scripture, when they are solely concerned with authorial intent, are unable to overcome the postmodern accusation against the Christian faith, namely, that it has served and continues to serve as an instrument of violence. Modern exegetes who advocate a strictly literal reading of the text are faced with a stark choice: to justify the violence inherent in the Old Testament or to abandon the Old Testament as Christian Scripture. Since either option seems to me detrimental to the church, I suggest that a serious look at the third-century exegesis of Origen is well worth our while.[23]

Scripture as Incarnate Logos

For much of the Great Tradition, the term "mystery" functioned as a synonym for the word "sacrament." Susan Wood, in her book *Spiritual Exegesis and the Church in the Theology of Henri de Lubac*, makes the point that for de Lubac—and, we could add, for many of the fathers and medieval theologians— "the structure of allegory is fundamentally sacramental."[24] She explains this statement as follows:

22. See also Origen, *On First Principles* 4.2.1 (Butterworth, 269–71). Here Origen takes issue first with "the hard-hearted and ignorant members of the circumcision," then with "the members of the heretical sects," and finally with "the simpler of those who claim to belong to the Church," all for their literalist readings of the Old Testament Scriptures.

23. I do not mean to suggest that violence can never be justified. I have argued elsewhere that I think it does, in fact, play a role in the divine economy. See *Violence, Hospitality, and the Cross*. Still, if we restrict ourselves to a literal reading of Joshua, we miss out on typological/ allegorical elements in the text that prevent us from taking elements such as incitements to genocide as timeless principles valid for all times.

24. Wood, *Spiritual Exegesis*, 39.

The content or signification of both the historical event and the future historical
reality of Christ and the Church to which the allegorical meaning refers exceed
what is observable within history. Just as what is observable within history does
not limit the mystery it embodies, so too, Christian allegory is not limited to
the historical dimension. That is, allegory points not only to future historical
realities, but to future mysteries which, belonging to the fulfillment of history,
surpass history. Thus the concept of *mysterium*, that which is hidden within,
is proper to both the past historical event and the future reality it prefigures.[25]

Two comments may help clarify what it is that Wood is suggesting about
spiritual interpretation. First, when allegorical exegesis insists that Old Testament events point to New Testament realities, it is not just moving from
point A to point B on a chronological timeline. Allegory is not just like a
prophecy-fulfillment scheme. Instead, Wood maintains, both point A and
point B have a signification that exceeds or goes beyond what is observable
within history.[26] Historical events are never *just* historical events. Particularly,
salvation-historical events always carry an extra dimension. They always point
beyond history.

Second, when Old Testament events point to future events—referring to
Christ or to the church—they point, says Wood, to "future mysteries." She
uses the term *mysterium*. This is a sacramental term, and we would not go
wrong by translating it simply as "sacrament." Sacraments are often described
as visible signs of invisible realities. They make present God's invisible grace
in our visible reality. Or if we take our starting point in this tangible world,
we could say that inasmuch as created realities function as sacraments, they
carry an extra, mysterious dimension. That is to say, if one were to take all
the measurements of a particular object that one possibly could—if one were
to map its DNA, so to speak—one still would not fully grasp or comprehend
the object. The reason is this: there's a sacramental mystery to the object that
simply isn't subject to measurement. It belongs to the invisible, eternal realm,
to which we do not have access by means of the senses. Wood calls *mysterium*
"that which is hidden within." We could also say it is "that which exceeds or
transcends" the empirically observable.

Mysteries point from Old Testament events to New Testament realities—
but not as if these were unconnected events, like sign A pointing to reality
B. Rather, the notion of *mysterium* or *sacramentum* means that the New
Testament reality B already lies embedded within the earlier, Old Testament
event A. Event A carries a mysterious presence B that is unobservable by

25. Ibid.
26. I discuss this in more detail in *Heavenly Participation*, 21–23.

the senses but is no less real. Event *A* carries the "real presence" of event *B*. Wood's expression "future mysteries," borrowed from the Great Tradition, is paradoxical in character, since it combines horizontal, chronological connections with vertical, spiritual links. Old Testament events point both forward in time (hence the word "future") and upward toward the invisible realm (hence the term "mysteries").

For Origen, all divine revelation functions in a thoroughly sacramental fashion. Robert J. Daly makes this clear in his foreword to an anthology of Origen's work edited by Hans Urs von Balthasar and entitled *Spirit and Fire*. The Word or Logos of God, Daly explains, is central to Origen's theology. When God reveals himself in history, the eternal Logos takes on the form of earthly, temporal existence. Daly's summary of the various "incarnations" of the Logos is worth quoting in full:

> When Origen speaks of the biblical WORD, the WORD incarnate in the scriptures, at least four interconnected levels of meaning are in play. *First*, this WORD is the pre-existent, eternal, divine Logos, the Logos proclaimed in the prologue of John's gospel and expounded in extraordinary detail and depth in Origen's commentary on this prologue. *Second*, this same divine Logos is the one who took flesh of the Virgin Mary, lived and worked among us, suffered, died, rose again and ascended to the Father, where he continues to intercede for us and to work until all things have become subjected to the Father who is all in all. *Third*, this same eternal WORD who took flesh of Mary has also become incarnate in the words of scripture. *Fourth*, this same divine WORD, born of Mary and also incarnate in the scriptures, also dwells and is at work within us, espoused to our souls, calling us to make progress toward perfection, and to work with him in ascending to and subjecting all things to the Father.[27]

Daly explains that there are four levels of meaning in connection with the word "Logos." The starting point is the Logos itself, the eternal, preexisting Son of God. This eternal Word takes on the characteristics of time and space in three different ways; or, we could also say, there are three incarnations of the eternal Word: (1) *the* incarnation of Jesus Christ in the Virgin Mary, (2) the incarnation in the Scriptures, and (3) the incarnation in our own souls (see diagram 1).

Daly's analysis is essentially right, I believe—though, of course, the differences between these various "incarnations" do have to be kept in mind.[28] It is fascinating to see how for Origen the second incarnation (the Word's

27. Daly, foreword to Origen, *Spirit and Fire*, xiv.
28. It seems to me that the "incarnations" in Scripture and in the soul can only be termed "incarnations" in an analogical sense.

Diagram 1

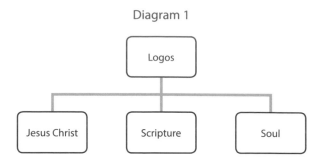

presence in Scripture) is intimately linked to the third (the birth of Christ in our souls). Daly adds that this final level of meaning is the "dominating" one, as it constitutes Origen's "central hermeneutical principle."[29] And, indeed, for Origen the Logos that is present in Scripture is the same Logos that dwells also in the believer. Henri de Lubac reflects on this in his book *History and Spirit*. He makes the point that, according to Origen, we need to read the soul in a similar manner to the way we read Scripture. De Lubac comments: "What we call the spiritual sense in Scripture we name the image of God in the soul. And if the divine Logos is planted in each soul as he is inserted into the fabric of Scripture, are the inspired words not as engraved 'with the image of the great King' as is the human soul? It is on both sides the same impression, or rather the same Presence."[30] As we read Scripture, we come to understand ourselves in the process—and, of course, vice versa: as we come to understand ourselves better, we become better equipped to read and understand Scripture. The same Word is active both in Scripture and in ourselves, explains de Lubac.[31]

We need to briefly pause here, because de Lubac's reflection is important in relation to the fear of arbitrariness that often arises in connection with Origen's allegorical exegesis. If it is true that Scripture and the soul have the same structure—if it is true that both are, in some sense, incarnations of the eternal Logos—then Spirit-guided exegesis can hardly be arbitrary. I do not mean, of course, that the presence of the Logos in the believing soul ensures that the believer will find just the right, objectively correct interpretation. For Origen, there is no such thing, and neither is there for de Lubac. Rather, as de Lubac puts it, "Every time I am faithful to the Spirit of God in the interpretation of the Scriptures, my interpretation is valid in some

29. Daly, foreword to Origen, *Spirit and Fire*, xiv.
30. De Lubac, *History and Spirit*, 397. De Lubac's statement contains quotations from Origen's *Commentary on Matthew* and his *Commentary on John*.
31. De Lubac, *History and Spirit*, 398.

respect."[32] Multiplicity of interpretation, on this understanding, is simply a reflection of the Spirit's plurality of gifts in the lives of believers. As long as the believer's soul reflects the "imprint" of the image of God, she will identify spiritual readings that reflect the presence of the eternal Logos.[33]

As already indicated, I believe Daly is fundamentally right in his understanding of a threefold incarnation. At the same time, his helpful discussion does need some amplification. We need to keep in mind that Origen was, as he himself says, a "man of the church" (*vir ecclesiasticus*): "I want to be a man of the church. I do not want to be called by the name of some founder of a heresy but by the name of Christ, and to bear that name which is called blessed on the earth. It is my desire, in deed as in Spirit, both to be and to be called a Christian."[34] This beautiful passage highlights an important concern for Origen.[35] De Lubac has strongly insisted that the individual quest for God is never *just* an individual quest. It is always *in*corporation *into* the body, or *corpus*, of the church.[36] So close, in fact, is the link between the church and the individual that it may be more appropriate to speak of the Word's incarnation in the church than of the Word's incarnation in the individual soul. Or, as diagram 2 makes clear, perhaps we could speak of a fourfold incarnation of the Logos: in Jesus Christ, in Scripture, in the believer, and in the church.[37]

The way in which Balthasar, in his anthology of Origen's work, structures the lengthy section on the "Word" captures this ecclesial element well. The first section, "Word with God," dealing with the eternal Logos, leads to a threefold incarnation: "Word as Scripture," "Word as Flesh," and "Church." As Balthasar puts it: "Incarnation in the scripture and in an individual body were both an image and means to the third incarnation which was the meaning and purpose of the redemption: the incarnation of the Logos in his mystical body."[38] This mystical body, the church, has existed, according to Origen, since the beginning of the world. The result is that throughout the Old Testament we see types or figures of the church. Adam and Eve's union, Noah's ark,

---

32. Ibid.
33. I have dealt at some length with the objection of arbitrariness in the previous chapter.
34. Origen, *Spirit and Fire*, 155 (§389).
35. See de Lubac, *History and Spirit*, 68–73.
36. See especially de Lubac, *Catholicism*.
37. De Lubac makes the point that the entire universe is also the "subject of spiritual interpretation" (*History and Spirit*, 401), so that it too is an incarnation of the Logos (ibid., 401–6). Furthermore, since the Eucharist is also the body of Christ, the bread and wine of the Eucharist are types or symbols of the church (ibid., 406–15). Thus, the Eucharist too is an incarnation of the Word.
38. Origen, *Spirit and Fire*, 148.

Diagram 2

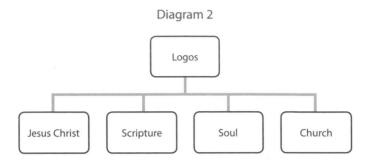

Abraham, Jael, the bride of the Song of Songs, and the Queen of Sheba all prefigure the church of the gentiles.[39]

The fact that the Word becomes incarnate both in Jesus Christ and in the church enables Origen to posit a close link between the two. What happens to the church happens to Christ and vice versa, since both share in the eternal Logos.[40] Balthasar's anthology pulls together some fascinating passages from Origen's writings that illustrate this close link. Referring, for example, to opposition coming from both Jews and pagans, Origen comments: "I see Jesus every day 'giving his back to the smiters' (Isa 50:6). Go into the Jewish synagogues and see Jesus being beaten by them with blasphemous tongue. Look at the pagan assemblies, plotting against Christians and how to capture Jesus. And he 'gives his back to the smiters.' . . . So many beat and strike him, and he is silent and says not a word. . . . And to this day, Jesus 'has not hid his face from shame and spitting' (Isa 50:6)."[41] According to Origen, Jesus' suffering, prophesied in Isaiah 50, continues in the church. In a real sense, for Origen the church *is* Christ, so that, along with Christ, the church is an incarnation of the eternal Logos.

De Lubac too draws attention to this unity between Christ and the church. In fact, he makes the daring point that the church is a "more perfect, fuller realization of the divine design" than the historical body born of the Virgin.[42] The reason for this is that the church is the reality of which the historical body of Christ is the type or symbol.[43] De Lubac captures Origen's understanding of

39. Ibid., 148–52 (§§368–75).

40. Saint Augustine's *totus Christus* theology—with Christ and the church together forming the "whole Christ"—functions in a similar manner. Cf. chap. 6, sec. "Harmony with the Voice of Christ."

41. Origen, *Spirit and Fire*, 170 (§407).

42. De Lubac, *History and Spirit*, 412. De Lubac's comment can be interpreted in a way that would render it acceptable. Still, his comment gives a one-sided impression, since it ignores the distinction between Christ and his church, along with his lordship over the church.

43. Ibid.

the Christ-church relationship as follows: "The historical life of Christ in his flesh and the mystical life in his Church are thus one and the same life under two different aspects, in two 'bodies,' one of which is symbolic and the other symbolized."[44] For Origen, both the historical body and the ecclesial body are incarnations of the one Logos. The historical body is a prefiguration of the completion of the Logos in the eschatological, full reality of the church. In short, what we have seen so far is that the existence of multiple incarnations of one and the same Logos implies a close relationship among these various incarnate, earthly realities. There is an intimate link between Scripture and the soul as well as between Christ and the church.

At the historical or horizontal level, there are, of course, all kinds of differences among these various incarnations of the Logos—differences that we can observe with the senses. Still, the close connection that we have already observed between Scripture and the soul, as well as between Christ and the church, shows that if we move beyond the observable to the eternal Word itself, we come to the point (an eternal, heavenly one) where the four are not just similar but actually identical. The multiple earthly words find their point of unity and their coherence in the eternal Word. For de Lubac, our purpose as believers is finally to reach beyond the multiplicity of words to the simplicity of the one Word. Thus, when in the incarnate Christ we reach beyond the human nature that we observe with the senses, we arrive at his divine nature, at the eternal Word of God. Likewise, when in Scripture we go beyond the literal sense of the text to the spiritual meaning, we come to the eternal Word itself. De Lubac summarizes Origen's thought as follows:

> In his Scripture as in his earthly life, Origen thought, the Logos needs a body; the historical meaning and the spiritual meaning are, between them, like the flesh and the divinity of the Logos. All of Scripture is, so to speak, "incorporated"; like the One whom it proclaims and prepares for, it is "non in phantasia, sed in veritate" (not in fantasy, but in truth). Certainly, just as one must not stop in Christ at the man who is seen but, through the flesh that veils him to carnal eyes, perceive by faith the God who is in him, so one must go through the external history that is offered to us in the Holy Books, particularly in the Old Testament, in order to penetrate to the "spiritual mystery" that is hidden there.[45]

According to Origen, in the spiritual sense of the Bible, as in the divinity of Christ, one arrives at one and the same eternal Logos. Origen's working assumption here is that "there are not two Words any more than there are two

44. Ibid.
45. Ibid., 105. See also ibid., 385–96; H. Boersma, *Nouvelle Théologie*, 161.

Spirits."[46] The Word of Scripture is none other than the eternal Logos. De Lubac explains that it is "still the same word, the same biblical word, and there is no play on words in that."[47]

The obvious implication—although to my knowledge de Lubac does not spell this out—is that the soul of the individual too, to the extent that she reaches perfection, finds her point of unity in the eternal Logos. And with regard to the church, Origen makes the same point. Not only is the body of Jesus Christ a type of the body of the church, but this connection between Christ and his church implies that the many members are eschatologically united in one body. Origen comments, for instance, that "when this resurrection of the true and perfect Body of Christ takes place . . . , then his multiple members will form a single body."[48] It seems as though Origen is suggesting that the full unity of the church in the eschaton is the fullness of the eternal Logos. We may fairly suggest, then, that on the great day of the resurrection, the incarnate Christ, the Holy Scriptures, the individual soul, and the body of the church all reach their unifying apex or climax in the fullness of the eternal Word of God. Diagram 3 thus makes clear that each of the four "incarnations," as they render present the reality to which they point (understood, respectively, as Christ's divine nature, the spiritual sense of Scripture, the image of God in the soul, and the fullness of ecclesial unity), find their point of unity in the eternal Logos.

Mysterii video sacramentum

So far I have described Origen's understanding of the temporal and sensible appearances of Christ, Scripture, the soul, and the church as embodiments or incarnations of the eternal Logos. This is certainly true to Origen's description of things. But with equal validity, we could describe the relationship between these four aspects and the eternal Logos as sacramental in character. Thus, we could say that Jesus' humanity is the sacrament of the eternal Logos and that the literal meaning of Scripture is the sacrament of the eternal Logos. After all, the Logos has a "real presence" in the incarnate Christ (by means of the divine nature) and in Scripture (through the spiritual meaning of the text). Likewise, we may add, the Logos has a "real presence" in the soul and in the church.

We need to note the implication of this sacramental viewpoint particularly with regard to Holy Scripture. Robert Daly states that there is a *"real*

46. De Lubac, *History and Spirit*, 385.
47. Ibid.
48. Origen, *Commentary on John* 10.35, quoted in de Lubac, *History and Spirit*, 412.

Diagram 3

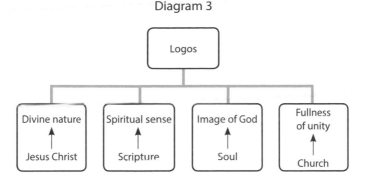

incarnation and hence 'real presence' of the eternal WORD in the scriptures."[49] He goes on to say: "It is thus not mere metaphorical language but precise theological description to speak of the 'sacramentality of the biblical word' according to Origen."[50] It seems to me that Daly is quite right. We have already seen that the term "mystery" has the sacramental connotation that we have just been tracing in connection with the Word's various incarnations. The events described in the biblical text are mysteries; they are sacraments. That is to say, the eternal Word or Logos of God shows up in them. There is a real presence of this eternal Word in the events that the Bible describes.

That Origen is firmly convinced of this real, sacramental presence of the Word in the Old Testament is something we can see throughout the *Homilies on Joshua*. The simple fact that Joshua's name in the Septuagint is rendered as "Jesus" and that Origen uses this Greek name throughout his homilies enables him to shift back and forth seamlessly from Old Testament type to New Testament reality, from the sacrament of the historical event to the mystical reality of the eternal Word.[51] Origen starts *Homily 1* magnificently with an allusion to Philippians 2:9: "God gave the name that is above every name to our Lord and Savior Jesus Christ. For this 'name that is above every name' is Jesus."[52] Noting that Moses was unable to lead the army and asked Jesus

49. Daly, foreword to Origen, *Spirit and Fire*, xiv–xv.

50. Ibid. Frances M. Young makes a similar point when she insists: "The biblical narratives, read imaginatively rather than literally, but accorded an authority greater than the merely metaphorical, can become luminous of a divine reality beyond human expression. This is not so much allegorical as sacramental." *Biblical Exegesis*, 143–44. While I am not persuaded of the differentiation between "allegorical" and "sacramental," Young's overall argument for a sacramental understanding of language is certainly insightful. See her chapter "The Sacrament of Language" in ibid., 140–60.

51. The fact that the names Joshua and Jesus are identical in Greek is employed both by Justin Martyr and by Origen. See O'Keefe and Reno, *Sanctified Vision*, 74–78.

52. Origen, *Homilies on Joshua* 1.1 (FC 105:26).

(Joshua) to choose mighty men (Exod. 17:9), Origen comments: "Therefore, when I become acquainted with the name of Jesus for the first time, I also immediately see the symbol of a mystery (*mysterii video sacramentum*). Indeed, Jesus leads the army."[53] The use of the terms *mysterium* and *sacramentum* right at the outset of his commentary illustrates that these two words came to function nearly as synonyms for his Latin translator, Rufinus, as they would for many of the church fathers and for the medieval tradition.[54] Throughout his homilies, Origen speaks of the literal sense as the mystery or sacrament of the spiritual sense.[55]

It may be worth our while to go through a few examples, in order to get a sense of how important this sacramental relationship between the divine Word and human words was for Origen. In *Homily 11*, the Alexandrian preacher comments: "But meanwhile Jesus destroyed the enemies, not teaching cruelty through this, as the heretics think, but representing the *future sacraments* in these affairs, so that when Jesus destroys those kings who maintain a reign of sin in us, we can fulfill that which the Apostle said, 'Just as we presented our members to serve iniquity for iniquity, so now let us present our members to serve righteousness for sanctification' [Rom. 6:19]."[56] We may notice in this passage both the paradoxical language of "future sacraments," which we saw Susan Wood borrowing from the Great Tradition, and the seamless way in which Origen moves from the historical to the spiritual meaning when he comments that "Jesus destroys those kings." When Origen first says that "Jesus destroyed the enemies," his words contain a certain ambiguity: the clause may speak either of Joshua the son of Nun or of Jesus Christ; both understandings are possible since the two names are identical in Greek. The rest of the passage, however, makes clear that Origen is really speaking of Christ. It is Jesus, not Joshua, who destroys our demonic enemies so that we can live holy lives in line with Romans 6.

In *Homily 22*, Origen observes that Joshua reports three times that the Canaanites live among the people of Ephraim. Origen then comments that if we investigate these three occurrences carefully, "we shall not doubt that these things were written not so that only a narration of exploits might be transmitted to us [i.e., the historical sense], but so that these things be filled with *divine sacraments* and things worthy of God."[57] The term "divine sacra-

53. Ibid., 1.1 (FC 105:27).
54. Since Origen's Greek text has not survived, it is not clear which terms he used. Quite possibly, the Greek word *mysterion* lies behind Rufinus's *mysterium*.
55. See also Origen, *Spirit and Fire*, 89–90 (§§161–69).
56. Origen, *Homilies on Joshua* 11.6 (FC 105:119) (emphasis added).
57. Ibid., 22.1 (FC 105:189) (emphasis added).

ments" speaks of the spiritual reality to which the historical accounts point. In the same homily, when Origen notes the command to "purge the Rephaites from among you" (Josh. 17:15), he comments: "We find Rephaites to be interpreted 'slack mothers.' According to that which is said in a mystery (*in sacramento*) concerning the soul as though concerning a woman, there is a certain power in our soul that brings forth perceptions and is, so to speak, the mother of those perceptions."[58] When the power of these perceptions is "slack and languid," this is indicated "under the name 'Rephaites,' so that we may purge ourselves of these languid mothers, who bear weak and useless thoughts."[59] Origen intentionally and explicitly identifies the Rephaites in sacramental fashion.

When in the next homily Origen discusses the drawing of lots to divide the conquered cities, he makes the point that this dividing of lots mirrors an angelic drawing of lots in heaven. He then comments: "Insofar as it was permitted, we have dared to offer to you these things concerning the distribution of the lots of the land of Judah by the invitation of Scripture, which calls Jerusalem and Mount Zion heavenly, and the rest of those places that are written to be in heaven. This gave us the opportunity to remark about all these passages because heavenly mysteries are described in them."[60] The reference to "heavenly mysteries" in connection with the various place names implies, according to Origen, that one should not think that the book of Joshua relates something "worthless" when it presents us with these many proper names. "Rather, know that ineffable things are contained in these mysteries and things greater than either the human word is able to utter or the mortal sense of hearing to hear."[61] Earthly events such as the drawing of lots, as well as the names of cities mentioned in Joshua, thus turn out to be sacramental "mysteries" of heavenly realities.

As he discusses the detailed description of the inheritance that the various sons of Levi receive, Origen interrupts himself in *Homily 25* with the words: "Who is able to follow and to comprehend all these things? Who can even remember and pay attention to the order of the mysteries (*mysteriorum*)? But if, according to the letter alone, we can explain the difficult text of the narration and unfold the confusion either of places or of persons that are bound together in the story, what do we say concerning those sacraments

58. Ibid., 22.4 (FC 105:192). The name Rephaites appears to be derived from the verb *rapah*, meaning "to sink, drop, relax, or slacken." The translation of Josh. 17:15 is taken from Origen's treatise.
59. Ibid.
60. Ibid., 23.4 (FC 105:201).
61. Ibid., 23.4 (FC 105:202).

(*sacramentis*) that are depicted through this, and in which the distributions of a future inheritance are dimly sketched?"[62] Again, Origen uses the terms "mysteries" and "sacraments" to denote the heavenly, eternal realities given in earthly, this-worldly descriptions.

Finally, in the next homily, when he discusses the Transjordanian tribes building an altar in imitation of that of Judah (Josh. 22:10–20), Origen first recounts the historical event and then immediately adds: "But let us see what sacrament lies within this deed."[63] This in turn leads to a spiritual interpretation of this particular chapter. The "sacrament" is obviously the spiritual explanation of the passage.

These examples from Origen's homilies on Joshua present us with a rather impressive number of occurrences of the words "sacrament" and "mystery." There is little doubt that for Origen the words of the biblical text, while they relate historical events, also carry a deeper meaning, one that is located in heaven and refers to Jesus Christ, the eternal Son of God himself. It is important to note that this sacramental interpretation is thoroughly christological. We need to keep this in mind in connection with the objections that we noted at the beginning of the chapter regarding Origen's allegorizing. Origen, I indicated, is often viewed as a moralist who jumps straight from the Old Testament to how we should live today. Certainly, he is concerned with the virtuous habits of the Christian life. But he is also thoroughly christological in his exegesis. The sacramental meaning of the historical event refers first and foremost to Jesus, who himself is the incarnation of the eternal Logos. Origen is a "man of the church," a *vir ecclesiasticus*. And as such, his prime concern is Jesus Christ. The Alexandrian tradition stemming from Origen is thus a sacramental tradition that takes Christology for its starting point.

History's Rightful Place

Still, the question is often raised: Does history receive its rightful place in Origen's reading of Joshua? In addressing this question, we should reflect carefully on what we mean by history's "rightful place." If we regard as the purpose of biblical exegesis to find out what the human author really meant, this often tends to imply, as Oxford critic Benjamin Jowett famously put it in 1860, that we read Scripture "like any other book."[64] Seeing as authorial intent is a historical matter, such a quest inevitably yields varying degrees of

62. Ibid., 25.4 (FC 105:212–13).
63. Ibid., 26.3 (FC 105:218).
64. See Barr, "Jowett," 433–37.

probability. If, with such an understanding of biblical interpretation, we ask whether Origen gives history its "rightful place," the answer must be negative. Origen is singularly *un*concerned with the kinds of historical questions modern scholars tend to put to the text. He is almost oblivious to what the original author may have meant with the text of the book of Joshua. The reason is this: Origen doesn't so much look backward as forward. For Origen, biblical interpretation is not first and foremost a historical discipline. Such an approach would have struck him as an oddly reductionistic enterprise.

Furthermore, when it comes to history itself, unlike many modern historians, Origen does not reduce history to measurable cause-and-effect, to that which we can observe with the senses. This means that he regards history as open to a providential ordering of events. His sermons are predicated on the notion that the history of salvation is divine in character. He does not begin with attempting to ascertain the historicity of particular events. Instead, he takes them for granted (most of the time), and he reads them as guided by God himself.

When, for example, Origen turns in *Homily 23* to the drawing of the lots for the seven tribes as described in Joshua 17–19, he engages in a theological discussion of providence. He begins by discussing the drawing of lots in Leviticus 16, where one lot was taken for God and another for the scapegoat (Lev. 16:8).[65] Origen observes that Caleb was assigned a share *not* by lot, but "according to the commandment of the Lord" (Josh. 14:13).[66] Many others on the west side of the Jordan River, however, received their portions through the casting of lots. And Origen adds the theologically weighty comment that the "lot is not tossed by chance, but according to that which was predestined by God."[67] Origen then goes through several additional biblical occurrences of the lot: Jonah was selected by lot to be cast into the sea, Solomon appeals to the lot in the book of Proverbs, and the apostles filled the place of Judas by casting the lot. Again, Origen concludes that "when prayer preceded, it was no longer by chance but by providence that the lot announced divine judgment."[68]

Next, he relates this providential ordering of the lot to Christology: "But still I sought in the New Testament if anywhere the lot is mentioned in relation to Christ or to the Church, or even to mystic things that seem to relate to the soul."[69] Origen then observes that several New Testament passages speak

65. Origen, *Homilies on Joshua* 23.1 (FC 105:195).
66. Ibid., 23.1 (FC 105:196).
67. Ibid.
68. Ibid., 23.2 (FC 105:197).
69. Ibid.

of believers' predestination "by lot."[70] Origen insists that these passages too should be understood not just in their historical sense: "But according to the inner understanding, as Paul seems to indicate when he says, 'in the portion of the lot of the saints' [Col. 1:12], and 'called by lot in Christ' [Eph. 1:11], it must be seen whether perchance the lot is drawn not only among humans, but also among the celestial powers."[71] All of Scripture, including the New Testament, is subject to spiritual interpretation for Origen. The New Testament too points to eternal realities.

When we draw lots here on earth, the results are in line with lots drawn in heaven. This explains, according to Origen, why Deuteronomy 32:8–9 can say that God divided the nations and fixed the boundaries of the nations "according to the number of the angels of God." "We must not think," comments Origen, "that it was by accident that it indeed fell to one angel to receive by lot one nation, for example, that of the Egyptians, but to another, the nation of the Idumeans, and to another, the nation of the Moabites and to another, India or every single nation on earth."[72] Origen thus arrives at the conclusion "that not even for a single one of us does anything come to pass except by a lot of this kind that is dispensed by the judgment of God."[73] It now becomes clear that when by lot Benjamin received Jerusalem and Mount Zion, this was not an accidental matter: "Doubtless, it is because the nature of that heavenly Jerusalem established it that the earthly Jerusalem, which preserved a figure and form of the heavenly one, ought to be given to none other than Benjamin."[74] (Origen here has in mind Hebrews 10:1 and 12:22, which he has just quoted.) It is divine providence that arranges human affairs by heavenly lots, so that earthly arrangements are in line with heavenly ones.

It should be clear at this point that history was not insignificant for Origen. We may even say that he had a higher view of history than do many modern historical exegetes. The reason is that he refused to reduce history to immanent cause-and-effect. Because history was for Origen a matter of providential ordering, it was much more than just inner-worldly cause-and-effect observable by the senses. A view of history as purely autonomous and this-worldly would have struck him as terribly reductionistic. History, to Origen, had significance because it was the outcome of God's eternal providential ordering.

70. Ibid. Eph. 1:11 uses the verb *klēroō* (to cast a lot); Col. 1:12 speaks of a "share in the allotment" (*klēros*).
71. Ibid., 23.3 (FC 105:198).
72. Ibid., 23.3 (FC 105:198–99).
73. Ibid., 23.3 (FC 105:199).
74. Ibid., 23.4 (FC 105:200).

It seems unlikely, therefore, that when Origen allegorized, he meant to suggest thereby that the historical event never occurred. His spiritual reading can hardly be meant to *deny* history, at least not across the board. Both Origen's sacramental understanding of interpretation and his insistence on the providential ordering of history militate against this. If it is *historical events* that carry a sacramental dimension, then this means that the spiritual reality is present *in historical events*. And if God orders history providentially, then, again, this implies an acknowledgment of its significance. Accordingly, Henri de Lubac, in his book on Origen's biblical interpretation, shows at length that usually Origen affirms the historicity of the events. "All that happened," explains de Lubac, "happened 'in mystery': but the mystery presupposes the real event. One must believe 'the testimony of the history.'"[75]

In his book *On First Principles*, Origen distinguishes a threefold interpretation, and he makes clear that *each* of the three levels is integral to a full-orbed understanding of the text. One must portray, says Origen,

> the meaning of the sacred writings in a threefold way upon one's own soul, so that the simple man may be edified by what we may call the flesh of the scripture, this name being given to the obvious interpretation; while the man who has made some progress may be edified by its soul, as it were; and the man who is perfect and like those mentioned by the apostle: "We speak wisdom among the perfect; yet a wisdom not of this world, nor of the rulers of this world, which are coming to nought; but we speak of God's wisdom that hath been hidden, which God foreordained before the worlds unto our glory" [1 Cor. 2:6–7]—this man may be edified by the spiritual law [cf. Rom. 7:14], which has "a shadow of the good things to come" [Heb. 10:1]. For just as man consists of body, soul and spirit, so in the same way does the scripture, which has been prepared by God to be given for man's salvation.[76]

There are three levels of meaning, according to Origen, corresponding to the various aspects of the human person: the literal level corresponds to the body, the moral level to the soul, and the spiritual level to the spirit.[77] The historical level of interpretation is part and parcel of an overall interpretive

---

75. De Lubac, *History and Spirit*, 106. I am inclined to think that de Lubac overstates his case somewhat. As we will see, there are instances where Origen does deny the historicity of the events narrated in Joshua.

76. Origen, *On First Principles* 4.2.4 (Butterworth, 275–76).

77. Karen Jo Torjesen has objected to the link that is commonly made between Origen's distinction between body, soul, and spirit and his distinction between literal, moral, and spiritual reading ("'Body,' 'Soul,' and 'Spirit,'" 22). I agree with Torjesen's overall argument that Origen hopes to transform his readers from fleshly to spiritual readers and that the multiple ways of reading Scripture serve this purpose (see chap. 1, sec. "Retrieving Sacramental Reading: Meaning,

approach with various levels. For Origen, one cannot interpret Scripture without doing justice to history. The common assumption, therefore, that allegory is a jumping *away from* history is, to put it bluntly, simply based on a lack of familiarity with the fathers. Reading the fathers makes one recognize quickly that historical realities are an integral part—although by no means the most important part—of the reading of the text.

This is not to say that Origen never devalued or even discounted the literal meaning. There "are certain passages of scripture which, as we shall show in what follows, have no bodily sense at all," he insists in *On First Principles*.[78] Sometimes "the scripture wove into the story something which did not happen, occasionally something which could not happen, and occasionally something which might have happened but in fact did not."[79] Even when speaking of the Gospels and the writings of the apostles, Origen comments that "the history even of these is not everywhere pure, events being woven together in the bodily sense without having actually happened; nor do the law and the commandments contained therein entirely declare what is reasonable."[80] On Origen's understanding, the Spirit sometimes includes along with the historical account descriptions of things that are either contradictory or immoral, and which God thus intends as obstacles, deliberately placed in the text in order to drive people to the benefit of a spiritual reading.

We see such nonhistorical readings also in the *Homilies on Joshua*. A few examples will suffice to clarify the point. In *Homily 7*, Origen comments: "I would like to inquire of the Jews and of those who are called Christians, but who still preserve the Jewish interpretation of Scriptures, how they explain that 'Rahab the prostitute was joined to the house of Israel up to this very day' [Josh. 6:25]. How is Rahab said to be 'joined up to this very day'?"[81] Similarly, when Joshua defeats the alliance of Jabin, king of Hazor, he destroys all his people—"so that no one remained there who might recover"

Virtue, Progress, and Providence"), but I am still inclined to think that Origen intends to draw a connection between the body-soul-spirit distinction and the threefold reading of Scripture.

We may well wish to criticize both the order of the three levels of interpretation and Origen's linking of these levels to the human faculties. After all, by placing the moral level before the spiritual level, Origen gives at least the impression that we may arrive at the moral meaning without being concerned with Christology. At the same time, we need to keep in mind that in his actual exegesis Origen often doesn't move from the historical via the moral to the spiritual. Instead, as de Lubac has made clear, most often Origen moves straight from the historical to the spiritual. See de Lubac's discussion in *History and Spirit*, 159–71. Cf. H. Boersma, *Nouvelle Théologie*, 164–68.

78. Origen, *On First Principles* 4.2.5 (Butterworth, 277).

79. Ibid., 4.2.9 (Butterworth, 286).

80. Ibid., 4.2.9 (Butterworth, 287).

81. Origen, *Homilies on Joshua* 7.5 (FC 105:79).

(Josh. 11:11)—and he hamstrings their horses. Noticing the order of events, *first* the destruction of every single person and *then* the hamstringing of their horses, Origen comments in *Homily 15*: "Concerning this, we say first of all to those who wish these things to be understood only according to the letter, that if any of the enemies had survived, it seemed reasonable that the horses be hamstrung so that no one could use them for flight. But here, when it is said that no one was left among the enemies who could take a breath, why were the horses still commanded to be hamstrung, especially those that were able to be of use and service to the victors?"[82] Origen takes the logical improbability of these passages as sufficient reason to move to a spiritual reading. He does the same thing on at least five other occasions.[83] The reason is, no doubt, that his relative neglect of history (or, we might say, his urge to get beyond history to the spiritual meaning) is such that he cannot bother taking the time to investigate possible solutions to the apparent contradictions that he finds in the literal meaning of the text. I don't think there is an adequate defense for such neglect. But if we ask which neglect is more serious, the nearly wholesale neglect of spiritual levels of interpretation in a great deal of modern historical exegesis or the occasional neglect of history in Origen and other practitioners of allegorical exegesis, the answer seems to me fairly evident.

From History to Spirit: Biblical Rationale

This leads us to the question, on what biblical basis does Origen move from history to spirit? What is his rationale for this sacramental approach to Scripture? Doesn't such a move from history to spirit lead to a supersessionism in which the New Testament simply supersedes and replaces the Old? Put sharply, what real use can Origen possibly have for the Old Testament? Of course, we have already seen his main motive for the move from history to spirit: he holds to a sacramental view of history and of the Scriptures. Furthermore, we have seen that on occasion, when the text appears problematic, Origen jumps straight to the spiritual meaning without worrying about the historical event. So, we know why it is that Origen distinguished multiple levels of meaning in the text: his sacramental view of reality demanded as much. But the question we have not yet asked is this: How does Origen ground this sacramental view biblically? Does the Bible support his allegorical exegesis?

82. Ibid., 15.2 (FC 105:139).
83. Ibid., 6.1 (FC 105:70), 15.7 (FC 105:150), 16.1 (FC 105:152), 20.4 (FC 105:179), 21.1 (FC 105:184).

Interestingly, Origen's homilies often discuss and justify his hermeneutical moves as he presents his understanding of the text. On various occasions, the text's very meaning, according to Origen, refers to the principle of allegorizing. In other words, he sees the biblical text as addressing the question of interpretation. Such is the case in *Homily 2*, when God promises Joshua (or Jesus) that he will give him every place, "wherever [he] will ascend with the soles of [his] feet" (Josh. 1:3).[84] Origen insists: "The letter of the Law is placed on the ground and lies down below. On no occasion, then, does the one who follows the letter of the Law ascend. But if you are able to rise from the letter to the spirit and also ascend from history to a higher understanding, then truly you have ascended the lofty and high place that you will receive from God as your inheritance."[85] The very phrase "ascend with the soles of your feet" carries, for Origen, a hermeneutical principle, namely, that we are to ascend from the historical to the spiritual level. Apparently, when we read the text allegorically, the allegorical level gives us the justification for the very practice of allegorical exegesis in which we have just engaged.[86]

It may seem hard to avoid the conclusion that this involves a form of circular reasoning: Origen assumes the results of spiritual interpretation to justify its practice; it is an allegorical reading of Joshua's ascent "with the soles of [his] feet" that shores up Origen's allegorical approach. I am not so sure, however, that Origen asks us to take his reading of Joshua 1:3 in a strictly logical or demonstrative sense. I suspect that his desire to delight the reader and to bring to the fore readings that allude to God's eternal beauty drives him (as well as other fathers) to engage in this sort of exegetical practice.[87] Exegetes such as Origen would hardly consider this particular reading of Joshua 1:3 as the definitive meaning of the text. Instead, Origen would likely regard it as one of many possible readings, a reading that particularly delighted him, that was consonant with the overall faith of the church, and that made sense only for those already convinced of the need for spiritual interpretation.

Origen often reaches beyond such self-referential Old Testament interpretations to look for New Testament texts that directly assert the requirement of spiritual interpretation. I do not need to rehearse these New Testament passages in detail.[88] When Origen turns to passages such as 1 Corinthians

84. Ibid., 2.3 (FC 105:39).

85. Ibid.

86. See also the interpretation of Josh. 5:2 in ibid., 5.5 (FC 105:63), and of Josh. 15:17–19 in ibid., 20.6 (FC 105:182).

87. Cf. Byassee, *Praise Seeking Understanding*, 97–148.

88. In his *Homilies on Joshua*, Origen refers to John 5:46 (18.2 [FC 105:164]); Rom. 7:14 (which he mentions no fewer than five times); 1 Cor. 10:4 (5.4 [FC 105:63–64], 15.3 [FC 105:144]); 1 Cor. 10:11 (mentioned four times); 2 Cor. 3:5 (also used several times); 2 Cor. 3:14–15 (3.1

10:4 ("For they drank from the spiritual Rock that followed them, and the Rock was Christ"), Galatians 4:24 ("Now this may be interpreted allegorically [*allēgoroumena*]: these women are two covenants"), and others, he simply steps into the exegetical precedent set by the apostle Paul himself. As Peter Martens puts it: "Throughout his entire career, Origen repeatedly invoked Paul's name as the practitioner and guide par excellence to the allegorical interpretation of Israel's Scriptures."[89] In doing so, Origen wasn't particularly unique. Other church fathers often used the same biblical passages. The reason is that they, like Origen, were preoccupied with the spiritual progress that the hearers must make, a spiritual progress that they saw expressed in various New Testament passages.

But again, this spiritual progress does not come at the expense of the letter. To be sure, in some sense the letter and the law are disregarded: Moses "cannot lead the army" into the promised land.[90] Jesus needs to do this. And "if we do not understand how Moses dies, we shall not be able to understand how Jesus reigns."[91] Origen goes on at some length about the rites of the law having become obsolete now that Jesus holds the leadership. But he immediately adds that the law does hold its rightful place among Christians. Appealing to the *Assumption of Moses*, Origen comments that "two Moseses were seen: one alive in the spirit, another dead in the body. Doubtless, in this was foreshadowed that, if you consider the letter of the Law empty and void of all those things we have mentioned above [the Old Testament sacrificial rites and the like], you have the Moses who is dead in the body; but if you are able to draw back the veil from the Law [2 Cor. 3:16] and perceive that 'the Law is spiritual' [Rom. 7:14], you have the Moses who lives in the spirit."[92] For Origen, Moses is both dead and alive. As long as we read him spiritually, he remains alive for us. So, yes, in an important sense, the New Testament does supersede the Old, just as the new covenant supersedes the old. At the same time, however, the New Testament also renders the fullest and truest meaning of the Old Testament, by drawing out its deepest mystery, its sacramental meaning. Thus, Origen spots a greater treasure in the Old Testament than it had been possible to find prior to the coming of Christ.[93]

[FC 105:41]); Gal. 4:22–24 (9.8 [FC 105:103]); Heb. 8:5 (17.1 [FC 105:157], 17.2 [FC 105:160]); and Heb. 12:22 (23.4 [FC 105:200–201]).

89. Martens, *Origen*, 158.

90. Origen, *Homilies on Joshua* 1.1 (FC 105:27).

91. Ibid., 2.1 (FC 105:37). Origen here comments on Josh. 1:2.

92. Ibid., 2.1 (FC 105:38).

93. For a more elaborate exposition of Origen's understanding of the relationship between Old and New Testaments, see de Lubac, *History and Spirit*, 190–204.

Conclusion

It is not the purpose of this chapter either to defend each and every exegetical choice that Origen makes or to suggest that he investigates the historical meaning of the Scriptures with the kind of care with which one perhaps would have liked him to do so. Nonetheless, the common objections to Origen's interpretation of Scripture remain largely unconvincing because they are predicated on a view of history that approaches it without regard either for its providential ordering or for its sacramental functioning. By abandoning the notion that history is anchored within divine providence, much contemporary historical exegesis can no longer answer the question of why history is important. It is because he recognized the sacramental function of history—as well as of the Scriptures that record the historical events—that Origen saw in history much greater significance than do his modern-day detractors.

The fortunate expression "future sacraments" (*futura sacramenta*) indicates, on the one hand, that the Alexandrian preacher regarded the historical progression of salvation history to be of great significance. Origen recognized that it is only by advancing from the Old to the New Testament that God's people obtain salvation. It is as the culmination of the Old Testament narrative that Christ brings redemption. On the other hand, the same expression also makes clear that Origen—rightly, I believe—regarded the historical level of the Joshua narrative as subordinate. Its indispensable role consists, for Origen, precisely in pointing from Joshua to Jesus, from the letter to the spirit, from the field to the treasure. For Origen, therefore, Joshua, the letter, and the field function as sacraments that contain the hidden presence of Christ.

6

HARMONIOUS READING

Clement of Alexandria, Athanasius, Basil, Gregory of Nyssa, and Augustine on the Music of the Psalms

Tuning People with the Psalms

The psalms were tremendously popular throughout the period of the early church. Brian Daley, patristics scholar from the University of Notre Dame, has pointed out: "Early Christian commentaries on the psalms easily exceed in number those on any other book of the Old or New Testament; we still possess partial or complete sets of homilies or scholarly commentaries on the psalms—sometimes more than one set—by at least twenty-one Latin or Greek Patristic authors, and this interest did not abate in the medieval Church."[1] As a result of this popularity, we have a great deal of material from which we can infer how early Christians read the psalms theologically or spiritually.

We are particularly fortunate to have two fairly lengthy fourth-century writings that explain *how* we are supposed to read the psalms. I am thinking of the *Letter to Marcellinus* by Athanasius (ca. 296–373), the ardent defender of the doctrine of the Trinity against Arian heresy, and of the *Treatise on the Inscriptions of the Psalms*, written by the mystical theologian Gregory of

1. Daley, "Patristic Exegesis," 204.

131

Nyssa (ca. 335–ca. 394). There is also an introduction to the psalms written by Basil of Caesarea (ca. 329–379), Gregory's elder brother, that considers the principles of interpretation that one should bring to bear on one's reading of the psalms.[2]

These and other patristic writings allow us to reflect not only on interpretive strategies employed in reading Scripture (in this case the psalms)—which is the main question we are asking throughout this book—but also on how music functions in terms of metaphysics and theology. The church fathers were keenly interested in what music is and how it functions. What is more, they were convinced that the musical form and the theological contents of the psalms were closely related. According to the fathers of the early church, music—particularly the musical accompaniment and the singing of the psalms, but also other good music—participates in the harmony of the universe and in Christ himself. Music, therefore, has the ability to make one grow in virtue and to heal the emotions; music tunes people and makes them more harmonious. The theology of the psalms does much the same thing, the fathers maintained. Entering into the contents of the psalms, we participate in the reality of Christ that they represent. As a result, we grow in virtue and move toward the happiness that awaits us at the end of the journey. For the fathers, both the music and the theology of the psalms turn us into better people, as we learn to move in harmony with the universe and with Christ toward the ultimate sacramental reality of divine happiness.

Harmony in the Platonic Tradition

In contemporary society, music is underrated: we typically regard its beauty as merely a matter of personal taste, we doubt its ability to signify truths that take us beyond the here and now, and we consider its moral impact negligible. Each of these three limitations stems from metaphysical assumptions that are widely shared in our society. As Julian Johnson, Regius professor of music at Royal Holloway, University of London, observes in his book *Who Needs Classical Music?*, we have come to question the idea that there is good as well as bad music, and we are quick to insist that our appreciation of music comes down to a matter of personal taste. The reason, says Johnson, is "the pseudo-democracy of a commercial culture that accords equal validity and equal status to all of its products."[3] In reality our "personal taste" isn't nearly as personal as we'd like to think it is. It is usually deeply indebted to the

2. Basil of Caesarea, *Exegetic Homilies* 10.1–2 (FC 46:151–54).
3. Johnson, *Who Needs Classical Music?*, 14.

vagaries of commodity capitalism. "In this context," writes Johnson, "the objection that 'it's all a matter of taste' takes on a rather different aspect. Our musical choices are rarely the wholly free and independent actions of a sovereign individuality, surveying the products of world music from on high. They are more often our responses to the continual demands to select from a changing but always determined musical choice."[4] The bottom line, according to Johnson, is this: "Music sells because it is popular. It is popular because it is sold."[5] Regardless of evidence to the contrary, we continue to insist on music being just a matter of taste because we link music with feeling, authenticity, and self-expression.[6] In other words, we regard music as primarily something subjective rather than objective: "At each stage the essential idea is self-expression; the composer writes and the performer plays in order to express themselves through the music, and listeners, too, find something of themselves expressed in the music."[7] Johnson quotes nineteenth-century music critic Eduard Hanslick, who laconically suggested that "to judge music solely by the emotions it aroused was like trying to judge a wine while getting drunk."[8] Taste, according to Johnson, is not necessarily a good judge of the quality of music.

The notion that music is a matter of taste didn't always dominate. Throughout most of the history of Christianity, taste was something to be developed and brought up to par rather than something to be taken as starting point and norm. The reason, Johnson makes clear, is that music was regarded as primarily objective in character: "To an earlier age, our contemporary idea of a complete relativism in musical judgment would have seemed nonsensical. One could no more make valid individual judgments about musical values than about science. Music was no more 'a matter of taste' than was the orbit of the planets or the physiology of the human body. From Plato to Helmholtz, music was understood to be based on natural laws, and its value was derived from its capacity to frame and elaborate these laws in musical form. Its success was no more a matter of subjective judgment than the laws themselves."[9] As we will see, Johnson quite deliberately refers to the "orbit of the planets" and the "physiology of the human body." For much of the Christian tradition, including the patristic era, music was directly linked with the revolutions of the planets and the makeup of the human body. In contrast, today we typically

4. Ibid., 15.
5. Ibid., 16.
6. Ibid., 40.
7. Ibid.
8. Ibid., 41.
9. Ibid., 12.

don't think of music as taking us beyond the here and now: our insistence that music speaks of our feelings and subjective experiences means that we usually regard its value as dependent on our emotional state.

Johnson wants to open our eyes to what I would call the sacramentality of music. That is to say, music (at least, some music) conveys to us something that we cannot find on the "surface" of things. According to Johnson, starting at the turn of the nineteenth century, we began increasingly to "objectify" music, first through the printing of sheet music, and later especially through commercial sound recordings.[10] The result is that we've learned to treat music as a physical object that we can control and incorporate into our everyday lives as we see fit.[11] Johnson sharply criticizes this embrace of what he terms a "blank and depthless surface":[12] "The emphasis on the surface of things is essentially inhumane. It is pornographic because it fetishizes the materiality of human existence and denies the spiritual personality that vivifies it from within. . . . Perhaps my use of the term 'pornographic' seems inappropriate and sensationalist in relation to music. But the central category of pornography is perhaps not sex but the process by which the humane is reduced to the status of things. The theoretical term for this is 'reification.'"[13] Johnson is worried that we have reified music, that we have reduced it to a mere object, a thing, so that we no longer believe there are hidden depths underlying the sounds that we hear.

Johnson's overall argument is a defense of the modern classical canon of music, which he believes is grounded within Enlightenment humanism. It's not a defense I would underwrite in every respect, and it's important to keep in mind that Johnson doesn't advocate a return to the sacramentalism of the Christian Platonist tradition.[14] Still, he shares the language of "surface" with the fourth-century Cappadocian interpreter Saint Gregory of Nyssa, who, as we saw in chapter 2, speaks of the "surface level" (*to procheiron*) of the biblical text and insists that we dare not reduce the meaning of the biblical text to this level.[15] Johnson, similarly, invites us to be open to the "transcendent." Music-as-art, he argues, "resists the everyday because its function is to be Other. . . . The way art treats its materials implies that its content lies

10. Ibid., 52–53.
11. Ibid., 54–57.
12. Ibid., 58.
13. Ibid., 58–59.
14. Johnson's uncritical embrace of "Enlightenment values"—he mentions individuality, freedom, and self-identity (ibid., 31)—doesn't comport well with his desire for transcendence. It seems to me precisely Kantian subjectivism that is the cause of many of the problems in aesthetic philosophy that Johnson rightly critiques.
15. See chap. 2, sec. "Gregory's Literal Reading as Theological."

elsewhere, *through* its materials but at the same time *beyond* them."[16] Johnson concludes his book with an explicit appeal to move beyond the physical to the spiritual. In projecting something beyond its acoustic materials, maintains Johnson, music-as-art "does not deny its physical aspect but redeems it as the vehicle of something that exceeds the physical. In doing so, it offers us not only a symbol of our transcendent nature but also a means for its repeated enactment."[17] Though he doesn't use the language of sacramentality, it is clear that Johnson has in mind the idea that music makes present a reality greater than its own embodied self.

Johnson doesn't discuss in any detail either the Platonic or the patristic view of music as linked to the transcendent. It is in these traditions, however, that we find the resources for an aesthetic that upholds the sacramental character of music. Through much of the Middle Ages, music was taught as part of the *quadrivium*, the four disciplines of arithmetic, geometry, astronomy, and music, which prepared the student for the *trivium*, which consisted of grammar, rhetoric, and dialectic.[18] To the modern mind, it seems odd to classify music in the same rubric as arithmetic, geometry, and astronomy, and the reason for this is precisely the modern reduction of music to taste and to the here and now. The medieval curriculum traced music's roots to Pythagorean and Platonic approaches to reality, which recognized the mathematical structure of music and, along with that, its objective character.

Albert Blackwell, whose book *The Sacred in Music* is an extended argument for the sacramental character of music, makes clear that the Christian musical tradition is based on two sacramental strands, the Pythagorean and the incarnational. The former emphasizes the imperceptible, focuses on eternal truth, and takes its starting point in Wisdom 11:20: "But thou hast arranged all things by measure and number and weight" (RSV). The latter highlights the beauty of the sensible sights and sounds around us, zeroes in on the subjective response of love, and comports well with Wisdom 13:5: "For from the greatness and beauty of created things comes a corresponding perception of their Creator" (RSV).[19]

Blackwell's distinction is helpful, but we should not oppose these two strands to one another.[20] True, the sacramentalism of the Christian tradition has differing emphases, some highlighting the creature's upward move in and

16. Johnson, *Who Needs Classical Music?*, 128.
17. Ibid., 130.
18. For a helpful discussion, see Caldecott, *Beauty for Truth's Sake*, 20–27.
19. The foregoing summary is mostly taken from Blackwell, *Sacred in Music*, 37–48.
20. Blackwell himself rightly accentuates that both traditions are sacramental and that they are complementary rather than opposed to each other.

through the material toward the spiritual, and others focusing on the real presence of the spiritual in the visible and audible realities around us. But many of the theologians of the incarnational tradition would recognize their indebtedness to the Pythagorean tradition. Both strands of the sacramental musical tradition are anchored in Pythagoras's discovery of the numerical patterns of musical pitch.[21] Blackwell summarizes Pythagoras's contribution: "Pythagoras co-ordinated the sounds of hammers on an anvil with the hammers' proportional weights to discover the principle that musical pitches are related by numerical ratios. Thus far his accomplishment represented epoch-making science. He also discovered that consonant musical pitches—that is, pitches that please our ears when they sound together—are related by simple numerical ratios of whole numbers."[22] Blackwell exposits at length the musical consequences of these initial Pythagorean discoveries, particularly the contribution of the early eighteenth-century discovery of the musical overtone series.[23] Music systems, Blackwell maintains, inescapably "come under the sway of its basic principles," regardless of the immense variety of the ways in which they give expression to it.[24]

The Pythagorean understanding of music as essentially mathematical in character traveled via Plato's *Timaeus* and Plotinus's *Enneads* into the Christian faith. Plato, in chapter 35 of the *Timaeus*, argues that God created the intellectual reality of the world soul with proportions of double intervals (1, 2, 4, 8) and of triple intervals (1, 3, 9, 27).[25] God did this, according to Plato, by separating a portion of the whole and then doubling and tripling it, so as to arrive at a series of seven terms (1, 2, 3, 4, 8, 9, 27). Plato relates the seven intervals to the seven planets: "When God had made the bodies of each of them He placed them in the orbits along which the revolution of the Other was moving, seven orbits for the seven bodies."[26] For Plato, then, the cosmos is designed rationally, according to harmonious intervals. The significance of this insight is far-reaching. As Quentin Faulkner puts it: "The 'harmony

21. Cf. Caldecott, *Beauty for Truth's Sake*, 53–71. Reflecting on Augustine's use of Wis. 11:20, Thomas O'Loughlin describes Augustine's view as follows: "Measure, weight and number are at the base of being and function as the fundamentals of knowing; and in being these basic principles they are sacramental of the one who is unknown beyond them who creates both them and what they measure." "Mysticism of Number," 402.

22. Blackwell, *Sacred in Music*, 54.

23. Ibid., 56–71. The overtone series, also known as harmonic series, is the series of notes one hears (or feels vibrating) along with the basic note that's being played. As one goes up the series, the overtones appear closer and closer together, following mathematical proportions, so that the harmony becomes increasingly complex.

24. Ibid., 71.

25. Plato, *Timaeus* 35b–c (LCL 234:67).

26. Ibid., 38c (LCL 234:79).

of the spheres,' then, was more than simply a mathematical or astronomical theory. It formed the basis for a unified world-view, a vision of all existence as interrelated and interdependent. For the arts in particular it assumed a unifying role, giving impulse, direction, and form, not just to music, but to other arts such as architecture as well."[27] Harmony's unifying role extended from the cosmic spheres to the arts, including music. Music's purpose was to imitate and so to participate in the proportions that were observable in the cosmos as a whole. Through music—as well as through the practice of a well-lived, harmonious life—people themselves too could fall in line with cosmic harmony. Plato puts this as follows:

> Music too, in so far as it uses audible sound, was bestowed for the sake of har-
> mony. And harmony, which has motions akin to the revolutions (*periodois*) of
> the Soul within us, was given by the Muses to him who makes intelligent use
> of the Muses, not as an aid to irrational pleasure, as is now supposed, but as
> an auxiliary to the inner revolution of the Soul, when it has lost its harmony,
> to assist in restoring it to order and concord with itself. And because of the
> unmodulated condition, deficient in grace, which exists in most of us, Rhythm
> also was bestowed upon us to be our helper by the same deities and for the
> same ends.[28]

Music, for Plato, has the purpose of bringing the human soul into rational harmony with the cosmos. The revolutions (*periodoi*) of the soul—the changing phases of human life—are patterned on the revolutions of the planets.[29] If one wishes to nurture a harmonious soul, then, he will be careful to listen to music that displays the harmony of the universe.[30] Typically, for Plato, this meant that one should be careful to note how the various modes of music affect the soul:

> So whenever someone submits himself to the musical art to beguile and pour
> down upon his soul through his ears, as it were through a funnel, the sweet, soft
> and mournful harmonies which we were describing just now, and he passes his
> whole life humming, gladdened by the song, if he has any passion, would he
> not first of all soften it as he would iron, and make it usable instead of useless
> and hard? But whenever he does not stop pouring in the music and is bewitched,
> then the immediate result is that he melts and liquefies until he has dissolved

27. Faulkner, *Wiser Than Despair*, 36.
28. Plato, *Timaeus* 47c–d (LCL 234:109).
29. Cf. Spitzer, "World Harmony," 419.
30. Karen C. Adams discusses Jacobus Obrecht, the fifteenth-century Renaissance composer, as an example of someone who consciously composed music patterned on the harmony of the universe as reflected in Pythagorean number theory. "Neoplatonic Aesthetic Tradition," 17–24.

away his spirit, and he cuts out the sinews of his soul, as it were, and makes himself a "fainthearted spearman."[31]

Plato is often thought to have had a negative view of music. It is certainly true that he was suspicious with regard to the effects that music could have. But the reason for his caution is not that he disparaged music per se. Rather, it is precisely Plato's *high* view of music that made him vigilant in how we use it. In and through the music to which we listen, Plato believed, it is possible to enter into contact with the creator's harmonious purposes for the universe. Put in Christian terms, music has a potentially sacramental function.

Not only did Plato's *Timaeus* prove influential for the Christian tradition, but so also did Plotinus's *Enneads*. The third-century Neoplatonic philosopher had high regard for music, distinguishing it sharply from painting, sculpture, and dancing. The latter he regarded as just "imitative arts," which copy models found in the material world, so that they relate to the intellectual sphere only indirectly, via the Reason-Principle in human beings.[32] In contrast, he maintained, music's harmonies have a participatory character, which unites them to cosmic harmonies: "But if any artistic skill starts from the proportions of [individual] living things and goes on from there to consider the proportions of living things in general, it would be a part of the power which also in the higher world considers and contemplates universal proportion in the intelligible. And certainly all music, since the ideas which it has are concerned with rhythm and melody, would be of the same kind, just like the art which is concerned with intelligible number."[33] For Plotinus, then, audible music directly represents the inaudible rhythms of the intellectual world. Again, translating this into Christian theological idiom, we could say that for Plotinus, music's participatory quality renders it sacramental in character.

Harmony in the Early Church

The Platonic and Plotinian understanding of music proved tremendously influential in the Christian tradition. Lewis Rowell comments: "Plotinus' vision of music as the earthly image of harmony, proportions, and the motions of the eternal cosmos—when supplemented by the doctrines of Christian theology—became the standard medieval explanation."[34] Music, according to

31. Plato, *Republic* 411a–b (LCL 237:317).
32. Plotinus, *Ennead* 5.9.11 (LCL 444:311).
33. Ibid., 5.9.11 (LCL 444:311–12).
34. Rowell, *Thinking about Music*, 88. Even in the twentieth century, French philosopher Simone Weil recognized the abiding validity of the Christian Platonist approach, as she comments

the early church, is primarily not a matter of taste but participation in eternal structures—though, of course, this could take place through numerous different styles and musical traditions. And music was not just an expression of unconnected sounds ricocheting back and forth on the flat surface of pure immanence. Rather, music gave expression to transcendent truth, which in turn gave ultimate validation of its aesthetic quality.

Both Augustine's *On Music* (387–391) and Boethius' *Fundamentals of Music* (ca. 520) built on the Pythagorean and (Neo-)Platonic tradition in their articulations of a philosophy of music.[35] Although Boethius wrote somewhat later than the theologians I am primarily interested in here, his approach to music is instructive, seeing as earlier church fathers such as Clement of Alexandria and Gregory of Nyssa in the East and Augustine and others in the West were broadly in line with Boethius' later articulation of Pythagorean principles. Boethius distinguishes between three types of music: "The first is cosmic (*mundana*), whereas the second is human (*humana*); the third is that which rests in certain instruments (*instrumentis*), such as the kithara or the aulos or other instruments which serve melody."[36] *Musica instrumentalis*—the only one of Boethius' three types that we usually call "music"—is meant to reflect the harmony of the planets. As Calvin Stapert puts it: "Ideally, *musica instrumentalis* should be a reflection of *musica mundana*: that is, it should be an audible manifestation of the order and harmony of the universe if it is to fulfill the function Plato gave it of tuning our out-of-tune souls."[37] Music, both according to the Platonic tradition and according to the early church, is a reflection of cosmic harmony.

Stapert, whose book *A New Song for an Old World* traces the impact of a Platonic metaphysic on the early church, shows both the continuity with and the divergences from classical thought in the Christian tradition. Early third-century theologian Clement of Alexandria (ca. 150–ca. 215) is particularly instructive here. On the one hand, his view of music fit squarely within the Platonic approach that linked cosmic harmony, the harmony of the soul, and the harmony of music. In that sense, his approach reflected the philosophical mindset of the

---

in her book *Intimations of Christianity among the Ancient Greeks*: "To be precise, there is here below but one single beauty, that is the Beauty of the Word. All other beauties are reflections of that alone, be they faithful and pure, deformed and soiled, or even diabolically perverted. . . . This cluster of marvels is perfected by the presence, in the necessary connections which compose the universal order, of divine verities symbolically expressed. Herein is the marvel of marvels, and as it were, the secret signature of the artist." *Intimations of Christianity*, 191, as quoted in Blackwell, *Sacred in Music*, 90.

35. For a brief but helpful discussion, see Faulkner, *Wiser Than Despair*, 76–78.

36. Boethius, *Fundamentals of Music* 1.2 (Bower, 9).

37. Stapert, *New Song*, 53.

time. Clement, however, reached beyond this when in *The Exhortation to the Greeks* he refers to the eternal Word as the author of the cosmic harmony: "He who sprang from David and yet was before him, the Word of God, scorned those lifeless instruments of lyre and harp. By the power of the Holy Spirit He arranged in harmonious order this great world, yes, and the little world of man too, body and soul together; and on this many-voiced instrument of the universe He makes music to God, and sings to the human instrument."[38] For Clement, the eternal Word of God composed both the entire cosmos and humanity as a microcosm, and in so doing, he manifested himself as the great musician of the universe. But if with respect to the world the Word of God is a musician, in relation to God, Clement maintains that in relation to God the Word serves as an instrument, as "an all-harmonious instrument of God, melodious and holy."[39] As such, the Word is the mirror opposite of Orpheus, who had used music to entice people to idolatry.[40] The Word of God introduces something altogether new; he is the "New Song,"[41] whose music, like that of David, chases the demons and heals us of our wickedness.[42] Stapert makes the point that Clement diverged from the Platonic tradition also by explicitly placing the *musica humana* of the soul above the *musica mundana* of the cosmos:[43] "Plato's god made the cosmos, and then, using the same proportions but on a lower level, he made the human soul. Clement's God made the cosmos, but created man in his own image, thereby making him the crown of all creation."[44] Only *musica humana*, Clement maintained, was made in the image of God.

When the Alexandrian theologian Athanasius discusses the psalms in his *Letter to Marcellinus* (probably dating from around 367), he reflects on the relationship between the harmony of the psalms that are sung and the harmony of the soul. "It is important," he writes in his letter, "not to pass over the question of why words of this kind are chanted with melodies and strains."[45] As he addresses this question, Athanasius explicitly rejects the notion that singing in church would simply be for aesthetic pleasure. Some, he writes, imagine that "on account of the sweetness of the sound" "the psalms are rendered musically for the sake of the ear's delight. But this is not so."[46]

---

38. Clement of Alexandria, *Exhortation to the Greeks* 1 (LCL 92:13).
39. Ibid., 1 (LCL 92:15).
40. Ibid., 1 (LCL 92:9).
41. Ibid., 1 (LCL 92:7, 11, 15, 17).
42. Ibid., 1 (LCL 92:13–15).
43. Stapert, *New Song*, 58.
44. Ibid.
45. Athanasius, *Letter to Marcellinus* 27 (Gregg, 123).
46. Ibid. A little later he reiterates, "The Psalms are not recited with melodies because of a desire for pleasant sounds." Ibid., 29 (Gregg, 125).

Plato and Plotinus would have agreed. At the same time, Athanasius had a specifically Christian motivation for downplaying the role of aesthetic pleasure. The purpose of liturgical music, for the Egyptian bishop, was not a sensual or material one; its purpose was spiritual. It is, says Athanasius, "for the benefit of the soul."[47]

Athanasius points to two particular benefits of singing the psalms. First, he comments that in singing the voice "is richly broadened."[48] He seems to mean by this that the sounds of the words are lengthened, dragged out, as it were, while at the same time they span various tonal inflections of the human voice. He links this musical feature with the life of the soul. The broadening of the soul, says Athanasius, enables people "to love God with their whole strength and power."[49] Second, for Athanasius, the melody accompanying the words serves as "a symbol of the spiritual harmony of the soul."[50] Just as the soul has different faculties, so music combines various sounds into one. Music's harmony, we could say, is analogous to that of the soul. And the way in which the faculties of the soul are ordered is no less important than the way in which the various sounds of a song are ordered. Following Plato, Athanasius holds that human beings have three faculties: reason (*logistikon*), affections (*thymētikon*), and passions or desires (*epithymētikon*).[51] For those three faculties to be in harmony, it is important that reason govern the passions. After all, says Athanasius, "the most excellent things derive from reasoning, while the most worthless derive from acting on the basis of desire."[52]

Athanasius doesn't just posit an external analogy between the harmony of the psalms and the harmony of the soul's faculties. Thomas Weinandy points out that the Egyptian bishop detects a much closer link between the two: "Christ's heart and mind were perfectly conformed to the Psalms. He prayed the Psalms in a perfect manner because his interior heart and mind—the seat of his emotions—corresponded perfectly with what the Psalms professed. For Athanasius, the Christian must acquire the same harmonious conformity. The Christian achieves this harmonious conformity in singing the Psalms. In praying the Psalms, the Christian conforms his heart and mind to the truth that is professed and so assumes and expresses an emotional state that is appropriate to the Psalm."[53] For Athanasius, harmonious psalms make for

47. Ibid., 27 (Gregg, 123).
48. Ibid.
49. Ibid.
50. Ibid., 28 (Gregg, 125).
51. Cf. Smith, *Passion and Paradise*, 52–58.
52. Athanasius, *Letter to Marcellinus* 27 (Gregg, 124).
53. Weinandy, "Athanasius's Letter to Marcellinus," 399.

harmonious people.[54] As a result, he argues that there is an intimate, typological connection between the two. "The harmonious reading of the Psalms,"
he claims "is a *figure and type* of such undisturbed and calm equanimity
of our thoughts."[55] A little later again, he comments that the harmonious
combination of cymbals, harp, and ten-stringed instrument is a *"figure and
sign* of the parts of the body coming into natural concord like harp strings,
and of the thoughts of the soul becoming like cymbals."[56] The harmonious
character of the melodies of the psalms and of musical instruments serves
as a figure, a type, or a sign of the harmonious character of the body and of
the faculties of the soul. This means that the two are closely linked: the harmony of music, for Saint Athanasius, has the ability to harmonize the soul.
"Blessed David, then," comments Athanasius, "making music in this way
for Saul, was himself well pleasing to God, and he drove away from Saul the
troubled and frenzied disposition, making his soul calm."[57] For Athanasius,
theological aesthetics recognizes that outward (aesthetic) beauty leads to inner
(spiritual) harmony; as a type—perhaps we could say, as a sacrament—the
former makes present the latter.

A similar concern for harmony, along with the language of typology, pervades Gregory of Nyssa's discussion in his *Treatise on the Inscriptions of the
Psalms*. This treatise, written perhaps between 376 and 378, is meant as an
exposition of the Septuagint headings above the psalms. Gregory also takes the
opportunity, however, to reflect on the role of music and on the structure of
the Psalter. Like Clement and Athanasius, he makes reference to the narrative
of David playing the harp and thereby soothing King Saul's troubled disposition, restoring harmony among his soul's faculties (1 Sam. 16).[58] Gregory
observes that people tend to sing the psalms on all sorts of occasions, including
"banquets and wedding festivities."[59] He then deals with the question of what
it is that makes people take such pleasure in what the psalms teach. It is not
just the fact that we *sing* the words that causes this pleasure, insists Gregory.[60]
The profound reason people love the psalms is that singing them puts them
in line with the order of the universe. The universe itself constitutes what the

54. Cf. the observation of Carol Harrison: "Athanasius' description of the natural resonance
which exists between the soul and the Psalms is clearly based on his conviction that both are
the work of God and that both resonate, in microcosm, with the measured music of his entire
creation." "Enchanting the Soul," 211.
55. Athanasius, *Letter to Marcellinus* 28 (Gregg, 124) (emphasis added).
56. Ibid., 29 (Gregg, 125–26) (emphasis added).
57. Ibid., 29 (Gregg, 125).
58. Ibid., 29 (Gregg, 125). Gregory of Nyssa, *Treatise on the Inscriptions* 1.33 (Heine, 92).
59. Gregory of Nyssa, *Treatise on the Inscriptions* 1.30 (Heine, 88).
60. Ibid.

Cappadocian theologian calls a "diverse and variegated musical harmony,"[61] so that it sings a "polyphonic tune."[62] One can perceive in creation a rhythmic oscillation between rest and motion. The combination of rest and motion that we observe in the planets creates a musical pattern in praise of God. Nyssen calls this cosmic harmony "the primal, archetypal, true music."[63]

Gregory then moves from the cosmos to humanity. Human beings, he insists, are a microcosm, for human nature reflects the musical harmony of the cosmic archetype.[64] Even the human body, insists Gregory, shows this harmony: "Do you see the flute in the windpipe, the bridge of the lyre in the palate, the music of the lyre that comes from tongue, cheeks, and mouth, as though from strings and a plectrum?"[65] Saint Gregory, who often insists that our physical bodies will have to undergo a drastic transformation so as to be fitted for the hereafter, obviously does not disdain the human body as such: it is an intricate work of divine art, reflecting the musical order of the cosmos.

For Gregory, then, we may discern musical harmony both in the cosmos (the archetype) and in the human person (the microcosm). It is with good reason, therefore, that we *sing* the psalms: the teaching of the psalms is meant to harmonize the faculties of the soul. "In this singing," says Gregory, "nature reflects on itself in a certain manner, and heals itself."[66] Singing "symbolically" (*di' ainigmatōn*) points to the "proper rhythm of life," to a virtuous life in which the passions have been subdued.[67] At this point, Gregory has finished dealing with the question he has set out to address, namely, why it is that people take such pleasure in what the psalms teach. The reason is that harmonious singing puts us in harmony with the cosmos, with human nature, and therefore ultimately with the teaching about the virtues, which is the main focus of the book of Psalms.[68] Harmony and virtue, beauty and goodness, go together for the Cappadocian father.

Gregory's elder brother, Basil of Caesarea, presents similar reflections in the broad-ranging introduction to his homily on Psalm 1. The two Cappadocian theologians share a focus on the cultivation of virtue as the purpose of the psalms. Music, for both, does not exist for its own sake but serves to support the promotion of virtue. Basil charmingly comments: "The delight

61. Ibid., 1.30 (Heine, 89).
62. Ibid., 1.31 (Heine, 89).
63. Ibid., 1.32 (Heine, 90). See on this topic and its relation to mathematics Caldecott, *Beauty for Truth's Sake.*
64. Gregory of Nyssa, *Treatise on the Inscriptions* 1.32 (Heine, 90–91).
65. Ibid., 1.33 (Heine, 91).
66. Ibid.
67. Ibid.
68. For similar reflections, see ibid., 2.75–76 (Heine, 129–30).

of melody He [i.e., the Holy Spirit] mingled with the doctrines so that by the pleasantness and softness of the sound heard we might receive without perceiving it the benefit of the words, just as the wise physicians who, when giving the fastidious rather bitter drugs to drink, frequently smear the cup with honey."[69] For Basil, the psalms' teaching on virtue is the bitter but beneficial drug, and the melody is the honey that makes it palatable.

In fact, Basil considers the musical harmony of the psalms not just conducive to ridding oneself of sinful passions; he also has an eye for the communal benefits of the psalms. "A psalm," he says, "forms friendships, unites those separated, conciliates those at enmity."[70] The result is that the harmony of the psalms produces harmony among the congregation: "Psalmody, bringing about choral singing, a bond, as it were, towards unity, and joining the people into a harmonious union of one choir, produces also the greatest of blessings, charity."[71] The harmony of the choir produces the virtuous harmony of love.

The four theologians that we have looked at—Clement, Athanasius, Gregory, and Basil—all recognized the significance of musical harmony. They did not see musical harmony as a matter of mere taste, and they certainly would have approved of Johnson's excoriation of such a reductive view of music. In line with the Pythagorean and Platonic tradition, they assumed harmony is something that characterizes not just music but also the human person, the church community, and the universe. By incorporating their theory of music and of harmony into a broader metaphysic, the church fathers presented a much more integrated cosmology than is common in the modern era. The reason is that their theology is undergirded by a metaphysic in which the realities of music, the human person, the church, and the cosmos are harmoniously connected. The sacramentality of this mindset is impossible to ignore: through the harmony of music, the human soul grows in harmony and becomes attuned to the harmony of the entire cosmos, arranged by the Logos as the great musician. Music is thus a sacramental means that enables one to participate ever more deeply in the harmonious reality of God himself.

Restoring Harmony: Virtue and Emotions in the Psalms

The foregoing discussion makes clear that, for the fathers, virtue was not only a moral category; it was also an aesthetic one. Virtue beautifies the soul,

69. Basil of Caesarea, *Exegetic Homilies* 10.1 (FC 46:152).
70. Ibid., 10.2 (FC 46:152).
71. Ibid.

producing a person whose character and life are in tune with the melodic principles of the universe. It is quite understandable, therefore, that virtue took center stage as a hermeneutical category in biblical interpretation. The church fathers were quick to ask how the biblical text can instill virtue. They asked this question not because they were preoccupied with God as the divine lawgiver, whom we are to obey in everything we do—though saying this would obviously not be wrong in itself. Rather, they highlighted the notion of virtue as a key to interpretation because they believed that the biblical text, much like music, serves as a sacramental means uniting our lives with the harmonious character of the universe and so ultimately with God himself.

The emphasis on virtue is particularly clear in the Alexandrian tradition (notably Clement and Origen) and among the Cappadocians (Basil the Great, Gregory of Nyssa, and Gregory of Nazianzus), who in this respect built, at least in part, on the first-century Jewish philosopher from Alexandria, Philo. Gregory of Nyssa casts his entire *Treatise on the Inscriptions of the Psalms* as a treatise on virtue, writing in the preface, "You enjoined us to investigate the meaning to be observed in these inscriptions, so that their capacity to lead us to virtue might be obvious to all."[72] Gregory begins the first chapter of part 1 with the words, "The goal of the virtuous life is blessedness."[73] He then explains the five books of the psalms as five stages of ascent in the growth of virtue. And in part 2, where he explains the Septuagint's headings above the psalms, he begins by insisting that also these inscriptions are meant to lead us on in virtue: "For these too make a significant contribution to us in respect to the way of virtue, as can be learned from the meaning itself of the words which have been inscribed."[74] Gregory was convinced that the psalms are all about teaching us the virtuous life; as a result, the theme of virtue runs throughout his commentary. Gregory's brother Basil is hardly different. Commenting on the two "ways" depicted in Psalm 1, Saint Basil explains: "Leading us on wisely and skilfully to virtue, David made the departure from evil the beginning of good."[75] Both Cappadocians regarded virtue as an important aspect, perhaps even as the leading theme and purpose, of the Psalter.

This emphasis on virtue is not restricted to the Alexandrians and the Cappadocians. It is also present among the Antiochenes. When Theodoret of Cyrus (ca. 393–ca. 458/466)—who likely wrote his *Commentary on the Psalms*

---

72. Gregory of Nyssa, *Treatise on the Inscriptions* 1.24 (Heine, 83).
73. Ibid., 1.25 (Heine, 84).
74. Ibid., 2.69 (Heine, 124).
75. Basil, *Exegetic Homilies* 10.4 (FC 46:157). See also ibid., 10.5 (FC 46:160–61).

between 441 and 448[76]—comments on the word "blessed" in Psalm 1, he explains that this epithet "constitutes the fruit of perfection as far as virtue is concerned."[77] "The practice of virtue has as its fruit and goal the beatitude from God."[78] And speaking of the psalm's metaphor of a tree growing by the riverbanks, he explains: "You see, champions of virtue reap the fruit of their labors in the future life; but like a kind of foliage they bear sound hope constantly within them."[79] At least in part, the church fathers let their exegesis be guided by the question of how a particular reading advances one's growth in virtue. Interpretation for them was less a matter of historical investigation (what the text *meant*) than it was the pursuit of a spiritual purpose.[80] Sometimes the fathers may make us feel uncomfortable by their relative neglect of the historical level of meaning. They were right, however, to search the Scriptures to see how they can be "useful" in ridding ourselves of earthly passions and how they can assist our growth in the life of God;[81] in other words, they rightly focused on what the text *means*.

Personal appropriation is not only a matter of growth in virtue, however, even if that is the overriding and ultimate concern, especially for the Cappadocians. The church fathers were also keenly aware that the book of Psalms reflects a broad range of human emotions, and they believed it quite legitimate to appropriate the psalms by locating one's own inner experiences in them. Athanasius' *Letter to Marcellinus* contains a long section in which he reflects on how one can make the psalms one's own. Athanasius praises the Psalter for having "a certain grace of its own."[82] He then comments that

> it contains even the emotions of each soul, and it has the changes and rectifications of these delineated and regulated in itself. Therefore anyone who wishes boundlessly to receive and understand from it, so as to mold himself, it is written there. For in the other books one hears only what one must do and what one must not do. And one listens to the Prophets so as solely to have knowledge of

76. R. Hill, introduction to *Commentary on the Psalms*, 4.

77. Theodoret of Cyrus, *Commentary on the Psalms 1–72* 1.4 (FC 101:47).

78. Ibid.

79. Ibid., 1.8 (FC 101:49). See also ibid., 1.9 (FC 101:50).

80. Cf. John J. O'Keefe's comment: "When Theodoret says that interpretations of the psalms that overemphasize *historia* help the Jews but offer nothing nourishing to those who have faith, he means these interpretations are insufficiently Christian." "Theodoret's Unique Contribution," 196.

81. The "usefulness" of the biblical text is an important consideration for many of the church fathers in determining its meaning. See Sheridan, *Language for God*, 226–29; H. Boersma, *Embodiment and Virtue*, 68–69.

82. Athanasius, *Letter to Marcellinus* 10 (Gregg, 107).

the coming of the Savior. One turns his attention to the histories, on the basis of which he can know the deeds of the kings and saints. But in the Book of Psalms, the one who hears, in addition to learning these things, also comprehends and is taught in the emotions of the soul.[83]

Athanasius puts himself forward here as a pastor and physician of the soul, who is aware that one cannot read the psalms without making the various emotions of the psalms one's own. And so he comments that "the one who hears is deeply moved, as though he himself were speaking, and is affected by the words of the songs, as if they were his own songs."[84] Recitation of the psalms, for Athanasius, leads to deeper knowledge also of oneself.[85]

Athanasius links this interest in therapy of the soul with the presence of Christ in the psalms.[86] Just as the psalms provide examples for us that mirror the emotions of our souls, so also Christ serves as a "type" (*typos*) providing an "image" (*eikōn*) or "model" (*paradeigma*) for our acting.[87] Christ, says Athanasius, "offered himself as a model (*typon*) for those who wish to know the power of acting. It was indeed for this reason that he made this resound in the Psalms before his sojourn in our midst, so that just as he provided the model (*typōn*) of the earthly and heavenly man in his own person, so also from the Psalms he who wants to do so can learn the emotions and dispositions of the souls, finding in them also the therapy and correction suited for each emotion."[88] Christ, according to Athanasius, is the one who stands behind the descriptions of our emotional life in the psalms; what is more, his very life itself offers a description of the life of the soul. Athanasius goes on to offer page upon page of references to the psalms, connecting them to the various emotional states of the believer. There are psalms for nearly every situation one may encounter and for nearly every emotional expression to which one may wish to give voice.[89] The psalms, for Saint Athanasius as well as for the other church fathers, offer a glimpse into one's own soul. Thus, the psalms become a means for the healing of one's emotional life.

83. Ibid., 10 (Gregg, 108).

84. Ibid., 11 (Gregg, 109).

85. Paul R. Kolbet notes that Athanasius prescribes psalm recitation for therapeutic purposes as an integral part of his overall ascetic program. "Athanasius," 75–96.

86. To be sure, Athanasius carefully distinguishes in the psalms prophecies about the Savior, on the one hand, and passages in which we may see our own emotions reflected, on the other hand. *Letter to Marcellinus* 11 (Gregg, 109–10).

87. Ibid., 13 (Gregg, 112).

88. Ibid.

89. Ibid., 14–26 (Gregg, 112–23).

Harmony with the Voice of Christ

For the church fathers, the recognition of Christ's presence in the psalms made them particularly apt for spiritual interpretation. Perhaps no church father is more emphatic about this than Saint Augustine (354–430). Michael Fiedrowicz, in his introduction to Augustine's *Expositions of the Psalms*, mentions five kinds of patristic christological interpretations of the psalms. He explains that they were interpreted as (1) a word to Christ (*vox ad Christum*); (2) a word about Christ (*vox de Christo*); (3) a word of Christ, spoken by him (*vox Christi*); (4) a word about the church (*vox de ecclesia*); and (5) a word of the church, spoken by the church (*vox ecclesiae*).[90] Of course, only the first three were strictly christological, and I will focus only on these three: Augustine treats the psalms as words *to* Christ, *about* Christ, and *of* Christ. This christological focus of Augustine makes clear that it is not just music and virtue that can unite us to the eternal harmony of God, but that a christological reading of the psalms does much the same thing.

We should keep in mind that, for Augustine at least, Christ and church should always be viewed together as the "whole Christ" (*totus Christus*).[91] Christ, in his reprimand of Saul—"Saul, Saul, why are you persecuting me?" (Acts 9:4)—appeared to Augustine to be identifying himself with his church.[92] The head (Christ) and the body (church) make up the one, total Christ for Augustine. Jason Byassee, author of a wonderful book on Saint Augustine's interpretation of the psalms, notes that Augustine's commentary presents "a 'christo-ecclesiological' form of exegesis, premised on the *totus Christus*, the 'whole Christ,' who speaks throughout the Psalter."[93] So, when the psalms speak about Christ, this often needs to be applied to those united to him—the church as well as individual believers. Conversely, what the psalms say about individual believers or the church, we often need to understand as referring to Christ himself as well. Augustine was convinced, then, that proper interpretation of the psalms takes into account not *just* Christology; they also speak a word about the church (*vox de ecclesia*) and a word spoken by the church (*vox ecclesiae*).

Let me first make a brief comment about the psalms as words *to* Christ (*vox ad Christum*). When the psalms address God, the fathers (including

90. Fiedrowicz, general introduction to *Expositions*, 44–45.

91. See Cameron, "Emergence of *Totus Christus*," 205–26; G. Boersma, "Augustine's Psalter," 27–34.

92. See also Matt. 25:40; 1 Cor. 10:16–17; 12:2; Col. 1:24. Cf. Fiedrowicz, general introduction to *Expositions*, 53–54.

93. Byassee, *Praise Seeking Understanding*, 63.

Augustine) had little hesitation in seeing in these words prayers addressed to Christ. Since Christ is the incarnate Son of God, the fathers considered it entirely legitimate to address him as God through the words of the psalms. So, when the psalmist appeals to God for help, for forgiveness, for justice, and so on, all of these petitions may be interpreted as petitions addressed to Christ.[94] In this way, the fathers consciously allowed theological convictions to influence their reading of the text.

The psalms also speak *about* Christ (*vox de Christo*). Psalm 1 may again serve as an example. "Blessed is the man who walks not in the counsel of the wicked," begins Psalm 1. The immediate question is, who is this "man," who is the object of the psalmist's speech? Fascinatingly, the very first words of Augustine's commentary on the book of Psalms are Christ-filled words. "This statement," he says, "should be understood as referring to our Lord Jesus Christ, that is, the Lord-Man."[95] He then speaks about Christ's faithfulness in contrast to Adam's lack thereof: "'Blessed is the person who has not gone astray in the council of the ungodly,' as did the earthly man who conspired with his wife, already beguiled by the serpent, to disregard God's commandments."[96] When Augustine reflects on this "man" of Psalm 1 not "standing" in the way of sinners (1:1), he takes this as an opportunity to comment on the incarnation: "Christ most certainly came in the way of sinners by being born as sinners are; but he did not stand in it, for worldly allurement did not hold him."[97] Augustine distinguishes here between "coming" and "standing": Christ "came" in the way of sinners (since in the incarnation he came in the likeness of sinful flesh), but he did not "stand" in the way of sinners (which is to say, he did not become sinful himself). Without any hesitation, therefore, Augustine immediately starts off with a christological reading of the psalm. The psalmist's voice is here a *vox de Christo*, a voice about Christ.

To be sure, there was no unanimity on this point among patristic interpreters. The earlier fourth-century defender of orthodox trinitarian thought, Hilary of Poitiers (ca. 315–ca. 368), explicitly disagreed with the approach that Augustine later took. "I have discovered," writes Hilary, "either from personal conversation or from their letters and writings, that the opinion of many men about this psalm is, that we ought to understand it to be a description of our Lord Jesus Christ, and that it is His happiness which is

94. Ibid., 45.
95. Augustine, "Exposition of Psalm 1," in *Expositions of the Psalms 1–32*, 67.
96. Ibid. Here and elsewhere I have replaced Boulding's use of italics in rendering Augustine's biblical quotations with quotation marks.
97. Ibid.

extolled in the verses following."[98] Of course, we just saw that this is exactly the approach of Saint Augustine. And, judging by Hilary's words, this must have been a common patristic approach. Hilary, however, disagrees. "But this interpretation is wrong both in method and reasoning," he comments, "though doubtless it is inspired by a pious tendency of thought, since the whole of the Psalter is to be referred to Him."[99] We must carefully take note: Hilary is not objecting to a christological reading, for "the whole of the Psalter is to be referred to Him [i.e., Christ]." Reading the Psalter christologically was a given for the church fathers.

Saint Hilary nonetheless does not think that the comment "Blessed is the man" is a reference to Christ, and he gives two basic reasons. First, the Son is the one who *gave* the law, while, according to the psalm, this man's happiness or blessedness depends on his "desire" being in the law of the Lord. How can one attribute such desire to Christ? His desire, insists Hilary, is not in the law of the Lord; rather, as the one who gives it, Christ is the law's Lord.[100] Second, the psalmist compares the blessed or happy man to a tree. This means, Hilary explains, that the tree is the greater standard by which the blessed man is measured. How could a tree be happier than the Son of God? How could Christ be happy by becoming like the objects that he himself has created? We must infer, concludes Hilary, that the psalmist is speaking not about Christ but about believers: "We must suppose him, who is here extolled as happy by the Prophet, to be the man who strives to conform himself to that body which the Lord assumed and in which He was born as man."[101] We see from this comparison between Hilary and Augustine that the church fathers, while unanimous in their opinion that the psalms must be read christologically, were not always agreed on the details of *how* to do so.

Athanasius, in his *Letter to Marcellinus*, provides numerous examples of words *about* Christ (*vox de Christo*) in the Psalter. Thoroughly at home in the psalms, Athanasius moves back and forth among them with amazing alacrity, and as he does so, he identifies in the psalms many of the particular moments within the economy of the Son's work. For instance, Athanasius reads in the psalms the teaching that the Savior will come as one who is God (Pss. 49 [50]:3; 106 [107]:20; 117 [118]:26–27). He reads here about the eternal generation of the Son (Pss. 44 [45]:1; 109 [110]:3). He reads about the incarnation of God's Son in the flesh (Pss. 44 [45]:6–7; 86 [87]:5). He reads about the virgin birth (Ps. 44 [45]:10–11). He reads about the suffering of the Savior (Ps. 2:1–2), about his

98. Hilary of Poitiers, *Homilies on the Psalms* 1 (NPNF[2] 9:236).
99. Ibid.
100. Ibid.
101. Ibid. (NPNF[2] 9:237). See below for the discussion of the psalmist as a prophet.

death on the cross (Ps. 21 [22]:15–18), and about the representative character of his suffering (Pss. 68 [69]:4; 71 [72]:4, 12; 87 [88]:16; 137 [138]:8). He also reads about Christ's ascension into heaven (Pss. 23 [24]:7; 46:6 [47:5]) and about his session at God's right hand (Pss. 9:7–8; 109 [110]:1). Furthermore, he reads here a prophecy of Christ's return as judge (Pss. 49 [50]:4; 71 [72]:1–2; 81 [82]:1). And, finally, he reads in the psalms about the calling of the nations (Pss. 46 [47]:1; 71 [72]:9–11).[102] Athanasius considered the *vox de Christo* to be nearly omnipresent in the book of Psalms. Saint Basil of Caesarea, while not nearly as extensive in his analysis as Athanasius, is in line with him when he heaps praise on the psalms with the comment: "Therein is perfect theology, a prediction of the coming of Christ in the flesh."[103] The idea that the psalms present a "word about Christ" received the unanimous support of the fathers.

This approach implies great confidence in the inspiration of Scripture. Mark Sheridan comments that among the "most important presuppositions" of the fathers regarding the "nature of the Scriptures" is that they constitute "divine writing, not human," so that "God is the author of the text even in (what a modern writer might consider) its most insignificant details."[104] In line with this conviction of divine authorship, the fathers believed that the Spirit so shaped the contents of the Old Testament that it already contained New Testament christological realities. Divine inspiration is what allowed the fathers to read the book of Psalms prophetically. The notion that the Psalter is a book of prophecy is perhaps one of the distinguishing characteristics of patristic exegesis. Interpreters such as Augustine often referred to the psalmist as "the prophet." Or, more radically yet, in an unencumbered sort of way, Augustine and others would simply mention the Holy Spirit as the speaker of a particular psalm.[105] Our contemporary sermons and commentaries tend to be much more reserved, not usually identifying "the prophet" or "the Spirit" as saying something in the text. This circumspection goes hand in hand with a reluctance to read the psalms prophetically, as speaking about Christ. The modern restriction of exegesis to a search for the intent of the human author tends to limit our horizons of interpretation to this-worldly realities. In such an interpretive context, it is difficult to draw out the Spirit's overarching intentions within the text. My hunch is that if we were to expand our attention beyond this-worldly realities and acknowledge the Spirit's providential guidance in the authorship and the interpretation of Holy Scripture, we would likely also regain confidence in identifying the presence of Christ in the Old Testament.

102. Athanasius, *Letter to Marcellinus* 5–8 (Gregg, 103–6). See also ibid., 26 (Gregg, 123).
103. Basil, *Exegetic Homilies* 10.2 (FC 46:153).
104. Sheridan, *Language for God*, 223.
105. Fiedrowicz, general introduction to *Expositions*, 24.

Not only did the church fathers allude to the *vox ad Christum* and the *vox de Christo* in the psalms, but they also heard here the *vox Christi*, the voice *of* Christ—Christ himself speaking through the voice of the psalmist. Fiedrowicz makes clear that one of the key elements of patristic exegesis was the attempt to figure out who it was that was speaking in a psalm. Fiedrowicz refers to this as "prosopological exegesis," derived from the Greek word *prosōpon*, meaning "person." Prosopological exegesis asked the question, which *person* is speaking in this psalm? Once this was established, much of the rest of the psalm would fall into place.[106] We see a striking example of such prosopological exegesis at the very beginning of Hilary's commentary on Psalm 1: "The primary condition of knowledge for reading the Psalms," he starts off—raising right at the outset the question of how to interpret—"is the ability to see as whose mouthpiece we are to regard the Psalmist as speaking, and who it is that he addresses."[107] By asking whose "mouthpiece" the psalmist might be, Hilary introduces prosopological interpretation.

We see something similar in Saint Augustine. As I already mentioned, for the bishop of Hippo, the doctrine of *totus Christus*—the "whole Christ" as a reference to Christ *and* his members—meant that in a particular passage Christ could be speaking either in his own person (*ex persona sua*) or in our person (*ex persona nostra*).[108] Fiedrowicz puts it this way:

> An important part of Augustine's thought is that the Church was already present in Christ's prayer. His exegesis of the frequently quoted verse of Psalm 21 (21:2 [22:1]) shows that for Augustine the cry of Christ on the cross was not only raised "in Adam's name" but had an ecclesial dimension too, in that Christ directed those words to the Father "in the name of his body" equally (*ex persona corporis*). By identifying the Church with even the earthly body of Christ Augustine was able to discover a mysterious involvement of humanity in the event of the cross. We were there (*nos ibi eramus*).[109]

---

106. The underlying assumption is that, for some reason, the prima facie speaker is not the one who is really speaking in the text. Matthew W. Bates, in a fascinating study on prosopological exegesis, defines it as "a reading technique whereby the interpreter seeks to overcome a real or perceived ambiguity regarding the identity of the speakers or addressees (or both) in the divinely inspired source text by assigning nontrivial prosopa (i.e., nontrivial vis-à-vis the 'plain sense' of the text) to the speakers or addressees (or both) in order to make sense of the text" (*Hermeneutics of the Apostolic Proclamation*, 221). Bates shows that prosopological exegesis was common among pagan, Jewish, and Christian interpreters (ibid., 183–221) and argues that Paul's Letters also make frequent use of it (ibid., 223–328).

107. Hilary of Poitiers, *Homilies on the Psalms* 1 (NPNF² 9:236).

108. Fiedrowicz, general introduction to *Expositions*, 52–55.

109. Ibid., 54; round brackets in original.

"We were there," writes Augustine. This statement shows what was at stake for the African theologian—and, we may add, for the fathers in general—in prosopological exegesis. By seeing the psalms as referring to Christ, the church fathers allowed God's people to make these psalms their own.[110] According to the fathers, the church is present in the psalms because Christ himself is present there. That is to say, the christological exegesis of the psalms was for them a sacramental practice. Spiritual or sacramental interpretation was required inasmuch as it was nearly synonymous with christological interpretation. Thus, for the fathers it was not only music and virtue that could sacramentally unite us to the harmonious reality of God. Reading the psalms christologically did much the same thing. Singing the psalms, reading the psalms, and living the psalms served to bring one in harmony with the reality of God in Christ.

Gregory of Nyssa on the Order of the Psalms[111]

Gregory of Nyssa, like Augustine and Athanasius, was deeply concerned with the healing of the soul in his interpretation of the psalms. As he unfolds the meaning of the psalms, Nyssen takes the structure of the entire Psalter as his guide for the spiritual life of virtue. Here, as in many of his other works, Saint Gregory was interested in the purpose (*skopos*) of the Psalter, as well as in the order (*taxis*) or sequence (*akolouthia*) of its various sections.[112] By taking these elements seriously, Gregory believed that he not only could perceive the genuine purpose and structure of the book of Psalms but also was able to discern the purpose and structure of the journey of the soul. As we will see, these two—interpretation and the soul's ascent—were for Gregory two sides of the same coin.

Gregory begins his *Treatise on the Inscriptions of the Psalms* by identifying the harmonious aim of the Psalter. He does this through a procedure borrowed from the early fourth-century Neoplatonic philosopher Iamblichus. Nyssen insists that to understand the book "one must understand the aim (*skopon*) to which this writing looks. Next, one must pay attention to the progressive arrangements of the concepts in the book under discussion. These are indicated both by the order (*taxis*) of the psalms, which has been well arranged in relation to knowledge of the aim (*skopou*), and by the sections of the whole

110. Discussing Augustine's exegesis of Ps. 100 (101), Andrew Louth comments: "It is Christ's voice we hear in the psalm, and part of what is meant by understanding the psalm is learning how to join our voice to Christ's; the Christ singing in the psalm is Christ the head of the Church, of which we are the members." "'Heart in Pilgrimage,'" 303.

111. This section closely follows H. Boersma, *Embodiment and Virtue*, 71–74.

112. See Drobner, "Skopos – σκοπός," 681–82; Gil-Tamayo, "Akolouthia – ἀκολουθία," 14–20.

book, which are defined by certain distinctive conclusions."[113] Gregory, like Iamblichus before him, takes the aim (*skopos*) and the order (*taxis*) of the work as the starting point and guide of the interpretive process.[114]

Nyssen identifies the aim of the Psalter by turning to the beginning of Psalm 1 ("Blessed is the man"). Since he regards this "blessedness" or "happiness" as the "goal" (*telos*) of the virtuous life, Gregory takes the Psalter as a whole to be a means of attaining this eschatological blessedness. The Psalter, he insists, points the way to blessedness "through a skilful and natural sequence (*akolouthia*) in teaching which is simple in its appearance and lacking in artifice by setting forth systematically in various and diverse forms the method for acquiring the blessing."[115] Nyssen recognizes the common division of the Psalter into five sections as providing the sequence, since these five parts all "conclude in a similar manner with certain ascriptions of praise to God."[116] Thus, Gregory outlines in the first part of his commentary the "systematic order"[117] or the "orderly sequence" of the five books.[118] Gregory is remarkably interested in the compositional structure of the book, which he believes will help him understand its meaning.

Since the book of Psalms leads one to the "blessedness" first mentioned in Psalm 1 and victoriously celebrated in Psalm 150, Nyssen takes each section as a stage in what he calls the "ascent" (*anabasis*) to the blessedness of perfect harmony, when humanity will imitate perfectly "the harmony of the universe in the variety and diversity of the virtues, having become an instrument for God in rhythmical music."[119] And because, in line with Iamblichus, he assumes that the beginning of a work mentions its overall aim, the first psalm of each section must give insight into the section as a whole and thus enables one to grasp how the soul advances in each stage of her ascent. Gregory explains that Psalm 1 holds out for us the ways of virtue and vice, and thus shows the "first entrance to the good," which allows for an initial "participation" (*metochē*) in what is superior.[120] This initial participation leads to the ardent desire for virtue described in Psalm 41:2 (42:1), which forms the beginning of the second part of the Psalter. In this psalm, the soul, like the doe, is said to long or thirst for the living God. The participation in goodness that has

---

113. Gregory of Nyssa, *Treatise on the Inscriptions* 1.24–25 (Heine, 83).

114. See Margerie, "Saint Gregory of Nyssa," 213–39; Heine, introduction to *Treatise on the Inscriptions*, 29–43.

115. Gregory of Nyssa, *Treatise on the Inscriptions* 1.26 (Heine, 84).

116. Ibid., 1.38 (Heine, 95). Cf. ibid., 1.65 (Heine, 119–20).

117. Ibid., 1.39 (Heine, 96).

118. Ibid., 1.65 (Heine, 119).

119. Ibid., 1.65 (Heine, 120).

120. Ibid., 1.39 (Heine, 96).

now been attained, comments Nyssen, is transformed into the very fountain of water for which the soul has thirsted.[121]

Psalm 72 (73) opens up the third section of the Psalter, as it describes the kind of contemplation that has become possible for the person arriving at the third stage of ascent. Here one has obtained the divine ability to discern justice by examining "how the justice of the divine judgement will be preserved in the disparity of life" that the psalmist describes.[122] Proper "contemplation"[123] no longer looks at what is currently at hand: "When he enters the heavenly shrines he upbraids the lack of judgement of those who basely pervert the discernment of what is good to our physical members capable of sense-perception. This is why he says, 'For what do I have in heaven, and what do I desire on earth besides you? [Ps. 72 (73):25].'"[124] Thus, the third stage allows one to contemplate and participate in divine judgment.

In Psalm 89 (90), Moses, who according to the heading is the author, guides the soul to the next step. Since Moses himself became "unchangeable in the changeable nature," he is able to serve as a boundary (*methorios*) between the divine and human natures; he can mediate, leading the soul to the height that Moses himself has already reached.[125] No longer following the "delusion of the material life,"[126] the person who has ascended to this fourth stage has "removed himself from things that are inferior and earthly."[127]

The ascent finally arrives at its climax at the "mountain-peak" of the fifth step, which begins with Psalm 106 (107).[128] Since the psalm recounts the narrative of Israel's exodus and desert journey, Gregory sees here "a complete consummation and recapitulation of human salvation."[129] Having flown with the wings of an eagle to the highest mountaintop,[130] one can now look back and see how God has been faithful in dealing with all the obstacles on the journey of ascent. As a result, this fifth section of the book of Psalms naturally leads

121. Ibid., 1.40 (Heine, 98).
122. Ibid. Cf. Ps. 72 (73):17.
123. Ibid., 1.40 (Heine, 98), 1.41 (Heine, 99). Ps. 72 (73):1 states: "Truly God is good to Israel, to those who are pure in heart." The reference to "Israel," commonly interpreted as meaning "the man who sees God," along with the reference to the "pure in heart"—which according to the Beatitudes leads to the vision of God (Matt. 5:8)—allows Gregory to reflect on the soul's participation in divine contemplation.
124. Ibid., 1.41 (Heine, 99). Here and elsewhere I have replaced Heine's use of italics in rendering Gregory's biblical quotations with quotation marks.
125. Ibid., 1.45 (Heine, 103).
126. Ibid., 1.51 (Heine, 109).
127. Ibid., 1.45 (Heine, 103).
128. Ibid., 1.52 (Heine, 109).
129. Ibid.
130. Ibid.

into the eschatological song of praise of Psalm 150. The human nature is joined
with that of the angels when the psalmist sings, "Praise him with sounding
cymbals; praise him with loud clashing cymbals!" The clashing together of
the two cymbals indicates, according to Saint Gregory, the harmonious union
of the angelic and human natures: "The supernatural nature of the angels is
one 'cymbal'; the rational creation consisting of mankind is the other. But sin
separated the one from the other. Whenever, then, the mercy of God again
unites the two with one another, then what comes about from the two with
one another will cause that praise to resound."[131] The climax of the book of
Psalms represents the pinnacle of cosmic harmony. It is not just that there is a
similarity between the harmony of human virtue and the harmony of angelic
songs. For Gregory, the former sacramentally participates in the latter. The
harmonious virtue of human beings serves as a sacrament that participates,
in ever-greater degrees, in the harmony of the cosmos. For Gregory, attention to the technical details of Iamblichian exegesis—with its focus on the
aim and sequence of the biblical text—does not stand in conflict with the
spiritual purpose of biblical interpretation. Instead, the exegetical approach
of the Neoplatonic philosopher helps in the pursuit of spiritual harmony.[132]

Saint Gregory's attention to the structure and purpose of the text itself
means that he has little interest in the history behind the text. Several times,
Gregory draws attention to the fact that the psalms do not always follow a historical sequence. Psalms 50 (51) and 51 (52) present the most obvious example
of this difficulty. The former is connected with David's sin against Bathsheba
and Uriah (2 Sam. 11) and the latter with the incident involving Doeg the
Edomite (1 Sam. 22).[133] Although Gregory appears to take these historical
references at face value, the chronological sequence does not determine his
exegesis. Gregory argues that if chronology had been the principle structuring
the Psalter, the order of these two psalms would have to be reversed. And so
he reminds the reader that the psalms are not concerned with the "sequence
(*akolouthia*) of history," with the "chronological interval," with the "sequence
(*akolouthia*) of the events," or with the "order (*taxei*) of history."[134] After all,

131. Ibid., 1.66 (Heine, 121).
132. Even so, Marie-Josèphe Rondeau makes the case that there is "nothing arbitrary or
forced" in Gregory's exegesis ("Exégèse du Psautier et anabase spirituelle chez Grégoire de
Nysse," 519) and that Gregory makes a solid case for the various hinges that connect the
five sections of the Psalter, so that exegesis and spiritual theology influence each other in his
commentary (ibid., 531). Jean-Marie Auwers similarly argues that Gregory's identification of
"blessedness" as the *skopos* of the text is in line with the overall composition of the book of
Psalms. "Grégoire de Nysse, interprète du Psautier," 174–80.
133. Gregory of Nyssa, *Treatise on the Inscriptions* 2.133 (Heine, 178).
134. Ibid., 2.115 (Heine, 163).

as we have seen, Gregory believes that the aim of the Psalter is to reshape us by means of virtue into the divine likeness, so that Christ may be formed in us.[135] Gregory explains: "The order of the psalms is harmonious, therefore, since what is zealously pursued by the Spirit, as was said, is not to teach us mere history, but to form our souls in accordance with God through virtue."[136] Similarly, he comments: "But the spiritual Word is not concerned about the chronological and material order of things. For what great benefit is it to me to learn first that about the 'Edomite,' and then to be taught that about 'Bathsheba'? What virtue is there in this? What sort of ascent to that which is superior? What teaching that produces desire for things sublime?"[137] The fact that the Psalter doesn't follow the chronology of the historical narratives is of little consequence for the Cappadocian father; what matters is the spiritual *skopos* of the text, along with the virtue that allows one to obtain one's final end. The underlying assumption throughout is that the exegetical goal is identical to one's personal aim. Both set out for blessedness, and both end in harmonious praise of God. In the patristic reading of Scripture, interpretation and harmonious character are inseparable.[138]

Conclusion

Patristic exegesis of the psalms modeled a remarkable synthesis of Greek metaphysical thought and Christian theological convictions. On the one hand, the patristic understanding of music and its relation to anthropology and cosmology is unthinkable without the Pythagorean and (Neo-)Platonic understanding of the mathematical structure of the universe and of musical harmony. For the church fathers, as for the Greek tradition from which they borrowed, music serves to put us into contact with the creator's harmonious purposes for the universe, and as such it has a potentially sacramental role. Music, on this understanding, has an exalted function, and for this reason we do well to treat it with great circumspection. The Greek notion that human virtue tunes the soul to the cosmic structures of the world also deeply influenced the church fathers: virtue, they believed, enables one to enter into the divine life. According to the theologians of the early church, therefore, both music and virtue serve a sacramental purpose: they unite us with the harmony of the universe and in so doing draw us into the divine life.

135. Ibid., 2.116 (Heine, 164).
136. Ibid., 2.117 (Heine, 164).
137. Ibid., 2.133 (Heine, 178).
138. Fowl, "Virtue," 837. See also Briggs, *Virtuous Reader*; Treier, *Introducing Theological Interpretation*, 92–96.

On the other hand, we need to be cautious in the use of the language of "sacramentality" when it comes to the Greek mindset. At best, the Platonic tradition knows of sacramental beauty in a remotely analogous sense. True, the notion of participation is key to the Platonic tradition, and the church fathers adopt this language to give expression to the sacramental cast of the Christian faith. But it is only in the Christian tradition that the harmony of the universe is predicated on Christ as its composer. It is only in the Christian tradition that the harmonizing of the soul is also its renewal as the image of God. It is only in the Christian tradition that the musical aim of life is seen as a reunification of human beings with the angels. And, most emphatically, it is only in the Christian tradition that Christ himself is the one who encounters us as the climactic reality present in the Psalter's words.

For the church fathers, these words of the psalms were indispensable. The text of the Scriptures—to which neither Pythagoras nor Plato had access—was the gracious sacramental gift through which one could reach true harmony. The fathers detected a deep congruity between the process of interpretation and progress of the soul. The very purpose of Bible reading was to foster virtue, that is to say, to yield harmony for the soul. To read the psalms well, then, one had to read them with an eye to the summit of the Christian life: harmonious praise of God in Jesus Christ. It was, therefore, with good reason that the psalms were put to music in the church's liturgy: in the book of Psalms, the early church possessed a means of salvation so precious that it contained the very aim of the Christian life—the voice of Christ.

Music making, Bible reading, and moral living were all of a piece to the church fathers. They all had to do with the discovery of divine harmony. Through each of these activities, the believer entered into Christ. Through each of these activities, the believer joined the harmony of the cosmos. Each of these activities, therefore, was sacramental in a way that was unique to the Christian faith. With faith in Christ, the key to genuine harmony had finally been unlocked. When early Christians *sang* their psalms, they enjoyed the beauty of Christ. When early Christians *read* their psalms, they learned the truth of Christ. And when early Christians *lived* their psalms, they participated in the virtue of Christ. In each of these ways, they joined the perfect harmony of a new song.

7

DOCTRINAL READING

Athanasius and Gregory of Nyssa
on the Wisdom of Proverbs 8

Spiritual Interpretation and Christian Doctrine

Without exegesis of Holy Scripture, we do not have Christian doctrine. This point is crucial as we engage in a discussion of Proverbs 8. Thus far, we have looked at various biblical passages without concerning ourselves directly with specific theological or doctrinal implications. To be sure, I have already made the case that all proper interpretation of Scripture is spiritual or theological in character. That is to say, I have argued that we interpret the Bible for a certain purpose, a particular aim—eternal life in the Triune God. Any exegesis that doesn't aim at this purpose isn't interpretation of Scripture in the full, Christian sense. But an approach that takes this ultimate aim of exegesis into account carries an implication that I have not yet spelled out: exegesis provides the grounding for Christian doctrine; that is to say, biblical theology and dogmatic or systematic theology belong together.

Through what *kind* of reading, however, do we arrive at Christian doctrine? On my understanding, a Christian reading of the biblical text always moves from the letter to the spirit. Spiritual interpretation, then, is an absolute requirement for exegesis. Perhaps the most important reason for this is that the heritage of Christian doctrine is the result of this kind of reading of the Bible. Sacramental reading, so I will argue in this chapter, is not an optional extra but lies at the heart of trinitarian exegesis and theology. In terms of hermeneutics, the main difference between the Arian and the pro-Nicene traditions of reading Proverbs 8 is that only the latter read the chapter in a deliberately sacramental fashion. The difference in hermeneutical approach between Arian and pro-Nicene theologians is a strong indication that we need the spiritual or theological interpretation of the church fathers in order to uphold the truth of the Nicene faith. Anglican scholar Ephraim Radner, in an essay on nineteenth-century Anglo-Catholic John Keble, argues that if patristic exegesis "is genuinely rejected, so too must be any pretence to holding orthodox theistic convictions."[1] It is not the purpose of this chapter to argue this proposition in detail. After all, the fourth-century trinitarian disputes were wide-ranging, and the disagreements over Proverbs 8 formed only one small (though significant) element in the broader controversies.[2] By looking at disagreements over Proverbs 8, we do, however, get some sense of the importance that a sacramental hermeneutic held for pro-Nicene theology.

I need to make an important caveat at this point: it is not the case that those who reject spiritual exegesis invariably also object to the doctrine of the Trinity. In fact, this is quite obviously not the case. Many Christian scholars, convinced that we cannot follow patristic approaches to the reading of Scripture, are nonetheless wholeheartedly devoted to the dogma of the Trinity as the ecumenical councils of the fourth century articulated it. What I am arguing, however, is that a rejection of the sacramental exegesis of the church fathers makes it difficult to ground our trinitarian convictions in the text of the Old Testament witness. In other words, it seems to me that while we may still hold to Nicene trinitarian theology even when we do exegesis by means of a purely historical method, we will have lost an important plank in the defense of this theology.

Disagreements in the early church on how to read Proverbs 8 were, in one important respect, limited. All interpreters of Scripture—from strict adherents to Nicaea such as Athanasius and Gregory of Nyssa to radical subordinationists such as Aetius and Eunomius—agreed on one crucial point: Christ was

---

1. Radner, "Faith of Reading," 87. Cf. Byassee: "You cannot have patristic dogma without patristic exegesis; you cannot have the creed without allegory." *Praise Seeking Understanding*, 16. And Treier: "It seems odd to suggest that we can receive the doctrines of the apostles without accepting the legitimacy of the scriptural hermeneutics by which they developed and defended that teaching." *Introducing Theological Interpretation*, 50.

2. For a thorough treatment of the theological developments surrounding the fourth-century debates, see Ayres, *Nicaea and Its Legacy*.

somehow to be identified with the Wisdom of Proverbs 8. Khaled Anatolios rightly comments that a nonchristological interpretation was simply out of bounds: "A common adherence to the principle of the intertextual unity of Scripture prevented participants in the fourth-century debates from taking that route. If Jesus Christ is scripturally identified as God's Wisdom (cf. 1 Cor. 1:24), then anything predicated of Wisdom anywhere in the Scriptures must be appropriately predicated of Christ."[3] So, both the pro-Nicene and the anti-Nicene theologians of the fourth century saw in the Wisdom of Proverbs a reference to Christ. The reason, undoubtedly, is that all parties involved in the debates recognized that proper exegesis demands that the unity of the Scriptures be taken into account. It simply wasn't possible, either for the Arians or for pro-Nicene theologians, to read Proverbs 8 in isolation, independent of God's self-revelation in Jesus Christ and detached from the New Testament witness to him. The church's dogma—including her christological teaching—was grounded in the biblical text, and for the church fathers this included the Old Testament. To be sure, we will observe shortly that this unanimity about a christological reading isn't as profound as it may appear at first sight: not every christological reading was also a sacramental reading. Nonetheless, because today's biblical scholars are divided over precisely the question of a christological reading of Proverbs 8, it is a significant observation that Arians and pro-Nicenes agreed on precisely this point.[4]

From Origen to Eusebius

Early Christian theologians treated the trinitarian controversies as exegetical controversies. At stake, they believed, was the proper interpretation of the Scriptures—most notably, perhaps, Proverbs 8 (though, as I have already indicated, many other passages also entered the picture). At the same time, the road from exegesis to doctrine is one that the fathers knew to be strewn with obstacles. In this chapter we will see that different theologians—even those within the pro-Nicene camp—arrived at readings of Proverbs 8:22–25 that were at times remarkably different from each other. We will also see, however, that regardless of internal differences, the exegetical choices of pro-Nicene theologians such as Athanasius and Gregory of Nyssa were driven by sacramental convictions about the interpretation of the Scriptures.

3. Anatolios, *Retrieving Nicaea*, 132.
4. Gordon D. Fee rejects a christological exegesis of Proverbs 8 in "Wisdom Christology in Paul," 251–79. In contrast, N. T. Wright argues in favor of a christological reading in *Climax of the Covenant*, 110–13.

The passage from Proverbs 8, though it was by no means the only one leading to sharp exegetical disagreements in the fourth century, was central to the debates. Opinions clashed particularly with regard to verses 22–25:

> [22] The Lord created (*ektisen*) me as the beginning of his ways, for his works.
> [23] Before the ages, he established (*ethemeliōsen*) me in the beginning.
> [24] Before the earth was made, before the depths were made, before the springs of the waters came forth,
> [25] before the mountains were founded, before all the hills, he begets (*genna*) me.[5]

It is important to recognize that the fourth-century debates took place against the backdrop of an already developing tradition of interpretive engagement with this passage. This tradition goes back to the early third-century work of Origen (ca. 185–ca. 254). Reflecting on this passage in his book *On First Principles* (ca. 225), Origen refers every aspect of it to the eternal relationship between the Father and the Son. Speaking of the two natures of Christ, Origen explains that he wants "to see what the only-begotten Son of God is."[6] Origen then quotes the passage in question, along with Colossians 1:15, which refers to Christ as the "firstborn of all creation." The theologian from Alexandria straightforwardly makes the point that both passages refer to the eternal generation of the Son.[7]

This reading could easily lead to an erroneously subordinationist Christology; Origen (or his translator Rufinus) added, therefore, that the begetting of the Son mentioned in Proverbs 8:25 is an eternal begetting, so that we should not suppose that the Father "ever existed, even for a single moment, without begetting this wisdom."[8] God the Father "always had an only-begotten Son," claims Origen.[9] Begotten "of the Father's will,"[10] the Son is the invisible image and likeness of the Father, so that "there is no time when he did not exist."[11] In a comment that would reverberate throughout the later Arian controversies, Origen adds: "And when did the image of unspeakable, unnameable, unutterable substance of the Father, his impress, the Word who knows the Father, not exist? Let the man who dares to say, 'There was a time when the Son was not,' understand that this is what he will be saying, 'Once wisdom did not exist,

---

5. This is my own (rather wooden) translation of the Septuagint, the Greek translation of this Proverbs passage, which Arians and pro-Nicenes both used.
6. Origen, *On First Principles* 1.2.1 (Butterworth, 15).
7. Ibid.
8. Ibid., 1.2.2 (Butterworth, 15).
9. Ibid., 1.4.4 (Butterworth, 42).
10. Ibid., 4.4.1 (Butterworth, 314).
11. Ibid., 4.4.1 (Butterworth, 315).

and word did not exist, and life did not exist.'"[12] There was never a time when the eternal Son of God, the Wisdom of God, did not exist. And so, when in verse 22 Wisdom claims that she was created as "the beginning of his ways," Origen clarifies that she was "begotten beyond the limits of any beginning that we can speak of or understand."[13] So, on the one hand, he applied the entire passage of Proverbs 8:22–25 to the pre-incarnate, eternal Son of God, to the generation of the Son, and so to the immanent life of the Trinity. On the other hand, *On First Principles* also placed the eternal Wisdom of God firmly on the other side of the creator-creature divide: the Father was never without his Wisdom.

Origen did face a serious exegetical challenge: How could one say of the eternal Son of God that he was "created" in eternity without thereby putting his genuine divinity in jeopardy? We already noted Origen's claim that we shouldn't think of the Son's "beginning" as something we can understand. With regard to the "creation" of the Son (Prov. 8:22), Origen comments that Wisdom "fashions beforehand and contains within herself the species and causes of the entire creation."[14] Creation, that is, always existed "in form and outline" within the divine Wisdom.[15] Origen appears to suggest that to say that Wisdom was "created" means that the creatures preexisted eternally in the eternal Son of God. To some, this exegesis must have seemed strained: whereas the text suggests that *Wisdom* was created, Origen seemed to be saying that the *creatures* were created (preexisting from eternity in Wisdom).

I suspect that two factors convinced Origen that his approach was nonetheless justified. First, he must have thought it *theologically* legitimate to apply creaturely predicates to eternal Wisdom because of his high view of divine providence: all creatures have their origin and destiny already in the eternal Word of God. Likely, therefore, Origen would not have seen a theological obstacle to referring the "creation" language of verse 22 to the creatures' preexistence in the Son of God. Second, Origen must have realized that one's exegetical options are limited: (1) one can deny the christological character of Proverbs 8 altogether; (2) one can refer the "creation" language to the incarnation of the Word rather than to the eternal relations in the Godhead; (3) one can lower the divine status of the Son by explaining both the "creation" of Wisdom in verse 22 and her being "begotten" in verse 25 as speaking of a later (and lower) derivation of the Son from the Father; or (4) one can

---

12. Ibid. Again, several of the preceding (and following) comments may well be Rufinus's, in an attempt to claim Origen for the pro-Nicene camp.

13. Ibid., 1.2.3 (Butterworth, 16).

14. Ibid.

15. Ibid., 1.4.4 (Butterworth, 42).

read the "creation" language as a reference to the creatures' eternal origin in the Word of God. As we have already seen, the first option wasn't a serious option for any party in the third- and fourth-century christological debates. In what follows, we will observe that Marcellus of Ancyra, Athanasius (in part), and Gregory of Nyssa would take the second option, but this raised the question of how this passage could still be taken as a reference to the eternal generation of the Son. The third option was the one that the Arian party would typically take; Origen's *On First Principles*, however, rejected it explicitly, since it implies that there was a time when the Son did not exist. As a result, Origen settled for the fourth option, even though to some it may have appeared as contrived.

Origen's reflections on Proverbs 8 set the stage for the fourth-century trinitarian debates. Seven years before the Council of Nicaea (325), Arius, condemned by an Alexandrian synod, fled to the northwest of today's Turkey, to his friend Eusebius of Nicomedia, who at one time may have been a fellow student. Wishing to return to Alexandria, Arius wrote a letter to his bishop, Alexander of Alexandria, from Nicomedia in the year 320. Arius asked to be reinstated as a priest in Alexandria, with recognition for his christological views. His letter to Bishop Alexander begins—as a typical creedal formula would—with the words "We know one God."[16] The creedal letter was Arius's confession of faith, intended to serve as a word of self-defense.[17] It contains several references to Proverbs 8. Arius insists that when, in eternity, God begot an "only-begotten son," the result was an "immutable and unchangeable perfect creature of God."[18] Furthermore, Arius maintains that the Son had been "created by the will of God before times and ages."[19] Arius's creation language obviously echoes Proverbs 8. The Father, by his "will"—language that Origen had also used—"created" or "established" the Son "before the ages."[20] Arius's creedal statement used a lot of "begetting" (*gennaō*) language. The Son was "an offspring" (*gennēma*), Arius maintained, but not as one of those born.[21] The Son, he explained, was "begotten timelessly."[22] Clearly, Arius was referencing Proverbs 8:25: "Before the mountains were founded, before all the hills, he begets me." Arius appeared convinced that the orthodox claim of the Son's consubstantiality

16. See Behr, *Nicene Faith*, 2/1:150.

17. For Arius's letter, see "Arius's Letter to Alexander of Alexandria," in Rusch, *Trinitarian Controversy*, 31–32. For an analysis, see Böhm, "Exegesis of Arius," 692–94.

18. Rusch, *Trinitarian Controversy*, 31.

19. Ibid., 31.

20. Ibid., 31–32.

21. See Kelly, *Early Christian Creeds*, 237.

22. Rusch, *Trinitarian Controversy*, 32.

with the Father flew directly in the face of the language of verses 22 and 23: "The Lord created (*ektisen*) me" and "established (*ethemeliōsen*) me." The two key verbs seemed to make it obvious to Arius that Christ, as the eternal Wisdom of God, was a *creature* who had been *established* by God. A clear difference in origin and hence also in rank between the Father and the Son appeared to be implied. It would only stand to reason, then, that when verse 25 states, "he begets (*gennā*) me," this too implies that before this begetting, the Son did not exist—which is exactly the conclusion that Arius drew.

It is understandable that Proverbs 8 featured prominently in the Arian debates. The Arian side kept pressing what they thought was the obvious or plain reading of the text—which, as a result, became the key point of dispute with the pro-Nicene party. The Arianizing theologian Eusebius of Caesarea (ca. 263–ca. 339) pressed the need for literal exegesis in a sharp debate with Marcellus of Ancyra (ca. 280–374). Marcellus was a strong opponent of Asterius the Sophist (died ca. 341) and other Arian theologians, whom he denounced in his book *Against Asterius*, written shortly after the Council of Nicaea (325). Asterius, an ally of Arius, made essentially three christological claims.[23] The first was that God had created his Son, or the Word, before he created anything else, so that the Word could subsequently function as God's medium in creating the rest of creation. The Word, therefore, was a pre-temporal creation of God. The second claim was that the Son had to learn how to serve as this medium; he had to learn how to create the rest of the world. And the final claim was that the Father's own, internal Word should not be confused with God's Son, who in Scripture also gets the designation of "Word." The result is that Asterius seemed to posit two "Words": God's own, proper Word, which was internal to him, as well as the Son or the Word through whom God created the world. It is the latter Word whose proper divinity Asterius disputed.

Although Marcellus—along with Athanasius and others—was a strong opponent of Asterius, he became most well known not for his pro-Nicene stance but for his heterodox eschatological views (though Marcellus regarded the two as closely linked). Because of his strong convictions regarding the unity of the eternal Word of God with the Father, Marcellus could not accept that the human nature of Christ would have an abiding place in the eternal kingdom. One day, God would be "all in all" (1 Cor. 15:28), and this implied, according to Marcellus, that the kingship of Christ—and perhaps also his human

23. Asterius' position can be deduced in part from Athanasius' writings. For the three claims of Asterius, I am following Clayton, "Orthodox Recovery," 275–82.

nature—would come to an end.[24] Marcellus' position was condemned by the Council of Constantinople (381), which added to the Creed the words, "whose kingdom shall have no end." Ironically, Marcellus' deviating views on the consummation directly resulted from his stringent opposition to the Arian cause.

As a pro-Nicene theologian, Marcellus may well have thought that Origen's exegesis of Proverbs 8:22–25 insufficiently safeguarded the full divinity of the Son. Origen, after all, had interpreted the word "created" in verse 22 as a reference to the generation of the eternal Word of God. To be sure, he had added that this word refers only *indirectly* to the Son and that it is really the preexistent creatures that are in view in verse 22. But Marcellus probably worried that this exegetical qualification would not have come across very convincingly in debate with Asterius and other Arians. In other words, Origen's exegesis could easily be morphed into a subordinationist reading of the text. Marcellus therefore took a different approach, one that Athanasius and Gregory of Nyssa would later adopt as well: he took verse 22 as a reference to the incarnate Christ. Khaled Anatolios summarizes his position as follows: "Marcellus dealt with Proverbs 8:22 by locating the 'creation for the sake of the works' at the point of the incarnation and not in the absolute origin of the divinity of the preexistent Christ."[25] Marcellus, in short, transferred the reference of Proverbs 8:22 from theology (the trinitarian life)—where Origen had located it—to the economy (the history of salvation).

Eusebius of Caesarea, in his books *Against Marcellus* and *Ecclesiastical Theology* (both written between 337 and 339), vehemently attacked Marcellus.[26] Sympathetic to the Arian cause, the bishop of Caesarea believed that Proverbs 8:22–25 could easily be read as referring in its entirety to the eternal relationship between the Father and the Son. That is to say, unlike Marcellus, Eusebius followed Origen's line of thought and took the verbs "created," "established," and "begets" all as references to the Son's pre-temporal origin in the Father. Marcellus, so it appeared to Eusebius, simply didn't do justice to the "obvious" (*procheirou*) sense of the text.[27] Eusebius' main objection to Marcellus' exegesis, explains Christopher Beeley, is that the latter "strays from the plain and obvious sense of the text and is ignorant of the story that has been narrated."[28] In short, the Arian tradition of Eusebius and others highlighted the "plain" reading of the text and balked at the allegorizing tendencies of the pro-Nicene party.

24. Beeley, *Unity of Christ*, 78; Anatolios, *Retrieving Nicaea*, 90.
25. Anatolios, *Retrieving Nicaea*, 95.
26. See the account in Lienhard, *Contra Marcellum*, 104–35.
27. Eusebius, *Against Marcellus* 1.2; as quoted in Beeley, *Unity of Christ*, 329n44.
28. Beeley, *Unity of Christ*, 79.

Furthermore, according to Eusebius—and here he parted ways with Origen and instead aligned himself with Asterius—one had to distinguish between the Word that was internal to the Father's own being and the subordinate Wisdom or Son of God through whom God had created the world. It was the latter, Eusebius maintained, to which Proverbs 8:22–25 referred.[29] Eusebius, unlike Origen, distinguished between the internal Word of the Father and Christ as the created Wisdom of God. Also unlike Origen, he maintained that the word "created" in verse 22 speaks *directly* of the eternal Son of God himself (rather than of creatures preexisting eternally in the Son of God); Eusebius thereby introduced the subordinationism that Origen had kept at bay in his exegesis of the passage.

Athanasius: Interpretive Strategies

The Arian use of Proverbs 8 put the pro-Nicene party on the defensive. Saint Athanasius (ca. 296–373) was forced to deal with the passage in his dispute with the Arians, since his opponents kept using it as an argument. On several occasions, Athanasius embarked on an extensive discussion of the passage. He did so particularly in two writings, the *Second Discourse against the Arians* (the various segments probably dating from between 337 and 342) and *On the Nicene Council* (also known as *De decretis*, dating from around 353), both of which give evidence of how Athanasius read the Scriptures.

The most noteworthy—as well as most controversial—aspect of Athanasius' rebuttal of the Arians' interpretation of Proverbs 8 was the sacramental cast of his exegetical approach. Challenged by the Arians' claim that the three verbs of Proverbs 8:22–25—"create," "establish," and "beget"—must all have one and the same point of reference, Athanasius disputes his opponents' interpretive starting point. "We must not," he avers in his *Second Discourse*, "expound [these proverbs] nakedly in their first sense, but we must inquire into the person (*prosōpon*), and thus religiously put the sense on it. For what is said in proverbs is not said plainly (*ek phanerou*), but is put forth latently (*kekrymmenōs*), as the Lord himself has taught us in the Gospel according to John, saying, 'These things have I spoken unto you in proverbs, but the time cometh when I shall no more speak unto you in proverbs, but openly' [John 16:25]."[30] Athanasius does two things in this passage. First, he inquires after the person (*prosōpon*) to which the text alludes—a point to which we will

29. For a clear overview, see ibid., 77–83.
30. Athanasius, *Four Discourses* 2.44 (NPNF[2] 4:372).

return shortly.[31] Second, he maintains that we will gain insight into the identity of this person if we keep in mind the genre of the text. Proverbs, argues Athanasius, demand from us that we not look for the "plain" or "manifest" (*ek phanerou*) meaning. Instead, they give us their intended meaning in a "latent" or "hidden" manner (*kekrymmenōs*). Accordingly, we should not explain them as if they were given "plainly," lest, Athanasius insists, "by a false interpretation we wander from the truth."[32]

As we will see, by insisting that we should move from the "plain" to the "hidden" meaning of the text, Athanasius suggests that the christological reality of the economy of salvation lies hidden in the text. Whereas the Arians insisted on a "plain" reading of the text as referring to a pre-temporal origin of the created Wisdom of God, Athanasius turned to the New Testament to find there the reality of the Christ who is only obliquely hinted at in the Wisdom of the book of Proverbs. He was convinced, in other words, that the proverbs serve as sacramental containers for a reality that comes fully into the open when God reveals himself in the incarnation of Jesus Christ.

Among the most notable positions that Athanasius staked out hermeneutically is that biblical exegesis must be faithful to what the early church called the "canon of truth," or its "rule of faith"—the basic trinitarian and christological confession of the church.[33] Athanasius' starting point for interpretation was that the Scriptures have their place within the church and thus should be read in line with the church's basic confession. In other words, the sacramental reality of God's revelation in Jesus Christ—confessed in the rule of faith—rightly stamps one's exegesis of the biblical text. Frances Young, in her 1997 book *Biblical Exegesis and the Formation of Christian Culture*, makes the comment: "Athanasius is confident that his interpretation is correct because he has received insight into the 'mind' of scripture through the Canon of Truth received from his predecessors."[34] Athanasius' reading of Scripture in line with the rule of faith implies that from the outset some readings—in particular the Arian ones—are excluded as exegetical possibilities. This is not to say that Athanasius wasn't guided by the Scriptures or that he simply imposed his own preconceived opinions on the text; his meticulous exegesis clearly proves differently. It is to say, however, that when one already knew the overall mind (*dianoia*) of Scripture from the rule of faith, this inevitably ruled out interpretations that were in conflict with it. For Athanasius, the truth of

31. See the discussion of prosopological exegesis in chap. 6, sec. "Harmony with the Voice of Christ."

32. Athanasius, *Four Discourses* 2.44 (*NPNF*² 4:372).

33. Cf. chap. 2, sec. "Theological Literalism in Saint Augustine."

34. Young, *Biblical Exegesis*, 44–45.

Jesus Christ, as the reality of the biblical witness confessed in the church's rule of faith, governed the plausibility (or lack thereof) of one's interpretation of the biblical text.

Athanasius engaged in a form of exegesis, therefore, that was, at least to some extent, predetermined: it was shaped by what he believed to be the basic truth of the gospel, namely, the rule of faith. In other words, Athanasius' exegesis was influenced by his creedal position; interpretation was theological in nature. John Behr provocatively puts it as follows: "The true 'sense' of the text, therefore, is not determined by such modern considerations as its history, redaction, or literary setting, but by the apostolic perspective which sees Scripture . . . as referring to Christ."[35] Perhaps Behr exaggerates slightly; as we will see, Athanasius was quite interested in questions of genre, and he applied various technical interpretive strategies to the biblical text. Nonetheless, Behr makes an important point: Athanasius was not interested in the history behind the text, and he was convinced that the interpretation of the Scriptures could be faithful and true only if it was in line with the confession of the church—in line, that is, with the rule of faith, which centers on the Triune God revealed in Jesus Christ through the Spirit.

Allan Clayton's excellent 1988 dissertation on Athanasius' use of Proverbs 8 points to several hermeneutical strategies that the Alexandrian bishop consciously employed. One of them is what Clayton calls the "tripartite exegetical formula."[36] According to Clayton, Athanasius, in reading the text, looked for three elements: time (*kairos*), person (*prosōpon*), and purpose (*pragma*).[37] Clayton makes clear that Athanasius' use of these three elements was an adaptation of a well-known contemporary interpretive approach. With regard to time, a biblical passage could speak either of the eternal relations of the immanent Trinity (theology) or of the history of salvation (economy). If the "time" referred to the immanent Trinity, this in turn shed light on how to read the passage christologically. The "person" referred to in the passage would then be the eternally preexistent Son of God. If, however, the "time" was the economy of salvation, this meant that the "person" of the passage was the Son of God in the flesh. It was the task of the exegete, according to Athanasius, to divide or partition statements regarding Christ between those that refer to the immanent Trinity and those that refer to the economy of salvation. John Behr, in his three-volume work *The Nicene Faith*, refers to

---

35. Behr, *Nicene Faith*, 2/1:208–9.

36. For this discussion I rely on Clayton, "Orthodox Recovery," 220–32.

37. In addition to Clayton, see Behr, *Nicene Faith*, 2/1:208–15. Athanasius also referred to the purpose of a text as its "cause" (*aitia*) or "need" (*chreia*).

this as "partitive exegesis."[38] Passages that allude to the eternity of the pre-existent Son use "absolute terms," according to Athanasius, and as a result they do not mention any "purpose." In contrast, passages that speak of the economy of the incarnate Son of God typically include a reference to our salvation as the purpose of the incarnation. Trying to come to grips with Athanasius' exegetical approach, therefore, we need to keep in mind that he entered the text differently than we typically do today. He approached the text with the question, what does it say about the three elements that gram-marians and rhetoricians tell us are of particular importance with respect to understanding the text?

Athanasius' interpretation was also heavily dependent on the scope or intention (*skopos*) of a particular passage.[39] Much like "time" and "per-son" could refer either to the preexistent Son or to the incarnate Son in the economy of salvation, so also the "scope" or overall intention of Scripture was twofold: "Now the *scope* and character of Holy Scripture, as we have often said, is this,—it contains a double account of the Saviour; that He was ever God, and is the Son, being the Father's Word and Radiance and Wisdom; and that afterwards for us He took flesh of a Virgin, Mary Bearer of God, and was made man. And this *scope* is to be found throughout in-spired Scripture, as the Lord Himself has said, 'Search the Scriptures, for they are they which testify of Me.'"[40] For Athanasius, the scope or overall purpose of Scripture was christological. The Scriptures testify to Christ. The task of the exegete, therefore, was to try to understand *how* a given passage refers to Christ.

Clayton makes clear that searching for the *skopos* of a work was very much a Neoplatonic preoccupation. Neoplatonic philosopher Iamblichus (ca. 245–ca. 325) had argued that one should turn from the many to the one, not only in cosmology but also in interpretation. As Clayton puts it: "Neoplatonism's fundamental philosophical imperative was to discern how the One was in the Many at every stage of reality. Iamblichus thought this imperative could function as an exegetical device as well."[41] Just as there was unity in the multiplicity of the cosmos, so the single *skopos* of a work, its overall intent, could be discovered in its many parts.[42]

38. Ibid., 2/1:210, 212.
39. Here I rely on Clayton, "Orthodox Recovery," 232–51. See also Leithart, *Athanasius*, 39–41. We encountered the importance of the *skopos* in the previous chapter in connection with Gregory of Nyssa (sec. "Gregory of Nyssa on the Order of the Psalms").
40. Athanasius, *Four Discourses* 3.29 (NPNF[2] 4:409) (emphasis added).
41. Clayton, "Orthodox Recovery," 236.
42. Ibid., 242.

Athanasius' appropriation of the Neoplatonic concern for the *skopos* of a passage fit well with his interest in trying to locate the elements of time, person, and purpose. This triad, explains Clayton, was "the means by which the *skopos* was discovered."[43] It will be clear that this Neoplatonic interest—the attempt to find unity in the midst of multiplicity—lent itself to a sacramental approach to interpretation: for early Christians, exegesis was the attempt to find the spiritual, christological point of unity in the midst of the historical multiplicity of the Old Testament text. Christ, according to Athanasius, is the *skopos* of the biblical text, and the reference to Wisdom in the book of Proverbs must be read accordingly.

Athanasius: Exegesis 1 and 2

Faced with the argument that the word "created" in Proverbs 8:22 demands a subordinationist Christology, Athanasius makes a distinction between theology and economy. He applies this distinction in sections 44–60 of his *Second Discourse*. Clayton, building on Charles Kannengiesser, refers to this as "Exegesis 1"[44] (which is followed by a different interpretation, which he labels "Exegesis 2"). Throughout sections 44–60, in presenting Exegesis 1, Athanasius uses the theology-economy distinction in his explanation of Proverbs 8: he applies his "partitive exegesis" to the three verbs in question. Athanasius places the words "created" and "established" (vv. 22 and 23) under the rubric of the economy, while classifying the word "begets" (v. 25) under that of theology. "For had [the Son] been a creature," explains Athanasius with reference to verse 25, "He had not said, 'He begets me,' for the creatures are from without, and are works of the Maker; but the Offspring is not from without nor a work, but from the Father, and proper to His essence."[45] From eternity, according to the Alexandrian bishop, the Son was begotten—not created or established—and as such he is of the same essence as the Father.

By way of support, Athanasius points to a peculiarity in verse 22: "The Lord created me as the beginning of his ways, *for his works.*" Although the Word has existed from all eternity ("in the beginning was the Word" [John 1:1]), it is much later, in the incarnation, that he is "sent *'for the works'* and the Economy towards them."[46] According to Athanasius, then, the incarnation

43. Ibid., 250.
44. As outlined in Clayton, "Orthodox Recovery," 257–74. The division between Exegesis 1 and Exegesis 2 is derived from Kannengiesser, *Athanase d'Alexandrie évêque et écrivain.*
45. Athanasius, *Four Discourses* 2.57 (NPNF² 4:379).
46. Ibid., 2.51 (NPNF² 4:376) (emphasis added).

in the economy of salvation happened "for God's works." In time, in history, the Word was created "for us," says Athanasius, for "if He was not created for us, we are not created in Him; and, if not created in Him, we have Him not in ourselves but externally; as, for instance, as receiving instruction from Him as from a teacher."[47] Athanasius here appeals to Saint Paul's use of "creation" language: "For we are God's workmanship, created in Christ Jesus" (Eph. 2:10). God's "creating" Wisdom in Proverbs 8:22 *must* refer to the incarnation, argues Athanasius, or else we are not created in Christ and so are not truly saved. Put differently, by linking Christ's "creation" in the economy of salvation to our "creation" in Christ, Athanasius underscores that our relationship to Christ is participatory rather than just external in character.

The Alexandrian theologian does much the same with the word "established" in verse 23 ("Before the ages, he established me in the beginning"). "This too," explains Athanasius, "is said after the way of proverbs."[48] Accordingly, he comments, "Wisdom Itself is founded for us, that It may become beginning and foundation of our new creation and renewal."[49] Since God founded or established Wisdom *for us and for our salvation*, the term "established" or "founded" must refer to the economy, the incarnation—not to theology, the eternal inner-trinitarian life. As Athanasius explains, "The Lord also did not when founded take a beginning of existence; for He was the Word before that; but when He put on our body, which He severed and took from Mary, then He says, 'He hath founded me . . .'"[50] Athanasius' argument at this point is somewhat less than convincing: it is essentially an argument from silence. He points out that the text does *not* say, "Before the ages, he established me *as Word or Son*" (as a reference to trinitarian relations) but simply "he established me." The point, argues Athanasius, is that this founding was *for us*, in line with the Pauline statement "For no one can lay any foundation other than the one already laid, which is Jesus Christ" (1 Cor. 3:11). We are precious stones built into a temple on the foundation of Jesus Christ.[51] Using verbal association— what theologians today might call "intertextual echoes"—Athanasius takes the christological "creation" and "foundation" discourse from elsewhere in Scripture (Eph. 2:10 and 1 Cor. 3:11) to support his position that this same language in Proverbs 8:22–23 refers to the economy of God.[52] By contrast,

47. Ibid., 2.56 (*NPNF*[2] 4:378).
48. Ibid., 2.74 (*NPNF*[2] 4:388).
49. Ibid., 2.73 (*NPNF*[2] 4:388).
50. Ibid., 2.74 (*NPNF*[2] 4:389).
51. Ibid., 2.74 (*NPNF*[2] 4:388).
52. Cf. the discussion of "associative" reading in chap. 2, sec. "Gregory's Literal Reading as Theological."

Athanasius sees the "begetting" language of verse 25 as referring to the inner life of God itself, the immanent Trinity.[53]

Just as it seems that we have arrived at the conclusion of the exposition, Athanasius starts all over again. Between sections 77 and 78, a break occurs in his exposition, and it is at this point that he moves to Exegesis 2.[54] This second section—comparatively brief—takes a rather different approach to the same biblical passage. So different are the two interpretations that Charles Kannengiesser has suggested that Athanasius wrote the original version of his *Discourse* between his first and second exiles (337–339), while writing the final few paragraphs (along with the preface) somewhat later, during his second exile (340–342).[55] Be this as it may, it is clear that we have here, side by side, two quite different interpretations of Proverbs 8.

The main difference between Exegesis 1 and 2 concerns the way in which the two approaches connect the second element of the "tripartite exegetical formula" (the identity of the person or *prosōpon*) to verses 22 and 23. As we have seen, according to Exegesis 1, the "creating" and "establishing" language of these two verses refers to the incarnation, and thus to the economy of salvation; in this context, Athanasius speaks about salvation in terms of incarnation and our inclusion in Christ's "creation" and "founding." Exegesis 2 has a rather different theological focus: here Athanasius speaks of God's Wisdom as the image of God. This Wisdom, explains the Alexandrian bishop, came to us not just in the incarnation but earlier, already in our initial creation as human beings: from the beginning, the impress of God's Wisdom placed its stamp on us as created in Wisdom's image. What Athanasius does here is to read the Genesis narrative christologically. The reason, he explains, that verse 22 speaks of Wisdom as if it were created is that human beings—who *are* actually created and who carry its stamp—reflect Wisdom. As a result, we may predicate, analogically as it were, "creation" language also of God's eternal Wisdom.[56] Clayton puts it as follows:

> From this angle, Wisdom, contemplating the creation of her image in all creation, says that she was herself "created" in Prov 8:22. It is not that Wisdom was in fact "created"; but since her image was "created" in humans upon their creation, she can metaphorically speak of herself as "created" (*CA* 2.78). The parallel texts are Matt 10:40 ("He who receives you receives me. . . .") and Acts

53. Saint Augustine, similarly, applies verse 22 to the Son in the form of a servant and verse 25 to the Son in the form of God. *On the Trinity* 1.12.24 (WSA I/5:87–88).
54. Clayton, "Orthodox Recovery," 282–88.
55. See ibid., 255.
56. Athanasius, *Four Discourses* 2.78–79 (NPNF[2] 4:390–91).

9:4 ("Saul, why do you persecute me?"; *CA* 2.78, 80). The reception or persecution of a disciple is the same as receiving or persecuting the Lord himself
because the Lord's impress is on the disciple. Likewise, the creation of beings
stamped with the impress of Wisdom is the creation of Wisdom herself. Prov
8:22 is a testimony to the intimate interconnection of image and archetype.[57]

The person (*prosōpon*) of verse 22, according to Exegesis 2, is the eternal
Wisdom of God (to whom, in some way, we attribute human characteristics).
The implication is that, according to Athanasius' Exegesis 2, verse 22 places
us in the realm of theology, not that of the economy.

Likewise, the "establishing" or "founding" of Wisdom in verse 23 does
not, in Exegesis 2, refer to the incarnation. Also here, there is a shift between
Exegesis 1 and 2 from the incarnation to creation. Athanasius now maintains
that the language of "establishing" implies that "the works remain settled and
eternal."[58] The reason for this is, again, that eternal Wisdom has imprinted
her image on creation. The one who is truly eternally "established" and as
such immovable is of course the eternal Son of God himself. But because the
Son of God allows the creation, as his image, to participate in his wisdom,
God's works can also be said to be "settled and eternal." In verse 23, as in
verse 22, therefore, the focus turns away from the incarnation to creation, and
in both cases the exegesis pivots on the notion of the image of God, which
links creation with Christology. According to Exegesis 2, both verses 22 and
23 refer to theology rather than to the economy: we may say that Wisdom
is "created" and "established" inasmuch as the creation is "created" and
"established." The image of God in his works allows us to transfer these notions from the creature to eternal Wisdom itself. The only exegetical point
that remains the same between Exegesis 1 and 2 is the "begetting" language
of verse 25: in Exegesis 2, it continues to refer to Wisdom as the eternally
begotten Son of the Father.[59]

The overall result of Athanasius' shift is that, in Exegesis 2, each of the three
verbs—"created," "founded," and "begets"—refers primarily to the eternal
Son of God. That is to say, in each verse the person (*prosōpon*) is one and the
same. The reference is now to the inner-trinitarian life (theology) rather than
to the salvific work of Christ (economy). By making this shift, Athanasius
achieved two purposes. First, he was able to underscore the participatory link
between Christ and his creature. In Exegesis 2, the focus is on the participation of the image of God in its eternal prototype. Athanasius' basic claim (in

57. Clayton, "Orthodox Recovery," 284.
58. Athanasius, *Four Discourses* 2.80 (*NPNF*[2] 4:392).
59. Ibid., 2.80 (*NPNF*[2] 4:392).

explaining vv. 22 and 23) is that human beings, since they're created in the image of God, participate in the Wisdom of God. The focus here is not on Christ's work in and through the economy of salvation. Rather than emphasize soteriology, Athanasius now focuses on creation and explains that Proverbs 8:22–23 refers to the works of creation (especially human beings) as sharing in the eternal wisdom and knowledge of the Son. It is the image of God that allows us to predicate of the Son language (such as "created me" and "established me") that, properly speaking, is true only of the creature. We already saw Origen make a similar exegetical move, when he suggested that according to verse 22 the *creatures* were created, despite the text's claim that *Wisdom* was created. This approach of Origen and Athanasius fits remarkably well with Augustine's later *totus Christus* theology, which would also predicate of Christ what is true of the creature, and which would also use the Acts 9 passage ("Saul, Saul, why are you persecuting me?") to illustrate the point.[60]

Second, with Exegesis 2, Athanasius dealt a blow to the exegesis of his Arian opponents. It will be recalled that they applied the three words in question to the Father's creating, establishing, or begetting a Son before time, thereby reducing the Son's status to that of a mediating, less than fully divine creature. Perhaps the greatest drawback of Athanasius' Exegesis 1 is that it introduced a split between verses 22–23 as speaking of the economy and verse 25 as referring to theology proper. This use of "partitive exegesis" can hardly have satisfied Athanasius. It is one thing to insist that a text may refer either to theology or to the economy; it is another to divide up three verbs in close proximity according to different persons or *prosōpa*. Exegesis 2 fixed this difficulty. Athanasius still used here the traditional Iamblichian mode of exegesis, asking to which person (*prosōpon*) the text refers. But by assigning each of the three verbs to the eternal Son of God, Athanasius reinforced the coherence of the passage as a whole. What is more, in a masterstroke, he now followed not only Origen but also the entire Arian tradition in attributing the three verbs to theology rather than to the economy. And by doing this, he demonstrated that it was possible to read the entire passage in terms of "theology" without lapsing into subordinationism. Athanasius must have thought he was defeating the Arians on their own turf: that of a strictly "theological" reading of verses 22–25.

Interestingly, it appears that Athanasius was content to have Exegesis 1 and 2 stand side by side as two complementary readings of the text. Athanasius, Clayton rightly insists, believed that "words could have multiple meanings," since "passages were capable of sustaining two different interpretations. One

60. See chap. 6, sec. "Harmony with the Voice of Christ."

exposition focused on the eternal Son while the other centered on his economic enfleshment. It was the 'nature' or 'essence' of Christ—that his one divine nature had existed both eternally in the bosom of the Father and incarnately in man—that enabled the exegete to treat Scriptural language as signs that derived their meaning from the symbols to which they pointed."[61] Clayton suggests that partitive exegesis made it possible for Saint Athanasius to allow for both interpretations ("theology" and "economy") of verses 22 and 23 at the same time. This may well be correct, though I suspect we will never quite know why it is that Athanasius kept both interpretations of the passage alongside each other in his *Second Discourse*. In any case, this juxtaposition of the two approaches does make clear that he took the "hidden" meaning of the proverbs seriously. For Athanasius, the genre of a proverb meant that the text does not speak "plainly" (*ek phanerou*). Since proverbs give us their intended meaning in a "hidden" way (*kekrymmenōs*), they call not for a scientific determination of the one meaning but for a theological exploration of their christological depth in line with the church's rule of faith. The latter approach, it seems, allowed for various exegetical options to stand unresolved beside each other. For Athanasius, both readings of the text were orthodox, in line with the rule of faith, and as such at least potentially legitimate as explorations of the hidden, sacramental meaning of Proverbs 8.

Gregory of Nyssa: Turning the Peacock

Gregory of Nyssa (ca. 335–ca. 394) was forced to deal with the Proverbs 8 passage in debate with Eunomius of Cyzicus, a theologian from Cappadocia and a student of the well-known neo-Arian theologian Aetius.[62] Eunomius maintained in his *Apology* (ca. 360) that only the first of the three divine beings was "unbegotten" (*agennētos*) and that this term, as applied to the Father, defined the divine essence.[63] Since the Son was begotten, he was unlike the Father and not properly divine. Because of his insistence that the Son is unlike (*anomoios*) the Father, Eunomius is often regarded as the leader of

---

61. Clayton, "Orthodox Recovery," 249.

62. Timothy D. Barnes objects to the label "neo-Arians" on the grounds that the views of Aetius and Eunomius were altogether new and as such must be understood against their own intellectual backgrounds a generation after Arius. *Athanasius and Constantius*, 139. It may be true that the conflicts with Aetius and Eunomius reflect rather different circumstances from those of the earlier Arian controversy, but in both conflicts the true divinity of Christ was at stake. As such, the term "neo-Arian" does not seem out of place.

63. For detailed discussion of Eunomius's theology, see Vaggione, *Eunomius of Cyzicus*. For a helpful entry into the thought of Aetius and Eunomius, see also Ayres, *Nicaea and Its Legacy*, 144–49.

the so-called Anomoians.[64] Eunomius's own writings are no longer extant, but we can partially reconstruct them from the refutations written by Basil (particularly his *Against Eunomius*, written shortly after the publication of Eunomius's *Apology*) and from the three books *Against Eunomius*, published by Basil's younger brother, Gregory of Nyssa, shortly after the Council of Constantinople (381), in which he took up the baton from his elder brother after the latter's death in 379.[65]

For Gregory, the disagreement regarding Proverbs 8 centered on a hermeneutical question: Should we read this biblical passage at a literal or at a spiritual level? We already saw this issue come to the fore in connection with Athanasius, who insisted that the text does not speak "plainly" (*ek phanerou*) but yields its meaning in a "hidden" way (*kekrymmenōs*). Gregory's approach is quite similar: "It is generally agreed that in scriptural usage the word 'proverb' is not applied to the manifest (*phanerou*) meaning, but is used of some improper (*katachrēsei*) sense. Thus the Gospel calls puzzling and obscure sayings 'proverbs,' so that the proverb, if one considers a rule to understand this word, is an expression which indicates through words, which literally (*procheiron*) mean one thing, another hidden (*krypton*) meaning, or an expression which does not directly draw out the intention (*skopon*) of the thought, but delivers its teaching obliquely by some indirect meaning."[66] Gregory, like Athanasius, distinguishes between the "plain" or "obvious" meaning of the text and its "improper" or "hidden" sense. The reason he believes he is entitled to do this is that we are dealing with the genre of proverbs. Nyssen turns to the beginning of the book of Proverbs, which, he says, tells us how we are to read it. Proverbs 1:3 makes clear that the book is not to be taken in its "obvious" sense.[67] The Greek text, which uses the word *strophē* ("turning" or "subtlety"), seems to suggest that the purpose is to grasp the proverbs' "subtlety." Gregory therefore is convinced that we get to the purpose or *skopos* of the text by means of a "turn."[68] He explains that Solomon refers to the "manifestation of hidden things" as a "verbal 'turn.'"[69] Saint Gregory compares this spiritual interpretation to the plumage of a peacock: "The same happens with the feathers which the peacock displays in its tail. If one sees the back of the feathers one would,

64. See Hildebrand, *Trinitarian Theology*, 20–23; H. Boersma, *Embodiment and Virtue*, 24–25.

65. Eunomius's works have been edited by Vaggione in a critical text, *Eunomius: The Extant Works*.

66. Gregory of Nyssa, *Against Eunomius* 3.1.23 (Hall, 47); translation slightly adjusted.

67. See H. Boersma, *Embodiment and Virtue*, 61.

68. Gregory of Nyssa, *Against Eunomius* 3.1.24 (Hall, 47).

69. Ibid., 3.1.25 (Hall, 47).

because of the unattractive and plain appearance, certainly dismiss the spectacle as uninteresting; but if one turned it round (*anastrepsas*) and exposed its other side, one sees the varied artwork the species has, the semi-circle brilliant in the middle with purple tint, and the golden radiance round the edge alive and shining with many-coloured rainbows."[70] Just as one can see the peacock's brilliant colors only by turning from the back to the front, so one can discern the beauty of the text only by turning from the outside to the inside. Gregory explains with a reference to the well-known messianic Psalm 44:14 (45:13)—"'All the glory,' as it says, 'of the king's daughter is on the inside'"—that "there is no beauty in the literal (*procheirō*) meaning of the term" and that Solomon is "lighting up the hidden beauty with golden thoughts."[71]

The reason for Gregory's extended reflections on the need for a "turn" is that he saw Eunomius as being in opposition to a spiritual reading of the text. Eunomius, Gregory caustically comments, is a "slave of the letter," who "attends in Jewish fashion to the mere sound of syllables"[72] and is a mere "scribbler."[73] Gregory was worried, of course, that Eunomius's appeal to the "plain" meaning of the text would convince some people that the Father had "created" or "begotten" the Son at a particular point, prior to which the Son would not have existed.[74]

Eunomius's subordinationist reading of Proverbs 8, reliant on the literal meaning of the text, was not new. Eusebius' interpretation, in debate with Marcellus, had adumbrated this reading.[75] Gregory, in opposition to what he regarded as the wooden literalism of this approach, insisted on a "turn" from the literal to the hidden meaning. That is to say, Nyssen wanted to move beyond the sacrament (*sacramentum*) to its christological reality (*res*), and his main hermeneutical objection to Eunomius was that the latter refused to recognize the sacramental depth of the book of Proverbs.

70. Ibid., 3.1.25–26 (Hall, 47).
71. Ibid., 3.1.26 (Hall, 47).
72. Ibid., 3.1.33 (Hall, 48–49).
73. Ibid., 3.1.83 (Hall, 59).
74. Cf. Leemans's comment: "We can follow Gregory's exchange with Eunomius in his *Contra Eunomium*, in which he gives long quotations from the writings of his opponent. In the Trinitarian debates of the fourth century Eunomius defended a radical subordinationist position, thereby often capitalizing on a literal reading of the Scriptures. Proverbs 8:22 ('The Lord created me before his ways') is a crucial text which was taken by many to imply that Father and Son could not possibly be co-eternal whereupon authors such as Athanasius of Alexandria and later Gregory of Nyssa countered that one must not interpret the text too literally and apply it not to the divine Son of God but only to his humanity, to the period that he was in the flesh." "After Philo and Paul," 443.
75. Beeley, *Unity of Christ*, 82–83.

To be sure, Eunomius's emphasis on the "plain" meaning of the text didn't preclude him from adopting a christological reading. As we have already seen, every theologian in the fourth-century controversies read Proverbs 8 christologically; Eunomius was no exception. The hermeneutical issue between Eunomius and Gregory, therefore, didn't concern the acceptability of seeing Christ in Proverbs 8. The real issue, rather, was whether it is legitimate to move beyond what the text seems to convey about the pre-temporal origins of Wisdom (or of the Son of God). Controversy emerged when Gregory interpreted verses 22–25 as referring not to the eternal generation of the Word of God—as the "plain" meaning seemed to suggest—but instead to the economy of salvation. For Gregory, as we will see shortly, it was legitimate to read Proverbs 8 as referring to the sacramental reality of the Son's incarnation in the flesh and to the life of believers in the dispensation of the New Testament church. It was this "turn" to a "hidden" meaning that Eunomius's partiality toward the "plain" reading could not tolerate.

Gregory of Nyssa: Christ Created, Established, and Born in Us

The details of Gregory's exegesis followed rather naturally from the sacramental hermeneutical principles as I have just outlined them. Since the greatest difficulty for the pro-Nicenes was the association of Wisdom with the word "created" in verse 22, Gregory begins his discussion of Proverbs 8 in book 1 of *Against Eunomius* by observing that the Anomoeans "do not give reasons why we must refer that text to our Lord at all"—though, as we will see, he doesn't actually end up opposing a christological reading of this verse.[76] Gregory then notes that the original Hebrew behind the Greek text—the word *qanani*—can be translated not only as "created me" (as the Septuagint renders it) but also as "possessed me."[77] That, in fact, is how other known Greek translations (Aquila, Theodotion, and Symmachus) render the word. Such an alternate translation would dissolve much of the strength of Eunomius's argument. Gregory observes that if we translated the text so that the Lord "possessed" wisdom, this could be read "in the allegorical language of the Proverbs" as referring to the one who, according to Philippians 2:7, took the form of a slave, so that he became a "possession."[78] The weight that the Septuagint carried in the church, however, may have made it difficult for Gregory to rely

76. Gregory of Nyssa, *Against Eunomius* 1.22 (NPNF[2] 5:63).
77. Ibid., 1.22 (NPNF[2] 5:63), 2.10 (NPNF[2] 5:117). Cf. H. Boersma, *Embodiment and Virtue*, 64.
78. Gregory of Nyssa, *Against Eunomius* 2.10 (NPNF[2] 5:117).

too much on this argument from the Hebrew text; it plays only a minor role within his overall discussion.

Even if we don't translate *qanani* as "possessed" and instead read it, with the Septuagint, as meaning "created," Gregory maintains that the term—taken allegorically—still connotes slavery. After all, Nyssen reminds us, according to the New Testament, "all creation is in bondage" (Rom. 8:21). By taking on human flesh, the Word was "created after God" as a "new man" (Eph. 4:24).[79] Because this "new man" is Christ (Rom. 13:14), he becomes for us "the beginning of the ways of salvation" when we "put him on" as the new man.[80] It is clear what Gregory is doing here: because Wisdom is described in Proverbs 8:22 as "created," Gregory scours the New Testament for a place where Christ is described as "created." Much like Athanasius before him, Gregory concludes from this "associative" reading that the created Wisdom of Proverbs 8:22 is a reference to Christ in the flesh (in slavery). In other words, Proverbs 8:22 refers to the incarnation, not to the eternal generation of the Son.

In book 3, chapter 1, Gregory makes a theological argument for this reading. Like Athanasius (in Exegesis 1), he maintains that the expression "created me" refers not to "the one who is purely divine" but to the economy, "the one combined in the Economy with our created nature."[81] If Wisdom were something created in eternity, as the Arians would have it, then God "possessed Wisdom as something acquired," so that at one time the bosom of the Father would have been empty, without Wisdom, which could not possibly be true.[82] Gregory argues here from what is (or is not) "fitting" theologically. "So," he exclaims sharply,

> since Christ is Wisdom, let the intelligent reader study the account given by our opponents and our own, and let him decide which is more religious, which better preserves the thoughts befitting God (*theoprepeis*) in the text, the one which stipulates that the Creator and Lord of the universe was made, and argues that he is of like standing with the servile creation, or rather the one which looks to the Economy, and keeps intact what is due to the understanding of the divine and the human, where the doctrine is supported by the testimony of great Paul, who sees createdness in the new man, but in the true Wisdom the power of creating.[83]

Gregory's harsh rhetoric makes clear what is at stake for him: exegesis must be in line with what is "befitting God." Eunomius's notion that the creator

---

79. Ibid., 2.10 (*NPNF*² 5:117). See also 3.1.52 (Hall, 52–53).
80. Ibid., 2.10 (*NPNF*² 5:117); 3.1.52 (Hall, 52–53).
81. Ibid., 3.1.50 (Hall, 52).
82. Ibid., 3.1.49 (Hall, 52).
83. Ibid., 3.1.54 (Hall, 53).

(the eternal Word of God) was "created" obviously does not fall into this category.[84]

Saint Gregory's interpretation of the second key word in the debate—the verb "established" or "founded" (*ethemeliōsen*) in verse 23—follows along similar lines. Here too the Cappadocian father combs the New Testament for a verbal analogy in a christological setting. He finds one in 1 Corinthians 3:11. The text reads, "For no one can lay a foundation (*themelion*) other than that which is laid, which is Jesus Christ." The "foundation" of which Saint Paul speaks is the incarnate Christ. Christ has been laid as a "foundation" in our hearts in order that we might build on this foundation.[85] Just as we are to put on the incarnate Christ as "created after God," so we are to build on him as the "foundation" that has been laid.[86] Nyssen concludes from the verbal similarities that Proverbs 8:22–23 refers to the salvific economy rather than to the immanent Trinity. Both the "creation" language of verse 22 and the "foundation" language of verse 23 must be taken allegorically.

Remarkably, perhaps, Gregory also reads the word "begets" of verse 25 spiritually or allegorically. Reflecting on verses 24 and 25 ("Before the earth was made, before the depths were made, before the springs of the waters came forth, before the mountains were founded, before all the hills, he begets [*genna*] me"), Gregory makes clear that we should not see here a reference to the eternal generation of the Son. Instead, he insists, these verses speak of Christ's birth in us: "For the great David calls righteousness the 'mountains of God' [Ps. 35 (36):6], His judgments 'deeps' [Ps. 35 (36):6], and the teachers in the Churches 'fountains,' saying 'Bless God the Lord from the fountains in Israel' [Ps. 67 (68):26]; and guilelessness he calls 'hills,' as he shows when he speaks of their skipping like lambs [Ps. 113 (114):6]. Before these therefore is born in us He Who for our sakes was created as man, that of these things also the creation may find place in us."[87] Again by way of associative reading, Gregory establishes that Christ is born in individuals *before* their lives begin to flourish in the form of "righteousness," "judgments," "teachers," and "guilelessness." In this instance, Gregory's associative reading does not appeal to New Testament references to *Christ*; the reason is that he is searching for characteristics of *believers*, whose Christian lives take shape *after* Christ has been born in them. Gregory finds it easiest to locate these characteristics in the book of Psalms. Put differently, it is only *after* Christ

---

84. Cf. H. Boersma, *Embodiment and Virtue*, 64; Meredith, "God-Fittingness in Gregory of Nyssa," 507–15.

85. Gregory of Nyssa, *Against Eunomius* 2.10 (NPNF² 5:117), 3.1.55 (Hall, 53).

86. See H. Boersma, *Embodiment and Virtue*, 64.

87. Gregory of Nyssa, *Against Eunomius* 2.10 (NPNF² 5:118); cf. 3.1.56 (Hall, 53).

is born in us that the various christological virtues, depicted in verses 24 and 25, take shape in us.

Gregory even goes so far as to suggest that the three disputed verbs—all referring, as he sees it, to the economy of salvation—follow one another chronologically, so that we can detect an order (*taxis*) in the text.[88] First, through the virgin birth, God created the "new man" (Christ) as the beginning of the ways of salvation (v. 22; cf. Eph. 4:24). After this, Saint Paul, as a "skilled master builder," laid the foundation (Christ) for the church (v. 23; cf. 1 Cor. 3:10–11). And finally, the church's believers receive the many gifts of the Holy Spirit (vv. 24–25).[89] Gregory felt justified in allegorizing the various elements of these last two verses on the basis, first, of the verbal associations with the psalms and, second, of the "order" of the text. This allegorizing is thus a meticulously thought-through procedure. It is only after associating the "creating" and "establishing" language of verses 22–23 with the Pauline use of these words—justified by the christological setting of both passages (Eph. 4:24 and 1 Cor. 3:11)—that Gregory then also allegorizes verse 25, again by means of verbal associations, and deliberately in a way that coheres with the christological allegorizing of verses 22–23. Entirely consistent with this, Nyssen concludes his exegesis of Proverbs 8 by interpreting verses 26–31 as a paragraph that allegorically speaks of the life of the church.[90] Taken on their own, these allegorical readings would seem quite arbitrary. Gregory, however, has made a number of prior exegetical choices in connection with verses 22–25—all established with painstaking attention to textual detail—that provide a framework of interpretation within which the allegorical readings of verses 26–31 are naturally at home and, in fact, seem like the obvious corollary of the earlier exegetical choices.

The upshot is that Gregory presents an interpretation that is internally coherent, with each of the three disputed verbs referring to the economy of salvation. He thus ends up at almost the opposite end of the exegetical spectrum from Athanasius' Exegesis 2. The latter maintained that each of the three verbs of verses 22–25 reference the eternal Son of God. By contrast, for Gregory, it is the economy of salvation that the passage has in view throughout. Gregory's approach came at a cost, of course: Proverbs 8:25 could no longer

---

88. Ibid., 3.1.55 (Hall, 53). Cf. H. Boersma, *Embodiment and Virtue*, 64.

89. Gregory of Nyssa, *Against Eunomius* 3.1.55 (Hall, 53).

90. Gregory sees the "land" of verse 26 as that which "accepts the sowing and ploughing of the Word," and the "desert" of verse 26 as the "heart that admits evil residents"; he regards the "winds" of verse 27, denoting "spiritual conduct," as the throne of the believer; the "clouds" of verse 28 are the instructions of the church; the "sons of men" in verse 31 are "godly thoughts"; and the "joy" of verse 31 speaks of the joy of Christ, who rejoices over the salvation of the believers. Ibid., 3.1.57–60 (Hall, 54). Cf. H. Boersma, *Embodiment and Virtue*, 64–65.

function as a proof text for the eternal generation of the Son. But Nyssen was likely relatively unconcerned about this. Using verse 25 ("begets") as a proof text was less important to him than being able to defend himself against Eunomius's literal reading of verse 22 ("created"). Furthermore, by applying a "turn" to each of the three verbs of Proverbs 8:22–25, Gregory avoided the problem that Athanasius' Exegesis 1 had faced, namely, the odd disjunction between verses 22–23 (referring to the economy) and verse 25 (referring to theology). Gregory's solution was remarkably harmonious, even though the "slave of the letter" must have shaken his head at what he would have regarded as allegorical flights of fancy.

Reading Wisdom Sacramentally

The interpretive tradition of Proverbs 8 in the early church charts a winding, perhaps even tortuous, path, as numerous theologians tried to come to grips with the relationship between the Christ they had come to know in the church and the descriptions of Wisdom in the book of Proverbs. As we negotiate the many twists and turns of the multiple debates, it is easy to lose sight of an obvious observation: every one of the theologians, regardless of where he situated himself in the midst of the often sharp controversies, read the book of Proverbs through the lens of the Christ whom the church had come to know in faith. Neither Arian nor pro-Nicene theologians could fail to recognize in Proverbs 8 the presence of Christ. This observation seems of particular importance in our contemporary context, in which historical exegesis has made many reluctant to acknowledge any kind of Christology in the book of Proverbs.

As we have seen, however, the across-the-board agreement on a christological interpretation by no means produced unanimity about the *manner* of christological exegesis. The most important fault line, it seems, lies between interpretations of the Arian tradition and those of the Nicene tradition. Theologians such as Arius, Eusebius, Asterius, and Eunomius favored a literal interpretation of Proverbs 8. Again, this does not mean that they failed to read the text christologically. But it does mean that they failed to acknowledge the sacramental depth of the book of Proverbs. When "slaves of the letter," such as Eunomius, read Proverbs 8, they were intent on determining the "plain" or "literal" meaning of the text. As a result, they saw in the passage references to a shadowy figure called "Wisdom," whom God had "created," "established," or "begotten" long before time began. This figure—who later had become incarnate in Jesus Christ—must have been God's very first and

highest creature, considering that Wisdom had its origin long before the creation of the material world. By all accounts, then, theologians in the Arian
tradition—though Gregory of Nyssa disparagingly referred to them as mere
"scribblers"—appear to have been careful readers of the text of Proverbs.

They were not, however, sacramental readers of the text. That is to say, they
did not believe that the passage contained a deeper, sacramental reality, which
one would only be able to identify in light of the incarnation of Jesus Christ.
The reading strategies of theologians such as Marcellus of Ancyra, Athanasius of Alexandria, and Gregory of Nyssa were grounded in the sacramental
conviction that the genre of the book of Proverbs demands that we recognize
a "hidden" meaning, one that becomes clear to us only in and through God's
economic self-revelation in Jesus Christ. The reason pro-Nicene theologians
reacted vehemently to the Arian readings of Proverbs 8 is, of course, that
the latter ran counter to the church's rule of faith. But the pro-Nicenes were
also disturbed by the kind of exegesis that their opponents practiced. In fact,
they were convinced that the latter's faulty hermeneutic served to justify their
christological errors: a strictly literal, nonsacramental reading of Proverbs 8
was problematic, according to the pro-Nicene theologians, in that it failed to
recognize the sacramental reality (res) of Christ and his church as really present
in the Wisdom passages of the book of Proverbs. By refusing to allegorize, the
Arian tradition was unable to recognize within Proverbs the doctrinal truth
of God's full self-disclosure in Jesus Christ.

The result of this disagreement is that pro-Nicene theologians typically
demanded attention to the specific genre of a proverb as containing a particular
truth that is not immediately evident. This explains Athanasius' search for
the time (kairos), person (prosōpon), and purpose (pragma) of the text, as
well as his interest in partitive exegesis, all of which he believed would help
him find the main intention (skopos) of the text. For Athanasius, the text's
intention was the deeper reality that was not immediately manifest but that
lay embedded in a "hidden" way (kekrymmenōs) in proverbial sayings. This
same attention to the genre of a proverb lay behind the key notion of a "turn"
(strophē) in Saint Gregory of Nyssa's approach to the book of Proverbs.
Gregory's strategy of "turning" the text of Proverbs 8 provided insight into
the sacramental reality of the economy of salvation: the incarnation of Christ,
the apostolic foundation of the church, and the gifts of the Holy Spirit in the
lives of believers.

Some of the terminology that theologians such as Athanasius and Gregory used to describe their sacramental exegesis was part of the stock-in-
trade of exegetical procedures in late antiquity. They spoke of "allegorizing"
(allēgoreuein), of "going up" (anagōgē), of reading "figuratively" (tropikōs),

and so forth. They contrasted a "plain" (*ek phanerou*) or "surface" (*procheiron*) level meaning with a "hidden" (*krypton*) or "improper" (*katachrēsis*) meaning of the text. They looked for the presence of the one "intention" (*skopos*) in the midst of the many words of the Scriptures. And they insisted that the nature of a proverb requires that one "turn" (*anastrephō*) to the hidden meaning of the text. There is little doubt that such interpretive strategies influenced pro-Nicene theologians as they read the book of Proverbs. The reason, however, that they found these strategies helpful is that they enabled them to discern within the outward sacrament (*sacramentum*) of the text the inward reality (*res*) of the Christ event revealed in the economy of salvation.[91]

Obviously, the shared sacramental hermeneutic of the pro-Nicenes did not prevent them from widely differing among themselves with regard to their exegetical choices. Athanasius initially (in Exegesis 1) used his partitive approach to distinguish between the "creation" and "establishing" language of verses 22–23 and the "begetting" language of verse 25, with the former referring to the economy and the latter to trinitarian theology. Probably dissatisfied with the internal inconsistency of this exegesis, he later argued (in Exegesis 2) that each of the three verbs spoke of Christ as God's eternal Wisdom: the language of creatures being "created" and "established" could be predicated also of Christ, since creatures, as created in the image of God, participate in the eternal wisdom and knowledge of the Son. By taking the entire passage (8:22–25) as speaking of the eternal Wisdom of God, Saint Athanasius ended up adopting a line of interpretation common to the Arian tradition—referring each of its verbs to trinitarian theology rather than the economy—while at the same time recognizing the sacramental participation of creatures in the eternal Word of God.

Gregory of Nyssa took the opposite approach, insisting that each of the three disputed verbs—along with the rest of the Proverbs 8 passage that followed—refers to the economy of salvation. Nyssen's sacramental reading means that he assigned to many of the passage's details allegorical meanings taken from the life of Christ and of the church. Far from arbitrarily reading moral virtues or other aspects of believers' lives into the words of the passage, however, Nyssen—and here he was at one with the approach of Athanasius—allegorized by looking in the New Testament for words that he could associate with the christological references that he saw in Proverbs 8. By thus establishing

---

91. I am not arguing that the pro-Nicenes used the actual sacramental language of *sacramentum* and *res* to describe their hermeneutical approach. Much of the later tradition, especially the Western tradition building on Saint Augustine, would do exactly that and, in so doing, was in line with the implicitly sacramental approach of theologians such as Athanasius and Gregory of Nyssa.

the allegorical meaning of the key verses (8:22–25) through intertextual verbal associations, Nyssen believed he could even detect a chronological order in these three verses, which then allowed him also to put in place the subsequent allegorical details of verses 26–31.

Conclusion

The pro-Nicene interpretation of Proverbs 8 is hardly a foolproof scientific bulwark against subordinationist interpretations. The Arians clearly put Athanasius on the defensive with their reading of verse 22. And Athanasius' initial solution of dividing the exegesis of the passage between verses 22–23 (economy) and verse 25 (theology) makes clear that he had great difficulty coming up with a reading that would turn the tables on the Arians. And while Nyssen managed to counter Eunomius's troubling reading of verse 22, he could do so only by abandoning any reference to the eternal generation of the Son in verse 25. While they were convinced that reading in line with the church's rule of faith demanded a sacramental reading of the text, Athanasius and Gregory did not arrive at a shared interpretation that would unambiguously give the lie to the Arian tradition of interpretation. But then again, seeing as the sacramental reality was a treasure "hidden" in the recesses of the proverbs' sayings, such clarity was something they would hardly have expected.

The "plain" reading of the Arians had a commonsense appeal: it did not require one to turn to New Testament verbal links in order retroactively to shed light on the hidden meaning of Proverbs 8. The principle of Ockham's razor—which asks that we adopt the simplest possible explanation, so that the fewer assumptions we bring to the solution, the better—does not favor the pro-Nicene sacramental approach. Indeed, long before William of Ockham's fourteenth-century logic demanded that unnecessary suppositions be "shaved off," the lure of the simplicity in the "plain" reading approach enticed Arian interpreters to embrace a simple exegetical literalism. As a result, the pro-Nicenes faced an uphill battle, and the fact that it is their sacramental exegesis, rather than the "plain" readings of the Arians, that set the stage for the subsequent history of interpretation is something that I can only see as an act of divine providence. If any hermeneutical rule can be deduced from the fourth-century battles over the meaning of Proverbs 8, it would seem to be that Ockham's razor is a dangerous tool in exegesis: by excising the sacramental depth from the treasure of the biblical text, it can sever its devotees from the Old Testament roots of trinitarian orthodoxy and ultimately from the theological foundations of the Nicene church.

8

NUPTIAL READING

Hippolytus, Origen, and Ambrose on the Bridal Couple of the Song of Songs

Contemporary Readings of the Song of Songs

Disagreement over the appropriateness of allegorical interpretation is perhaps nowhere more pronounced than when it comes to the Song of Songs. Few contemporary biblical scholars advocate for an allegorical reading of this book.[1] Yet the earlier tradition was virtually unanimous on the need for an allegorical reading of the Song of Songs. As Tremper Longman—who himself understands the Song strictly as an anthology of love poems—acknowledges, "No matter what the particular brand, the evidence is overwhelming that the dominant interpretative approach to the Song up to the mid-nineteenth century was allegorical."[2] The only obvious exception in the patristic period was Antiochene theologian Theodore of Mopsuestia (ca. 350–428), who argued that in the Song of Songs Solomon celebrated his relationship with an Egyptian bride, and who for that reason insisted that the book was unworthy of being included in the canon.[3]

1. But some recent publications counter this common trend: Norris, *Song of Songs*; Jenson, *Song of Songs*; Griffiths, *Song of Songs*.
2. Longman, "Song of Songs," 759.
3. See Hill, introduction, in Theodoret of Cyrus, *Commentary on the Song of Songs*, 7n22, 12. William E. Phipps relates that Sebastian Castellio, an advocate of religious toleration in Calvin's Geneva, held a similar view in the sixteenth century. "Plight," 96.

In modernity, however, allegorical readings of the Song have come to be viewed with suspicion and, in some cases, derision. William Phipps, for example, comments: "It is one of the pranks of history that a poem so obviously about hungry passion has caused so much perplexity and has provoked such a plethora of bizarre interpretations."[4] And Tremper Longman comes to the harsh judgment: "The Song of Songs is an unfortunate example of the tendency to use theology/philosophy to skew the interpretation of a text."[5] These examples could easily be multiplied, and today's insistence on a strictly historical reading of the Song is almost as universal as the premodern agreement on allegorical interpretation once used to be. It is probably fair to say that by defending an allegorical reading of the Song of Songs, a contemporary exegete would place himself outside the accepted boundaries of the guild of biblical scholarship. While recent interest in theological exegesis may be changing attitudes here and there, many continue to find the insistence on the "plain sense" of the text obvious and the alternative patently ludicrous.

Throughout this book, we've looked at objections to patristic exegesis, much of it focused on the allegorical approach common among the church fathers. The case of the Song of Songs, however, is particularly noteworthy. The objection here is not just that allegory arbitrarily twists the original meaning of the text but also that it denies the intrinsic goodness of the body and of sexuality. The denial of the body for the sake of the soul, and of earthly pleasures for the sake of heavenly joy, ties in directly, so it is thought, with the rejection of a literal reading of the Song in favor of a spiritual reading. In other words, the assumption is that a fundamental dualism affects attitudes toward sexuality as well as the interpretive stance vis-à-vis the Song of Songs.

Longman, for instance, claims that the Song's canonical significance depends on the disavowal of earlier dichotomous readings: "Once the false dichotomy between body and spirit is rejected, it becomes clear why such a book might be found in the canon. God loves his human creatures as whole people, not just as temporarily embodied spirits. Love is a powerful emotion and sexuality a large part of the human experience, bringing great joy and pain. The book's affirmations and warnings about love express God's concern for his people."[6] At stake in a literal interpretation of the Song of Songs, ac-

---

4. Phipps, "Plight," 82.
5. Longman, "Song of Songs," 759.
6. Ibid., 760. The notion that the Song of Songs would be in the canon because of its celebration of temporal love and sexuality is historically highly dubious. Considering the earlier unanimity regarding an allegorical reading of the Song, Frances Young's assessment is far more likely. She claims that modernity's reaction against allegory should "provoke puzzlement as to why it [i.e., the Song] should ever have got into the canon, let alone stayed there. Faced by dispute on this very question as early as the first century at the council of Jamnia, Rabbi

cording to Longman, is the genuine affirmation of temporal love and sexuality. On this view, the allegorizing of the Song is particularly egregious inasmuch as it warps the meaning of the Song into its opposite: a rejection of the love and sexuality that are celebrated therein.

In one important respect, the objection to allegorical readings of the Song makes a valid and important point: the way we approach interpretation (including but not only that of the Song of Songs) often says a great deal about how we view the body and sexuality, and vice versa. And a dichotomy between body and spirit—whether physically or hermeneutically—would indeed be problematic. But such a dichotomy can take different forms, since it is not just a neglect of the body in favor of the spirit that is problematic; equally dubious would be a materialist focus on the body at the expense of the spirit. On a sacramental view of reality, visible things point to and make present invisible things. The two interpenetrate. So, whether we're dealing with a "spiritualist" or a "materialist" dichotomy, in either case we have lost sight of the sacramental mindset that I am defending in this book. In this regard, it bears pointing out that most modern interpretations settle for a strictly historical reading of the Song, and it is fair to ask whether this doesn't constitute a lapse into the mirror opposite of the dichotomy that has allegedly stained most of the Christian tradition.

It is not my purpose, however, to turn the tables on contemporary detractors of spiritual readings of the Song of Songs. My aim in this chapter is a more limited and defensive one: I simply wish to dispute the claim that it is escapism—a rejection of the physical or textual body—that drove the allegorical exegesis of the Song of Songs in the Christian tradition. At a fundamental level, patristic readings of the Song were sacramental. This doesn't mean that the history of interpretation of the Song is without its problems, perhaps even at times problems of a dichotomous character; it is simply to say that by and large it is not such dichotomizing but rather a sacramental approach that shaped the impetus for and practice of the allegorizing of the Song of Songs.

In order to make this argument, I will focus on the exegesis of three patristic theologians: Hippolytus of Rome, Origen of Alexandria, and Ambrose of Milan. Considering the popularity of the Song of Songs in the early church, this is a relatively limited overview, but it will nonetheless enable us to draw several conclusions. First, there is a clear development from Hippolytus via Origen to Ambrose. While Hippolytus's ecclesial reading of the

---

Aqiba stated: 'No man of Israel ever disputed about the Song of Songs. . . . The whole world is not worth the day on which the Song of Songs was given to Israel, for all the Scriptures are holy, but the Song of Songs is the Holy of Holies.' This love-poem is canonical because it has evoked that kind of response." "Sexuality and Devotion," 83.

Song interpreted the bride as the church, Origen complemented this reading with a personal interpretation that took the bride to be the soul. Ambrose, accepting both of these approaches—though more enamored with the latter than the former—added his own distinct ascetic emphasis.

Second, patristic allegorizing of the Song was profoundly shaped by Jewish exegesis and took its starting point in Old Testament nuptial metaphors for the relationship between God and Israel. As a result, the interpretations of Hippolytus and of Origen—and to some extent also of Ambrose—were grounded in the historical narrative of salvation. That is to say, they located the deeper or allegorical meaning of the Song within the historical and ecclesial realities of Israel and the church. None of these authors used allegory as a way to avoid God's historical dealings with his people in history.

Third, even the personal readings of the Song, certainly in Origen (but, we will see, in some way even in Ambrose), cannot be said simply to result from overzealous asceticism. Origen shunned almost all moralizing when it came to the Song of Songs and avoided all discussion of physical virginity and of sexual purity. To be sure, he did refuse to treat sexuality and the body as ultimate, insisting that both the erotic "letter" of the text and the physical body serve their own proper function inasmuch as they bring the soul to spiritual union with Christ. On the whole, Origen's personal allegorizing of the Song was, theologically, the almost inevitable by-product of an ecclesial interpretation.

Finally, though the early Ambrose used the Song of Songs to promote the consecration of virgins, and though matters of personal morality and asceticism were important to him, his use of the Song of Songs was nonetheless remarkably sacramental. It is precisely Ambrose's much-criticized moralizing that allowed him to link the erotic language of the Song to questions surrounding sexuality and virginity. Also, Ambrose wasn't interested in virginity just for its own sake: he regarded it as symbolic of the church's purity, and he saw the bride's desire for her groom as coming to fulfillment in the church's sacraments. What is more, in a number of instances the bishop's use of the Song's erotic imagery was rather daring, and as such it grounded the spiritual relationship between Christ and the soul within the actual sensuous language of the text.

In order to make this study somewhat manageable, I will give particular attention to the opening verses (1:1–6), where the groom's kisses, breasts, and ointment, as well as the bride's being "black and beautiful" were occasion for much patristic speculation.[7] Exegetical expositions of this passage took a vari-

---

7. English translations typically use the word "love" instead of "breasts" in Song 1:2. The Septuagint's *mastoi* (breasts) translates the Hebrew word *daddekha* rather than *dodekha*. Since

ety of forms. Hippolytus's *Commentary on the Song* was probably in origin a set of three Easter sermons. Origen's surviving work consists of two homilies along with the first three books of a ten-book commentary on the Song of Songs. Saint Ambrose, while he doesn't offer a full-fledged commentary on the Song of Songs, does refer to it repeatedly in his early books *Concerning Virgins* and *On Virginity*, though we need to keep in mind that these are not really works on the Song of Songs per se. By contrast, his work *Isaac, or the Soul*—which in origin was likely a series of Easter sermons—purports to give an explanation of Genesis 24, but turns out to be a fairly detailed interpretation of the Song of Songs. Ambrose again returns to the Song later in life with his *Homilies on Psalm 118* as well as with his mystagogical works, *The Sacraments* and *The Mysteries*, which are basically treatises on the typology of the liturgy, initially preached as homilies to newly baptized Christians at Easter. This variety of literary forms does not really present an obstacle to our investigation, but it is nonetheless good to keep in mind the genre of the various texts as we read along with Hippolytus, Origen, and Ambrose.

Hippolytus: Allegory and Economy

Saint Hippolytus of Rome (170–235) was one of the leading theologians and preachers of the third century.[8] He wrote the first extant commentary on the Song of Songs and perhaps all of Scripture.[9] His *Commentary*, which ends at Song 3:8, likely first served as an Easter homily—or perhaps a series of three homilies[10]—in which Hippolytus introduced newly catechized and baptized believers to the mysteries of the Christian faith.[11] After elaborating in his

---

the two words have identical consonants and the Greek translators had a Hebrew text without vowels, the reading of "breasts" is theoretically possible (though contextually unlikely). The term *mastos* is used to speak both of a woman's breasts (e.g., Luke 11:27) and of a man's chest (e.g., Rev. 1:13).

8. Ronald E. Heine comments that "Hippolytus is one of the most enigmatic figures in the history of the early Church. He appears to have been a man of great importance, but both his identity and his writings are surrounded with problems." "Hippolytus," 142.

9. The authorship of the *Commentary on the Song of Songs* is much disputed. J. A. Cerrato has suggested that Hippolytus was a bishop in the Eastern Mediterranean, perhaps Laodicea or Ephesus (*Hippolytus*, 25, 258), but Yancy Smith has presented a lengthy refutation of Cerrato and maintains that the traditional attribution of the *Commentary* to Hippolytus of Rome remains plausible, seeing as there are good reasons to link the author to Rome (*Mystery of Anointing*, xvi, 15–17, 59–80).

10. This is the suggestion of Smith, *Mystery of Anointing*, 266–70, 412, 416.

11. Hippolytus's commentary, initially written in Greek, is mainly extant in a Georgian translation made of an Armenian text prior to the ninth century, though a thirteenth-century Greek paraphrase that has survived also sheds light on the meaning of the text. Richard, "Une

introduction on the three books of Solomon—Proverbs, Ecclesiastes, and the Song of Songs—Hippolytus discusses the king's wisdom, insisting that Solomon himself shouldn't simply be identified with Wisdom, but that instead "the Word, who was himself Wisdom, was crying out through him."[12] Wisdom, brought forth by the Father before all creation, spoke the following words to Solomon: "I, Wisdom, have lived with you as counsel and knowledge."[13] Hippolytus presents Solomon as Wisdom's instrument.

The term "mystery" is an important one for Hippolytus. The original Greek, which likely has the word *mystērion*, is significant here.[14] Hippolytus seems to indicate with it that the depth of meaning that once was hidden—also in the words of Solomon—has been revealed in Christ. Wisdom, Hippolytus points out with an appeal to 1 Corinthians 1.24, is Jesus Christ, the Son of God.[15] Solomon was "announcing (or foreshadowing) a mystery of revelation, from which it becomes understandable [that he] spoke what would later happen."[16] Hippolytus claims that this mystery was long "hidden,"[17] but that it was already revealed typologically in the Song of Songs: "Now the Spirit sings what has been ordained in the church, since in various portions it reveals to us the economy in types which we must declare to those who are able to listen with faith."[18] This economy (*oikonomia*) of salvation is for Hippolytus a plan that God in his Wisdom (i.e., in Christ) has mapped out before time, a plan that the three books of Solomon reveal by means of certain types.

Because Saint Hippolytus takes his starting point in what we may call an "economy of types," his approach to the Song of Songs is focused squarely on history. The redemptive economy is announced beforehand, in part through the Song, and it climaxes in Christ. Yancy Smith rightly comments, therefore, that for Hippolytus Scripture does not

> simply reveal a series of eternal truths in allegory that could have been distilled apart from the history of God's relationship with human beings. Rather, the history of God's relationship with Israel in Scripture reveals God's οἰκ[ο]νομία

paraphrase greque résumée du Commentaire d'Hippolyte sur le Cantique des Cantiques," 137–54. Throughout, I will use Smith's translation of the Georgian text, in *Mystery of Anointing*, 418–561.

12. Hippolytus, *Commentary on the Song of Songs* 1.6 (Smith, *Mystery of Anointing*, 425).

13. Ibid., 1.7 (Smith, *Mystery of Anointing*, 426).

14. Smith points out that the Armenian word for "counsel" (*xorhurd*) has a similarly broad range as the Greek *mystērion*: "thought," "intention," "counsel," "mystery," "symbol," "sacrament." See Smith, *Mystery of Anointing*, 47, 426n32.

15. Hippolytus, *Commentary on the Song of Songs* 1.8 (Smith, *Mystery of Anointing*, 427).

16. Ibid., 1.9 (Smith, *Mystery of Anointing*, 428); square brackets in original.

17. Ibid., 1.11 (Smith, *Mystery of Anointing*, 430).

18. Ibid., 1.16 (Smith, *Mystery of Anointing*, 441–42).

(economy). . . . The mode of theologizing that Hippolytus follows depends upon a narrative in time and space that has to do with the redemption of physical beings of flesh and blood.[19]

As we will see, this affirmation of God's economic unfolding of history—and, as Smith suggests, of embodiment—means that Hippolytus's allegorical exegesis of the Song finds its *telos* or purpose in the incarnation and in the church.

This historical grounding of Hippolytus's allegorizing shows up clearly when he explains Song 1:2 ("May he kiss me with kisses of his mouth, for your breasts are better than wine").[20] Hippolytus immediately zeroes in on the longing of God's people Israel for the coming of Christ. The imagery of the bride pleading for the bridegroom to kiss her is, according to Hippolytus, a "type" of "the people that entreats the heavenly Word to kiss them."[21] In other words, the Song depicts the Old Testament people of God as praying for the Christ to appear. As Gertrud Chappuzeau puts it, Hippolytus sees the plea for kisses as "a prayer of the people Israel that is waiting for the Messiah."[22] The Old Testament people of God are asking for the mouth of God to pour out the love and power of the Spirit. While the commandments, much like wine, gladden the heart (cf. Song 1:2), Hippolytus is convinced that the combination of law *and* gospel (the breasts of Christ) provides "eternal nourishment."[23]

Here as elsewhere in his *Commentary*, explains Chappuzeau, Hippolytus appears concerned with the "facts of redemptive history. This is not about facts in the sense of objectively given facts, such as the birth of Jesus in Bethlehem or his entry into Jerusalem, but about the acts of God for the salvation of humanity, about the redemptive economy."[24] In other words, Hippolytus is after what I called earlier the "economy of types." While it is obvious that Hippolytus allegorizes the text, he does so against the backdrop of the economy of salvation. So, when he looks for the deeper meaning of the Song, he finds it in the historical narrative of the Scriptures as it comes to its climax in Christ.[25] The historical unfolding of the economy of salvation forms the

---

19. Smith, *Mystery of Anointing*, 393–94.

20. Here and elsewhere, I quote the Greek translation of the Septuagint from Brannan, *Lexham English Septuagint*. However, when discussing Origen and Ambrose, I will follow the English rendering used in the published translations of their works.

21. Hippolytus, *Commentary on the Song of Songs* 2.2 (Smith, *Mystery of Anointing*, 443).

22. Chappuzeau, "Auslegung des Hohenliedes," 52. (All translations from Chappuzeau are my own.)

23. Hippolytus, *Commentary on the Song of Songs* 2.4 (Smith, *Mystery of Anointing*, 444).

24. Chappuzeau, "Auslegung des Hohenliedes," 57.

25. Brendan McConvery rightly comments: "For Hippolytus, as for all Patristic exposition of the Old Testament, the hermeneutical starting point for interpreting the scriptures of Israel was the Christ-event as expressed in lapidary fashion by Luke the Evangelist: 'beginning with

framework for Hippolytus's allegorical exegesis. For Hippolytus, therefore, history and spirit are closely connected. One finds the deeper meaning by searching within the history of salvation itself.

In a lengthy exposition on Song 1:3 ("and the scent of your ointment better than all spices; your name is an ointment poured out"), Hippolytus maintains that here the prayer of the previous verse has been answered: in the incarnation the Father has smashed open the vessel of oil. Now, therefore, the oil—the Word—spreads its aroma.[26] What has apparently happened is that the Father has kissed his bride in the incarnation by opening his mouth (a "vessel of joy") so that in the descent of Christ (the outpouring of the oil) the prophets are fulfilled.[27] Hippolytus then presents a litany of Old Testament saints who already desired this anointing oil: Noah, Eber, Abraham, Jacob, Tamar, Joseph, Moses, Aaron, Phinehas, Joshua, David, Solomon, Daniel, the trio of Shadrach, Meshach, and Abednego, and Joseph and the Virgin Mary—they all longed for this anointing oil. The mystery of the incarnation, as the apex of salvation history, is at the center of Hippolytus's attention.

It is certainly true that Hippolytus allegorizes the smallest details of verse 3. (He even mentions and allegorizes details that are *not* in the text, such as the "vessel" containing the oil.) But his allegorizing has a clear logic: he determines the meaning of each of the details against the backdrop of the previous verse (Israel's prayer for the coming of the Messiah) and with an eye to the salvation of God's people in Christ. As Chappuzeau puts it: "The meaning isn't derived point by point from the text; rather, a redemptive event is attributed in analogous fashion to the clear semantic contents of the image."[28] The result is that Hippolytus treats the biblical passage as a unit, with the flow of thought depicting the coming of the incarnate Word.

A variety of factors likely influenced Saint Hippolytus's allegorical choices. First, we must keep in mind that the Old and New Testaments contain numerous nuptial references to God's relationship with his people. In the Old Testament, passages such as Isaiah 50:1; 54:5–8; 62:4–5; Jeremiah 2:2–3; 3:1, 6–15; Ezekiel 16:1–63; and 23:1–48 all speak of God's covenant with Israel as a love relationship between husband and wife, and they allude in different ways to Israel's repeated betrayal of her husband and to God's responses both of anger and of covenant renewal. And of course much of the book of

---

Moses and all the prophets, he interpreted to them the things about himself in all the scriptures' (Luke 24:27)." "Hippolytus' *Commentary*," 215.

26. Hippolytus, *Commentary on the Song of Songs* 2.5 (Smith, *Mystery of Anointing*, 447–48).

27. Ibid., 2.6 (Smith, *Mystery of Anointing*, 449).

28. Chappuzeau, "Auslegung des Hohenliedes," 48.

Hosea is an extended reflection on the rocky marital relationship between God and Israel.[29] New Testament passages such as Matthew 9:15; 2 Corinthians 11:2; Ephesians 5:22–33; Revelation 19:7–9; 21:2, 9; and 22:17 build on this Old Testament imagery as they depict the relationship between Christ and his church as one between a bridegroom and his bride. It wouldn't seem to require a great leap of the imagination for Hippolytus to depict the relationship between the groom and the bride in the Song of Songs in terms of the relationship between Christ and his church.

Second, Hippolytus may well have built on an earlier commentary on the Song of Songs written in the previous century by Irenaeus of Lyons.[30] Saint Irenaeus engaged in exactly the kind of exegesis that we see at work in Hippolytus's *Commentary*. Karl Shuve points out that it is Irenaeus who first established the typological pattern for reading Old Testament nuptial texts as prophetic witnesses to Christ's redemption of his people.[31] For example, in *Against Heresies* 5.9.4, Irenaeus speaks of the Holy Spirit delighting in the temple—in fleshly existence—as a bridegroom delights in his bride; and in 4.20.12, the bishop of Lyons refers to Hosea's marriage to a prostitute and Moses' marriage to an Ethiopian woman (Num. 12:10–14) as types of Christ's relationship with the gentiles.[32] Shuve makes the interesting point that Irenaeus, against gnostic denials of the goodness of the created order, treats particular, historical marriages in the Old Testament as types of the relationship between Christ and the church. Shuve comments that "far from being an attempt to repress the corporeal, sexual, and social dimensions of marriage, Irenaeus develops this typological pattern to uphold the essential goodness of embodied existence."[33] Indeed, there is nothing either in Irenaeus or in Hippolytus that would suggest the early church started allegorizing the Song of Songs to escape its erotic contents.[34]

Third, Jewish exegetes also read the Song allegorically as describing the relationship between God and Israel, and they also did so in a historically

29. See Patterson, "Metaphors of Marriage," 691–98.

30. Irenaeus's commentary is no longer extant, though a small Syriac fragment remains. See Smith, *Mystery of Anointing*, 137n9. Smith points to Irenaeus's influence in a number of exegetical respects. Ibid., passim.

31. Shuve, "Irenaeus's Contribution," 82.

32. Ibid., 85–86.

33. Ibid., 87.

34. Cf. Robert Jenson's comment: "It need not—as some modern commentators have assumed—be prudery that moves us to ask what such lyrics are doing there. . . . All other books of the Old Testament in some way concern Israel's relation to her God; the supposition is not immediately likely that a collection of sheerly secular lyrics came among them by pure accident." *Song of Songs*, 5.

conscious manner. Jonathan Kaplan has recently argued that in the first few centuries after Christ, rabbinic sages (the Tannaim) interpreted the Song of Songs by means of what he calls a "typological historicization." He shows that the traditions of these early Jewish interpreters "correlated" the Song of Songs to a variety of events in Israel's history. "What makes this process unique," argues Kaplan, is that the Tannaitic midrashim "employed a form of figural interpretation of Song of Songs in order to achieve this correlation."[35] Rabbi Joshua ben Levi, a contemporary of Hippolytus, explained the bride's plea for kisses as a petition from the people of Israel for God to speak with them and to give them his commandments, so that they might obey them.[36] As we have seen, Hippolytus similarly saw God's gift of the commandments reflected in the opening words of the Song, but he deemed the commandments to be mere wine compared to the milk that flows from the breasts of the groom. Rabbi Yohanan, who wrote perhaps several decades after Hippolytus—and did so in polemical dialogue with Origen[37]—saw the vessel with "ointment poured out" in Song 1:3 as a reference not to Christ but to Abraham. Abraham was like a vessel lying in a corner that could not spread its fragrance until someone placed it out in the open. The patriarch had to travel, so that his name might grow in reputation throughout the world.[38] The only real difference between Rabbi Yohanan and Hippolytus is that the former read Abraham where the latter read Christ. This doesn't necessarily mean that Hippolytus took his exegesis here directly from Jewish contemporary exegetes, though this is possible.[39] It seems likely that there was a polemical cross-fertilization between Jews and Christians. The main point is that the kind of allegorical exegesis in which Hippolytus engaged was common also among rabbinic exegetes.

Controversy over the identity of the true people of God—the synagogue or the church—was important, therefore, as early Christians read the Song of Songs. And, as I already observed, this stands to reason against the backdrop of biblical depictions of the nuptial relationship between God and his people. This polemical context helps us understand why Hippolytus gives such detailed attention to the place of the Jews in God's economy of salvation. He brings this out particularly in his reflections on Song 1:5–6, where the bride says she is "black and beautiful" and implores the daughters of Jerusalem not to gaze

35. Kaplan, *My Perfect One*, 56.
36. Chappuzeau, "Auslegung des Hohenliedes," 50.
37. Urbach, "Homiletical Interpretations," 247–75; Kimelman, "Rabbi Yohanan," 567–95; Hirshman, *Rivalry of Genius*, 83–94.
38. Chappuzeau, "Auslegung des Hohenliedes," 58; Kimelman, "Rabbi Yohanan," 583.
39. Kimelman, for instance, suggests that with regard to the comparison between breasts and wine, Rabbi Yohanan likely responded to Origen rather than vice versa. "Rabbi Yohanan," 581.

on her because she is dark. Hippolytus depicts the bride here as the Jewish people boasting that despite being black from sin, they are "beautiful"— beloved by God.[40] Hippolytus is convinced that the Jews deceive themselves with this claim. Israel doesn't remain God's beloved people regardless of her behavior. "Indeed, God is able from stones to raise up children for Abraham [cf. Matt. 3:9], so do not beguile yourself now about the promise of the patriarchs," warns Hippolytus.[41] Israel, so he argues, appears to have lost her status as the people of God.

Next, however, Hippolytus presents Israel in verse 6 as engaging in an act of repentance. She pleads with the church of the gentiles (the "daughters of Jerusalem") not to look on her, as she admits that the sun's rays have burnt her—meaning that Christ, as the "sun of righteousness" from Malachi 4:2, is looking down on her. Israel acknowledges that the prophets used to urge her to return to God and to guard her identity ("The sons of my mother fought in me. They made me a guard in the vineyards"[42]). And she admits she has failed to do so: "I have not guarded my vineyard."[43] By putting a confession of sin and an acknowledgment of Christ in the mouth of the Jews, Hippolytus upholds his claim that the church has become the true bride, while holding out hope that the Jews may be saved in and through Christ. Hippolytus doesn't despise the Jews; he calls for their repentance: they must accept the new economy of salvation in Christ to be saved.[44]

For Hippolytus, the Song of Songs is about ecclesial identity: Who makes up the true bride, the true people of God? His answer is that it is those who confess their faith in Christ and accept the economy of salvation that he has introduced. Hippolytus makes his case by means of detailed allegorical

---

40. Hippolytus, *Commentary on the Song of Songs* 5.1 (Smith, *Mystery of Anointing*, 466), 7.2 (Smith, *Mystery of Anointing*, 470).

41. Ibid., 7.2 (Smith, *Mystery of Anointing*, 470).

42. I have slightly changed the Septuagint translation of *emachesanto en emoi* from "fought with me" to "fought in me," since Hippolytus seems to suggest that the prophets fought *in* Israel in order to make her return to the law. The notion of the vineyard as a reference to Israel goes back to Isa. 5:1–7.

43. Hippolytus, *Commentary on the Song of Songs* 5.3 (Smith, *Mystery of Anointing*, 467–68).

44. So also Chappuzeau, "Auslegung des Hohenliedes," 67. Joel Marcus very much overstates the case when he suggests Hippolytus believed that Israel remains God's chosen people and that perhaps even non-Christian Jews may be saved. "Israel and the Church," 394–95, 402. It is true that Hippolytus hoped that Israel will be saved, but as it is, she has clearly lost her status as the people of God and can be saved only by turning to Christ. Roland Murphy puts it better, therefore, when he comments that "the Song is seen as a prophecy by Solomon of the end of the Old Covenant, as Israel is replaced by the Church. This interpretation reflects a hermeneutical principle of the NT and the early Church: the OT is applied in a transferred meaning; Israel becomes the Church." "Patristic and Medieval Exegesis," 507.

exegesis, but it is an exegesis driven by questions about ecclesial identity and grounded in an "economy of types"—the biblical narrative as it centers on Christ and the mystery of salvation that he has brought about. Hippolytus displays no fear of the erotic language of the Song, nor does he allegorize because he dichotomizes body and soul or history and spirit. His approach is very much a sacramental one, in which the historical narrative of salvation is the locus where we can find the deeper meaning of the Song.

Origen: Ecclesial and Personal Readings

Origen of Alexandria's (ca. 185–ca. 254) *Two Homilies on the Canticle of Canticles* (likely preached in 241 or 242) and his *Commentary on the Canticle of Canticles* (completed several years later) owe a great deal to Hippolytus,[45] perhaps as the result of meeting him in Rome.[46] Several of Origen's exegetical choices are similar to those of Hippolytus. Origen's allegorizing, like that of Hippolytus, takes place against the backdrop of the developing economy of salvation. Further, as I already mentioned, Origen has an ongoing dialogue with the synagogue, whose repentance he hopes will fulfill the Pauline promise of the salvation of all Israel (Rom. 11:26). As a result, the Alexandrian theologian treats historical realities as indispensable, focuses repeatedly on the ecclesiological implications of the Song, and respects (even if he treats it minimally) the literal meaning of the Song of Songs.

In no way does this turn Origen into a carbon copy of Hippolytus. Origen does caution against carnal readings that he believes can cause trouble to fleshly readers, and this warning is connected to the duality he posits between the outer, carnal man and the inner, spiritual man, between the bodily and the spiritual senses, and between visible and invisible things. This duality, however, is not a form of dualism. Origen's acknowledgment of a duality does not separate the visible and the invisible in antithetical fashion.[47] Instead, Origen believes that the body has a limited but positive role to play—though of course it can also hinder the anagogical or upward journey of the believer.

---

45. I am following J. Christopher King in terms of the relative dating of the *Two Homilies on the Canticle of Canticles* and *The Commentary on the Canticle of Canticles* (*Origen*, 9–11). Eusebius mentions that Origen wrote the first five books of *The Commentary on the Canticle of Canticles* on his journey to Athens (around 245) and the last five books after he came back to Caesarea (in 246 or 247). *Ecclesiastical History* 6.32.1–2; cf. King, *Origen*, 9.

46. Eusebius speaks of a visit to Rome, which would have taken place around the year 215. *Ecclesiastical History* 6.14.10–11; cf. Tzamalikos, *Origen*, 7–8.

47. See my discussion in chap. 1, sec. "Metaphysics and Hermeneutics: Origen, Hobbes, and Spinoza."

He simply downplays the role of the physical body, since he is convinced that ascent to the perfection of union with Christ is much more important. In short, Origen's allegorical reading of the Song works with a sacramental relation between history and spirit in which he aims to give each its proper due.

Origen is aware, I think, of the down-to-earth character of the Song of Songs as a literal marriage song. It is important to reaffirm this, particularly since J. Christopher King has recently argued that Origen reads the Song as a "total allegory," by which he means that every aspect of the text is meant to be allegorical, "with no surplus whatsoever of a conventional, obvious, or corporeal meaning remaining behind."[48] The result, according to King, is a treatment of the Song of Songs as a "bodiless" or "asomatic" text, in which all duality between letter and spirit has disappeared.[49] The reason for this, he thinks, is that Origen believed that in the Song the "letter" of "bodiless" texts becomes identical to its allegorical or figurative meaning. The coincidence of the two, explains King, "would seem to mean nothing less than that the literal meaning, which stands apart and inferior in most other Scriptures, is the spiritual meaning in the 'bodiless' text. . . . In the Song, it would appear that the 'letter' has been transformed into 'spirit.'"[50] According to King, Origen treated the Song as a "bodiless" text not because he wanted to protect the reader from the sensuality of the erotic text but because he regarded the Song "as nothing less than *the spirit of Scripture itself*, revealed in its essential nature as Christ the Word's eschatological song of nuptial love."[51]

I am not quite persuaded.[52] Origen did, in fact, intend to give the literal or historical understanding of the text its due, and the distinction he makes between the inner and the outer man—between body and soul—in the prologue of the *Commentary* shows that he meant to give a place to both (though obviously he regarded the latter as more important than the former). Origen explains that Scripture often calls "the members of the outer man by the same names as the parts and dispositions of the inner man,"[53] and that this distinction corresponds to that between carnal and spiritual love.[54] Similarly, when in book 3 he explains what allegorical exegesis does, he begins by distinguishing

48. King, *Origen*, 39.
49. Ibid., 45–59.
50. Ibid., 55.
51. Ibid., 269.
52. King himself recognizes the novelty of his approach: "To date, no studies of the great *Commentary* have taken notice of the peculiar spiritual character that Origen attributes to the *sensus literalis* of the Song." Ibid., 60.
53. Origen, *Commentary on the Canticle of Canticles*, prologue (ACW 26:26).
54. Ibid., prologue (ACW 26:29). Cf. chap. 1, sec. "Metaphysics and Hermeneutics: Origen, Hobbes, and Spinoza."

between visible and invisible things, and he then suggests that "the invisible things of God are understood by means of things that are visible."[55] Origen explains that earthly creatures are created after the likeness of "heavenly patterns."[56] Thus, we are taught by visible things to understand invisible things. What is true for metaphysics in general also holds for interpretation, so Origen continues. Historical events in Scripture have "the aspects and likeness of certain hidden things."[57] Of course, the hidden, heavenly things are much more important to Origen than the historical events. But it is through the latter that we arrive at the former. This is true for the Song of Songs no less than for other biblical texts.

So in what way does Origen acknowledge a distinct, literal meaning of the Song? In his *Commentary* he repeatedly distinguishes three meanings of a passage. The first is the "literal" (*historicam intelligentiam*)[58] or "surface" (*historicum drama*)[59] meaning of the "simple story" (*historiae speciem*)[60] in its "dramatic form" (*dramatis in modum composita historica*).[61] The second is the "inner meaning" (*interior intellectus*),[62] the "spiritual interpretation" (*spiritalis intelligentia*),[63] or "mystical exposition" (*ordinem mysticum*).[64] Finally, Origen repeatedly refers to what he calls the "third explanation," which speaks of the life of the soul.

To get an impression of how Origen treats the "surface" meaning of the text, let's follow along with his understanding of the opening verse of the Song:

> Reading it as a simple story, then, we see a bride appearing on the stage, having received for her betrothal and by way of dowry most fitting gifts from a most noble bridegroom; but, because the bridegroom delays his coming for so long, she, grieved with longing for his love, is pining at home and doing all she can to bring herself at last to see her spouse, and to enjoy his kisses. We understand further that the bride, seeing that she can neither be quit of her love, nor yet achieve what she desires, betakes herself to prayer and makes supplication to God, whom she knows to be her Bridegroom's Father.[65]

55. Ibid., 3.12 (ACW 26:218).
56. Ibid., 3.12 (ACW 26:219).
57. Ibid., 3.12 (ACW 26:223). Cf. chap. 1, sec. "Metaphysics and Hermeneutics: Origen, Hobbes, and Spinoza."
58. Ibid., 1.2 (ACW 26:63), 1.5 (ACW 26:84).
59. Ibid., 2.1 (ACW 26:91). I have changed Lawson's rendering of "superficial" meaning.
60. Ibid., 1.1 (ACW 26:58), 1.2 (ACW 26:63).
61. Ibid., 1.1 (ACW 26:59).
62. Ibid., 1.1 (ACW 26:59).
63. Ibid., 1.1 (ACW 26:58).
64. Ibid., 2.1 (ACW 26:92).
65. Ibid., 1.1 (ACW 26:58–59).

Clearly, the drama in Origen's epithalamium is hardly erotic, and Origen emphasizes the bride's modesty by quoting 1 Timothy 2:8–9, saying that the bride makes her request by "'lifting up holy hands without anger or contention, . . . in decent apparel with modesty and sobriety,' adorned with the worthiest of ornaments, such as befit a noble bride."[66] Further, Origen gives precious little space to the literal reading of the text. In fact, when he comments that the bride "betakes herself to prayer and makes supplication to God," he almost lets the literal reading slide directly into the allegorical one.[67] Still, he doesn't ignore the former altogether. He deals with it up front because it is the indispensable ground for his (much more important) spiritual understanding of the text.

Origen's "inner meaning" of the text—an exposition of the relationship between Christ and the church—is fairly similar to Hippolytus's interpretation: the progress in salvation history is central in Origen's allegorizing of the text. Although there are obvious differences—Origen pays much closer attention to the details of the text and is far more sophisticated than Hippolytus in drawing on other biblical passages to elucidate the Song—their underlying approaches are quite similar. Already in the prologue of his *Commentary*, when he discusses the title of the Song, Origen draws attention to the salvific history. He explains that "the songs in relation to which this song is called 'The Song of Songs'" are introductory songs sung by the bridegroom's friends—prophets and angels.[68] There were six such songs: the song that Moses and the Israelites sang after crossing the Red Sea (Exod. 15:1–18); the song about the well that the Israelites sang after God provided water for them (Num. 21:17–18); Moses' final song just before his death (Deut. 32:1–43); the song of Deborah and Barak (Judg. 5:2–31); David's song of victory over his enemies (2 Sam. 22:2–51); and David's song of thanksgiving after the ark was placed in the tent (1 Chron. 16:8–36).[69] The bride—and Origen sees her at this point both

66. Ibid., 1.1 (ACW 26:59). Lawson uses italics to indicate Origen's biblical quotations, a practice that I have removed; instead I enclose biblical quotations in quotation marks, here and elsewhere.

67. I suspect the reason for this is that Origen saw the allegorizing of the Song as something that the canonical text itself invites us to do. Jenson, therefore, goes so far as to suggest that the rabbinic and Christian interpretations are in some way "plain sense" readings rather than allegory, and he goes on to say: "If the rabbis and the Fathers were right in their judgment about genre, then construing theological allegory for the Song's overtly secular poems is in fact plain-sense reading, and is an allegorizing reading just in the sense that allegory is that sort of interpretation which the text invites the interpreter to employ." *Song of Songs*, 6. Jenson makes an interesting point, but we need to keep in mind that Origen himself does distinguish between "historical" and "mystical" readings of the Song.

68. Origen, *Commentary on the Canticle of Canticles*, prologue (ACW 26:46).

69. Ibid., prologue (ACW 26:47–50). Origen speculates that perhaps the song of the vineyard (Isa. 5:1–7) and the songs found in the book of Psalms could be added to this. He includes Isa.

as the church and as the individual soul—must progress through each of the stages of these songs to arrive at the climactic Song of Songs itself. There the bride enters the nuptial chamber of the bridegroom, the heavenly reality itself.[70]

Origen recognizes in the bride who desires her groom's kisses (Song 1:2) the church that "longs for union with Christ."[71] Angels have already given her the law as a betrothal gift, and the prophets have also already ministered to her.[72] But the bride is no longer satisfied with God speaking to her through his servants; she desires that he

> may come Himself, directly, and kiss me with the kisses of His mouth—that is to say, may pour the words of His mouth into mine, that I may hear Him speak Himself, and see Him teaching. The kisses are Christ's, which He bestowed on His Church when at His coming, being present in the flesh, He in His own person spoke to her the words of faith and love and peace, according to the promise of Isaias who, when sent beforehand to the Bride, had said: "Not a messenger, nor an angel, but the Lord Himself shall save us" [Isa. 33:22].[73]

Origen makes clear that the bride—here the Old Testament people of God— longed for the time when God himself would come to his people in Christ.

The next words of the Song, according to Origen, place us at a later point in history: here Christ has already come, and the church enjoys his breasts. The wine mentioned in the text stands for the teaching of the Law and the Prophets; the Savior's breasts are better than this wine and conceal treasures (*thesauri*) of wisdom and knowledge (cf. Col. 2:3).[74] Origen carefully elucidates how it is that breasts can contain wisdom and knowledge: John in his Gospel uses the term "bosom" or "breast" when people recline at table as a way of referring to the ground principle of Jesus' heart (John 13:23–25); furthermore, in Leviticus the "little breast of separation" and the "shoulder" are set aside to serve as the "ground of the heart" for the priests (Lev. 10:14–15).[75]

Origen recognizes the verbal similarities between Colossians 2:3 and Matthew 13:44, with the former speaking of Christ in whom are "hidden" (*apokryphoi*) all the "treasures" (*thēsauroi*) of wisdom and knowledge, and the latter comparing the kingdom of heaven to a "treasure" (*thēsaurō*) "hidden"

5:1–7 instead of 1 Chron. 16:8–36 in *Two Homilies on the Canticle of Canticles* 1.1 (ACW 26:267).

70. Origen, *Commentary on the Canticle of Canticles*, prologue (ACW 26:50, 53).

71. Ibid., 1.1 (ACW 26:59).

72. Ibid.

73. Ibid., 1.1 (ACW 26:60).

74. Ibid., 1.2 (ACW 26:65).

75. Ibid., 1.2 (ACW 26:64).

(*kekrymmenō*) in a field. Origen exploits this link, and he associates both passages, in turn, with Song 1:2. It is "certainly possible," he suggests, that the field mentioned by Jesus contains vineyards to produce wine.[76] Better than this wine, however, is the treasure that the man in Jesus' parable purchases. Likewise, says Origen, the breasts of the bridegroom—"who is hidden like a treasure (*thesaurus absconditus*) in the Law and the Prophets"—are better than the wine of the Law and the Prophets.[77] In short, Origen identifies Christ (along with his wisdom and knowledge) as the treasure hidden within the vineyard of the Old Testament.[78]

When the bride says that the fragrance of the groom's ointments is better than all spices (Song 1:3), she intimates to Christ, who by this time is in her presence, that while she used to have the Law and the Prophets (the spices) as pedagogues, now he, the only begotten Son, has been sent into the world by the Father and has been anointed with the Holy Spirit.[79] Origen suspects that this anointing refers to the priestly ointment mentioned in Exodus 30:22–25, since Christ is not only bridegroom but also priest. Origen then gives a detailed explanation of each of the four spices mentioned in Exodus 30—myrrh, cinnamon, sweet reed, and cassia—showing how each refers to Christ.[80] All these spices used to be blended together with olive oil (Exod. 30:24), which Origen maintains is either a reference to the Son of God taking on the form of a servant or to his anointing with the Holy Spirit.[81]

When the bride then says that Christ's "name is an ointment poured out," Origen claims that these words are "a certain prophecy" regarding Christ's name being spread throughout the world so as "to make it an odour of sweetness in every place."[82] In other words, at this point in the history of salvation we move from the life of Christ to the growth of the church. And so the young maidens—"young souls growing up in years and beauty"[83]—come to love the Savior and run after him, in line with the words: "Therefore have the maidens loved Thee, have they drawn Thee. We will run after Thee into the fragrance of Thine ointments" (Song 1:3–4). The bride then enters into the king's chamber, where she sees all his royal riches: the very mind of Christ, "in which," says

76. Ibid., 1.2 (ACW 26:69).
77. Ibid.
78. Origen returns once more to Colossians 2:3 when he explains that the soul enters the king's chamber, "in which are hid the treasures (*thesauri*) of His wisdom and knowledge." Ibid., 1.5 (ACW 26:85).
79. Ibid., 1.3 (ACW 26:70).
80. Ibid., 1.3 (ACW 26:71–72).
81. Ibid., 1.3 (ACW 26:72–73).
82. Ibid., 1.4 (ACW 26:74).
83. Ibid., 1.4 (ACW 26:75).

Origen with a reference to Colossians 2:3, "are hid the treasures (*thesauri*) of His wisdom and knowledge."[84] The maidens, though they too have made some progress, have not yet attained the bride's "summit of perfection,"[85] and they cannot quite enter into the king's chamber so as to drink directly from the Savior's breasts. And so they are looking forward to a time when they *will* love the groom's breasts better than wine (Song 1:4).

As he moves to book 2 of his *Commentary*, Origen begins by reflecting on the bride's comment that she is dark and beautiful (Song 1:5). Here the bride—who now, after the incarnation and the spreading of Christ's name across the world, clearly is the church of the gentiles—responds to the daughters of Jerusalem (the Jews) vilifying her ignoble birth. The Jews "call her black, as one who has not been enlightened by the patriarchs' teaching."[86] In an ingenious excursus on the place of Ethiopians in the Scriptures, Origen shows that at least five Old Testament passages contain "types foreshadowing this mystery" (*sacramenti hujus forma*) of the church coming from the gentiles.[87]

Origen makes clear that he is not thinking of the "natural blackness" of the Ethiopian race.[88] Instead, this is a blackness that originates from the disobedience of the gentiles. And unlike physical blackness, this spiritual black identity isn't in any way cast in stone: Origen turns the tables on the "daughters of Jerusalem" and claims that while the church of the gentiles has become white—in line with the words of Song 8:5, "Who is this that cometh up, having been made white, and leaning upon her Nephew?"[89]—the synagogue now stands exposed to the Sun of Justice (Jesus Christ; cf. Mal. 4:2) and risks being blackened by its rays. The Sun of Justice either gives light or scorches one's face, depending on how one responds to Christ. Following the logic of Saint Paul in Romans 11 (as well as that of Hippolytus), Origen comments that Israel has become "disobedient and unbelieving," and that the Sun of Justice has darkened and even blinded the Israelites (Rom. 11:25).[90] Clearly,

84. Ibid., 1.5 (ACW 26:85).
85. Ibid., 1.5 (ACW 26:87).
86. Ibid., 2.1 (ACW 26:92).
87. Ibid., 2.1 (ACW 26:93). Origen discusses Num. 12:1; 1 Kings 10:1–13; Ps. 67:32 (68:31); Zeph. 3:10; and Jer. 45 (38):7–13. Ibid., 2.1 (ACW 26:93–104).
88. Ibid., 2.2 (ACW 26:107). It is important to keep in mind that Origen is dealing here with the mystical or ecclesial interpretation of the Song of Songs and therefore is not thinking in racial terms. Mark S. M. Scott rightly emphasizes that Origen uses black imagery to convey soteriological truth, not racial stereotypes. "Shades of Grace," 65–83. Just as Origen has no intention of affirming the physical sexual suggestions in the Song, so also he doesn't express any negative judgments about racial characteristics.
89. Origen, *Commentary on the Canticle of Canticles* 2.1 (ACW 26:106), 2.2 (ACW 26:107).
90. Ibid., 2.2 (ACW 26:108).

Origen is hoping that the synagogue will yet turn to Christ.[91] Meanwhile, however, it is the church that is the legitimate bride, who despite her "black" origin is in the process of becoming white through her acceptance of Christ as the Sun of Justice.

Origen's ecclesial reading of the first five verses of the Song of Songs is obviously allegorical. At the same time, his allegorical choices are governed by the unfolding narrative of redemptive history. It is within these parameters that Origen searches the Scriptures for appropriate intertextual connections that will allow him to move from the historical to the spiritual level of interpretation. Without the historical unfolding of the economy of salvation, which culminates in the Christ event, Origen's entire exegetical approach would fall apart. Thus, it is the historical and ecclesial anchor of his exegesis of the Song that renders it sacramental rather than dualistic. The Alexandrian exegete believes that salvation—the spiritual dimension of the text—is an event that unfolds in history, in Christ, and in the church as the people of God.

To be sure, Origen's main innovation vis-à-vis the earlier tradition is that he adds to this ecclesial reading of the Song a personal interpretation. The "third interpretation" that he repeatedly mentions in his *Commentary* reads the relationship between the bridegroom and the bride as the bond between Christ and the soul. It is, of course, particularly in connection with such a personal reading of the Song that ascetic interests would come to the fore in the later tradition. We must ask, therefore, how Origen's personal reading unfolds: Is it ascetic? Does it avoid the Song's erotic language? Does it disparage the body? In short, does Origen actually maintain a sacramental approach also in his personal reading of the Song?

We should perhaps first take a quick tour of the exegetical choices that Origen makes in his personal reading. He maintains that the soul's dowry, which she brings to her quest for union with Christ, consists of natural law, reason, and free will.[92] Earlier, she received interpretations ("kisses") from her teachers, but now she approaches the Word of God directly for the enlightening of her mind (Song 1:2).[93] As the soul matures and moves beyond childhood, she leaves behind the wine of other people's teachings, and having taken a Nazirite vow of abstinence (Num. 6:3), she instead drinks directly from the

---

91. Origen repeatedly refers to Rom. 11; see ibid., 2.1 (ACW 26:103); *Two Homilies on the Canticle of Canticles* 1.6 (ACW 26:277). Cf. Elizabeth A. Clark's comment: "When read with an historian's eye, Origen's *Commentary on the Canticle of Canticles* resembles nothing so much as Romans 9–11, in which Paul's argument for the union of Jew and Gentile in Christianity reaches its climax." "Uses of the Song of Songs," 390.

92. Origen, *Commentary on the Canticle of Canticles* 1.1 (ACW 26:61).

93. Ibid., 1.1 (ACW 26:61–62).

breast of the Word of God.[94] She recognizes the superiority of "knowledge of the mysteries and the divine judgements" over the "spices" of mere ethics and natural philosophy (Song 1:3).[95] The sense of smell through which she is drawn to Christ (Song 1:4) "denotes not a bodily faculty but that divine sense of scent which is called the sense of the interior man."[96] Although in his *Commentary* Origen is so preoccupied with the Jew-gentile relationship that he doesn't come around to a personal reading of the bride being "black and beautiful," in his *Homilies* he does take time to warn his hearers against the darkness of sin, telling them to "take heed lest *your* soul be described as black and ugly, and you be hideous with a double foulness—black by reason of your past sins and ugly because you are continuing in the same vices!"[97]

Such moral injunctions, however, are the exception rather than the rule in Origen's reflections on the Song. Notably absent from his exposition are any warnings against the passions or any language about the dangers of sexuality or of bodily preoccupations more broadly.[98] Origen's exegesis instead centers on christological mysticism; he is affective in his approach, wanting his reader to be united to Christ. One reason for the absence of ascetic warnings may be that Origen regards the Song of Songs as the third and most perfect of the three books authored by King Solomon. The first (the book of Proverbs) discusses matters of morality. The second (Ecclesiastes) deals with natural philosophy and physics.[99] And in Solomon's last book, the Song of Songs, "he instills into the soul the love of things divine and heavenly."[100] Therefore, to make moral exegesis the focus in one's reading of the Song of Songs would, for Origen, be to miss out on the purpose of the book. It has a higher, more ultimate aim.

Origen recognizes that reading the Song of Songs at a surface level carries certain dangers. And it is fair to say that in connection with the Song of Songs, Origen is particularly cautious not to dwell at any length upon the "simple story" of the dramatic encounter of the groom and the bride. Part of the reason is, again, that the Song is aimed at describing the climactic spiritual union between Christ and the church or the soul. But an additional reason is probably the sensual contents of this particular Bible book. In his prologue to the *Commentary*, Origen warns that if someone

94. Ibid., 1.2 (ACW 26:69–70).
95. Ibid., 1.3 (ACW 26:73).
96. Ibid., 1.4 (ACW 26:80–81).
97. Origen, *Two Homilies on the Canticle of Canticles* 1.6 (ACW 26:276).
98. Clark, "Uses of the Song of Songs," 401–2.
99. Origen, *Commentary on the Canticle of Canticles*, prologue (ACW 26:40).
100. Ibid., prologue (ACW 26:41).

who lives only after the flesh should approach it, to such a one the reading of this Scripture will be the occasion of no small hazard and danger. For he, not knowing how to hear love's language in purity and with chaste ears, will twist the whole manner of his hearing of it away from the inner spiritual man and on to the outward and carnal; and he will be turned away from the spirit to the flesh and will foster carnal desires in himself, and it will seem to be the Divine Scriptures that are thus urging and egging him on to fleshly lust![101]

The Song of Songs can be misused, so Origen notes. He warns, therefore, that people who are "not yet rid of the vexations of flesh and blood" should stay away from it.[102]

Origen certainly means for his readers to take his admonition to heart. But his word of caution doesn't set the stage for an exegesis focused on ascetic concerns. Roland Murphy rightly observes that "the actual course of Christian interpretation [of the Song of Songs] is not to be explained as a pathological rejection of sex. Sex is simply seen in a different framework, indeed, it is hardly seen at all, due to the exegetical principles which we find in Origen, who wielded such great influence on later interpreters."[103] For Origen, by the time we're contemplating the soul's mystical union with Christ, the fleshly passions have long disappeared from the horizon. Put differently, for Origen the soul's quest for Christ is less a matter of avoiding the passions than of being drawn to the heavenly groom.

Several scholars have commented on the fact that Origen's distinction between ecclesial and personal readings of the Song isn't very clear-cut. R. P. Lawson comments that the two types of reading—which he calls spiritual and psychic—are closely linked: Origen "is saturated with the idea of the compenetration of the life of the Church and the life of the soul, of the mystery of the Church and our life under grace: in the final analysis, the two—inseparable—stand for true participation in the Divine-Human nature of the Logos."[104] Lawson suggests that what Christ is for the soul, he is also for the church, and vice versa. Similarly, Aidan Nichols has suggested that because Origen sees the soul as ecclesial (*anima ecclesiastica*), he often intermingles the two readings.[105] What counts for Origen, explains Frances Young, is the wisdom and understanding that come through Christ, which are "granted to the Church and also to the individual believer, the latter both receiving from

---

101. Ibid., prologue (ACW 26:22).
102. Ibid., prologue (ACW 26:23).
103. Murphy, "Patristic and Medieval Exegesis," 508.
104. Lawson, introduction to *The Song of Songs*, 15.
105. Nichols, *Lovely, Like Jerusalem*, 236.

the Church and in a sense representing the Church."[106] Each of these authors recognizes that the soul and the church are closely linked, inasmuch as they both receive their identity in and from Christ.

This close connection between the church and the soul is important. It suggests that, for Origen, Christ is the climax both of the ecclesial economy of salvation (*historia salutis*) and of the personal journey of faith (*ordo salutis*). This implies that there is an analogy between the church's attitude toward the letter (of the Old Testament narrative) and the soul's attitude toward the body. Neither letter nor body is evil in and of itself, and neither is to be avoided as such (though Origen is keenly aware of the close link between the body and the passions). But for Origen the letter and the body don't exist for their own sake; they are in no way ultimate. They serve rather to lead to Jesus Christ in such a way that the ecclesial history of salvation leads one forward (horizontally) to Christ, while the personal order of salvation leads one upward (vertically) to Christ. Insofar as the letter and the body fulfill this role, Origen wants us to affirm them; but to get stuck on the letter of the Song or on bodily concerns would be to miss the Song's purpose. So while it is true that the sensual character of the Song plays a subordinate role in Origen's vertical or anagogical (upward-leading) personal interpretation, this doesn't betray a lack of sacramentality or a dichotomizing of body and soul or letter and spirit. What it shows instead is that the erotic descriptions of the Song fulfill their proper, created purpose: to lead the soul to union with Christ.

Ambrose: Ecclesial Asceticism

If Origen added a personal reading to the earlier ecclesial interest in the Song, Ambrose of Milan (ca. 340–397) built on this by turning to the Song for the sake of moral purity in general and physical virginity in particular. Appropriating both Origen's ecclesial and personal readings of the Song, Ambrose took the latter in a direction that Origen had almost studiously avoided: deeply concerned with dangers to the soul's purity, Ambrose moved the Song into the realm of moral theology and asceticism.[107] To be sure, it's not as though Ambrose read the Song of Songs allegorically simply out of fear for its erotic language and the moral perils that this entails for the reader of Scripture. He was convinced that the Song speaks of Christ's relation to the church, and his personal reading—including his asceticism and even his early preoccupation with virginity—stands in the service of an ecclesial reading.

106. Young, "Sexuality and Devotion," 87.
107. Clark, "Uses of the Song of Songs," 404–5.

In Ambrose, the soul is never isolated, and sexual purity isn't just a matter of individual purity. That said, Ambrose's interest in morality did bring a new element into the tradition of the Song's interpretation, one that would leave a significant imprint upon later medieval theology and practice.

Ambrose's accentuation of morality in general and sexual purity in particular has some interesting consequences. On the one hand, it means that, in comparison with Origen, Ambrose took the Song back to earth, as it were, to the day-to-day dangers and pitfalls of the moral lives of his congregants, something that reinforces the basic sacramental sense of his exegesis. For him, spiritual union with Christ was closely patterned on physical union, such that Ambrose used the Song's erotic language in ways that Origen had been hesitant to do. Ambrose's exegesis is therefore sacramental, in that it doesn't leave behind the erotic contents of the Song but uses such contents to instill in his listeners a passionate desire for Christ. On the other hand, Ambrose, unlike Origen, loudly voiced his apprehensions with regard to the body and its passions, and it is perhaps at this point that he made himself vulnerable to the charge of dualism in a way that Origen did not. My criticism of Ambrose in this regard will be muted: as I have already noted, for the most part he rejected not the body per se but the illicit passions that it incites; he linked virginal purity to the purity of the church; and he used precisely the erotic letter of the text to elucidate its spiritual aim.[108] It also seems to me that as a pastor Ambrose rightly recognized the powerful force of sexuality in the lives of his congregants; not all warnings against sexual impurity are signs of a dichotomous anthropology.

There's little doubt that Ambrose was a staunch defender of virginity, both physical and ecclesial. His early works *Concerning Virgins* (377) and *On Virginity* (377–78) make clear that he believed physical virginity is worthy of the highest praise. From early on in his career, Karl Shuve points out, the bishop of Milan tried to defend the physical integrity (*integritas*) of the virgins in his community, actively promoting the ceremony of the "veiling of virgins" (*velatio virginum*), which consecrated virgins to Christ and set them apart from the rest of the ecclesial community.[109] Understandably, this active promotion of a secluded group of virgins had political implications. While many in Ambrose's congregation resented the bishop's encouraging young women to

108. The erotic language is suitable to describe the divine-human relationship precisely because we already know what erotic love between a man and woman is like. Ambrose recognizes, in other words, that the Song of Songs's erotic language serves to make God's love for us somewhat understandable. We could even say that it is precisely the erotic character of the Song that gives it its mystagogical role. I am grateful to Silvianne Aspray for her helpful insights on this point.

109. Shuve, *Song of Songs*, 118.

reserve their bodies for Christ, the practice may nonetheless have shored up Ambrose's authority. David Hunter makes the point that by presiding over the consecration ceremony, "the bishop took on a public, quasi-parental role in relation to the consecrated virgin. He became, in effect, a new *paterfamilias*."[110] Virginity, for Ambrose, resulted from a deeply held theological conviction and had potent political implications.

Ambrose makes clear, early on in his three books of *Concerning Virgins*, that he considers physical virginity to represent the purity of the church: Aaron's sister, Miriam, was a "type (*speciem*) of the church" as she gathered people together in song (Exod. 15:20).[111] The Virgin Mary's life, as he puts it a little later, is "as it were virginity itself."[112] On the last day, she will commend many other virgins to the Lord.[113] At that time, Mary—who now appears as the antitype of Miriam—"taking her timbrel, shall stir up the choirs of virgins, singing to the Lord because they have passed through the sea of this world without suffering from the waves of this world."[114] This Mariological construal of the church implies that the church herself is a virgin, "ignorant of wedlock, but fertile in bearing . . . in chastity a virgin, yet a mother in offspring."[115] Saint Ambrose's encomium on virginity is rooted in an identification of the consecrated virgins with Mary and with the church: Miriam, Mary, the church, and the virgins in his audience—they are all one and the same.[116]

It doesn't come as a surprise, therefore, that Ambrose identifies the virgins of his congregation also with the bride in the Song of Songs.[117] He quotes Song 1:2–3 and applies it directly to the consecrated virgin, who runs toward the king's chamber (1:5) so that she may be protected in his safety.[118] There she is guarded by the "wall" and the "battlements" of Song 8:9: "She who sported with kisses now builds towers that, encircled with the precious battlements of the saints, she may not only render fruitless the attacks of the enemy, but also erect the safe defences of holy merits."[119] The cloistered virgin is a "garden enclosed" and a "fountain sealed" (Song 4:12), maintains Ambrose.[120] The

---

110. Hunter, "Virgin," 156.
111. Ambrose, *Concerning Virgins* 1.3.12 (*NPNF*[2] 10:365).
112. Ibid., 2.2.6 (*NPNF*[2] 10:374).
113. Ibid., 2.2.16 (*NPNF*[2] 10:376).
114. Ibid., 2.2.17 (*NPNF*[2] 10:376).
115. Ibid., 1.6.31 (*NPNF*[2] 10:368).
116. Cf. Shuve's comment that the virgin "quite literally embodies the grace of Christ, the purity of the church, the life of the angels, and the hope of redemption." *Song of Songs*, 123.
117. Ambrose, *Concerning Virgins* 1.7.38–39 (*NPNF*[2] 10:369).
118. Ibid., 2.6.42 (*NPNF*[2] 10:380).
119. Ibid., 2.6.43 (*NPNF*[2] 10:380).
120. Ibid., 1.9.45 (*NPNF*[2] 10:370).

water of this fountain, so the bishop impresses on his readers, shines with the image of God, "lest its streams mingled with mud from the wallowing places of spiritual wild beasts should be polluted. For this reason, too, that modesty of virgins fenced in by the wall of the Spirit is enclosed lest it should lie open to be plundered."[121] And the preacher reminds the virgins from what worldliness they are escaping: "Look at the ears pierced with wounds, and pity the neck weighed down with burdens. That the metals are different does not lighten the suffering. In one case a chain binds the neck, in another a fetter encloses the foot."[122] Similarly, he warns against the dangers of dancing: "Is anything so conducive to lust as with unseemly movements thus to expose in nakedness those parts of the body which either nature has hidden or custom has veiled, to sport with the looks, to turn the neck, to loosen the hair?"[123] Ambrose looks to protect the consecrated virgins within the safe environs of the monastery and so to shield them from the worldliness outside its perimeters.

In *On Virginity*, Saint Ambrose again speaks up for the special place that consecrated virgins have within the church—clearly in defense against those who oppose his policy—and again the bishop has recourse to the Song of Songs to shore up his position. Using the full force of the erotic images of the Song of Songs, Ambrose imagines the virgin sleeping in her cell with her garment taken off (Song 5:3) as she hears Christ knocking (5:2) and reaching in through the window (2:9).[124] The virgin is to wait in her cell for this coming of Christ,[125] and when the door opens up and he enters in, the virgin should be ready: "So embrace whom you have sought; approach him to be filled with light; hold him and ask him not to depart quickly, pleading with him not to go away."[126] Ambrose is not afraid to use the erotic imagery of the Song of Songs to highlight the mutual desire between Christ and the consecrated virgin.

As Shuve points out, in this second book on virginity Ambrose places greater emphasis on the soul and on its spiritual purity than in his earlier work.[127] The virgin almost becomes a metaphor for the Christian soul, and Ambrose's warnings against immorality have a general applicability beyond the virgins he addresses. Christ, he insists, "is the bloom of lowliness, not of luxury, voluptuousness, of lasciviousness."[128] He maintains that Christ isn't impressed by "golden clothing, a precious necklace, or exquisite tiaras sparkling with

---

121. Ibid.
122. Ibid., 1.10.55 (*NPNF*[2] 10:372).
123. Ibid., 3.6.27 (*NPNF*[2] 10:385).
124. Ambrose, *On Virginity* 9.55 (Callam, 30).
125. Ibid., 9.68 (Callam, 35).
126. Ibid., 12.74 (Callam, 38).
127. Shuve, *Song of Songs*, 132, 134.
128. Ambrose, *On Virginity* 9.51 (Callam, 29).

jewels."[129] He lambasts the practice of curling one's hair.[130] And he warns the virgin against adultery: "Off with eye cosmetics and other follies of artificial beauty. Off with the allurements of an adulterous affection."[131]

Indeed, the virgin comes to embody the church as a whole (though Ambrose doesn't develop this point with the kind of typological detail that he explored in his book *Concerning Virgins*). The soul, he claims, is "one of the nation, one of the people."[132] He addresses the soul by saying, "You are one of the virgins the splendour of whose mind illuminates the grace of your body. For this reason are you compared to the Church."[133] The virgin's chastity and her longing for Christ are paradigmatic for the entire church's purity and spiritual fervor.[134] By so linking the virgin and the church, Ambrose not only elevates the status of the virgin within the ecclesial community, but he also powerfully links the personal and ecclesial interpretations of the Song.

When a number of years later (probably between 386 and 391) Ambrose returned to the Song of Songs in his book *Isaac, or the Soul*—likely a baptismal treatise originating in sermons preached to catechumens during Easter week[135]—he did so no longer in the context of a defense of virginity. Instead, the now much more experienced preacher explains the Song in the course of discussing Isaac's encounter with Rebekah by the well. Remarkably, Ambrose hardly deals with Genesis 24. Rebekah's encounter with Isaac becomes a straightforward allegory of the soul's union with Christ, which for Saint Ambrose is reason to turn the treatise into an extended commentary on the Song of Songs.

In several ways, the commentary is reminiscent of Origen's. Ambrose follows Origen in treating the bride as an image both of the church and of the soul. Regarding the former, he comments: "What does it mean, then: 'Let him kiss me with the kisses of his mouth'? Think upon the Church, in suspense over many ages at the coming of the Lord, long promised her through the prophets." And he immediately adds, "And think upon the soul, lifting herself up from the body and rejecting indulgence and fleshly delights and pleasures, and laying aside as well her concern for worldly vanities."[136]

It is the personal exegesis of the Song that really matters to Ambrose—though it is in the church (and in baptism) that the soul obtains her true

129. Ibid., 12.68 (Callam, 35).
130. Ibid., 12.71 (Callam, 37).
131. Ibid., 13.79 (Callam, 40).
132. Ibid., 12.68 (Callam, 35).
133. Ibid.
134. Shuve, *Song of Songs*, 111–12.
135. This is the judgment of Karl Schenkl in the introduction to the critical edition of *De Isaac vel anima* (CSEL 32/1, ii–iii).
136. Ambrose, *Isaac, or the Soul* 3.8 (FC 65:15).

identity.[137] The soul's union with Christ precludes bodily and material preoccupations. And so, when the soul drinks from the breast of the Word (Song 1:2), Ambrose doesn't just mention her enjoyment of the "knowledge of God" but adds that this knowledge is "richer than the joy of any bodily pleasure."[138] When the soul is drawn by the fragrance of the groom's ointments (Song 1:4) and the groom takes her into his royal chamber, the soul obtains her greatest blessing, seeing as she now rises from the body and scorns visible and material things.[139] For Ambrose, the reason the soul is "black and beautiful" (Song 1:5) is that she "has been darkened by her union with the body."[140] The soul admits that "the passions of the body have attacked me and the allurements of the flesh have given me my color."[141] Ambrose very much wants the bride to overcome the bodily passions, leave behind the lust of the body, and learn to resist the temptations of the world. Indeed, as Shuve puts it, "Unlike Origen . . . Ambrose is thoroughly preoccupied with the ascetic renunciation of the body, which marks his exegesis at every turn."[142]

As a mature theologian, Ambrose preached his *Homilies on Psalm 118* probably in the years 388 and 389.[143] The Song is never far from his mind as he preaches on the psalm, and in the first two sermons he deals with the Song's opening verses in some detail. Ambrose is again clearly dependent on Origen, and he reiterates that the betrothed virgin (the church) has been burning with desire for her betrothed for a long time: "At the world's beginning she was betrothed in paradise. She was prefigured in the flood, proclaimed in the Law, and called through the prophets. She has long awaited the redemption of man, the grace of the Gospel and the coming of the beloved. Now,

---

137. For Ambrose the human person is an ecclesially shaped person. Gerald P. Boersma, in a forthcoming essay ("Baptismal Identity in Ambrose's *De Isaac*"), argues persuasively that *Isaac, or the Soul* has for its overriding theme the renewal of the soul's identity in and through baptism.

138. Ambrose, *Isaac, or the Soul* 3.9 (FC 65:17).

139. Ibid., 4.11 (FC 65:19).

140. Ibid., 4.13 (FC 65:19). Similarly, Ambrose advises the soul: "Go out from the body and divest yourself of it wholly" (ibid., 5.47 [FC 65:38]). In *On Virginity*, Ambrose speaks of the four affections of the soul (anger, desire, pleasure, and fear) as the four horses of a chariot, and he explains that "the soul, weighed down by its perishable body, hardly knows herself" (*On Virginity* 15.95 [Callam, 47]). The chariot soul is meant to rise "above earthly things" (ibid., 17.111 [Callam, 54]) and to "fly away from earthly things" (ibid., 18.115 [Callam, 55–56]). It's important to keep in mind that in this context Ambrose also speaks of "bodily passions" (ibid., 15.95 [Callam, 47]), "worldly things" (ibid., 17.108 [Callam, 53]), and "bodily lusts" (ibid., 17.111 [Callam, 54]). He is more troubled by the body misdirecting the soul's affections than by the body per se. For a full discussion of Ambrose's understanding of the body-soul relationship, see G. Boersma, *Augustine's Early Theology of Image*, 102–11.

141. Ambrose, *Isaac, or the Soul* 4.13 (FC 65:19).

142. Shuve, *Song of Songs*, 138.

143. I am following the dating of Íde Ní Riain in Ambrose, *Homilies on Psalm 118 (119)*, x.

impatient at delay, she runs to receive his kisses and cries out: 'Let him kiss me with the kisses of his mouth' [Song 1:2]. She rejoices in these kisses and says: 'Your love is more delightful than wine' [Song 1:2]."[144] Ambrose adopts both Origen's identification of the bride as the church and his salvation-historical understanding of the opening lines of the Song.

When he turns to the "moral truth" of the Song's introduction, however, the Milanese preacher charts his own path. He depicts the bride's sordid history with reference to the haughty and lewd behavior of the "daughters of Zion" described in Isaiah 3:16. The bride, mindful of the prophets' many warnings to her, repents, and she "is now on fire with desire" and is troubled by her past behavior.[145] "She is dressed now in comely robe. No longer does she curl her hair. No longer does she wear gold, pearls, or gorgeous robes. Instead she clothes herself in modesty and simplicity."[146] The bride wants Christ to kiss her, which is what happens "whenever the Spirit of knowledge lights up our understanding."[147] She desires to keep the Lord's precepts, and recognizes that the "dreadful odour" that came from the pollution of sins has disappeared since Christ's name has been poured out like oil (Song 1:3).[148] The result is that now the world has become "everywhere redolent of the charm of chastity, the sweet perfume of faith, and the flower of integrity."[149] At that point in the Song, claims Saint Ambrose, Solomon finally abandons his moral instruction, as the bride turns from morals to mysteries, explaining that the king has brought her into his bridal chamber (Song 1:5).[150]

In his second homily, Ambrose reflects on the "young man" who corrects his ways (Ps. 118 [119]:9), and he uses John, the beloved disciple, as an example. While he used to be a fisherman, when Christ called him John instead followed the Lord (Matt. 4:21–22), "behaving as Christ's words prescribe: 'Let us love your breasts more than wine [Song 1:2].'"[151] Ambrose then pictures John as leaning his head on Jesus' breast (John 13:25), with the disciples amazed at the audacity of "sinful flesh" reposing on "the temple of the Word."[152] And so John's soul replies to his fellow disciples:

144. Ambrose, *Homilies on Psalm 118 (119)* 1.4 (Riain, 4).
145. Ibid., 1.5 (Riain, 4).
146. Ibid., 1.5 (Riain, 4–5).
147. Ibid., 1.5 (Riain, 5).
148. Ibid.
149. Ibid.
150. Ibid.
151. Ibid., 2.7 (Riain, 14). Riain uses italics to indicate Ambrose's biblical quotations, a practice that I have removed; instead I enclose biblical quotations in quotation marks, here and elsewhere.
152. Ibid., 2.8 (Riain, 15).

"I am dark but beautiful, daughters of Jerusalem" [Song 1:5], dark through sin, beautiful through grace. The flesh says: "I am dark but beautiful." Dark with the dust of the world, brushed off on me even though I strove against it! Beautiful with the oil of the spirit, which wiped off the dust of a sordid world. Dark through vice, but beautiful now through baptism, which has washed away all sin. I am dark because I have sinned, beautiful because Christ loves me. Rejected in the person of Eve, I have been restored through the Virgin and acknowledged in Mary.[153]

Ambrose's playful exegesis puts John in the position of the psalm's "young man," and the preacher links the young man's correcting of his ways with the grace received through the sacraments of the church and through the Virgin Mary.

Ambrose next moves to discuss the synagogue, for the bride's words in 1:5 are the synagogue's too. Here again, Ambrose develops Origen's initial reflections. He has the synagogue acknowledge that she is dark because she has sinned, yet beautiful because of the law (cf. Rom. 9:4). And so the synagogue asks not to be spurned for being dark (Song 1:6).[154] Thankfully, the Jewish bride's discoloring, which Ambrose explains as the result of the sun having left her, is not irreversible: "Do not think that because I am discoloured, the sun has utterly abandoned me, and that now that I am dejected it neither sees nor regards me. He has hidden himself from me because I did not keep his commandments. He will be reconciled with me when he sees me repent of my sins."[155] Saint Ambrose, like Hippolytus and Origen before him, hoped for Israel's repentance.

Ambrose probably wrote his two great mystagogical works, *The Sacraments* and *The Mysteries*, shortly after he preached on Psalm 118 (119), around 390 or 391.[156] It is in these two works that he most clearly relates the Song of Songs to the church's liturgy. In *The Sacraments* the bishop instructs newly baptized Christians in the faith by means of six short homilies.[157] He beautifully explains the sacraments of the church typologically by relating each of them to various Old Testament passages. In his fifth homily, preached on Saturday, the bishop

---

153. Ibid.

154. Ibid., 2.9 (Riain, 15).

155. Ibid. In Sermon 12, Ambrose places these same words of the bride in the mouth of the church: "As the orb of the Church says: 'Do not despise me because I am dark, the sun has not respected me.' She means that for a long time she lay blighted by winter's cold and frost, for the Sun of justice did not consider her worthy to be washed in the serene light of his face. Does it not seem to you like the icy cold of winter, all those ages when God was known to the Jews alone?" Ibid., 12.25 (Riain, 171).

156. Deferrari, introduction to *Saint Ambrose*, 267.

157. See the discussion in Shuve, *Song of Songs*, 153–55.

continues the instruction on the Eucharist that he had started the day before. Fairly quickly, the preacher turns to the Song of Songs: "You have come to the altar; the Lord Jesus calls you—both your soul and the Church—and He says: 'Let him kiss me with the kiss of his mouth [Song 1:2].'"[158]

Ambrose is quite personal in his homily, addressing the need for the soul of each of the neophytes or catechumens to come to Christ by means of the sacrament: "Your soul sees that it is cleansed of all sins, that it is worthy so as to be able to approach the altar of Christ. . . . It sees the marvelous sacraments and says: 'Let him kiss me with the kiss of His mouth,' that is, 'Let Christ impress a kiss upon me.'"[159] The reason the soul prays for Christ's kiss is that she recognizes that his breasts (the sacraments) are better than wine ("worldly pleasure") (Song 1:2).[160] Ambrose then depicts the "young maidens" of the next verse (Song 1:3) as renewed souls[161] whom Christ draws into his bedchamber (1:4)—or, as Ambrose informs his listeners, "'into his storeroom' or 'into his pantry,'" as the Greek text renders it.[162] The many dishes of this well-supplied pantry will make the meal—the Eucharist—a pleasant one.[163]

The Mysteries similarly consists of homilies preached during Easter week, and it bears many similarities to *The Sacraments*.[164] Also in *The Mysteries* the bishop of Milan explains by means of Old Testament typologies the sacramental mysteries through which the newly baptized Christians are entering the church. When the homily arrives at the point where the neophytes receive their white garments after being baptized, Ambrose is reminded of the change that the black bride undergoes in the Song of Songs: "The Church, having assumed these vestments through the laver of regeneration, says in the Canticles: 'I am black but beautiful, O ye daughters of Jerusalem' [Song 1:5], black through the frailty of human condition, beautiful through grace; black, because I am made up of sinners, beautiful by the sacrament of faith. Perceiving these vestments, the daughters of Jerusalem in amazement say: 'Who is this that cometh up made white?' [Song 8:5]. She was black; how was she suddenly made white?"[165] Ambrose doesn't just speak here of the souls of individual Christians. He clearly identifies the *church* with the bride who has turned white. And in what follows the bishop continues to

158. Ambrose, *Sacraments* 5.2.5 (FC 44:311).
159. Ibid., 5.2.7 (FC 44:311).
160. Ibid.
161. Ibid., 5.2.9 (FC 44:311).
162. Ibid., 5.2.11 (FC 44:312).
163. Ibid.
164. See the discussion in Shuve, *Song of Songs*, 152–53.
165. Ambrose, *Mysteries* 7.35 (FC 44:17–18).

reflect on Christ's praise of the church's beauty elsewhere in the Song of Songs.[166]

When he arrives at his discussion of the Eucharist, Ambrose emphasizes that after the consecration, the bread and wine really are the body and blood of Christ.[167] He then continues with a reference to Song 4:10, where the bride's breasts are said to have become more beautiful from wine. Ambrose sees here a reference to the blood that Christ gives his church to drink in the Eucharist, and so he has Christ address the church with the words, "How beautiful thy breasts have become, my sister, my spouse, how beautiful they have become from wine."[168] The union with Christ obtained in the Eucharist is for Ambrose the typological fulfillment of the Song's relationship between the bridegroom and the bride.

Ambrose assimilated Origen's twofold reading of the bride as both church and soul, but he did so by adding an ascetic dimension that was absent from Origen's reading of the Song. Interestingly, Ambrose was able to combine his asceticism with a broadly sacramental reading of the text, in which he addressed the economic and bodily conditions of his listeners, in which the erotic letter of the text played an indispensable role, and in which the sacramental life of the church functioned as the great archetype of the relationship between the groom and the bride.

Conclusion

Hippolytus, Origen, and Ambrose, despite the obvious differences in their readings of the Song of Songs, were united in their view that it must be read as an allegory. The Song is in the canon not because it is a love song celebrating the love between the king and the Shulamite but because it depicts the relationship between Christ and his people. This basic framework of the interpretation of the Song, shared by exegetes throughout the Great Tradition of the church, does not separate the physical and the spiritual, body and soul, letter and spirit. Quite the contrary: as we have seen, patristic theologians largely read the Song of Songs in a sacramental manner.

A number of elements in our three theologians' interpretation of the Song display this sacramentality: (1) the presence of the Song's spiritual meaning within the historical economy of salvation (Hippolytus and Origen); (2) the close link between the church and the soul—with both the history of the Old

166. Ibid., 7.37–39 (FC 44:18–19).
167. Ibid., 9.54 (FC 44:26).
168. Ibid., 9.55 (FC 44:26).

Testament (the letter) and the physical body serving their purpose when they aim at union with Christ (Origen); (3) the virgins' connection with the church and the Song's typological fulfillment within the liturgical celebration of the church (Ambrose); (4) concern for the moral integrity of the daily lives of the congregation (Ambrose); and (5) the use of the Song's sensual language to describe the relationship between Christ and the soul (Ambrose). Each of these characteristics counters the charge of a dichotomous reading of the Song.

This is not to say that dichotomous elements never entered into the exegesis of the Song. As we have seen, particularly Ambrose sometimes used language about the body and earthly life that is at least infelicitous. Still, I am somewhat suspicious of the relative ease with which late patristic and medieval authors are sometimes criticized for the way they treated the body and sexuality (as well as the letter of the text). Perhaps we ought to cut these early Christian readers a little slack. After all, as I mentioned earlier, the problem of dichotomizing cuts both ways. Today's nearly pandemic objectification of the body in advertising and pornography means that the pendulum has swung far in the opposite direction: we have become materialists, if not in theory then at least in practice. In such a context, a sacramental reading of the Song—one that recognizes that there's more to the Song than the physical eroticism that we see in the letter—is a welcome antidote. Yes, the Song of Songs is a "simple story," as Origen would put it; it's an ordinary love song. Sung within the church, however, its purpose is not to celebrate sexual union; it is to lead the reader to a closer union with Christ. That a love song served this purpose throughout the patristic period witnesses to the transformative power of a sacramental reading of Scripture.

9

PROPHETIC READING

Irenaeus, Cyril of Alexandria, Origen,
Eusebius, Gregory of Nyssa, Jerome, Ambrose,
and Augustine on the Servant Songs of Isaiah

Prophecy and Fulfillment: A Sacramental Bond

No Old Testament book plays as prominent a role in the New Testament as Isaiah. According to one estimate, "194 NT passages contain allusions to verses from 65 of Isaiah's 66 chapters."[1] It is fairly evident, when we look at some of the New Testament references to Isaiah, that the main reason for its popularity is its amenability to christological interpretation. In this chapter I will look at patristic exegesis of Isaiah, and in particular of Isaiah's Servant Songs, with a focus on the church fathers' christological reading of these poems.[2] It will be my argument that patristic readings of the Servant Songs should influence our understanding of the nature of biblical prophecy. It will become clear that the church fathers regarded prophecy not just as a

1. Schultz, "Isaiah, Book of," 342.
2. I will avoid language of "Deutero-Isaiah" or "Second Isaiah" for chaps. 40–55, which contain the four well-known Servant Songs. I do so not out of any strong conviction on the unitary authorship of Isaiah, but because it seems counterproductive to focus our exegesis on historical-critical questions; along with patristic authors, I am more interested in the canonical unity of the book of Isaiah and in its links with the New Testament witness about Jesus Christ and hence the overall biblical canon.

fore-telling of future events but, more importantly, as a *forth*-telling of the New Testament reality of Christ (and his church), a reality that the fathers believed is deeply embedded within the promissory words of the prophets themselves.

Prophecy, for the church fathers, was not just a matter of looking ahead—horizontally—to an entirely separate event within an entirely new context. Prophecy and fulfillment, though obviously chronologically distinct from one another, were connected through an intimate, sacramental bond. This close connection between prophecy and fulfillment, ultimately grounded in the providence of God, means that the church fathers believed the New Testament truth or reality (*alētheia* or *res*) to be nestled within the Old Testament shadow or sacrament (*skia* or *sacramentum*).[3] This means that for them the most important connection between prophecy and fulfillment was not historical or horizontal but participatory or vertical: they saw the New Testament fulfillment as the transcendent reality (to use an upward metaphor) or the depth dimension (to use a downward image) of Old Testament prophecy—the treasure hidden in the field of prophecy. With regard to the Servant Songs, this means that the church fathers regarded *Jesus Christ as the original truth or reality on whom the prophetic imagery of the servant was patterned*. The prophecies of Isaiah therefore required a sacramental approach to interpretation, so the church fathers believed. Only by taking the sacramental reality of Christ as one's starting point could one hope to come to an understanding of the Old Testament prophecies.

Before analyzing the church fathers' writings, I will begin by clarifying in greater detail what patristic sacramental reading of prophetic literature implied, which I will do by means of a discussion of nineteenth-century Tractarian Edward Pusey.[4] Pusey, greatly enamored of the church fathers' understanding of prophecy, can help us grasp some of the key insights that inspired their christological approach to Old Testament prophecy. Next, I hope to make clear that the fathers approached Isaiah's prophecies (and in particular the Servant Song of Isaiah 53) from the starting point of their faith in Jesus Christ. This in turn leads to a discussion of how the history of interpretation can be of help to us as we follow the fathers' lead in reading the prophets christologically. Turning therefore to their reading of the Servant

3. For the significance of providence in spiritual exegesis, see Matthew Levering's excellent book *Participatory Biblical Exegesis*.

4. The Tractarians were a group of high-church Anglicans, also known as the Oxford Movement, who published the *Tracts for the Times* between 1833 and 1841 as they turned to the early church in order to promote a more sacramental approach to the liturgy and theology. Other well-known Tractarians were John Henry Newman and John Keble.

Songs, I will finally analyze how the fathers discovered the real presence of Christ in the servant depicted in Isaiah.

Edward Pusey's Sacramental Typology

During the winter of 1836–1837, Edward Pusey, Hebrew scholar at Christ Church, Oxford, delivered his "Lectures on Types and Prophecies in the Old Testament."[5] Pusey had studied in Germany between 1825 and 1827, and he was troubled by the historicist approach to biblical studies that he witnessed among contemporary German scholars.[6] He became convinced that this same rationalist approach was taking hold among theologians in England as they were influenced by the deist mindset of the previous century.[7] Pusey was troubled, however, not just by the critical, rationalist theology that increasingly came to dominate the nineteenth-century theological world, but also by the reaction to it among conservative scholars as they used an equally rationalist, apologetic approach to Old Testament prophecy: they attempted to prove the truth of the Christian faith rationally by providing evidence from Old Testament prophecy in favor of the Christian faith. For Pusey, the two approaches seemed each other's mirror opposites.

The rationalist methodology of conservative apologetics approached prophecy with a view to securing rationally and definitively the truth of the Christian faith: the fact that Old Testament prophecies were fulfilled in the New Testament was treated as evidence of the truth of the Christian faith. William Van Mildert, bishop of Durham, maintained in his 1814 Bampton Lectures (*The General Principles of Scripture-Interpretation*) that only Old Testament types expressly authorized by Scripture should be regarded as genuine.[8] Thomas Hartwell Horne's influential 1818 publication, *An Introduction to the Critical Study and Knowledge of the Holy Scriptures*, also argued that there were rational criteria that one should use to determine the legitimacy (or illegitimacy) of treating something in the Old Testament as a type. Horne maintained that for something to function as a type, the Old

---

5. I am much indebted to George Westhaver, principal of Pusey House in Oxford, who introduced me to Pusey's lectures on typology through his excellent dissertation, "The Living Body of the Lord: E. B. Pusey's 'Types and Prophecies of the Old Testament,'" and who also kindly directed me to Pusey's lectures themselves.

6. Pusey critiqued German rationalism in his book *An Historical Enquiry into the Causes of the Rationalistic Character Lately Predominant in the Theology of Germany* (1828).

7. Pusey had in mind scholars such as Richard Whately, Thomas Arnold, and Renn Hampden. See Westhaver, "Living Body," 32–33.

8. Ibid., 146.

Testament author must have *designed* or *intended* it to function as a pre-figuration.[9] And John Davison's *Discourses on Prophecy* (1824) presented a plea for "clear, apparent and undeniable" criteria to assess what constitutes genuine prophecy.[10]

Pusey was convinced that these rationalist apologetic approaches could not function as a proper bulwark in defense of the Christian faith. George Westhaver, in his dissertation on Pusey's lectures, explains that "Pusey's analysis of German theology and orthodoxism lies behind his criticism of an evidence-based approach to prophecy in the 'Lectures.' The rigid insistence that prophecy must conform to analytic categories and serve as evidence is also a 'dry dialectic system.'"[11] The scholastic orthodoxy of the apologetic approach, Pusey argued, made the mistake of trying to combat historical critics by accepting the very rationalist methodology that the latter employed. This means that the battle had been conceded before it had even started. In particular, Pusey objected to the assumption of common, neutral ground, with prophecy being treated as something to be analyzed and dissected in order thereby to determine its possibly divine origin:

> In the apologetic use, prophecy is addressed to those who believe not, or, as if men believed not; the truth of the prophecy, which was "assumed" or rather accepted and believed as the very word of God in the former case becomes now the very point at issue. People disclaim or set aside for the time all knowledge of it as being the word of God, all except its previous existence, and would produce belief by the abstract argument that an event, not cognizable by human foresight, could only have been predicted by God, and that consequently the system wherein such predictions were found, came from God.[12]

Pusey maintained that a proper reading of prophecy is sensitive to the presence of Christ in the prophetic message and as such takes its starting point in the divine character of the prophetic message rather than trying to argue for this on purely rational grounds.

By treating the divine character of Old Testament prophecy as something established rationally and a posteriori rather than accepted a priori by faith, the apologetic school ended up focusing strictly on the linear character of chronologically separate events: the point was to see whether or not prophecies were in fact fulfilled later in history. Pusey noted that this approach moved

9. Ibid., 144.
10. Pusey, "Lectures," 10. Cf. Westhaver, "Living Body," 48–49.
11. Pusey, "Lectures," 36.
12. Ibid., 4.

the focus away from Christ as the religious contents of prophecy.[13] The basic problem, as Pusey saw it, was that the apologetic method "limited prophecy to the office of 'foretelling,' abstracted from the subject foretold."[14] It is the absence of a genuine focus on the christological reality of the prophetic witness that concerned Pusey the most. And so he insisted that a rationalist defense of Christianity, centered on prophecy fulfillment, would ironically end up losing the very heart of the Christian faith.

Pusey therefore set out to establish a third way of approaching Old Testament prophecy. Encouraged by discussions with his friend August Tholuck, a Pietist professor of theology at Halle, Pusey developed what he believed to be a more robust treatment of Old Testament prophecy, one that was in line with the church fathers' earlier approach. He countered the apologetic use of prophecy with the comment "Prophecy is given to direct and guide faith, not to create it."[15] As a result, Pusey, from the outset, focused on the christological contents of Old Testament prophecy. He maintained that the christological archetype was always already present in the Old Testament prophetic type. Westhaver summarizes Pusey's approach as follows: "In addition to the historical or horizontal correspondences between Old Testament types and their New Testament fulfillment, Pusey emphasizes a vertical dimension, the way in which types participate in the reality of the eternal Archetype, the Son of God, in whom all types are fulfilled."[16] The co-inherence of type and archetype was key to Pusey's view of Old Testament prophecy.

Pusey developed what we may characterize as a sacramental approach to prophetic interpretation. He draws attention to the sacramental relationship between prophecy and fulfillment when he comments: "It has been well said, that God has appointed, as it were, a sort of sacramental union between the type and the archetype, so that as the type were nothing, except in as far as it represents, and is the medium of conveying the archetype to the mind, so neither can the archetype be conveyed except through the type. Though the consecrated element be not the sacrament, yet neither can the soul of the sacrament be obtained without it. God has joined them together, and man may not and can not put them asunder."[17] For Pusey, there was a sacramental

---

13. Cf. Pusey's comment: "The religious element of prophecy was of necessity withdrawn from their sight, for although it has more persuasiveness, it has less of demonstration. The facts were considered apart from their religious meaning, men argued when they should have worshipped." Ibid., 1.

14. Ibid.

15. Ibid., 4.

16. Westhaver, "Living Body," 18.

17. Pusey, "Lectures," 23. Pusey also speaks of Melchizedek's sacrifice (ibid., 73) and of the Red Sea crossing and the gift of manna (ibid., 26) as sacraments, and he refers to the general

link between the shadow of the Old Testament type and the reality of the christological archetype in the New Testament, and on his understanding the two were inseparable. As Westhaver summarizes: "For Pusey the principle of typology is fundamentally a sacramental principle by which spiritual or eternal truth is communicated by typical elements consecrated through Christ's self-emptying in the Incarnation."[18] Perhaps the deepest reason Pusey objected to the apologetic school of Old Testament prophecy is that he regarded its representatives as antisacramental: they ignored or set aside the christological reality as something indifferent and extraneous to the rational and apologetic purposes that they had in mind for Old Testament prophecies. For Pusey, in contrast, a sacramental reading approached Old Testament prophecy with the question of where the prophetic text reveals the real presence of Christ.

Looking for Christ in Isaiah's Prophecies

The christological reading advocated by Pusey appears to have solid grounding in the New Testament's own treatment of Isaiah, and in particular of the Servant Songs. Robert Wilken, whose volume on Isaiah in The Church's Bible series I will be following in much of this chapter, mentions five Gospel passages that connect the story of Christ with Isaiah.[19] Matthew's Gospel refers to John the Baptist's preaching of the kingdom as the fulfillment of the prophecy of Isaiah 40: "The voice of one crying in the wilderness: 'Prepare the way of the Lord; make his paths straight'" (Matt. 3:3). The same Gospel writer reads Isaiah 7:14 as referring to the virgin birth ("Behold, the virgin shall conceive and bear a son, and they shall call his name Immanuel" [Matt. 1:23]). In Luke's Gospel, Jesus appropriates Isaiah 61 with the words "Today this scripture has been fulfilled in your hearing" (Luke 4:21); he claims that it is in him that the freedom of the Year of Jubilee (legislated in Lev. 25:10) finds its true reality. When in Matthew 11 John sends his disciples to Jesus to ask him whether he really is the Messiah, Jesus' reply—"Go and tell John what you hear and see: the blind receive their sight and the lame walk, lepers are cleansed and the deaf hear, and the dead are raised up, and the poor have good news preached to them. And blessed is the one who is not offended by me" (Matt. 11:4–6)—includes references to three Isaianic passages.[20] Finally,

---

18. Westhaver, "Living Body," 182–83.

19. Wilken, *Isaiah*, xx.

20. The Isaiah passages echoed in Jesus' words are Isa. 29:18 ("In that day the deaf shall hear the words of a book, and out of their gloom and darkness the eyes of the blind shall see"); 35:5–6

"sacramental character of the Old Testament" (ibid., 136 [p. 199 of Pusey's 1851 letter to the bishop of London]).

in Matthew 12, Jesus warns people not to tell anyone who he is (12:16), which for Matthew identifies him as the servant of Isaiah, who "will not quarrel or cry aloud" (12:19; cf. Isa. 42:2). The quiet way in which the servant establishes justice is something that finds its true reality (*res*) in Jesus' insistence that his identity as Messiah be kept quiet. Each of these Gospel passages reads Isaiah christologically. When Pusey took Christ as the key to the interpretation of Old Testament prophecy, it seems he was simply following New Testament precedent.

Particularly, the four Servant Songs lend themselves to such christological interpretation, and this too is reflected already in the Gospels as well as in the remainder of the New Testament. Wilken mentions that the first Servant Song (Isa. 42:1–4) is quoted in Matthew 12:18–21.[21] The second Servant Song (Isa. 49:1–6) is referenced in Acts 13:47; 2 Corinthians 6:2; and Revelation 7:16–17.[22] The third Servant Song (Isa. 50:4–9) is cited in Matthew 26:67.[23] And the last Servant Song (Isa. 52:13–53:12) is prominent throughout the New Testament: Matthew 8:17; Luke 22:37; John 12:38; Acts 8:32–33; Romans 10:16; 15:21; and 1 Peter 2:22–24 all refer back to the suffering servant of Isaiah 53.[24] In each of these quotations from the Servant Songs, the suffering servant is linked to Jesus Christ or to the New Testament realities of faith. According to the New Testament authors, therefore, Isaiah's servant poems find their reality in Christ and in the church. When these writers reflected on the person and work of Jesus Christ in the light of the Old Testament, time and again they felt the need to turn to the Servant Songs, simply because they observed the remarkable fact that Christ's identity and mission fit, almost hand in glove, with the depictions of Isaiah's servant of the Lord.[25]

That many of these passages from Isaiah have become popular in the church, and that many Christians read them naturally in the light of Christ's coming, is largely because already in the New Testament itself they are both popular and treated christologically. But because we're so inundated with

---

("Then the eyes of the blind shall be opened, and the ears of the deaf unstopped; then shall the lame man leap like a deer, and the tongue of the mute sing for joy"); and 61:1 ("The Spirit of the Lord GOD is upon me, because the LORD has anointed me to bring good news to the poor").

21. Wilken, *Isaiah*, 294.

22. Ibid., 366–67.

23. Ibid., 382.

24. Ibid., 414–16.

25. As Fr. John Behr pointed out to me, it is also true that this similarity between the Servant Songs and the mission of Jesus Christ stems from the fact that the language of Isaiah shaped the way the evangelists and apostles understood the Christ event, and so they drew on Isaianic language in their depiction of him. In other words, the faith of the early Christian church is grounded, from the outset, in a christological reading of the Old Testament.

these christological readings of Isaiah, we can easily fail to notice the controversial nature of this interpretive move, something of which, by contrast,
people in the early church were keenly aware. In what follows, I will briefly
reflect on how one early Christian—Philip the evangelist, in Acts 8—read
Isaiah in the light of Christ *without* the advantage of having a copy of the
New Testament in his back pocket, which means he was undoubtedly aware
of how radical and controversial an explanation he was proposing to the
Ethiopian eunuch. Controversial or not, christological readings were of the
essence for early Christians as they were trying to come to grips with their
identity. The question of whether or not the various moments of Jesus' life
could actually be found back in Isaiah was not just an interesting academic
question: without Isaiah being read christologically, it was impossible for
early Christians to maintain that Jesus was the one that the church *claimed*
he was. After all, the church could only make her claims about Jesus on the
basis of the Scriptures—and, at least until well into the second century, this
meant on the basis of the Old Testament.

Christopher Seitz—who as a student of Brevard Childs and the Yale school
of interpretation wants to read Isaiah in its broad, canonical context—refers
in his 2001 book, *Figured Out*, to the second-century dialogue between Christian convert Justin Martyr and his Jewish counterpart, Trypho. Central to the
exchange chronicled in *Dialogue with Trypho*, explains Seitz, was the identity
of Jesus. Justin recognized that as a Christian he was obliged to argue—on the
basis of the "oracles of God" (the church's Old Testament)—that Jesus was
the Messiah and had divine status. Seitz comments: "When the New Testament
emerged in the form we know it now, the Gospels in genre are essentially about
what Justin was about in his dialogue with Trypho: sustained argument with
the larger purpose of showing that Jesus is who the scriptures of Israel had in
mind. He is the One God promised. At God's name, at Jesus' name, every knee
shall bow, an exegetical move which reveals later *homoousia* logic."[26] The early
Christians turned to the (Old Testament) Scriptures, often in spirited dialogue
with Jewish detractors, in order to prove from this public witness that Jesus was
who the church claimed he was. "It was important," explains Seitz, "that Jesus
was who God said he was and would be, and that reference to some inherited,
public witness could validate this."[27] What Seitz calls the "inherited, public witness" validating Jesus' identity was of course the Old Testament. And within
this inherited, public witness, Isaiah—and within Isaiah, particularly the Servant
Songs—was the most notable of the documents revealing the identity of Jesus.

26. Seitz, *Figured Out*, 108.
27. Ibid., 104.

Christ as the Suffering Servant of Isaiah 53

The fourth and most well-known Servant Song (Isa. 52:13–53:12) makes for an interesting case study in this respect. It functions, both in the subsequent Scriptures and in the patristic tradition, as an important witness to the identity of Jesus Christ.[28] As already indicated, however, christological or messianic readings of this passage are by no means uncontroversial. Also today, many disagree on whether or not we should identify Isaiah's suffering servant—bearing our sins (53:4), wounded for our transgressions (53:5), led like a sheep to the slaughter and silent as a lamb before its shearer (53:7)—as the coming Messiah.[29] For Christian readers, this question is of particular importance, since, as we have seen, the New Testament frequently identifies Christ with the suffering servant.

The most significant passage in this regard is perhaps Acts 8, where Philip meets the Ethiopian eunuch. When the eunuch reads Isaiah 53:7–8 and asks Philip who the prophet means by the sheep that is led to the slaughter and by the lamb that is dumb before its shearers, Philip, "beginning with this Scripture . . . told him the good news about Jesus" (Acts 8:35).[30] Perhaps the one point to take note of is that Philip's engagement with the prophetic text is rather different from what today we typically understand exegesis to be. Let's look at this more closely. The eunuch has been reading Isaiah 53:7–8 ("Like a sheep he was led to the slaughter and like a lamb before its shearer is silent, so he opens not his mouth. In his humiliation justice was denied him. Who can describe his generation? For his life is taken away from the earth" [Acts 8:32–33]). He asks Philip the obvious question, which still occupies contemporary exegetes: "About whom, I ask you, does the prophet say this, about himself or about someone else?" (Acts 8:34). Put in contemporary exegetical parlance, the eunuch is asking about the identity of the suffering servant. Philip's answer, as we have already seen, is direct and to the point: "Then Philip opened his mouth, and beginning with this Scripture he told

---

28. Treating this passage (Isa. 52:13–53:12) as a distinct unit—the fourth Servant Song—is not without its problems. After all, the next verse (54:1) sings of the "barren one" who will have more children than the one who is married. Saint Paul quotes this text in Gal. 4:27 and applies it to the missionary success of the New Testament church. Following this Pauline appropriation of Isa. 54:1, the subsequent tradition often regarded the church's proliferation throughout the world as the outcome of Christ's passion (described in Isa. 52:13–53:12). I thank Fr. John Behr for pointing out to me that the modern delimitation of the fourth Servant Song limits our christological and ecclesial appreciation of the broader context of the passage.

29. See Goldingay and Payne, *Commentary on Isaiah 40–55*, 2:284–88.

30. I have discussed the meeting between Philip and the Ethiopian eunuch on two previous occasions, and so I will be relatively brief here. See H. Boersma, *Heavenly Participation*, 130–36; H. Boersma, *Sacramental Preaching*, 1–12.

him the good news about Jesus" (Acts 8:35). In other words, *Jesus* is the suffering servant. Although the eunuch wants to understand the passage he is reading, or at least would like to know who the servant is, Philip does not respond by interpreting Isaiah 52:13–53:12 in a way that would satisfy most contemporary standards of exegesis. Instead, he proclaims Jesus, using the Servant Song simply as his starting point. Then again, perhaps this is how Luke wants us to understand exegesis: not as a historical reconstruction of the precise original intent of the biblical author but as an uncovering of the God-given christological contents of the "good news about Jesus" in any given biblical passage that we're trying to understand.

The church fathers unanimously saw the presence of Christ throughout Isaiah 53's description of the suffering servant. But the verses that the eunuch read in his chariot (vv. 7–8) were the most celebrated of the entire poem. Already Saint Irenaeus referred back to this episode and these verses in the late second century, when in *Against Heresies* he argued that Christ fulfilled the Old Testament prophecies. Quoting the same passage that the eunuch was reading, Irenaeus comments that "Philip easily persuaded him [i.e., the eunuch] to believe in him, that he was Christ Jesus, who was crucified under Pontius Pilate and suffered what the prophet had predicted, and that he was the Son of God who gives eternal life to all." Once he believed and was baptized, explains Irenaeus, the eunuch "went his way rejoicing to be the herald in Ethiopia of Christ's coming. Philip had to exert little effort with this man because he had already been trained in the fear of God by the prophets."[31] Irenaeus insists that the conversion of the Ethiopian eunuch was easy precisely because the fourth Servant Song so obviously prepares the way for faith in Christ.

As they read about the silence of the servant (who "does not open his mouth")—which Isaiah illustrates by means of the metaphors of a sheep about to be slaughtered and a lamb ready to be shorn—the church fathers took the same approach that Philip took: beginning with the biblical text, they reflected on the good news of Jesus. Origen (ca. 185–ca. 254), in expositing John 1:29, was interested especially in the sacrificial death by which the "Lamb of God" takes away the sin of the world. Taking silence as an indication of purity, he comments that Isaiah describes the Lamb of God as a sheep dumb before its shearers "because by his death we have all been purified."[32] And he goes on to say: "Like a magical charm his death is an antidote against the powers of evil and the sin of those wishing to receive the truth. For the death of Christ has made ineffectual the powers who make war on the human race, and by its

---

31. Irenaeus, *Against Heresies* 4.23.2, quoted in Wilken, *Isaiah*, 425.
32. Origen, *Commentary on John* 1.233–34, quoted in Wilken, *Isaiah*, 426.

ineffable power has delivered the life of every believer from the hold of sin."[33] Origen also turns to Revelation 5:6, which speaks of "a little lamb 'standing as though slain,'" and he comments that "the Lamb offered himself as a victim on behalf of the world and purchased us with his own blood from him who had taken possession of us when we had sold ourselves by our sins."[34] Significantly, the theologian from Alexandria speaks of the sacrifices of the law as a "symbol" (*symbolon*), and he insists that they are "like this sacrifice."[35] Origen doesn't say that Christ's sacrifice is like the symbolic sacrifices of the law, but says that the latter are like the former. Christ's sacrifice is for him the great archetypal paradigm, on which the preceding symbols are modeled.

Saint Augustine (354–430), in a short sermon on the sacraments that must rank as a rhetorical masterpiece, explains how it is that the truth has sounded forth to the ends of the world (Ps. 18 [19]:3–4). He begins by quoting 1 Corinthians 5:7: "Christ, our Passover, has been sacrificed."[36] The bishop of Hippo immediately adds, "This has been previously foretold by the prophet"—which he follows up by quoting Isaiah 53:7. Again, much like Philip and Origen before him, Saint Augustine begins with the New Testament reality in order then to search for corroboration in the Old Testament shadows. That is to say, he assumes from the very outset that the lamb mentioned in Isaiah 53 is Jesus Christ, who has been sacrificed as our Passover lamb. The reason he feels at liberty to turn from 1 Corinthians 5 back to Isaiah 53 is, undoubtedly, that both chapters not only mention a lamb but also refer to its being slaughtered.[37]

With this basic framework in mind, Augustine then investigates the identity of the lamb more deeply. "Who is this?" he asks.[38] Since the next verse in Isaiah mentions that "in his humiliation his judgment was taken away," Augustine proceeds to explore the theme of Christ's humiliation and exaltation in the Scriptures—keeping in mind Isaiah's discourse of a lamb or a sheep that is slaughtered. (Augustine ignores the shearing of the lamb mentioned in verse 7.) He immediately turns to Revelation 5, reminding his hearers that the lamb (5:6) is at the same time a lion (5:5)—a king of "power and authority." He then plays on the dual theme of humiliation and exaltation, of lamb and lion: "Who is this, both lamb and lion? He endured death as a lamb; he devoured it as a lion. Who is this, both lamb and lion? Gentle and strong, lovable and

---

33. Ibid. (translation modified).

34. Ibid. Here and throughout I have replaced Wilken's use of emphasis (bold and italics for biblical quotations) with quotation marks.

35. Ibid.

36. Augustine, *Sermon* 375A.1–2, quoted in Wilken, *Isaiah*, 427.

37. Isa. 53:7 uses ordinary terminology for "sheep" and "lamb," while 1 Cor. 5:7 says that the "Passover lamb" (*to pascha*) has been sacrificed.

38. Augustine, *Sermon* 375A.1–2, quoted in Wilken, *Isaiah*, 427.

terrifying, innocent and mighty, silent when being judged . . . roaring when he comes to judge."[39] In other words, Saint Augustine sees Christ as a lamb in his passion and as a lion in his resurrection.

Then, however, the African preacher reverses himself. It cannot be right that Christ is first only a lamb and next only a lion. And so Augustine explains that Christ is both lamb *and* lion in both his passion *and* his resurrection. He argues this by means of two simple biblical quotations, from Genesis 49 and Revelation 14:

> Let us see him as a lion in his passion: Jacob said, "You have gone up; lying down you have slept like a lion" (Gen. 49:9). Let us see him as a lamb in his resurrection. the book of Revelation, when it was talking about the eternal glory of virgins, declared, "They follow the Lamb wherever he goes" (Rev. 14:4). The same book of Revelation says, what I mentioned just now, "The Lion from the tribe of Judah has conquered, to open the book" (Rev. 5:5). Why a lamb in his passion? Because he underwent death without being guilty of any iniquity. Why a lion in his passion? Because in being slain, he slew death. Why a lamb in his resurrection? Because his innocence is everlasting. Why a lion in his resurrection? Because everlasting also is his might.[40]

According to Augustine, the sleep of a lion mentioned in Genesis 49:9 implies that Christ was a lion not just in his resurrection but also already in his death. And the fact that a lamb takes the virgins' lead in Revelation 14:4 means that Christ was a lamb not only in his death but that he continued to be so in his resurrection. Theologically, the reason that Christ's exaltation begins already in his death is that it is precisely by dying that he conquered death, and the reason for his continued humiliation in the resurrection is that his lamb-like "innocence" continues into the resurrection.[41]

Saint Augustine's sermon, while playful in its rhetoric, makes a significant exegetical maneuver in the service of an equally important doctrinal point. Exegetically, the bishop of Hippo feels at liberty to identify Christ as the lamb of Isaiah 53 because both 1 Corinthians 5:7 and Revelation 5:6 describe Christ as a lamb undergoing sacrificial death. In other words, the intertextual echoes are so strong that Augustine cannot but tie the Old Testament

39. Ibid.
40. Ibid.
41. I am imposing the theological categories of humiliation and exaltation onto Augustine. For the most part this isn't a problem, but it is perhaps important to note that Augustine doesn't actually speak of a continued humiliation in the resurrection: Christ is the lamb also in the resurrection because of his "innocence," claims Augustine. The language of "innocence" doesn't quite map onto that of "humiliation."

prophecy directly to its New Testament fulfillment in Christ. This in turn allows him to balance the lamb metaphor with that of a lion, seeing as Revelation 5:5–6 identifies the risen Lord as both lion and lamb. Clearly, at this point Augustine has moved beyond the text of Isaiah 53. But this in no way bothers him: it is important to Augustine not just to establish the original meaning of the text but to give a full exposition of the theological meaning of Christ's humiliation, and he can do this only by elaborating also on the meaning of Christ's exaltation, which he does by means of the lion metaphor taken from the book of Revelation.

What stands out most clearly, perhaps, in the early church's approach to Isaiah 53 is the natural ease with which it assumed Christ to be the suffering servant. Of course, the church fathers took their cue from the numerous places in the New Testament that interpret this chapter christologically. But it seems to me that something more is going on than the church fathers merely following the New Testament lead. As we have seen, they never wavered in their christological reading; the identity of the suffering servant wasn't in doubt in any way. Much like the Ethiopian eunuch— who, we must keep in mind, read Isaiah without the benefit of numerous New Testament quotations of Isaiah 53—they were "easily persuaded" (as Irenaeus puts it) that the suffering servant is none other than Jesus Christ. I suspect that the reason is that the church fathers were like Philip (and like much of the New Testament) in the way they approached Isaiah: their starting point was the conviction that Jesus Christ is the sacramental reality already present within the prophetic descriptions of Isaiah's suffering servant.

Christological Reading and the *Wirkungsgeschichte* of the Text

We are prone to overlook the startling character of the church's use of Isaiah because of our familiarity with christological readings of the prophet. Most of us have been conditioned or habituated, as it were, to read the Isaianic passages quoted in the New Testament christologically. This makes it easier for us to accept the legitimacy of such christological readings. In class I sometimes do a thought experiment to illustrate that it is our deeply ingrained personal and cultural memories associated with a particular passage that determine to a large extent how comfortable we are with a certain interpretation. I read to my students Isaiah 40:1–2 ("Comfort, comfort my people, says your God. Speak tenderly to Jerusalem, and cry to her that her warfare is ended, that her iniquity is pardoned, that she has received from the LORD's hand double for all her sins") and then ask them what this passage is about. My mostly evangelical students typically respond that this passage speaks of the forgiveness of sins we receive through Christ, which leads to a discussion on why as a class we are pretty much in agreement that this is how the passage should be read. In the process I point out that the New Testament doesn't quote these verses anywhere, which adds some urgency to the question of why we see the atoning work of Christ referenced in this passage. Students usually—and rightly, I think—point to Handel's *Messiah* as the most likely reason they see the atoning suffering of Christ reflected in Isaiah 40:1–2. Most have heard the *Messiah* numerous times, are therefore intimately familiar with these opening words of Isaiah 40, and as a result interpret the passage in the light of Christ. It is the way we regularly sing along with Handel's *Messiah* that inclines us to read these lines as a reference to the work of Christ.

Admittedly, the thought experiment is a bit misleading: it is not just the *Messiah* that makes most of us read Isaiah 40:1–2 christologically; there are also good exegetical grounds for doing so. Most importantly, perhaps, even though verses 1 and 2 may not be quoted in the New Testament,[42] the verses that immediately follow *do* show up in the Gospels. Verse 3 ("A voice cries: 'In the wilderness prepare the way of the LORD; make straight in the desert a highway for our God'") is linked in each of the Gospels with John the Baptist (Matt. 3:3; Mark 1:3; Luke 3:4; John 1:23). His is the voice calling in the desert. If the Gospels take verse 3 of chapter 40 christologically, this would provide at least a good prima facie rationale for also reading the immediately preceding verses of Isaiah 40 in light of the christological reality of the New Testament. Handel appears to have had solid exegetical warrant for including Isaiah 40:1–2 in his *Messiah*.

The basic point of the thought experiment seems valid. When reading Isaiah 40:1–2, we interpret it christologically *not* because we know that the Gospels quote the next verse and relate it to the incarnation. (Very few of us, perhaps only New Testament scholars, have such intimate knowledge both of Isaiah and of the Gospels as to make these immediate associations.) The reason many of us read Isaiah 40:1–2 as a reference to Christ's work is, simply put, that Handel read these verses this way. It is our familiarity with the *Messiah* that predisposes us to read the opening verses of Isaiah 40 in the light of Christ.

There is a larger point to be made here: the way in which the church's tradition has read or received the biblical text over time colors the way we read it. Hermeneutical theorist Hans-Georg Gadamer refers to this reception history

---

42. Rev. 18:6 ("Pay her back as she herself has paid back others, and repay her double for her deeds") does quote the last line of Isa. 40:2 but refers to it not in relation to Christ's work but as a call of vengeance against Babylon.

as *Wirkungsgeschichte*—literally, the historical functioning of a particular text. Our interpretation of the biblical text depends in part on the way God's people have read it through the centuries. Gadamer's *Truth and Method*, first published in 1960, opposes the notion that we arrive at the meaning of a text (not just that of the Bible) by scientifically establishing what it is that the author originally had in mind.[43] Gadamer opposes the historicist notion that a certain "method" would enable one to arrive scientifically at the meaning of the text.[44] In opposition to Friedrich Schleiermacher and Wilhelm Dilthey, he maintains that we go wrong when we identify the meaning of a text with authorial intent and when we think that a scientific method gives us access to this meaning.[45] It is not that either the author or the text is irrelevant according to Gadamer; he doesn't reduce interpretation to the whims of a reader's subjective response. As Jens Zimmermann explains: "Gadamer's entire work rests on the premise that hermeneutics is not subjective since the interpreter strives to align himself with the horizon of the interpreted object. While prejudices are essential for our engagement of texts from the past, understanding comes into its own when the prejudgments it employs are no longer arbitrary but dictated by the object of interpretation."[46] Zimmermann's cautionary comment makes clear that Gadamer's hermeneutics does not allow a reader simply to impose his own notions onto the text. Meaning, Gadamer explains, is what happens when the reader's own horizon fuses with that of the text.

The consequence, according to Gadamer, is that the *Wirkungsgeschichte* of a text determines in part which readings are plausible and which are not.[47] "*Wirkungsgeschichte*," explains Mark Knight, "insists that the interpretative tradition, including the present, is active whenever we read and always needs to be taken into account."[48] The larger point with regard to biblical hermeneutics is that the way the church has read the Old Testament over time legitimately enters into its meaning. New Testament scholar Markus Bockmuehl, in his book *Seeing the Word*, makes a strong case for the importance of the *Wirkungsgeschichte* of the biblical text. On his understanding, the field of New Testament studies needs to reorient its focus on the biblical text's functioning in the history of the church:

43. Cf. Gadamer's comment: "Not just occasionally but always, the meaning of a text goes beyond its author. That is why understanding is not merely a reproductive but always a productive activity as well." *Truth and Method*, 296.

44. Ibid., 3–9, et passim.

45. Ibid., 184–97, 231–42.

46. Zimmermann, *Recovering Theological Hermeneutics*, 40.

47. Gadamer, *Truth and Method*, 300–307.

48. Knight, "*Wirkungsgeschichte*," 138.

My first suggestion is that New Testament scholars explicitly adopt the history of the influence of the New Testament as an integral and indeed inescapable part of the exercise in which they are engaged. Among the numerous benefits of this move would be a more historically embedded understanding of not just the background but also the foreground (so to speak) of the New Testament, including its reception and understanding in the patristic period and beyond. Instead of perpetually going behind the text, the whole battery of historical-critical and synchronic tools should usefully be applied to approaching the New Testament from its meaning and function "in front of the text," where it was in fact heard and heeded (or ignored).[49]

Bockmuehl makes his case with regard to the New Testament, but the point is equally valid with regard to the Old Testament. Instead of focusing only on what lies "behind the text" (its background), interpreters ought to focus also on what goes on "in front of the text" (its foreground); that is to say, they should keep in mind its *Wirkungsgeschichte*. The meaning of a text, insists Bockmuehl, "is in practice deeply intertwined with its own tradition of hearing and heeding, interpretation and performance."[50] Today's biblical readers stand within a long tradition of readers who have been shaped by the Scriptures; and it is the *Wirkungsgeschichte*—the powerful impact of the Scriptures on the faith and life of the church—that prevents a subjective free-for-all in the way that individual readers interpret the Bible and maintain its authoritative role within the church. Familiarity with the way the Scriptures have fruitfully been read throughout the church's history is not an obstacle to proper interpretation but is rather its sine qua non. In biblical interpretation, familiarity doesn't breed contempt; it breeds insight and understanding.

Gadamer's is a general reception theory of interpretation, and as such it proposes an approach that applies to all sorts of texts, not just the Bible. My argument is that Gadamer's reception theory also applies to the Scriptures.[51] If it is true that biblical interpretation too entails a fusion of horizons and that the *Wirkungsgeschichte* has a significant role in determining how we understand the meaning of the biblical text, then this raises the question

49. Bockmuehl, *Seeing the Word*, 64–65.
50. Ibid., 65.
51. A word of caution is in order. General hermeneutics (such as Gadamer's theory) does not regulate biblical hermeneutics. That is to say, the church's christological reading is determined first and foremost by faith in Christ, not by a general theory of interpretation. It is, therefore, the Christ event itself that gives Christians the rationale for a christological reading, and it is faith in Christ as the Lord of history that gives us a basic stance of trust vis-à-vis the church's tradition of interpretation. Still, inasmuch as nature is relatively autonomous in relation to the supernatural, a general theory of interpretation such as Gadamer's yields genuine insight into the functioning of interpretation and tradition.

of how we can secure a faithful reading of the biblical text. The objections would seem to be weighty: Isn't it possible for reception history to go astray? Isn't it true that there are multiple and sometimes contradictory interpretive traditions? And aren't such disagreements largely the cause of our ecclesial divisions? All of this is true, and it should caution us against treating the Bible's *Wirkungsgeschichte* as some deus ex machina that solves all our exegetical quandaries. The tradition of interpretation is not a monolithic whole, and it contains numerous aberrations and dead ends. The *Wirkungsgeschichte* of the Scriptures in the church, regardless of how inevitable and how important it may be, doesn't absolve us of our obligation to treat the biblical text with proper care and attention.

The *Wirkungsgeschichte* of the biblical text nonetheless renders crucial assistance in the exegetical process. To get an impression of just how significant this role is, it may be helpful to imagine a situation with little or no *Wirkungsgeschichte*: that of the first decades (or centuries) of the early church. How would we decide what difference the Christ event makes to our reading of the Old Testament? What would a christological reading of the Old Testament entail? We have already seen that this is the situation Philip faced as he tried to explain the meaning of the fourth Servant Song to the Ethiopian eunuch, and we saw that Philip's faith in Christ deeply shaped his reading of Isaiah. This shows us that it is not the *Wirkungsgeschichte* by itself that leads to a christological reading of Isaiah. It is first and foremost faith in Christ that shapes how we read the prophets. Still, as we have just seen, the subsequent history of interpretation also deeply impacts our reading of the Servant Songs.

Once the Gospels and the other New Testament writings began to function as an authoritative body of writings, they too helped to give shape to the christological reading of the Old Testament. To be sure, an established New Testament canon would have to wait until the fourth century, but from very early on the church regarded as authoritative many of the books that we now know as New Testament writings. These writings greatly assisted the church in developing an overall reading strategy with regard to the Old Testament. So while faith in Christ is sufficient warrant for a christological reading (as Philip realized), having the New Testament writings helps in determining what exactly such christological readings might look like in practice. In other words, being equipped with the New Testament is of immense help as we try to read the Servant Songs (as well as other parts of the Old Testament) christologically.

There is little doubt that also our two-thousand-year history of interpretation gives us a tremendous advantage in interpreting the Old Testament. Most notably, this is the case with regard to the trinitarian and christological dogmas that were secured in the fourth- and fifth-century councils of the church; the church fathers debated many Old Testament passages at great length in the period leading up to the Nicene Creed and the Chalcedonian Definition.[52] It is not just undesirable but in many ways also quite difficult (perhaps even impossible) for us to try to read the Scriptures without this interpretive tradition of the church's teaching: we often unconsciously assume the *Wirkungsgeschichte* of the text. In contrast, the early church had to learn to read the Old Testament Scriptures without centuries of interpretive insight at its disposal. Reading the Old Testament in a new situation—after Easter and after Pentecost—was a sensitive matter that required careful reinterpretation of the Scriptures in the light of Christ and of the church, which often put the church in sharp conflict with Jewish readings of these same Scriptures.

So if in today's situation Handel's *Messiah* encourages us to read Isaiah 40:1–2 as referring to Christ, then we should ask ourselves, what conditioned people in the early church to read Isaianic passages in the ways they did? I have already pointed to the importance of the centrality of Jesus Christ in the early church's faith and to the role that the New Testament soon came to play. Neither one's faith in Christ nor one's reading of the New Testament Scriptures, however, was for the early church a purely individual matter. Both faith and Scripture reading functioned primarily within the context of the church's liturgy. If familiarity breeds insight and understanding rather than contempt, it stands to reason that regular liturgical use of certain passages helped determine the way in which people came to understand them: ritual is tremendously influential in shaping our convictions. In important ways, therefore, the liturgical life of the church influenced the subsequent *Wirkungsgeschichte* of the Scriptures.

Robert Wilken gives an illuminating example of how the liturgy shaped people's (christological) reading of the Isaianic prophecies.[53] He refers to Isaiah 60:1–3:

> Arise, shine, for your light has come,
>   and the glory of the LORD has risen upon you.
> For behold, darkness shall cover the earth,
>   and thick darkness the peoples;
> but the LORD will arise upon you,
>   and his glory will be seen upon you.
> And nations shall come to your light,
>   and kings to the brightness of your rising.

52. For an example, see the discussion of Prov. 8 in chap. 7.
53. Wilken, *Isaiah*, xxii.

Quite understandably, the early church interpreted the "glory of the LORD" mentioned in the first verse as a reference to Christ. After all, the New Testament made it quite clear that Christ was shining like the light of the sun and that he had come with the knowledge of God. Christ was the glory of God. So when verse 2 refers to "darkness" covering the earth, early Christians saw in this a reference to the nations who used to be in darkness but who were now being enlightened by Christ—the glory of the Lord. As a result, Wilken explains, early Christians recognized in this passage a reference to the conversion of the gentiles: "In time it [i.e., this passage] became associated with the Feast of Epiphany, which celebrates the manifestation of God's glory in all the world, symbolized by the coming of the three wise men from the East to worship the infant Christ. To this day Isaiah 60:1–3 is read in most Christian churches on the Feast of Epiphany."[54] Through its place in the liturgy, people came to associate this passage with the magi worshiping the Christ child and hence with the gentiles' conversion to Christ and to the church. The very fact that a passage such as this from Isaiah 60 was read time and again in the liturgy habituated believers in the early church to read it in the light of Christ.

Christological Mystery Hidden in the Servant Songs

Now let's take a closer look at patristic readings of Isaiah's well-known Servant Songs to trace how the church fathers connected their faith in Christ to these passages. The four poems celebrate God's servant, who will judge the nations (Isa. 42:1–4), who has been called from his mother's womb to be a light to the nations (49:1–6), who obediently follows the Lord's instruction and trusts in his help (50:4–9), and who suffers and dies as a lamb that is led to the slaughter (52:13–53:12). I will take as the starting point for my analysis the excerpts that Robert Wilken provides in the *Isaiah* volume of The Church's Bible.[55] The excerpts are taken from several patristic commentaries and sermons. Careful reading of these patristic discussions of the Servant Songs makes clear that the church fathers overwhelmingly interpreted them christologically—though with varying details and interpretive strategies. In doing so, the fathers were not interested in positing an external link between two separate historical horizons (that of Isaiah and of Christ). Prophecy, they were convinced, did much more than predict events located in a distant future; the newness of the Christ event was already really present in the ancient

54. Ibid.
55. The relevant patristic commentary sections can be found in Wilken, *Isaiah*, 291–97, 363–74, 380–89, 412–30.

words of the prophet. Or, as Edward Pusey would have put it, the prophetic system of the Old Testament is full "of the rich treasure stored up within it."[56]

In their search for the sacramental presence of Christ in the prophetic text, the church fathers paid little attention to the kinds of questions that typically preoccupy contemporary scholarship on the Servant Songs. In particular, the question of whether the servant is Israel or the prophet or the coming Messiah is almost entirely ignored. In contemporary Old Testament studies, this question usually turns on the prophet's original intent: Whom did Isaiah have in mind when he gave his depictions of the servant figure? Was he thinking of Israel? Did he reflect on his own situation? Or was he already looking forward to the messianic future? These historical questions about Isaiah's intentions in writing are not illegitimate in themselves, but they assume a temporal separation between the prophetic act and its future fulfillment. By contrast, the sacramental cast of the patristic mindset operated on the a priori assumption that Christ is already present in the text. That is to say, prophecy had to be interpreted messianically, not just in the sense that the prophet looked forward to a future messianic age, but in the sense that this messianic future was, in a hidden fashion, already contained in the words of the prophetic promise.

Cyril of Alexandria (ca. 378–444) draws attention to the sacramental character of spiritual interpretation when he comments on the words of the second Servant Song, "From my mother's womb he called my name" (Isa. 49:1 LXX).[57] Cyril explains:

> A great and profound mystery (*mystērion*) is hidden (*synebalen*) in these words and can only be understood if one has been enlightened from above, as happened when it was revealed to blessed Peter that Jesus was "the Christ, the Son of the living God" (Matt. 16:16–17). The Word was and is God, of equal glory, sharing the throne of God the Father, coexistent and coeternal (cf. John 1:1). The names which he had by nature before his Incarnation are "God," "Wisdom," "Light," "Life," and "Might," and others besides these found in the Holy Scriptures. When he humbled himself, "being born in the likeness of men and being found in human form" (Phil. 2:7–8), he received a name like other names, "Christ" and "Jesus," or "God with us." The expression "with us" signifies that he shared our life. For it is written, "Look the virgin shall conceive and bear a son, and you shall name him Emmanuel" (7:14).[58]

56. Pusey, "Lectures," 8. Cf. Westhaver, "Living Body," 45.
57. Unless otherwise noted, I quote the Septuagint from the translation provided in Wilken, *Isaiah*.
58. Cyril of Alexandria, *Commentary on Isaiah* 49:1–3, quoted in Wilken, *Isaiah*, 367–68. Greek terms added in round brackets to Wilken's quotations are my own.

Cyril's language of a "mystery" that is "hidden" in—or, literally, "thrown together" with—the words of the text makes clear that he believed that the reality of the name of the incarnate Christ is somehow present in the text. Cyril, for whom the unity of the one person of Christ was important as he opposed the Antiochene separation of his divine and human natures, explains that Isaiah alludes to the mystery of the incarnation. Both the eternal names of the Son of God (God, Wisdom, Light, etc.) and the names he received through the incarnation (Christ, Jesus, and Emmanuel) apply to the one who has taken on human flesh. Restricting himself to the names derived from the incarnation, Cyril insists that there is no conflict between the prophet announcing that Mary's child will be named Emmanuel (Isa. 7:14; Matt. 1:23) and the angel saying that they are to call him Jesus (Matt. 1:21): "For the holy prophet, relating mysteries (*mystēria*) by the Spirit, announced that God would come among us and so named him from his divine nature and his sojourn in flesh. But the blessed angel gave him a name based on what he would do, for he saved his own people (Matt. 1:21). For this reason he is called Savior."[59] The mystery that, according to Cyril, lies wrapped up in the words of Isaiah 49:1 ("From my mother's womb he called my name") is the mystery of the incarnation. These words of the servant speak of the twofold character of the incarnate Lord: as Emmanuel, God "became man"; as Jesus our Savior, "he had to be God and become man."[60]

Cyril takes a keen interest in *how* to read the biblical text when he comments on Isaiah 50:4 ("He added to me an ear to hear. And the instruction of the Lord opens my ears"). It is obvious to Cyril that these words must be read typologically as speaking of the new insight that Christians gain through faith in Christ: people who come to faith "were given the addition of an 'ear,' that is, a faculty of hearing unlike anything we had previously."[61] Cyril objects to the way in which the Jews read the law: "They do not go beyond the shadow (*skian*) but are satisfied only with the types (*typois*)."[62] When Christians read Moses, however, they understand these same words "with a different kind of hearing, transposing the types (*typous*) into the truth (*alētheian*), the shadow (*skian*) becoming an occasion to contemplate on spiritual things."[63] Appealing to several well-known biblical passages (1 Cor. 2:14; John 5:39–40; and 2 Cor. 3:14–15), the Alexandrian bishop maintains that through the gift of a new ear, Christians are enabled to make the interpretive move from type to reality (or truth).

59. Cyril of Alexandria, *Commentary on Isaiah* 49:1–3, quoted in Wilken, *Isaiah*, 368.
60. Ibid.
61. Cyril of Alexandria, *Commentary on Isaiah* 50:4–5, quoted in Wilken, *Isaiah*, 385.
62. Ibid.
63. Ibid.

In the typological approach of Cyril and others, the immediate historical context of the prophetic message cannot provide the main framework for the interpretation of the Servant Songs. After all, the church fathers could not possibly understand either the nation of Israel or the prophet himself as the ultimate truth (*alētheia*) or the reality (*res*) conveyed in the poems. The only proper horizon for spiritual interpretation was found, therefore, in Christ and the church. At one point, Jerome (ca. 347–420) dismissively mentions "Jewish interpreters" who refer the third Servant Song "to the person of Isaiah because he said that he had received the word from the Lord to urge on a wary and wayward people and call them back to salvation."[64] Jerome wants nothing to do with such a historical approach: "Those who interpret the text in this way use every means at their disposal to turn the prophecy away from Christ and misunderstand it by distorting its interpretation."[65] The song itself gives ample reason for a christological reading, insists Jerome: "For he assumed a body at the time of the Incarnation and received 'a tongue of one who had been taught,' and he knew when 'he ought to speak' (50:4) and when to be silent."[66] In Jerome's opinion, the correspondence between the life of Christ and the words of Isaiah's prophecy demands a christological reading.

Similarly, when they deal with textual problems, the church fathers are concerned not so much with establishing the original text for its own sake as they are in seeking out the christological implications of textual variants. Eusebius of Caesarea (ca. 263–ca. 339), for example, observes a textual difficulty in the first Servant Song, which in the Septuagint begins with the words "Iakob is my servant, I will lay hold of him; Israel is my chosen, my soul has accepted him . . ." (Isa. 42:1). Eusebius observes that neither the Hebrew original nor two other Greek versions—Symmachus and Aquila—include the names of Jacob and Israel in the biblical text. Eusebius explains that the Septuagint must have imported the two names from Isaiah 41:8. He advises, therefore, that we abandon the Septuagint at this point and go with the other versions. The reason is christological: "But here a mightier personage has been introduced without being named, lest he be counted among those already referred to in 41:8 as 'Jacob or Israel or the offspring of Abraham.' This is plainly said of the Christ of God."[67] In short, Eusebius concludes from his text-critical discussion that Isaiah's servant is greater than Israel's ancestors.

Augustine displays a similar text-critical awareness, but he has a more positive attitude toward the Septuagint: "It is true, indeed, that the Hebrew

---

64. Jerome, *Commentary on Isaiah* 50:2–4, quoted in Wilken, *Isaiah*, 382.
65. Ibid.
66. Jerome, *Commentary on Isaiah* 50:2–4, quoted in Wilken, *Isaiah*, 382–83.
67. Eusebius, *Commentary on Isaiah* 40:1–4, quoted in Wilken, *Isaiah*, 294.

has 'my servant' in place of 'Jacob' and 'Israel,' but the Septuagint translators preferred to make the meaning more explicit, namely, that the prophecy refers to the 'form of a servant' (Phil. 2:7), in which the Most High showed himself in utter humility. To signify him they used the name of the man from whose stock Christ took the 'form of a servant.'"[68] Augustine, aware of the textual problem, prefers to give a meaning to the Septuagint passage that is in line with the christological dogma. Whereas Eusebius first establishes the original text and then proceeds to explain it, Augustine feels free to ignore what he knows to be the original Hebrew text. And while Eusebius uses the textual problem to allude to the servant's exalted status, Augustine uses it to draw attention to his humanity. The two authors obviously differ in their approaches, but both are intent on dealing with the text-critical problem in a christologically satisfying way.

Wounded by Love: Associations of the Chosen Arrow (Isa. 49:2)

The examples of christological exegesis that we have seen so far make clear that the church fathers were not satisfied with exegetical broad strokes. It was not enough for them simply to know that Christ is the suffering servant and as such fulfills the messianic prophecy of Isaiah's poems. Instead, the church fathers lifted out particular details from the Isaianic Servant Songs and maintained that the life of Christ is the reality after which the type of Isaiah's servant is patterned. As a result, Cyril saw the mystery of the divine-human identity of the incarnate Lord in the servant's name being called from his mother's womb (Isa. 49:1). Jerome recognized the Savior's silence in suffering (Mark 14:61) in the servant's receiving a "tongue of instruction" so that he might "know in season when it is necessary to speak a word" (Isa. 50:4). And both Eusebius and Augustine discerned a specific christological truth in the presence or absence of the names of Jacob and Israel from the biblical text. This means that although the church fathers knew that prophecy chronologically precedes fulfillment, they were convinced that *in a more important sense it is fulfillment that precedes prophecy*. Because they believed that the inward reality or mystery precedes the outward type or sacrament, the church fathers were confident that the types contain details modeled on specific aspects of Christ's life, death, and resurrection.

The church fathers believed that the providential link between reality (or archetype) and outward sacrament (or type) could be seen throughout the

---

68. Augustine, *City of God* 20.30, quoted in Wilken, *Isaiah*, 297.

biblical account. Earlier we noted their love of words and their interest in "associative reading"—a search for verbal similarities between biblical passages so as to link them theologically.[69] Patristic commentaries on the Servant Songs regularly employ this practice, and they do so out of a strong conviction that the relationship between the reality and the shadow—between the archetype and the types—is grounded in the faithfulness of a God who acts in analogous or similar ways throughout history. The church fathers believed that this faithfulness could be seen in different biblical authors using the same vocabulary despite being far removed from one another historically.

We see the church fathers working with such intertextual echoes when they deliberate on the servant's saying in Isaiah 49 that the Lord "made my mouth like a sharp sword, and under the shelter of his hand he hid me; he made me like a chosen arrow, and in his quiver he sheltered me" (49:2). Cyril of Alexandria begins his reflections on this verse by referring back to chapter 11: "He shall be girded with righteousness around the waist, and bound with truth around the sides, and with the breath from his lips he shall do away with the ungodly (Isa. 11:5, 4b)."[70] Chapter 11 allows Cyril to fill in some of the overtones that he thinks reverberate in the phrase "a sharp sword": it is a weapon that destroys the ungodly and establishes righteousness. This in turn reminds him of Ephesians 6, where the apostle combines these same two elements: spiritual forces that must be combated and the sword as the believer's weapon of choice (Eph. 6:12, 17). As a result, the Alexandrian bishop quotes both verses from Ephesians, commenting that the "divine and heavenly proclamation, the gospel which was spoken through the mouth of Christ, became a sharp and keen-edged sword against the devil's tyranny."[71] In this way, Cyril asserts, God transforms and justifies the ungodly, who now "rise up against those who were once their masters and run 'for the prize of the upward call' (Phil. 3:14) with no obstacle standing in the way."[72] Cyril completes his exegetical discussion by turning back to a place in Isaiah where the prophet too combines the language of a "sword" with spiritual warfare: "The prophet Isaiah makes clear that the spiritual teaching given by Christ puts an end to the devil's tyranny over those on earth when he states, 'On that day God will bring his holy and great . . . sword against the dragon, . . . the crooked serpent—and he will kill the dragon' (27:1)."[73] In essence,

69. See chap. 2, sec. "Gregory's Literal Reading as Theological."
70. Cyril of Alexandria, *Commentary on Isaiah* 49:1–3, quoted in Wilken, *Isaiah*, 368 (emphasis removed).
71. Ibid.
72. Ibid.
73. Ibid.

Cyril has used the verbal similarities between Isaiah 49 and Ephesians 6 to establish both the servant's identity as Jesus Christ and the sword as proclamation of the gospel in the power of the Spirit. The link with Ephesians 6 further strengthens Cyril's interpretation of the "sharp sword" in Isaiah 49 as a weapon in the spiritual battle with the evil one—something that he reinforces by his concluding reference to killing the dragon in Isaiah 27. The result is that Jesus Christ and his proclamation of the gospel become the very contents—the truth (*alētheia*) or reality (*res*)—of the Servant Song.

Not surprisingly, Cyril's exposition of the "chosen arrow" whom the Lord has "sheltered" in his "quiver" (Isa. 49:2) follows along similar lines. Though by his foreknowledge God had many arrows hidden in his quiver, Cyril claims that "the 'arrow' chosen above all is Christ, hidden in a 'quiver' as I have said by the Father's foreknowledge. He was known before the world's foundation (cf. Eph. 1:4) and he appeared among us when the whole world was on the verge of destruction."[74] Why does Cyril turn from Isaiah 49 to Ephesians 1? It seems to me that a combination of verbal and theological triggers makes him pull the two together. First, the language both of "choosing" (*eklegomai*) and of "hiding" (*kryptō*) occurs in both contexts. In Isaiah 49:2 we read, "Under the shelter of his hand he hid (*ekrypsen*) me; he made me like a chosen (*eklekton*) arrow, and in his quiver he sheltered me." The same terms appear in the broader context of Ephesians, which mentions that God "chose (*exelexato*) us in him [i.e., Christ] before the foundation of the world" (Eph. 1:4), and which says that the purpose of the preaching of the riches of Christ is "to bring to light for everyone what is the plan of the mystery hidden (*apokekrymmenou*) for ages in God" (Eph. 3:9). Cyril undoubtedly associates the "hidden" arrow (Isa. 49:2) with the Pauline mystery that once was hidden, and he recognizes that this hidden arrow is now "chosen" inasmuch as we are "chosen" in Christ. Thus, when God pulls out this arrow from his quiver, he makes known the christological mystery that used to lie hidden in his foreknowledge.

Cyril has not forgotten that both the "sharp sword" and the "chosen arrow" are martial metaphors. And so he immediately adds that the chosen arrow "routs Satan himself and his evil hosts" and "destroys the profane adversaries of his sacred teachings, the enemies of Truth."[75] These comments fit, of course, with the spiritual warfare theme that Cyril has already developed in connection with his discussion of the "sharp sword." Interestingly, however, Cyril isn't satisfied with depicting the arrow merely as an instrument of judgment. We already saw that the sharp sword of the gospel brings salvation, and the chosen

---

74. Cyril of Alexandria, *Commentary on Isaiah* 49:1–3, quoted in Wilken, *Isaiah*, 369.
75. Ibid.

arrow does the same thing: "But in wounding he brings health and salvation. Hence the passage in the Song of Songs where the smitten Bride says, 'I am wounded with love' (Song 2:5)."[76] Undoubtedly presupposing a christological interpretation of the Song of Songs, Cyril sees in the words "I am wounded with love" the bride's aching response to the groom having ravished her with the preaching of the gospel—the arrow mentioned in Isaiah 49. Interestingly, the Song of Songs doesn't even mention an arrow. The bride merely says that she is "wounded" with love. For Cyril, however, this is enough to bring about an association with Isaiah 49. Without question, the reason is that in Isaiah 49 Christ is the "chosen arrow" proclaiming the mystery once hidden in God's providence, while in Song 2:5 he is the groom creating a piercing wound of love in the beloved. Christ, it would appear, is both the archer and the arrow, wounding the beloved by placing himself within her heart.

Cyril is not alone in detecting a link between Isaiah 49:2 and Song 2:5. The fifth-century bishop is stepping into a well-established tradition, going back at least to Origen. This tradition reflected on the connection between the two passages in the context of commenting on the Song of Songs (rather than on Isaiah). Thus, Origen, in his *Commentary on the Canticle of Canticles*, suggests that the soul that is wounded by love is the person who has received the "sweet wound" of the chosen arrow of Isaiah 49:2, the one who has been "pierced through and through by the lovable javelin of the knowledge of him, so as to long for him by day and by night, to be unable to speak of anything else, to refuse to hear anything else, to know not how to think anything else, to have no inclination to desire or want or hope for anything else except him."[77] Origen goes on to reflect on the link between God's love for us (which creates the wound) and our love for him (the wound that responds with desire). Seeing as God is love (1 John 4:8), Origen suggests that it is fitting for God to smite souls and "transfix them with spears and darts."[78] The soul that has been wounded in this way is wounded also by wisdom, strength, and justice as well as by other divine attributes. The wound of love, however, is the greatest, according to Origen, because it includes each of the other attributes. The arrow of love, so it seems, creates a participatory bond between the character of God and that of the soul that has been touched by him. Wounded by love, the soul comes to participate in the life of God himself.

Gregory of Nyssa, who with his *Homilies on the Song of Songs* followed in the exegetical footsteps of Origen, does something quite similar—also linking the

76. Ibid. The same expression, "wounded with love," is repeated in Song 5:8.
77. Origen, *Commentary on the Canticle of Canticles* 3.8.3–15, quoted in Wilken, *Isaiah*, 370.
78. Ibid.

soul "wounded with love" with the servant as God's chosen arrow. The mystical Cappadocian preacher follows Origen in many respects: Gregory too makes the link with 1 John 4:8 and then immediately insists that God is the archer who sent the chosen arrow of Isaiah 49:2. Saint Gregory, however, speculatively introduces the mystery of the Trinity into his exegesis of the arrow that has wounded the bride. He explains that God sent his Son, "smearing [the arrow's] triple-tipped point with the Spirit of life."[79] Gregory doesn't clarify why he is speaking of a "triple-tipped point" on the arrow—though the threefold reference to God as the archer, the Son as the arrow, and the Spirit as the "poison" smeared on the arrow's tip makes clear that he is thinking of the Trinity. Gregory associates the triple-tipped point with faith, and it is faith in the Triune God that unites us with the three persons of the Godhead—the archer, the arrow, and the poison.

It is obviously Saint Gregory's pro-Nicene conviction that drives his exegesis of the "chosen arrow" of Isaiah 49. But it is likely that he also makes the association because in 2 Samuel 18:14, Joab kills Absalom with "three arrows." Nyssen comments on this narrative in his earlier *Treatise on the Inscriptions of the Psalms*, where he states, "And what is the triad of arrows (cf. 2 Sam. 18:14) that strikes the middle of the enemy's heart and brings death to the 'last enemy' (1 Cor. 15:26)?"[80] Gregory answers his question by saying that the triad of arrows is intimated by Isaiah's mention of a "chosen arrow." "This arrow," he comments, "is 'the living Word of God,' and is 'more piercing than any two-edged sword' (Heb. 4:12)."[81] Gregory (much like Cyril later on) links the arrow with the preaching of the gospel, and he does so through verbal association with Hebrews 4.

Of course, Isaiah 49 and Hebrews 4 speak of only one arrow and one sword, not of a triad of arrows. Gregory, however, is undaunted. If the triad of arrows in the narrative of Absalom's death is a reference to the Word (which Gregory has established by means of Heb. 4), then surely the doctrine of the Trinity must also be implied by the three arrows: "Now Christ is the Word, and the mystery of the Trinity is confessed by this name. The word teaches us about the one who anoints, the one who was anointed, and by what he was anointed. For if any one of these is omitted, the name of Christ, that is, the one who is anointed, loses its meaning."[82] For Gregory, it only makes sense that 2 Samuel 18 would refer to Christ as a "triad of arrows," since in any reference to Christ, the entire mystery of the Trinity is intimated. At this point, Nyssen has come full circle. Through verbal associations with 1 Corinthians

---

79. Gregory of Nyssa, *Homily 4 on the Song of Songs*, quoted in Wilken, *Isaiah*, 371.
80. Gregory of Nyssa, *Treatise on the Inscriptions* 2.11, quoted in Wilken, *Isaiah*, 371.
81. Ibid.
82. Ibid.

15:26 and Hebrews 4:12, he has linked the Old Testament "arrows" (2 Sam. 18:14; Isa. 49:2) with the preaching of the gospel, and he has established faith in Christ and in the Triune God as the true reality of the second Servant Song.

Finally, Ambrose of Milan (ca. 340–397), deeply influenced by Origen's allegorical exegesis, also pulls the "chosen arrow" of Isaiah 49:2 into his exegesis of the Song of Songs.[83] Saint Ambrose links our "wound of love" (Song 2:5) with the wound that Christ received on the cross.[84] He explains that Christ's wound is of benefit to the church: although Christ was wounded on the cross, he gives the church perfumed ointment and sweet fruit.[85] Ambrose is here thinking of the perfumes and the apples mentioned along with the wound of love in Song 2:5: "Strengthen me with perfumes, overwhelm me with apples, for I am wounded by love." The bishop points out that the context of the passage establishes the bridegroom (Christ) as the apple tree (Song 2:3). By eating of this fruit of the cross, the church comes to share in the Lord's perfume and in his wound: "We likewise confess this wound when 'we preach Christ crucified' (1 Cor. 1:23), and what's more, 'we are a sweet odor to God' (cf. 2 Cor. 2:15) since the cross of Christ is 'a stumbling block to Jews and folly to Gentiles' but to us it is 'the power and wisdom of God' (1 Cor. 1:23). The Church is wounded with this wound of love when she preaches the death of her Savior."[86] Once they've eaten from the apple tree, Christians pass on the "sweet odor" of Christ's perfume and preach the wound of the cross. Ambrose explains that this is also the meaning of Proverbs 27:6: "A wound from a friend is more beneficial than kisses freely given by an enemy."[87] The wound of Christ, our friend, benefits us, explains Ambrose. It is at this point that he mentions the second Servant Song: we should expose ourselves to the "good wound" from Christ by accepting the "chosen arrow"—which, again, is Christ—since "it is good to be wounded by this 'arrow.'"[88] At the same time, Ambrose cautions that sometimes the identification with Christ leads to a different kind of wound than the wound of love: preaching Christ, the apostles were stoned, Paul was beaten with rods on three occasions (2 Cor. 11:25), and the martyrs too are wounded for the name of Christ.[89]

83. Actually, Ambrose's comments occur in his *Homilies on Psalm 118*, but these homilies draw a great deal on the Song of Songs, and it is in the context of his reflections on the Song that Ambrose mentions Isa. 49.

84. The theme of union with Christ is an important aspect of Ambrose's overall participation theology. See G. Boersma, "Participation in Christ," 183–84.

85. Ambrose, *Homilies on Psalm 118* 5.16–17, quoted in Wilken, *Isaiah*, 372.

86. Ibid.

87. Ibid.

88. Ibid.

89. Ibid.

On some points, Ambrose's exegesis differs from that of Origen and Gregory; perhaps most significantly, only Ambrose links our being wounded with Christ's wound on the cross, and Ambrose is the only one to link this wounding with martyrdom. But his overall exegetical approach doesn't differ from that of his predecessors. He too interprets the Old Testament passages (Song 2:5 and Isa. 49:2) by verbally associating them both with other passages of the Old Testament and with various Pauline texts. In so doing, he makes clear that Christ is not just the one to whom Isaiah (along with other Old Testament passages) points by way of future reference, but that he is already present in the descriptions of the suffering servant. For Ambrose too, it is the sacramental reality that determines the meaning of the earlier shadows.

Conclusion

For the church fathers, the christological meaning of the Servant Songs is grounded in the overall providential structuring of history—which moves from shadows to reality—and so in the faithful character of God. Each of the fathers that I have discussed in this chapter was convinced that prophecy is more than just an advance announcement of a future event. They believed instead that the future event was Christ himself and that this climactic historical event retroactively shaped every event in sacred history that preceded it. Thus, the sacramental truth or reality (*alētheia* or *res*) was the archetype that determined and prepared the shape of the earlier type or sacrament (*typos* or *sacramentum*).

What is more, the church fathers saw the faithfulness of God not only in the similarities between the New Testament reality and God's earlier acts in history: they were convinced that these historical similarities left their traces also in the similarity between the biblical words that describe the shadows and those that depict their reality. In each instance, the church fathers make their case for the presence of Christ in the Servant Songs by mentioning New Testament references that shed light on the deeper meaning of the prophecy. The result is a sacramental reading of the Servant Songs (and of Old Testament prophecy in general) along the lines suggested in the nineteenth century by Edward Pusey. Though patristic exegesis does acknowledge that prophecies make forward-looking announcements of future events, more significantly, it aims to show that the future reality of Christ and the church is already present, though hidden, in the message of the prophets. Put differently, for the fathers prophecy is not only a *fore*-telling of future events; it is also a *forth*-telling of present realities.

Or again, putting the same thing in doctrinal language, we can express the church fathers' view by saying that God doesn't speak first, only to act later: God's word and his act are one and the same. God's promise is never an empty announcement, to which a later event may (or may not) correspond. God's speech act is always performative in character: in its very utterance it accomplishes what it proclaims. That is to say, God is always faithful.[90] For the church fathers, therefore, what was at stake in acknowledging the sacramental presence of Christ in Old Testament prophecy was nothing less than the faithfulness of God.

90. The language of "performative" discourse stems from speech-act theory. J. L. Austin understands "performative" utterances as statements that create the reality they describe. Austin speaks of promises as an example of performative statements: "In the particular case of promising, as with many other performatives, it is appropriate that the person uttering the promise should have a certain intention, viz. here to keep his word. . . . Do we not actually, when such intention is absent, speak of a 'false' promise? Yet so to speak is *not* to say that the utterance 'I promise that . . .' is false, in the sense that though he states that he does, he doesn't, or that though he describes he misdescribes—misreports. For he *does* promise: the promise here is not even *void*, though it is given *in bad faith*." *How to Do Things*, 11. Jim W. Adams (*Performative Nature*) discusses the four Servant Songs against the backdrop of speech-act theory. Unlike my chapter, however, Adams does not treat the Servant Songs as sacramentally making present their future fulfillment. Instead, his discussion of performative speech tends to focus on the Israelites' hoped-for involvement in the prophetic message.

10

BEATIFIC READING

Gregory of Nyssa, Augustine, and Leo the Great on the Beatitudes of Matthew 5

Spiritual Interpretation of the New Testament

So far we have been looking only at Old Testament books. There is good reason for this. Typological interpretation finds types in the Old Testament, types that are patterned on the New Testament antitypes (or archetypes) in which the types find their fulfillment. Spiritual interpretation represents, in many ways, a move from the Old to the New Testament, from truth that is veiled to the unveiling that takes place in Christ through the Spirit. So when we looked at Origen's *Homilies on Joshua*, we saw that at times he interprets the text as allegorically alluding to the distinction between the Old and New Testaments. The Alexandrian theologian does this, for instance, when he speaks of the Israelites' arrival in the promised land and about their being enjoined to make "knives out of rock" so as to receive their "second circumcision" (Josh. 5:2). Origen, we saw, explains that the instrument of the first circumcision is the law and that this refers to the putting aside of the worship of images, while the instrument used in the second circumcision is the rock, which is Christ, so that this second circumcision refers to the gospel faith.[1] Spiritual interpretation is about moving from promise to fulfillment, from

1. Origen, *Homilies on Joshua* 5.5 (FC 105:63). Cf. chap. 5, sec. "Origen's Polemical Context."

the outward to the inward, from the law to the gospel, from the letter to the spirit, from type to archetype, from sacrament to reality, and therefore from the Old Testament to the New Testament. As a result, questions surrounding spiritual interpretation often focus on how we are to read the *Old* Testament.

In this chapter I will focus on the Beatitudes of Matthew 5—a New Testament passage. We should pause briefly at this observation. It is one thing to argue that the Old Testament ought to be read spiritually, but it is something else to insist that we should do the same for the New Testament. Still, reading the New Testament text spiritually is exactly what the church fathers did. Regardless of whether they were reading the Old or the New Testament, their primary concern was forward looking rather than backward looking. This forward-looking approach in biblical exegesis seems to me exactly right. Just like Old Testament exegesis can never simply be a matter of trying to find the historical circumstances surrounding the text in hopes of determining scientifically what the author meant, so too in our reading of the New Testament, we are not concerned primarily with what the text *meant* but with what the text *means*. All biblical interpretation—also that of the New Testament—is (or should be) spiritual interpretation.

But isn't the gospel the very contents of the spiritual meaning? Isn't Christ the fulfillment of the Old Testament? And haven't we seen the church fathers arguing for a spiritual reading of the Old Testament on the very grounds that Christ is the sacramental reality that shines through in the historical realities depicted in the text of the Old Testament? Doesn't the notion that the New Testament must be read typologically or allegorically assume that even the New Testament writings are, as it were, carnal writings, whose deeper truth must be uncovered through spiritual exegesis? So then, if we read also the New Testament spiritually, doesn't this mean that we're looking for a yet greater reality, beyond God's self-revelation in Christ? How could there be a deeper truth than the very revelation of Jesus Christ, who is the contents of the New Testament gospel? What would it even mean for us to read the New Testament spiritually?

In his book on Origen, *History and Spirit* (1950), French Catholic theologian Henri de Lubac reflects on this question at length. He insists that there is also an "unceasing transformation of the Gospel at the level of the senses into the spiritual Gospel. Just as it cannot be determined by the work of scientific exegesis, even when carried out in the spirit of faith, it will never be fixed in a certain number of established and controlled results, in a series of objective meanings, capable of being inscribed in a kind of canon. This way of understanding it would allow its essence to escape. This spiritual understanding is, so to speak, the breathing of Christian reflection because it translates the rhythm of Christian life."[2] De Lubac's last sentence points to what is at stake in a spiritual reading also of the narrative of the gospel—and therefore of the Beatitudes. Spiritual reading, insists de Lubac, "translates the rhythm of Christian life." The very rhythm of our lives gets translated in our reading of the text. That is to say, it is not just the text but also the Christian who gets interpreted as we read the Scriptures. Spiritual understanding doesn't just look for a historical reconstruction—not even in the events described in the Gospels or in the theology and the injunctions presented by the apostle Paul. Christian reflection has a much more important task, namely, to translate the rhythm of a Christian mode of existence. That is to say, Christians see the church, and they see themselves, implicated in the New Testament Scriptures.

We already observed that for Saint Augustine, what is true for the head of the church is also true for the members. The reason is that the body of the church may be identified with Christ himself. The church *is*, in a real sense, Christ himself. De Lubac notes that this identification between Christ and the church is not new with Augustine but goes back to Origen.[3] The church—the members of Christ—is still on the way, traveling on its pilgrimage. This implies that tropology (the moral interpretation of the text) and anagogy (the eschatological reading) continue to be integral elements of the deepening insight into the Scriptures. Tropological reading of the New Testament is, for the fathers, a way of identifying with the virtues of Christ and of becoming more like God. And their anagogical readings of the New Testament stem from the recognition that, even though God has done a wonderful and climactic new thing in Christ to which nothing can be added, this new thing still needs to be brought to completion or perfection. The New Testament has given the fullness of the mystery of Christ. The treasure hidden in the field can now be seen. But the depth of this mystery and the contents of this treasure remain there for Christians to explore and perfect in their lives. De Lubac summarizes as follows: "It is the whole New Testament, understood as the complete progress of the Christian economy up to the last day, that also appears to him [i.e., Origen] to be oriented toward a more profound, absolutely and solely definite reality; a reality that it has the duty to make known by preparing for it, serving thus as intermediary between the Old Law and the 'eternal gospel.'"[4] The christological reality of the New Testament

2. De Lubac, *History and Spirit*, 240.

3. Ibid., 244.

4. Ibid., 248. De Lubac takes this use of the expression "eternal gospel" (Rev. 14:6) from Origen's *On First Principles*:

We must also see . . . whether the scriptures may not perhaps indicate this further truth, that just as the legislation is presented with greater clearness and distinctness in

is, for the church fathers, located between the law and what de Lubac terms the "eternal gospel" (Rev. 14:6), that is, the eschatological reality in which the fullness of the mystery and the reality of the person, the discourses, and the actions of Christ will become clear. The fullness of truth, on de Lubac's reading of Origen, remains in the future.

Interpreting between Cave and Mountain

We see this theological or spiritual dimension of the "eternal gospel" consistently on display in the church fathers' interpretation of the Beatitudes, particularly in the treatment of the Beatitudes by Gregory of Nyssa (ca. 335–ca. 394), Augustine of Hippo (354–430), and Pope Leo the Great (ca. 400–461). Most obviously and immediately, perhaps, this comes out in the way their homilies speak about the "mountain" on which, according to Matthew's Gospel, Jesus delivered his Sermon on the Mount (Matt. 5:1). As modern readers, we are perhaps inclined to read past a reference such as this. We may see it as a small geographical detail that we can skip in order to move on to more important matters. Or if we recognize similarities between Moses and Jesus in Matthew's Gospel, as many contemporary New Testament scholars do, the mountain may remind us of Mount Sinai, and we may conclude that Jesus is a second Moses, a second lawgiver.[5] Intrigued as they were with the very words of Scripture, the church fathers would certainly regard any oversight of the word "mountain" as seriously negligent. And while they wouldn't necessarily disagree with linking Jesus to Moses through this referencing of mountains, the concern for spiritual interpretation meant an interest to find eternal, heavenly truths—so that the fathers would consider the modern preoccupation with history and authorial intent as insufficiently attuned to the divine purpose of the text.

Deuteronomy than in those books which were written at the first, so also we may gather from that coming of the Saviour which he fulfilled in humility, when he "took upon him the form of a servant," an indication of the "more splendid and glorious second coming in the glory of his Father," at which coming, when in the kingdom of heaven all the saints shall live by the laws of the "eternal gospel," the figure of Deuteronomy will be fulfilled; and just as by his present coming he has fulfilled that law which has a "shadow of the good things to come," so also by that glorious coming the shadow of his first coming will be fulfilled and brought to perfection. For the prophet has spoken of it thus: "The breath of our countenance is Christ the Lord, of whom we said that under his shadow we shall live among the nations," that is, at the time when he shall duly transfer all the saints from the temporal to the eternal gospel, to use a phrase employed by John in the Apocalypse, where he speaks of the "eternal gospel." (*On First Principles* 4.3.13 [Butterworth, 309–10])

5. See Allison, *New Moses*, 172–80; Buchanan, *Gospel of Matthew*, 184; Leithart, "Jesus as Israel."

Gregory of Nyssa, the fourth-century Cappadocian spiritual master, immediately hones in on the "mountain" reference. Perhaps the most Platonic of the three preachers, Saint Gregory pretty much begins his first sermon by contrasting Matthew's mountain—a "spiritual mountain of sublime contemplation"—with Plato's cave: "This mountain leaves behind all shadows cast by the rising hills of wickedness; on the contrary, it is lit up on all sides by the rays of the true light, and from its summit all things that remain invisible to those imprisoned in the cave may be seen in the pure air of truth. Now the Word of God Himself, who calls blessed those who have ascended with Him, specifies the nature and number of the things that are contemplated from this height."[6] Gregory's reference to "those imprisoned in the cave" is striking. It is an explicit reference and appeal to Plato's allegory of the cave, which he relates in book 7 of *The Republic*. For Plato, if we want to be able to discern reality itself, we must be untied from our place in the cave of this earthly reality and learn to stand outside, gazing into the sunlight of the eternal Forms—a difficult thing to do after a lifelong imprisonment in the darkness of the cave.[7] Gregory links this notion of us living in a cave to the Sermon on the Mount's mirror-opposite depiction of Jesus (or, rather, "the Word of God Himself," as Gregory prefers to put it) teaching from the brightly lit-up heights of the mountain, the eternal place of truth. Within the framework of Saint Gregory's Christian Platonism, any mention of a mountain irresistibly drew his mind to the spiritual dimensions of such a reference.

This is not much different for Saint Augustine, especially during the first number of years following his conversion. Neoplatonism had played a significant instrumental role in this conversion, so when Bishop Valerius relieved Augustine from his priestly duties shortly after he had taken on his role as priest of Hippo Regius (ca. 393–395), Augustine too was eager to show the validity of Christian Platonism when writing his commentary on the Sermon on the Mount.[8] Matthew's reference to the "mountain" triggers Psalm 35 (36):6 in Augustine's mind: "Thy righteousness is like the mountains of God."[9] The bishop of Hippo takes this combination of "righteousness" and "mountains" to imply a reference to Jesus Christ. The psalm "may well mean," he comments, "that the one Master alone fit to teach matters of so great importance teaches on a mountain."[10] "For Augustine," comments Robert Wilken, "the

---

6. Gregory of Nyssa, *Beatitudes*, Sermon 1 (ACW 18:85).
7. Plato, *Republic* 514a–517a (LCL 276:106–15). For a good edition of the allegory of the cave, along with other myths, see Plato, *Selected Myths*.
8. Wilken, "Augustine," 45–46.
9. I am following the Septuagint translation used in Augustine, *Sermon on the Mount*.
10. Augustine, *Sermon on the Mount* 1.1.2 (NPNF[1] 6:4).

reason Jesus went up on a mountain is clear: he wanted to teach them about higher things. Seated on a mountain they were lifted above the quotidian affairs of their towns and villages, the cares and trials of life with family and friends and neighbors."[11]

Wilken is quite right, I think; Augustine directly links physical height with spiritual height. The "mountain," explains Augustine, is a reference to "the greater precepts of righteousness," and the bishop opposes these "greater precepts" to "lesser ones which were given to the Jews."[12] So he contrasts law and gospel, seeing in the "mountain" a reference to the latter. He then identifies this contrast with the juxtaposition of the kingdom of heaven to earthly kingdoms: "Nor is it surprising that the greater precepts are given for the kingdom of heaven, and the lesser for an earthly kingdom."[13] It is by means of remarkable mental agility and through a number of distinct exegetical steps, each of them presupposing the preceding one, that Saint Augustine finally arrives at his conclusion: when the Son of God teaches on the mountain, you know you're dealing with gospel teaching.

Around the same time as Augustine, Pope Leo the Great—known both for writing what we now know as Leo's Tome (which persuaded the Council of Chalcedon in the year 451 of the orthodox teaching on the two natures of Christ) and for meeting Atilla the Hun a year later and convincing him to withdraw from the city of Rome—wrote a short homily on the Beatitudes. Even in this brief address, Leo too takes time to refer to the great significance that, to his mind, the reference to a mountain must undoubtedly have. Jesus Christ, says Saint Leo, called his apostles to the mountain, "that from the height of that mystic seat He might instruct them in the loftier doctrines, signifying from the very nature of the place and act that He it was who had once honoured Moses by speaking to him."[14]

Three brief observations are in order. First, for Leo, the height of the mountain is indicative of the great mystical significance of the teaching that takes place there. Much like Gregory and Augustine, Leo takes the mere reference to height as indicative of spiritual significance—something we often see the fathers do, once we pay attention to it. Not surprisingly, this has to do with their understanding that the closer we come to heaven, the more spiritual we are. Physical proximity to heaven becomes symbolic of spiritual nearness.

Second, while Leo does pull Moses into the picture (as would many modern exegetes), he does this not in order to move typologically from Moses to Jesus.

11. Wilken, "Augustine," 43.
12. Augustine, *Sermon on the Mount* 1.1.2 (*NPNF*[1] 6:4).
13. Ibid.
14. Leo the Great, *Sermon XCV* (*NPNF*[2] 12:202).

Instead, he draws an analogy between Moses and the *apostles*. Just as Moses was once instructed on Mount Sinai, so the apostles now receive instruction on a mountain. The upshot of this is that it puts Jesus in the position of God himself. Just as God had once instructed Moses, so Jesus now instructs the apostles. The location of the mountain indicates, says Leo, "that He it was who had once honoured Moses by speaking to him."[15] The Beatitudes, for Leo, are the pronouncement of the Lord God himself.

Third, Leo takes the opportunity to dwell on the difference between law and gospel. He does so by observing not just the similarities but also the differences between God's speaking to Moses then and God's speaking to his apostles now: "There were no thick clouds surrounding Him as of old, nor were the people frightened off from approaching the mountain by frightful sounds and lightning."[16] These two differences—neither thick clouds nor thunder and lightning—are indicative, according to Leo, of the difference between what he calls the "harshness of the law" and the "gentleness of grace."[17] Pope Leo takes the church's convictions about the difference between law and gospel and reads the Beatitudes in the light of what the church already believes about the difference that the coming of Christ makes. Leo is even willing to pull in an argument from silence—the *absence* of clouds, thunder, and lightning—to make the case for his particular exegesis of the passage.

Gregory of Nyssa and Multiplicity of Meaning

A kind of typological exegesis appears to be at work in Leo's exposition of the meaning of the "mountain": Mount Sinai functions as the type, and the mountain of the Beatitudes as the antitype. We do need to be careful, however, with putting the label "typology" onto Leo's approach—and, indeed, onto the exegesis of the church fathers in general. The overall exposition of the three church fathers cannot be caught by the catchphrase "typology," as we commonly understand that term. Nor, for that matter, can we simply speak of "allegory," if by that we mean a *method* that the fathers apply to the text in order to arrive at a predetermined result. Instead, what we have here is really a form of contemplation—*theōria*—in which the plain sense of the text becomes the basis on which to reflect on God's providential dealings with the believers in Christ. In such contemplation, even the actions and words of Jesus take on implications beyond the ordinary sense that the words appear to convey.

15. Ibid.
16. Ibid. (*NPNF*[2] 12:203).
17. Ibid.

We can see the contemplative approach of *theōria* particularly in Gregory's repeated insistence on multiplicity of meaning in the text. On at least five occasions in his homilies on the Beatitudes—perhaps written during his exile, between 376 and 378—he insists that the text may have more than one meaning. Seeing that this is a controversial issue and an obstacle for much historical biblical scholarship, we should pause for a moment and analyze what is going on. How is it that Gregory can insist that the biblical text may have more than one meaning? What does this do to the authority of the text? How does this not justify arbitrary, subjective readings of the text?

To answer these questions, let's start by analyzing the five instances where Nyssen insists on a plurality of meaning. First, regarding the first beatitude ("Blessed are the poor in spirit, for theirs is the kingdom of heaven" [Matt. 5:3]), Gregory begins by explaining that poverty in spirit speaks of humility, the opposite of which is pride. Using passages such as 2 Corinthians 8:9 ("For you know the grace of our Lord Jesus Christ, that though he was rich, yet for your sake he became poor, so that you by his poverty might become rich") and Philippians 2:5–7 ("Have this mind among yourselves, which is yours in Christ Jesus, who, though he was in the form of God, did not count equality with God a thing to be grasped, but emptied himself, by taking the form of a servant, being born in the likeness of men"), Gregory contemplates the character of humility. He explains that humility is connatural to our earthly nature and then insists that "no other evil is so harmful to our nature as that which is caused by pride."[18] While these reflections on humility and pride are obviously important to Gregory, he nevertheless goes on to say that a more literal understanding of poverty—a reference to material possessions—should not be excluded: "Nor should you, my dear brethren, disregard the other interpretation of poverty which begets the riches of Heaven."[19] On this more literal understanding, being "poor in spirit" means, according to Nyssen, that one is "poor *for the sake of* the spirit."[20]

Second, the reference to "mourning" ("Blessed are those who mourn, for they shall be comforted" [Matt. 5:4]) may likewise be interpreted in a twofold fashion. Mourning may, on the one hand, refer to sorrow for sin, a mourning that brings repentance and leads to salvation (2 Cor. 7:10).[21] "But," Gregory continues, "it seems to me that the Word indicates something deeper than what has so far been said."[22] Noticing that the text doesn't speak of those who

18. Gregory of Nyssa, *Beatitudes*, Sermon 1 (ACW 18:90).
19. Ibid., Sermon 1 (ACW 18:95).
20. Ibid.
21. Ibid., Sermon 3 (ACW 18:107).
22. Ibid., Sermon 3 (ACW 18:108).

have mourned but of those who *are* mourning, and observing too that saintly people such as John and Elijah did not have any sin over which to mourn,[23] Gregory argues that in the beatitude "mourning" refers to sorrow over the absence of light in the cave—alluding again to Plato's allegory.[24] Recognizing that we cannot describe or grasp God—who, after all, is not circumscribed by time or place—Gregory comments: "And the more we believe the nature of the good to exceed our comprehension, the more should our sorrow grow within us, because we are separated from a good so great that we cannot even attain to its knowledge."[25] So Gregory uses the text to reflect both on the sorrow that comes from repentance and on the sorrow that comes from the recognition of our creaturely distance from God.[26]

In neither of these first two examples is Gregory concerned to limit his exegesis to one particular meaning. In fact, in his discussion of mourning, when he jumps to the second possible meaning, he does so by presenting two arguments—based on verb tenses as well as theological considerations—that appear in some way to plead *against* his first interpretation. Or, at the very least, the first form of mourning (that over sin) applies only to those who in their lives continue to struggle with sin. But for Saint Gregory this is not reason to oppose or reject his first reading; he is quite happy to let the first interpretation stand. The reason, no doubt, is that the first interpretation yields important moral insight: sorrow leading to repentance leads to a virtuous life. And, as we have seen before, Gregory will let pretty much any interpretation stand, as long as it leads to virtue. He shows no interest in establishing the one historical meaning of the text.

The other three instances in which Gregory argues for multiple meanings go beyond the mere observation that he is interested in multiplying rather than limiting possible meanings of the text. In each of these additional examples, Nyssen arrives at multiplicity of meaning by moving from a literal to a spiritual meaning. When discussing our hungering and thirsting after justice (Matt. 5:6), Gregory again has recourse to two distinct meanings. First, he maintains that hungering for justice means following Jesus, whose "food is to do the will of [the one] who sent [him]" (John 4:34), which really means that, along with Jesus, we hunger for our salvation.[27] Although justice is simply *one* of the virtues, Gregory maintains that all the others are included

23. Ibid., Sermon 3 (ACW 18:108–9).
24. Ibid., Sermon 3 (ACW 18:110–11).
25. Ibid., Sermon 3 (ACW 18:112).
26. For discussion of St. Gregory's broader attitudes toward grief, see H. Boersma, "'Numbed with Grief,'" 46–59.
27. Gregory of Nyssa, *Beatitudes*, Sermon 4 (ACW 18:124).

as well. "Every virtue," he explains, "is here comprised under the name of justice."[28] When he reaches this point, however, Gregory makes a jump. "If we would venture on a bolder interpretation," he comments, "it seems to me that through the ideas of virtue and justice the Lord proposes Himself to the desire of His hearers."[29] In other words, the beatitude concerning justice speaks not just of human virtue but also of our participation in divine justice. Gregory is convinced that since all virtue ultimately resides in the Second Person of the Trinity, in the Word, we must identify the Word as our food. God offers himself as the eternal bread and as the living water that satisfies us. God, the Logos himself—Virtue, that is, with a capital V—offers *himself* to us as our food and drink.[30]

The two meanings are connected. The first meaning presents the plain sense that we are to hunger and thirst for justice (or for virtue in general). Nyssen then moves from the various shapes that virtue takes in our lives—at a horizontal level among human beings—to the ultimate reality of Virtue itself. To reach for Virtue itself, Gregory's exegesis requires contemplation or *theōria*. He must make an anagogical or upward move, we might say; he must ascend, vertically, in order to identify the ultimate identity and meaning of Virtue in the eternal Word of God. Gregory reaches from *historia* to *theōria* by means of the Christian Platonist insight that the numerous human virtues unite in the unity of the one, eternal Word of God.

The remaining two examples function in similar fashion. When he explains the beatitude "Blessed are the merciful, for they shall receive mercy" (Matt. 5:7), Gregory explains that what he terms the "obvious" meaning calls us to mutual charity and sympathy.[31] A few paragraphs further down, however, he wants to "disregard the obvious meaning" in order "to let our mind penetrate the interior of the veil."[32] This language—both the reference to the "interior" and the reference to Moses' veil (2 Cor. 3:13–18)—makes clear that Gregory again has in mind a move from *historia* to *theōria*. The spiritual meaning, in this case, is the duty of the soul to have mercy not on disadvantaged people but on one's own soul. After all, "what is more pitiable than this captivity? Instead of enjoying paradise, we have been allotted this unwholesome place where to live and toil; instead of being impassible, we have been doomed to passions without number."[33] Our fall into sin, Gregory insists, requires that

28. Ibid., Sermon 4 (ACW 18:126).
29. Ibid., Sermon 4 (ACW 18:128).
30. Ibid., Sermon 4 (ACW 18:128–29).
31. Ibid., Sermon 5 (ACW 18:132).
32. Ibid., Sermon 5 (ACW 18:135).
33. Ibid., Sermon 5 (ACW 18:138).

we have mercy on our souls. The church's overall teaching—in this case the doctrine of sin—provides for Gregory the material from which to move to a higher, spiritual meaning of the text. Gregory is happy to accept both the "obvious" and the "interior" meanings of the text. "Either is equally good," he says, "to have pity on oneself in the matter aforesaid [i.e., *theōria*] and to sympathize with the misfortunes of our neighbours [i.e., *historia*]."[34]

Finally, the "peacemakers" who shall be called "sons of God" (Matt. 5:9) are first of all those who are peaceful in relation to other people. Peace—as opposed to hatred—refers to "a loving disposition towards one's neighbour."[35] In an attempt to highlight the great importance of peacemaking, Gregory presents a marvelous picture of the face of someone who, instead of being a peacemaker, falls prey to the passion of wrath. ("The eyes protrude from under their confining lids, staring bloodshot like dragons at the offending object; the inside is compressed, panting for breath, the veins in the throat swell and the tongue thickens. Since the windpipe is straitened, the voice automatically becomes rasping."[36] The description goes on at some length.) This surface meaning is the one on which Gregory focuses in particular: "Our sermon need not be too much concerned with the profound spiritual sense of the passage; the obvious meaning is all we need to acquire this marvellous thing."[37] Nonetheless, toward the very end, Gregory does explain that "perhaps" this beatitude does contain also a deeper theological truth; there may also be a reference to the peace between "flesh and spirit" in human nature, with the former obeying the latter, so that human nature becomes more like God, who himself is "not composite but simple."[38] Much as with the explanation of mercy, so also here Gregory's spiritual interpretation moves from outward, interpersonal relations to the inner nature of the human person.

Virtue and Salvation

The life of virtue is crucially important to the church fathers. This emphasis forms one of the greatest obstacles for today's readers to appreciate their writings. This is the case particularly for Protestants, who have learned to take the *sola gratia* (by grace alone) of the Reformation as their starting point. As a result, we are inclined to look askance at patristic writings that display

---

34. Ibid., Sermon 5 (ACW 18:139).
35. Ibid., Sermon 7 (ACW 18:159).
36. Ibid., Sermon 7 (ACW 18:161).
37. Ibid., Sermon 7 (ACW 18:159).
38. Ibid., Sermon 7 (ACW 18:165).

what we intuitively feel is too great an eagerness to instill virtue.[39] We worry such eagerness may fall prey to moralism, perhaps even to salvation by works. The grid with which, sometimes subconsciously, we approach the fathers can make it difficult for us to warm up to them.

There is no denying this emphasis on virtue. It ties in closely with the difference between symbol and sacrament. A symbol has no more than an external or nominal relationship to the reality that it symbolizes. Think of a driver encountering the road sign of a deer. He is not going to veer away from the road sign for fear of hitting the deer that is symbolized on it. In this scenario, there are no worries about confusing sign X with reality Y. To be sure, the two are related to each other, but the relationship is strictly an external or nominal one. A sacramental relationship, by contrast, implies real presence. Here sign X really participates in reality Y. The sacrament (*sacramentum*) participates in the reality (*res*) to which it refers. Or, taking our starting point in the reality, we could say that the reality has real presence in the sacrament. Moving well beyond positing a merely external or nominal relationship, sacramentalism argues for a participatory or real connection between sacrament and reality.[40]

This distinction between symbol and sacrament is of importance for our understanding both of salvation and of biblical interpretation. Let's begin with salvation. Earlier we saw X as a deer; but let's instead take X as Christ and Y as the believer. The question is, how can we say that something belonging to X belongs also to Y? For example, how can we say that Christ's righteousness (or Christ's virtue, for that matter) belongs also to the believer? The Reformation tradition has at times responded that in the case of Christ's righteousness or virtue, X relates to Y very much in the way the deer on a road sign relates to a deer in the forest. In both cases, there is an external or nominal relationship. Just as no one is going to confuse the deer on the road sign with a deer in the forest (since they're only nominally or externally related), so also no one should confuse the righteousness of Christ with the

---

39. Part of the problem is that in the ancient world (including that of the church fathers), different characteristics counted as virtues, and that virtue had different connotations—perhaps even a different meaning—than it does in modernity. See MacIntyre, *After Virtue*, 11. The church fathers typically understood a virtuous person as someone who, through habitual actions, had attained moral "excellence" as a skill with regard to his moral outlook and life, so that such a person had come to participate in God's own moral excellence (or virtue). It is the participatory link between divine and human "excellence" that was lost in the late medieval period, as a result of which the discourse of "virtues" inevitably took on moralistic connotations. Virtues thus turned into characteristics that human beings develop on their own strength, independently from participation in God and from the Spirit's guidance.

40. For greater elaboration on the foregoing paragraph, see H. Boersma, *Heavenly Participation*, 21–26.

believer himself truly turning into a righteous or virtuous person. Just because Christ himself led a righteous or virtuous life, that doesn't necessarily make the believer a righteous or virtuous person.

This becomes clear when we take the well-known Lutheran notion that the believer is at the same time righteous and sinner (*simul iustus et peccator*) [41] This notion makes clear that the relationship between X and Y (Christ's righteousness and that of the believer) is nominal in character.[42] Sure, the righteousness or virtue of Christ is legally considered to be that of the believer—and the Lutheran tradition has used the language of "imputation" to talk about this legal relationship—but personally, in himself, the believer remains a sinner. The righteousness of Christ is related to the believer only through the rule of law. The relationship is external or nominal. It is wrong, according to certain strands within the Reformation tradition, to insist that justification implies a real or participatory relationship of the believer with the virtues of Christ.

One can appreciate detractors of the Lutheran Reformation asking the question: But doesn't the grace of God change believers internally? Don't we actually *become* virtuous or righteous when we put on Christ? When Luther likened the relationship between X and Y (between the virtue of Christ and our virtue) to Boaz's cloak covering Ruth and to a mother hen's wings covering her chicks, these external metaphors did little to reassure the anxious worries of his Catholic opponents.[43] Boaz's cloak may have covered Ruth, but it didn't change her. The mother hen's wings may cover her chicks, but that doesn't change them. Opponents of the Lutheran Reformation wanted more than just a nominal or external relationship between the cloak and Ruth or between the hen's wings and the chicks: they insisted on a real or participatory relationship.[44]

It's no sense painting the Reformation tradition any darker than necessary. Many in the late Middle Ages did have the kind of focus on our own internal righteousness that gave the impression that people could earn their salvation simply by doing their natural best.[45] It was high time for protests of people

41. For the next few paragraphs I borrow from ibid., 92–93.
42. See Boulton, *God against Religion*, 138–44.
43. See ibid., 139–40. A more popular tale has it that Luther insisted that Christ's righteousness was like white snow covering the filthy dung hill of our unrighteous lives. I have not been able to find this metaphor anywhere in Luther himself—though in essence it is consistent with that of Boaz's cloak covering Ruth and that of a mother hen's wings covering her chicks.
44. Calvin, much like Luther, was intent on keeping justification distinct from human works. To do this, he too maintained that justification was a nominal or external judicial declaration rather than a real, internal transformation worked by the Holy Spirit. *Institutes* 3.11.13–23.
45. See Oberman, *Harvest of Medieval Theology*, 131–45.

such as Luther. Furthermore, the Wittenberg Reformer did recognize the need for good works, as can be seen from his strong opposition in the late 1530s to one of his erstwhile followers, antinomian theologian Johann Agricola.[46] Also, Luther and Calvin both recognized the importance of union with Christ, to the point that some scholars today insist that the notion of deification can be found in the magisterial Reformers.[47] Nonetheless, despite the importance of "union with Christ" language in the Reformers, I am not entirely convinced by this scholarship. While both Luther and Calvin no doubt recognized the importance of union with Christ, the question remains: Did they see this as implying that we come to participate in a *real* way in the righteousness of Christ? This is the old conflict between imputed righteousness (emphasized by the Reformers) and imparted righteousness (highlighted by the Catholic Church). It seems to me that the Reformers generally did not look at salvation in terms of human beings beginning to share or participate in the eternal virtue of Christ himself. And it is fair, I think, to ask whether perhaps Luther's own articulations of justification gave occasion for some of his followers to express their aberrant views.

Our approach to the virtues is colored by this sixteenth-century debate about whether our relationship to Christ and his righteousness is only nominal and external or also real and participatory. We need to keep in mind that this early modern debate was outside the scope of Gregory, Augustine, and Pope Leo. I am convinced that each of them (especially Saint Augustine) had a high view of divine grace. But they were not concerned with the dilemmas that arose at the time of the Reformation. These fathers assumed a participatory view of reality, and this allowed them to attribute a significant role to human virtues (as participating in divine virtue) without thereby capitulating to a Pelagian mindset. Sometimes this emphasis on the virtues and on free will appears (especially in Saint Gregory) as though it is quite optimistic with regard to our natural capacities.[48] This may well come across as problematic to later heirs of the Reformation. Again, we need to recall that the church fathers did not think of human virtue as autonomous and separate from God's grace: they regarded human virtue as sharing in the character of God. Any thought of earning one's own salvation would have been alien to them. Rather than read them through the lens of later sixteenth-century Protestant-Catholic debates,

46. See Brecht, *Martin Luther*, 156–71.
47. For Luther, see Mannermaa, *Christ Present in Faith*; Kärkkäinen, *One with God*. For Calvin, see Mosser, "Greatest Possible Blessing"; Billings, *Calvin, Participation, and the Gift*; McClean, "Perichoresis."
48. I defend Gregory against the charge of moralism in H. Boersma, *Embodiment and Virtue*, 211–46.

we should instead appreciate that, in terms of salvation, each of these fathers insisted on a real or participatory understanding of virtue.

What this means concretely is that for Gregory, Augustine, and Leo, growth in virtue is growth in perfection and as such growth in the life of God. This understanding makes salvation (our sharing in God's life) identical to growing in virtue. Salvation is, on this understanding, a process. So we would never read in Saint Augustine something like the following: "I got saved twenty years ago when I was in Milan listening to the preaching of Ambrose." This is not to deny that a truly miraculous, divine event took place in Milan. It is not to say Augustine didn't get converted in Milan. He quite clearly did. In an important sense, it is even true that for Augustine the process of salvation began in Milan. But precisely because that's where salvation *began*, this also meant for Augustine that the process itself had only just started. Salvation, for our authors, is a process of growing in virtue, and so a growing in perfection and in the life of God. Salvation is a process of changing ever more to become like God. Salvation, to go back to the terms I used earlier, is the process in which our real or participatory relationship with God gets worked out. For none of these authors is salvation something that has been decided once and for all simply by means of an external or nominal declaration.

Virtue and Interpretation

We need to take the application of the distinction between symbol and sacrament one step further: it is crucial not only for the doctrine of justification but also for the interpretation of Scripture. As we saw earlier, Stephen Fowl makes a distinction between "virtue-through-interpretation" and "virtue-in-interpretation."[49] With the former, virtue-through-interpretation, he means that in the fathers' understanding, interpretation *leads* to virtue. The latter, virtue-in-interpretation, speaks of the need to have developed proper virtues by the time we *come* to Scripture, if we are to read it rightly. I am interested here especially in virtue-through-interpretation, interpretation *leading* to virtue.

Virtue, for the fathers, is the *aim* of interpretation. Any interpretation that does not lead to growth in virtuous habits is, according to patristic exegesis, not interpretation that is worthy of God. If the Christian life is a journey into ever-deeper communion with God, then Scripture is the guide on this journey. "In this light," says Fowl, "Scripture plays a dual role. It articulates the shape and nature of the virtues. Further, as Christians interpret and embody their

---

49. See chap. 2, sec. "Gregory's Literal Reading as Theological." See also Treier, *Introducing Theological Interpretation*, 92–96; Briggs, *Virtuous Reader*.

interpretations of Scripture, Scripture becomes a vehicle to help in the formation of virtues, so that Christians are moved ever closer to their true end."[50] Scripture, for the fathers, is an aid—a means of grace (or a sacrament)—that assists in the development of virtue. If Scripture really has this function, it becomes imperative to approach the text with the question in mind of *how* it might assist in the development of virtue. It is because salvation is not just a nominal or external but also a real or participatory process that this becomes a central question.

It should not surprise us, then, to find that the Beatitudes, for the church fathers, are all about the virtues. The fathers don't see the Beatitudes as describing the plight of people who are going through a rough time here and now and as subsequently insisting that these same people will nonetheless be rewarded—either paradoxically in and through the very suffering they endure or in the promised life hereafter. Yes, the Beatitudes do talk about suffering—after all, they speak about mourning, about hunger, about persecution, all of which involve suffering of some kind. But Gregory, Augustine, and Leo all insist that when the Beatitudes speak of suffering, this suffering is primarily an occasion for the training and development of virtue. Far from taking our present circumstances (even situations of terrible suffering) as matters of ultimate concern, the church fathers were convinced that what is at stake is our need—regardless of the situation—to enter into and to develop a real, participatory relationship with God and with the virtues of God. Sometimes the readings of the church fathers may strike us as oddly single-minded in their approach. Especially when we read Saint Gregory of Nyssa, we may well wonder: Is there any passage that does *not* speak of the virtues? The answer to that question is: probably not. For Gregory, *everything* in Scripture relates to virtue; he took with utmost seriousness Saint Paul's claim that *all* of Scripture is useful for "training in righteousness" (2 Tim. 3:16).

If we turn to three of the descriptions that are obviously related to suffering (mourning, hungering, and thirsting), it is easy to see how the fathers read them as descriptions of virtue. For Gregory, we already saw, those who mourn are either people who mourn for their previous lives of sin or people who mourn because they are unable to grasp the ineffable God. Either way, the mourning is an incentive to continue on the path toward God. Augustine seems to oscillate between two understandings of mourning. First he explains that it refers to the mourning of people who have converted and are now grieving the things they used to hold dear.[51] A little later he suggests that what is mourned is "the loss of the highest goods," a loss of which one becomes aware once one

---

50. Fowl, "Virtue," 838.
51. Augustine, *Sermon on the Mount* 1.2.5 (*NPNF*[1] 6:5).

has attained the knowledge of Scripture.[52] On either reading, mourning has nothing to do with the suffering that others inflict on us, and has everything to do with repentance and the process of salvation. Finally, for Leo, mourning speaks about the "religious grief" that laments one's own iniquity.[53] Again, mourning is about repentance from vice and about turning to virtue. With this understanding of mourning, Leo takes the logical step of suggesting that "he that does wrong is more to be deplored than he who suffers it."[54] Leo goes so far as to exclude explicitly the notion that the mourning described by Jesus might be caused by other people inflicting suffering on believers.

None of the three church fathers interprets the promise of satisfaction for those who "hunger and thirst for righteousness" as expressing a desire for God to punish one's adversaries or to redress the injustice inflicted upon them. Gregory dismisses such an interpretation by rejecting the classical understanding of righteousness or justice as "the disposition to distribute equally to each, according to his worth."[55] This understanding of justice as rendering to each person what is due to him is "completely refuted by the inequality of life," insists Gregory.[56] Lazarus, entirely without authority to administer anything, could never be just if justice were a matter of fair distribution.[57] Gregory therefore spiritualizes justice as a reference to doing the will of the Father (John 4:34). Since the will of the Father is that all be saved (1 Tim. 2:4), Nyssen concludes that salvation is the justice for which we hunger.[58]

Saint Augustine uses the same text of John 4:34 ("My food is to do the will of him who sent me"), and he too explains that hungering and thirsting for righteousness means to long for eternal life. People who hunger and thirst for righteousness are "lovers of a true and indestructible good."[59] They "labour" with "vehement exertion" and "fortitude" to "wrench" themselves away from earthly entanglements.[60] The virtuous life is a process of hard labor. Along similar lines, Saint Leo maintains that the righteousness we seek is "nothing bodily, nothing earthly."[61] Instead, it has to do with being "filled with the LORD Himself," in accordance with the psalmist's words: "Taste and see that the LORD is sweet"

52. Ibid., 1.3.10 (*NPNF*[1] 6:6), 1.4.12 (*NPNF*[1] 6:7).
53. Leo the Great, *Sermon XCV* (*NPNF*[2] 12:204).
54. Ibid.
55. Gregory of Nyssa, *Beatitudes*, Sermon 4 (ACW 18:119).
56. Ibid., Sermon 4 (ACW 18:120).
57. Ibid. Gregory seems to ignore here that Lazarus might still desire to be the object of equal distribution of justice.
58. Ibid., Sermon 4 (ACW 18:124).
59. Augustine, *Sermon on the Mount* 1.2.6 (*NPNF*[1] 6:5).
60. Ibid., 1.3.10 (*NPNF*[1] 6:6), 1.4.12 (*NPNF*[1] 6:7).
61. Leo the Great, *Sermon XCV* (*NPNF*[2] 12:204).

(Ps. 33 [34]:8).[62] Hungering and thirsting for righteousness, each of these theologians maintains, has nothing to do with asking God to alleviate unjust material suffering; it has everything to do with the development of the virtuous life.

It is clear that we are dealing here with a theological or spiritual interpretation that is much more interested in the *purpose* of interpretation than in the historical meaning of the text. Furthermore, when we ask what kind of theology sets the agenda, it is obviously one in which salvation is a process of growth in virtue and perfection, so that one may be fitted for the kingdom of heaven. The theology of participation in the life of God dominates the way in which the text is approached and therefore determines also the range of possible meanings of the text.

Numbering the Steps of Virtue

The result of this link between virtue and interpretation is that for each of the three church fathers, the Beatitudes function as a pathway on the journey of salvation. Gregory, Augustine, and Leo all interpret the eight beatitudes as stages in the salvific process of the development of Christian virtue. If salvation is a process of entering into the mystery of God's being, then it becomes crucial to analyze the life of virtue as the path along which we do this. So, at the beginning of his second sermon, Gregory explains:

> When one climbs up by a ladder he sets foot on the first step, and from there goes on to the one above. Again the second step carries the climber up to the third, and this to the following, and hence to the next. Thus the person who goes up always ascends from where he is to the step above until he reaches the top of his ascent. Now why do I begin like this? It seems to me that the Beatitudes are arranged in order like so many steps, so as to facilitate the ascent from one to the other.[63]

Saint Gregory interprets the eight beatitudes as so many steps on a ladder, finally leading to what, in paradoxical terms, he calls the "supercelestial earth," which is "the inheritance of those who have led a life of virtue."[64] And at various points at the beginning of his other sermons in the series, he reiterates his understanding of the Beatitudes as steps in the virtuous ascent on the ladder to "the summit of the mountain."[65]

62. Ibid.
63. Gregory of Nyssa, *Beatitudes*, Sermon 2 (ACW 18:97).
64. Ibid.
65. Ibid., Sermon 3 (ACW 18:106). Cf. ibid., Sermon 4 (ACW 18:117), Sermon 5 (ACW 18:130), Sermon 7 (ACW 18:154).

Saint Augustine has a similar interest. He goes through the contents of the Beatitudes not just once but three times in a row. The first time, he simply gives a general explanation of each of the beatitudes.[66] The second time, he displays particular interest in how many beatitudes there are, insisting that there are really only seven, not eight, since the reward of the last one is identical to that of the first (namely, the kingdom of heaven).[67] Here he explains each of the seven beatitudes as consecutive "stages," beginning with humility in the first stage and ending in the perfection of wisdom in the seventh and final stage. He lists the seven stages as follows: (1) humility, (2) meekness in piety, (3) rejection of carnal custom and sins, (4) fortitude in the pursuit of righteousness, (5) assistance of those who are weak, (6) purity of heart through good works, and (7) wisdom, which is "the contemplation of the truth, tranquillizing the whole man, and assuming the likeness of God."[68] Augustine concludes: "Seven in number, therefore, are the things which bring perfection: for the eighth brings into light and shows what is perfect, so that starting, as it were, from the beginning again, the others also are perfected by means of these stages."[69]

The third time Augustine goes through the Beatitudes, he does it by way of a brief exposition on the gifts of the Spirit mentioned in Isaiah 11, of which (in the Septuagint) there are seven: wisdom, understanding, counsel, might, knowledge, piety, and fear of God.[70] Augustine encounters two problems, however, as he tries to match the gifts of the Spirit from Isaiah 11 with the Beatitudes of Matthew 5. First, while there are seven gifts of the Spirit, there are eight beatitudes. This is a relatively simple problem, and we have already seen how Augustine solves it: he insists that the final beatitude simply recapitulates the first, so that there are in essence only seven beatitudes. Second, Isaiah's list of the gifts of the Spirit begins with wisdom and ends with the fear of God. This presents a difficulty, since wisdom, in Saint Augustine's view, is the final end of the Christian life, while the fear of God is the beginning of this journey to wisdom, not its end. The Isaianic list not only doesn't quite fit with the Matthean one, but it almost appears as its mirror opposite, starting out with wisdom and ending with fear. The bishop of Hippo concludes, therefore, that Isaiah's progression begins at the

---

66. Augustine, *Sermon on the Mount* 1.1.3–1.2.9 (NPNF¹ 6:4–5).

67. Ibid., 1.3.10 (NPNF¹ 6:6).

68. Ibid. Although he clearly already has Isaiah 11 in mind in this second round through the Beatitudes in 1.3.10, Augustine discusses the seven gifts of the Spirit without at this point alluding to Isaiah.

69. Ibid.

70. The Hebrew Masoretic Text mentions only six gifts.

top of the ascent rather than at the bottom. We can summarize Augustine's exegesis, therefore, in table 1.

As we can see from this table, Augustine tries to show that the prophet Isaiah starts out at the end, while the Lord himself follows the natural progression of the ascent toward perfection.[71] In the process, Augustine displays remarkable ingenuity in linking the various beatitudes with the corresponding gifts of the Spirit.

We may well want to question both Augustine's use of the Beatitudes as stages in the Christian life and his attempt to match them with Isaiah's gifts of the Spirit. Robert Wilken suggests, however, that we need to understand what it is that the bishop of Hippo is doing: "Augustine's aim, of course, is to come up with a scheme that is simple and memorable. As a teacher of the church he wishes to present the Sermon not as a body of general moral principles but a workable guide to life."[72] Wilken's characterization of Saint Augustine's approach as giving a "workable guide to life" is certainly helpful. Augustine, after all, is interested more in how the text aids the Christian life than in what it says at the surface level. It is possible, however, to say more. Saint Augustine is interested in outlining the life of virtue, the life that leads to perfection. When he observes that it is by using the number seven that both the prophet Isaiah and Christ himself speak of the gifts of the Spirit (that is to say, the Christian's virtues), this is an indication to him that they are leading the Christian to perfection. After all, Augustine himself states explicitly, "Seven in number . . . are the things which bring perfection."[73] He goes even further by speculating rather extensively on the number eight. He is reminded that circumcision took place on the eighth day, that Christ's resurrection took place on the eighth day, that the liturgical calendar celebrates Easter (leading to the feast of baptism) over an eight-day period, and that we arrive at fifty, the number of Pentecost, by multiplying seven times seven and adding one, which gives us our inheritance of the kingdom of heaven, the very reality that the first and eighth beatitude mention as the reward.[74]

With a slightly different approach, Gregory does essentially the same thing. He alludes to the "mystery of the number eight" mentioned in the Septuagint headings of two psalms (Psalms 6 and 11), while pointing out that the eighth day is also the day of the feast of purification and of circumcision. Gregory too links the eighth beatitude with the day of Christ's resurrection. Jean Daniélou, the great French Gregory of Nyssa scholar, explains that the theme

71. Augustine, *Sermon on the Mount* 1.3.10 (*NPNF*[1] 6:6).
72. Wilken, "Augustine," 49.
73. Augustine, *Sermon on the Mount* 1.3.10 (*NPNF*[1] 6:6).
74. Ibid., 1.4.12 (*NPNF*[1] 6:7).

Table 1

		Beatitude (Matthew 5)	Gifts of the Spirit (Isaiah 11)	Description
1	*Virtue*	Poor in spirit	Fear of God	• Humility as opposed to pride
	Blessing	Kingdom of heaven		
2	*Virtue*	Meek	Piety	• Knowledge of Scripture • Teachability • Not resisting evil
	Blessing	Possession of the earth		• God as our portion
3	*Virtue*	Mourners	Knowledge	• Recognition of the loss of temporal things • Recognition of the loss of highest good
	Blessing	Comfort		• The Spirit's joy in eternal things
4	*Virtue*	Those who hunger and thirst after righteousness	Fortitude	• Love of indestructible good • Wrenching oneself away from earthly entanglements through vehement exertion
	Blessing	Satisfaction		• Doing the Father's will
5	*Virtue*	Merciful	Counsel	• Relieving the miserable • Giving and receiving counsel to get rid of entanglements • Forgiving others
	Blessing	Receiving mercy		• Being freed from misery
6	*Virtue*	Pure in heart	Understanding	• Singleness of heart • Good conscience through good works
	Blessing	Seeing God		• Seeing with the heart

7	*Virtue*	Peacemakers	Wisdom	• Proper order in God's kingdom
				  - No opposition to God
				  - Subjection of carnal lusts to reason
				  - Subjection of reason to the Son of God
				• Contemplation of God
				• Likeness of God

	Blessing	Being called sons of God		
8	*Virtue*	Persecuted	None	
	Blessing	Kingdom of heaven		

This table lists only those items that Augustine refers to explicitly in his exposition of the Beatitudes. Where Augustine does not mention anything, that space is left blank.

of the eighth day, the ogdoad, is important not only in these sermons on the
Beatitudes but also in Nyssen's *Treatise on the Inscriptions of the Psalms*
and in his homily entitled *On the Sixth Psalm*.[75] Daniélou explains that for
Gregory the eighth day is symbolic of the eschaton, because it follows after
the sensible world of the seven days, called the hebdomad.[76] For Gregory,
explains Daniélou, the theology of the ogdoad (the eighth day) expresses the
contrast between the finite, temporal character of creation and the eternity of
the hereafter. In Gregory's words, in the new creation "the true circumcision
of human nature will come to reality, in the removal of our bodily life and
the true purgation of our true uncleanness. This, then, is the way in which we
interpret the [biblical] law about the Eighth Day, the law of purification and
circumcision; namely, that when the time that is measured in weeks comes to
an end, an Eighth Day will come into being after the seventh— called 'eighth'
because it exists after the seventh, not because it is any longer capable of
numerical succession."[77] The temporal age of this world (time "measured in
weeks") must give way to the eighth day, to which Gregory alludes by speaking
of purification and circumcision. It is then that we will strip off the tunics of
skin with which we have been clothed since the fall, which in his sermons on
the Beatitudes Gregory calls the "dead skins."[78] Both for Saint Augustine and
for Saint Gregory, the theme of the ogdoad was rich with biblical echoes and
eminently suited to give expression to the life of the resurrection.

Seeing as we are dealing with a context of a salvation process leading to the
eighth day by means of the virtues, it is hardly surprising to see each of our
authors contrast temporality and eternity, as well as earth and heaven. After
all, on this view we are straining to reach the eighth day. Consequently, Gregory
repeatedly criticizes the luxury that he is worried may tempt his congregation.
Instead of hungering for what we need—justice and the will of the Father,
that is to say, our salvation—people often think of silver on the table and of
costly tripods and bowls for their drinks.[79] Gregory reminds his audience, in
a wonderful, rhetorical passage, of the final judgment: "When things such as
these shall be said, where will be the gold? Where the splendid vessels? Where
will be the security affixed to the treasures by seals? Where will be the dogs
that were assigned to watch by night, where the store of arms laid up against

75. Daniélou, *Bible and the Liturgy*, 270–75.

76. Ibid., 270.

77. Cited in Daley, "Training for 'the Good Ascent,'" 213 (square brackets in original).
Daniélou quotes this passage in *Bible and the Liturgy*, 273.

78. Gregory of Nyssa, *Beatitudes*, Sermon 8 (ACW 18:166). Cf. Daniélou, *Bible and the
Liturgy*, 274.

79. Gregory of Nyssa, *Beatitudes*, Sermon 4 (ACW 18:122–23).

burglars? Where will be the accounts entered into the books? What is all this against the weeping and gnashing of teeth? Who will lighten the darkness and extinguish the flame? Who shall turn away the undying worm?"[80] For Gregory, the goods of this temporal existence—while certainly goods—are by no means ultimate. How could they be if our real aim in everything we do is to train the virtues?

Saint Augustine argues no differently. Referring to the well-known messianic Psalm 44 (45), Augustine comments on the final, eighth beatitude: "Let any one who is seeking after the delights of this world and the riches of temporal things under the Christian name, consider that our blessedness is within; as it is said of the soul of the church by the mouth of the prophet, 'All the beauty of the king's daughter is within' [Ps. 44:14 (45:13)]."[81] The psalm, on Augustine's reading, refers to the church as the king's daughter. And her beauty has to do with internal, not external matters—or, we could also say, with eternal, not temporal affairs.

Saint Leo, much like Augustine, distinguishes between the "outward" and the "inward." In the introduction to his homily, he explains how Jesus rendered the hearts of his audience receptive to his teaching: "And therefore that the LORD might use outward healings as an introduction to inward remedies, and after healing bodies might work cures in the soul, He separated Himself from the surrounding crowd, ascended into the retirement of a neighbouring mountain, and called His apostles to Him there."[82] The "heavenly Physician" did not perform outward healings for their own sake, according to Leo. Instead, outward healing serves inward healing; the body serves the soul.

Conclusion

For each of the three theologians we have discussed, the Christian life aims at perfection or, we could also say, at ever-greater participation in the life of God. The doctrine of salvation aims at growth in virtue. Ultimately, the happiness or blessedness to which the Beatitudes point us is the eternal happiness or blessedness of God himself. Gregory makes this explicit when he says that "the one thing truly blessed is the Divinity itself."[83] This happiness is an infinite happiness that never changes, one that (in Gregory's understanding, at least) changeable human beings can never fully attain.

80. Ibid., Sermon 5 (ACW 18:142).
81. Augustine, *Sermon on the Mount* 1.4.12 (NPNF[1] 6:7).
82. Leo the Great, *Sermon XCV* (NPNF[2] 12:202).
83. Gregory of Nyssa, *Beatitudes*, Sermon 1 (ACW 18:87).

What *is* possible for human beings, however, is to *participate* in this happiness of God. When growth of virtue transforms our character into God's likeness, we come to participate in the virtue of divine blessedness or happiness. As Gregory puts it, "As He who fashioned man made him in the image of God; *in a derived sense* that which is called by this name should also be held blessed, inasmuch as he *participates* in the true beatitude."[84] Human happiness or blessedness is merely a derived and participatory blessedness. Gregory equates God, virtue, and blessedness. As a result, any blessedness or virtue that we attain is a participation in that of God. The aim of the Beatitudes is for us to come to share or participate in this blessedness.

84. Ibid., Sermon 1 (ACW 18:88) (emphasis added).

CONCLUSION

Becoming as the Face of Being

This book is a project of *ressourcement*. Not everyone will be convinced of the viability of such a retrieval of the sacramental sensibility that undergirds patristic exegesis.[1] But it is my hope that the biblical expositions of the church fathers discussed in this book will have proven winsome in convincing the reader that patristic exegesis has abiding vitality.[2] Still, we need to face head-on the question of whether it's possible in today's context to do the kind of exegesis that we have traced in this book. Isn't the bottom line that our age is simply too historical in outlook for patristic exegesis to function in any meaningful sense? Indeed, even many of those who wistfully glance back to the premodern era are nonetheless convinced there's no possibility of return.

Louis Dupré, for instance, is convinced there's no going back to premodernity. His book *Passage to Modernity* presents a perceptive and persuasive analysis of the philosophical and cultural changes that took place beginning with the late Middle Ages (though in some respects Dupré traces these changes

1. As I have tried to make clear throughout this book, I understand this retrieval not as a simple return to patristic interpretation but as a reappropriation of the sacramental sensibility that informed this exegesis. This will at times lead to similar (or even identical) exegetical results as those put forward by the church fathers. But the diversity of patristic exegetical approaches and choices, the willingness of the church fathers to entertain multiple meanings of any given text, and our own distinct social and cultural contexts all prevent a slavish following of the church fathers' exegesis.

2. Cf. John Webster's comment that "the future of Protestant divinity rests in some measure on its capacity to absorb and re-articulate the resources of the tradition(s) of Christianity—perhaps more than anything, its exegetical traditions and the modes of theological discourse in which they found expression." "*Ressourcement* Theology and Protestantism," 493.

to a much earlier period), and it is clear that he has a great deal of sympathy with the participatory cosmology that prevailed in premodern society. As he describes the birth of the modern period, he places what he calls the "fateful separation" between nature and the supernatural at the center of his analysis.[3] Dupré's discomfort with the resulting cultural changes is apparent throughout his discussion. Still, he resists the temptation of attempting a return to the past. "History," he claims, "carries an ontic significance that excludes any reversal of the present."[4] Dupré believes it is impossible to undo the features that have come to characterize modernity: "Its problems cannot be treated as errors to be corrected by a simple return to an earlier truth. That truth is no longer available; it has vanished forever."[5] The reason for this, Dupré believes, is that the modern age appears to have changed the very nature of Being itself.[6] Becoming, it turns out, "presents the real face of Being."[7]

A sense of inevitability pervades Dupré's analysis. There's no turning back the clock. Considering the passion with which Dupré describes the premodern participatory understanding of reality, it is hard to imagine him being unambiguously positive about the direction that Becoming has taken since the late Middle Ages. His book almost conveys a sense of reluctant resignation: the past will not come back, seeing as the nature of what's real has actually changed. Dupré counsels that we turn to panentheistic voices such as those of Nicholas of Cusa (1401–1464), Giordano Bruno (1548–1600), and others, in the hope that they will affect the direction of the future more than they have so far.

If Dupré were right, the project of this book would be fruitless. To be sure, Dupré doesn't discuss the pros and cons of patristic exegesis. But it seems clear that if Becoming is indeed the real face of Being, then it makes no sense to try to retrieve patristic interpretation. This book, however, is written on the premise that the basic sacramental cast of patristic interpretation can and will endure, so that a *ressourcement* is both possible and necessary. Notwithstanding Dupré's brilliant and convincing historical analysis, I am unconvinced of the need to accept his basic philosophical premise: that the modern age has changed the nature of Being itself. Nor am I convinced that patristic exegesis essentially belongs to a past age that simply won't return.

3. Dupré, *Passage to Modernity*, 167–89.
4. Ibid., 6.
5. Ibid., 7.
6. Ibid. Similarly, in his conclusion, Dupré writes that "the spiritual discovery of the moderns consists in understanding the active relationship of mind to cosmos as one that changes the nature of the real. As it directly affects the constituent relations of the real, this insight is itself transformative." Ibid., 252.
7. Ibid., 8.

The main reason for my hopeful stance vis-à-vis the prospects of patristic exegesis is that I believe this interpretive approach is based on a theologically informed metaphysic that is—to put it bluntly—true. Andrew Louth, whose book *Discerning the Mystery* presents a compelling apology for allegorical exegesis, points to the importance of the truth question. He discusses the preoccupation with a historical understanding of the Bible among the romantics, according to which people of every age were equally close to God. This historical consciousness of romanticism had no criteria, however, by which to determine truth and falsehood among ancient writers. By reducing the significance of ancient writers to their place within the organic development of history, the romantics, in effect, treated them all as false.[8]

Louth gives the example of how, on the basis of these philosophical underpinnings, the historical-critical method treats the history of philosophy. When the various philosophers of the past are simply located within their historical contexts, the truth question disappears. Louth rightly comments that in this approach "the philosophers are no longer of interest in themselves; they are interesting only as they contribute to the history of the subject. A gulf opens between history of philosophy and philosophy itself: philosophers need have no interest in the history of their subject and historians of philosophy certainly need not be philosophers."[9] This problem doesn't only beset philosophers: throughout the humanities a gulf has opened up between the history of the discipline and the discipline itself.

The consequence of this approach, explains Louth, is that we now typically treat the current state of any given discipline as having arrived at its highest point of development. We study previous practitioners of the discipline, not to gain from their insights, but simply to expose them as links in a historical chain of development. The result is that they will always and inevitably be superseded by the next link in the chain.[10] In the field of biblical studies, this means that the impact of contemporary historical exegetes is limited to what they contribute to the next generation of scholars within the discipline's historical development. This historicizing of the humanities tacitly assumes that all previous scholarship merely serves in a preliminary function, to bring us to where we are today. It's as though we imagine ourselves as having walked aboard a ship and, confident of our ability to take off on our own, we kick away the boarding plank that connected us to the shore. When the exegetical aim is to arrive at the one true meaning of the text, we inevitably condemn

8. Louth, *Discerning the Mystery*, 13.
9. Ibid., 14.
10. Ibid., 15.

our predecessors—and, in the not-too-distant future also ourselves!—to the dustbin of history.

Thankfully, the reality on the ground is usually not as black-and-white as I have just painted it. Even the most historicist of scholars usually still has favorites within the history of his discipline, and as a result some kind of *ressourcement* invariably takes place.[11] In practice, the gap between, say, the history of New Testament exegesis and the exegetical practice itself is rarely absolute. This shows simply that no discipline can function properly without the requisite confidence of distinguishing between true and false insights within the history of the discipline.

Christ as the Face of Being

The cultural moment that we face in North America is not conducive to sacramental interpretation. The reason for this is the cultural legacy of a separation between nature and the supernatural, between history and spirit, and between earthly and heavenly things. And since our culture typically focuses on the former elements, we live in a largely materialist context, which tends to spurn the spiritual interpretation of the church fathers. In that regard, the influence of (Neo-)Platonism in late antiquity made for much more favorable conditions for sacramental interpretation.

Unlike Dupré, however, I am not convinced that Becoming is the real face of Being. I believe that the flourishing of the historicist and materialist mindset of Western culture says nothing about its truth or falsehood. My Christian Platonist convictions imply that I will happily go back to the church fathers (or the Middle Ages or anywhere else) to look for insights that can contribute to the practice of sacramental reading today. After all, the question of whether a *ressourcement* of the exegesis of the church fathers is possible and worthwhile is, ultimately, a question of the truth or falsehood of its metaphysical and hermeneutical presuppositions. It is not popularity (or lack thereof) that determines the validity of the metaphysical undergirding of patristic exegesis.

Still, we may ask: Are these metaphysical presuppositions in some way borne out in the actual practice of theological or spiritual interpretation in today's situation? Do we have any actual evidence that sacramental exegesis is a live option today? It is one thing to illustrate the sacramental reading strategy of the church fathers; it is another to use it in today's context in sermons and

11. We already saw that Dupré, despite his acknowledgment that Becoming is the real face of Being, looks to certain panentheist philosophers of the past in the hope that they will contribute to future philosophical developments.

in commentaries. Thankfully, it is possible to point to a growing conviction, not only among dogmatic theologians but also among biblical scholars, that exegesis is not primarily a historical endeavor and that it first of all asks about the subject of the text—that is to say, about God and our relationship to him.[12] To be sure, not all theological interpretation of Scripture reads the Scriptures sacramentally. Still, it is fair to say that with the rise of theological interpretation over the past few decades, we are at least in a situation in which the possibility of sacramental reading can legitimately be raised.[13]

Over and over again, it has struck me how often the patristic interpretations are so similar to one another. I don't mean that there are no differences: the previous chapters have repeatedly drawn attention to the fact that the fathers were convinced that a text can have multiple meanings, and this obviously implies differences in exegesis—not just between different readers but also quite often within the corpus of one and the same reader of Scripture. I have also pointed out individual differences and varying approaches among several groups or schools of thought. Still, compared to the bewildering variety of exegetical choices among modern and postmodern interpreters, patristic exegesis comes across as remarkably homogeneous, and this is noteworthy considering that the emphasis on "method" in modern biblical scholarship was supposed to lead to greater certainty and unanimity with regard to the one true meaning of the text—such in contrast with the allegedly arbitrary (and therefore, one would think, wildly varying) readings of the church fathers.

Several factors give rise to this sense of continuity of interpretation within patristic exegesis. One of these is the frequent and at times unrestrained borrowing from predecessors that took place both in the patristic era and throughout much of the Middle Ages. At times, such borrowing was so extensive that in today's context it would be considered plagiarism.[14] The positive motivation for this reliance on one's predecessors, however, was the sense of tradition and the deep respect for one's theological forebears. The church fathers would look to earlier exegetes as well as to esteemed contemporaries for theological and exegetical models because they were convinced of the Spirit's continuing work within the tradition of the church. Along with this came the

12. Particularly noteworthy are the following commentary series: Brazos Theological Commentary on the Bible (Brazos), The Church's Bible (Eerdmans), Reformation Commentary on Scripture (InterVarsity), Two Horizons Commentary (Eerdmans), and the Catholic Commentary on Sacred Scripture (Baker Academic).

13. I have tried to show by means of a book of sermons that sacramental reading can also be practiced today: H. Boersma, *Sacramental Preaching*.

14. I have discussed one instance of this in the preaching of Caesarius of Arles (ca. 470–542), who borrowed extensively from Origen and from Saint Augustine. See H. Boersma, "Preaching through Many Voices."

recognition that one's own contribution was limited and that its originality was entirely subservient to the edification of the church. This same mindset made it unthinkable for premoderns to place a signature or initials at the bottom of a painting. Neither the commentary nor the painting was meant to point to the genius of its author; it is the described or depicted reality that was considered to be of utmost concern.

I suspect that an even greater factor in producing exegetical homogeneity, however, was the christological grounding of the church fathers' spiritual exegesis. Of course, it is possible for allegory to spin out of control. But the most important factor preventing this was that the church fathers read the Old Testament Scriptures as containing the sacramental presence of Christ. We saw that in the late second century, Irenaeus interpreted the parable of the treasure in the field (Matt. 13:44) allegorically by insisting that "Christ is the treasure that was hid (*thesaurus absconsus*) in the field,"[15] while in the 240s, Origen similarly insisted that Christ is "hidden like a treasure (*thesaurus absconditus*) in the Law and the Prophets."[16] It is quite likely that Origen read Irenaeus, and he may well have relied on the bishop of Lyons for his own interpretation. But I suspect that, in addition, something more significant is going on: both Irenaeus and Origen were determined to read the Scriptures within the church and as witnesses to the real presence of Jesus Christ. The result is an allegorizing of Scripture that centers on Christ. Because Christian allegorizing looks for Christ—and the salvation that he works in the history of the church—it is not surprising that exegetical outcomes often look rather similar.

Many of the details and peculiarities of an individual patristic author's exegesis are nonessential, and they need not and should not be retrieved. However, the sacramental metaphysical assumptions that give rise to a search for the mystery of Christ within the deeds and words of the biblical text lie at the very heart of patristic exegesis. For the church fathers, it is Christ himself who is the real face of Being. They would have argued that, as the *mysterium* hidden in the field of the biblical text, Christ's presence there depends not on the waxing and waning of historical sensibilities. The treasure is sacramentally present regardless of whether we search for it or find it. The viability of a *ressourcement* of patristic exegesis, therefore, depends not on its general appeal but on the continuing reliability of the gospel message itself. It is the church fathers' sacramental sensibility, grounded in a Chris-

15. Irenaeus, *Against Heresies* 4.26.1 (*ANF* 1:496). See chap. 1, sec. "Irenaeus's Recapitulation as Sacramental Reading."
16. Origen, *Commentary on the Canticle of Canticles* 1.2 (ACW 26:69).

tian Platonist ontology, that they believed distinguished their reading of the Scriptures from that of non-Christian interpreters (most notably Jewish and gnostic readers). It is this sacramental sensibility, as expressed in biblical exegesis, that shaped the doctrine of the subsequent tradition of the church. And it is this same sacramental sensibility that still has the vitality to renew the life of the church today.

BIBLIOGRAPHY

Primary Sources

Ambrose. *On Abraham*. Translated by Theodosia Tomkinson. Etna, CA: Center for Traditionalist Orthodox Studies, 2000.

———. *Concerning Virgins*. Translated by H. de Romestin, E. de Romestin, and H. T. F. Duckwort. In vol. 10 of *Nicene and Post-Nicene Fathers*, Series 2. Edited by Philip Schaff and Henry Wace. 1896. Reprint, Peabody, MA: Hendrickson, 1994.

———. *De Isaac vel anima*. In *Hexameron, De paradiso, De Cain, De Noe, De Abraham, De Isaac, De bono mortis*. Corpus Scriptorum Ecclesiasticorum Latinorum 32/1. Edited by Karl Schenkl. Prague: Tempsky, 1897.

———. *Homilies of Saint Ambrose on Psalm 118 (119)*. Translated by Íde Ní Riain. Dublin: Halcyon, 1998.

———. *Isaac, or the Soul*. Translated by Michael P. McHugh. In *Seven Exegetical Works*, edited by Bernard M. Peebles. Fathers of the Church 65. Washington, DC: Catholic University of America Press, 1972.

———. *The Mysteries*. Translated by Roy Joseph Deferrari. In *Saint Ambrose: Theological and Dogmatic Works*, edited by Roy Joseph Deferrari. Fathers of the Church 44. Washington, DC: Catholic University of America Press, 1963.

———. *The Sacraments*. Translated by Roy Joseph Deferrari. In *Saint Ambrose: Theological and Dogmatic Works*, edited by Roy Joseph Deferrari. Fathers of the Church 44. Washington, DC: Catholic University of America Press, 1963.

———. *On Virginity*. Translated by Daniel Callam. Peregrina Translations Series 7. 1980. Reprint, Toronto: Peregrina, 1989.

Arius. *Letter to Alexander of Alexandria*. Translated by William G. Rusch. In *The Trinitarian Controversy*, edited by William G. Rusch. Philadelphia: Fortress, 1980.

280

Athanasius. *Four Discourses against the Arians*. Translated by John Henry New-man. In vol. 4 of *Nicene and Post-Nicene Fathers*, Series 2. Edited by Archibald Robertson. 1891. Reprint, Peabody, MA: Hendrickson, 1994.

————. *The Life of Antony and the Letter to Marcellinus*. Translated and edited by Robert C. Gregg. Classics of Western Spirituality. New York: Paulist Press, 1980.

Augustine. *Confessions*. Translated and edited by Henry Chadwick. Oxford: Oxford University Press, 1991.

————. *De Doctrina Christiana*. Edited and translated by R. P. H. Green. Oxford: Clarendon, 1995.

————. *De Trinitate*. Translated by Edmund Hill. The Works of Saint Augustine: A Translation for the 21st Century I/5. Edited by John E. Rotelle. 2nd ed. Hyde Park, NY: New City, 2000.

————. *Expositions of the Psalms 1–32*. Translated and edited by Maria Boulding. The Works of Saint Augustine: A Translation for the 21st Century III/15. Edited by John E. Rotelle. Hyde Park, NY: New City, 2000.

————. *On Genesis: A Refutation of the Manichees; Unfinished Literal Commentary on Genesis; The Literal Meaning of Genesis*. Translated by Edmund Hill. The Works of Saint Augustine: A Translation for the 21st Century I/13. Edited by John E. Rotelle. Hyde Park, NY: New City, 2002.

————. *Our Lord's Sermon on the Mount*. Translated by William Findlay and revised by D. S. Schaff. In vol. 6 of *Nicene and Post-Nicene Fathers*, Series 1. Edited by Philip Schaff. 1888. Reprint, Peabody, MA: Hendrickson, 1994.

————. *The Retractations*. Translated by Mary Inez Bogan. Edited by Roy Joseph Deferrari. Fathers of the Church 60. Washington, DC: Catholic University of America Press, 1968.

Basil of Caesarea. *Exegetic Homilies*. Translated and edited by Agnes Clare Way. Fathers of the Church 46. Washington, DC: Catholic University of America Press, 1963.

————. *On the Human Condition*. Translated by Verna E. F. Harrison. Popular Patristics Series 30. Crestwood, NY: St Vladimir's Seminary Press, 2005.

Boethius. *Fundamentals of Music*. Translated by Calvin M. Bower. Edited by Claude V. Palisca. New Haven: Yale University Press, 1989.

Clement of Alexandria. *The Exhortation to the Greeks; The Rich Man's Salvation; To the Newly Baptized*. Translated by G. W. Butterworth. Loeb Classical Library 92. Cambridge, MA: Harvard University Press, 1919.

Eunomius of Cyzicus. *Eunomius: The Extant Works*. Edited by Richard Paul Vaggione. Oxford: Clarendon, 1987.

Gregory of Nyssa. *Against Eunomius*. Translated and edited by William Moore and Henry Austin Wilson. In vol. 5 of *Nicene and Post-Nicene Fathers*, Series 2. 1892. Reprint, Peabody, MA: Hendrickson, 1994.

————. *Against Eunomius Book Three.* In *Contra Eunomium III: An English Translation with Commentary and Supporting Studies; Proceedings of the 12th International Colloquium on Gregory of Nyssa,* translated by Stuart George Hall, edited by Johan Leemans and Matthieu Cassin, 42–233. Supplements to Vigiliae Christianae 124. Leiden: Brill, 2014.

————. *Gregory of Nyssa's Treatise on the Inscriptions of the Psalms.* Translated and edited by Ronald E. Heine. Oxford: Clarendon, 1995.

————. *Homilies on the Song of Songs.* Translated and edited by Richard A. Norris. Writings from the Greco-Roman World 13. Atlanta: Society of Biblical Literature, 2012.

————. *The Lord's Prayer; The Beatitudes.* Translated and edited by Hilda C. Graef. Ancient Christian Writers 18. New York: Paulist Press, 1954.

————. *On the Making of Man.* Translated by William Moore and Henry Austin Wilson. In vol. 5 of *Nicene and Post-Nicene Fathers,* Series 2. Edited by Philip Schaff and Henry Wace. 1892. Reprint, Peabody, MA: Hendrickson, 1994.

Hilary of Poitiers. *Homilies on the Psalms.* Translated by E. W. Watson, L. Pullan, et al. In vol. 9 of *Nicene and Post-Nicene Fathers,* Series 2. Edited by W. Sanday. 1899. Reprint, Peabody, MA: Hendrickson, 1994.

Hippolytus. *Commentary on the Song of Songs by the Blessed Hippolytus.* Translated and edited by Yancy Smith. In *The Mystery of Anointing: Hippolytus' Commentary on the Song of Songs in Social and Critical Contexts,* by Yancy Smith. Gorgias Studies in Early Christianity and Patristics 62. Piscataway, NJ: Gorgias, 2015.

Hobbes, Thomas. *Leviathan.* Edited by G. A. J. Rogers and Karl Schuhmann. 2 vols. London: Continuum, 2005.

Irenaeus. *Against Heresies.* In vol. 1 of *Ante-Nicene Fathers.* Edited by Alexander Roberts and James Donaldson. 1885. Reprint, Peabody, MA: Hendrickson, 1994.

————. *Fragments from the Lost Writings of Irenaeus.* In vol. 1 of *Ante-Nicene Fathers.* Edited by Alexander Roberts and James Donaldson. 1885. Reprint, Peabody, MA: Hendrickson, 1994.

————. *Proof of the Apostolic Preaching.* Translated by Joseph P. Smith. Ancient Christian Writers 16. New York: Paulist Press, 1952.

John Chrysostom. *Homilies on Genesis 1–17.* Translated by Robert C. Hill. Fathers of the Church 74. Washington, DC: Catholic University of America Press, 1986.

————. *Homilies on Genesis 18–45.* Translated by Robert C. Hill. Fathers of the Church 82. Washington, DC: Catholic University of America Press, 1990.

————. *Homilies on Genesis 46–67.* Translated by Robert C. Hill. Fathers of the Church 87. Washington, DC: Catholic University of America Press, 1992.

Justin Martyr. *The First Apology; The Second Apology; Dialogue with Trypho; Exhortation to the Greeks; Discourse to the Greeks; The Monarchy or The Rule of God.* Translated by Thomas B. Falls. Fathers of the Church 6. Washington, DC: Catholic University of America Press, 1948.

Leo the Great. *Sermon XCV: A Homily on the Beatitudes*. Translated by Charles Lett Feltoe. In vol. 12 of *Nicene and Post-Nicene Fathers*, Series 2. Edited by Charles Lett Feltoe. 1895. Reprint, Peabody, MA: Hendrickson, 1994.

Melito of Sardis. *On Pascha and Fragments*. Translated and edited by Stuart George Hall. Oxford: Clarendon, 1979.

———. *On Pascha: With the Fragments of Melito and Other Material Related to the Quartodecimans*. Translated and edited by Alistair Stewart-Sykes. Crestwood, NY: St Vladimir's Seminary Press, 2001.

Origen. *Commentary on the Canticle of Canticles*. Translated by R. P. Lawson. In *The Song of Songs: Commentary and Homilies*, edited by R. P. Lawson. Ancient Christian Writers 26. New York: Newman, 1957.

———. *On First Principles*. Translated and edited by G. W. Butterworth. 1936. Reprint, Gloucester, MA: Smith, 1973.

———. *Homilies on Genesis and Exodus*. Translated by Ronald E. Heine. Fathers of the Church 71. Washington, DC: Catholic University of America Press, 1982.

———. *Homilies on Joshua*. Translated by Barbara J. Bruce. Edited by Cynthia White. Fathers of the Church 105. Washington, DC: Catholic University of America Press, 2002.

———. *Spirit and Fire: A Thematic Anthology of His Writings*. Translated by Robert J. Daly. Edited by Hans Urs von Balthasar. 1984. Reprint, Washington, DC: Catholic University of America Press, 2001.

———. *Treatise on the Passover; and, Dialogue of Origen with Heraclides and His Fellow Bishops on the Father, the Son, and the Soul*. Translated and edited by Robert J. Daly. Ancient Christian Writers 54. New York: Paulist Press, 1992.

———. *Two Homilies on the Canticle of Canticles*. Translated by R. P. Lawson. In *The Song of Songs: Commentary and Homilies*, edited by R. P. Lawson. Ancient Christian Writers 26. New York: Newman, 1957.

Philo. *On Abraham*. In *The Works of Philo: Complete and Unabridged*. Translated by C. D. Yonge. Peabody, MA: Hendrickson, 1995.

———. *Supplement I: Questions and Answers on Genesis*. Translated by Ralph Marcus. Loeb Classical Library 380. Cambridge, MA: Harvard University Press, 1958.

Plato. *The Republic*. 2 vols. Edited and translated by Christopher Emlyn-Jones and William Preddy. Loeb Classical Library 237, 276. Cambridge, MA: Harvard University Press, 2013.

———. *Selected Myths*. Edited by Catalin Partenie. Oxford: Oxford University Press, 2004.

———. *Timaeus; Critias; Cleitophon; Menexenus; Epistles*. Translated by Robert Gregg Bury. Loeb Classical Library 234. Cambridge, MA: Harvard University Press, 1929.

Plotinus. *Ennead V*. Translated by A. H. Armstrong. Loeb Classical Library 444. Cambridge, MA: Harvard University Press, 1984.

Theodoret of Cyrus. *Commentary on the Psalms: Psalms 1–72*. Translated by Robert C. Hill. Fathers of the Church 101. Washington, DC: Catholic University of America Press, 2000.

———. *Commentary on the Song of Songs*. Translated and edited by Robert C. Hill. Early Christian Studies 2. Brisbane: Centre for Early Christian Studies, Australian Catholic University, 2001.

Thomas Aquinas. *Summa Theologica*. 5 vols. Translated by Fathers of the English Dominican Province. 1948. Reprint, Notre Dame, IN: Christian Classics, 1981.

Secondary Sources

Adams, Jim W. *The Performative Nature and Function of Isaiah 40–55*. New York: T&T Clark, 2006.

Adams, Karen C. "Neoplatonic Aesthetic Tradition in the Arts." *College Music Symposium* 17, no. 2 (1977): 17–24.

Allert, Craig D. *A High View of Scripture? The Authority of the Bible and the Formation of the New Testament Canon*. Grand Rapids: Baker Academic, 2007.

Allison, Dale C. *The New Moses: A Matthean Typology*. Minneapolis: Fortress, 1993.

Anatolios, Khaled. *Retrieving Nicaea: The Development and Meaning of Trinitarian Doctrine*. Grand Rapids: Baker Academic, 2011.

Arruzza, Cinzia. "La Matière immatérielle chez Grégoire de Nysse." *Freiburger Zeitschrift für Philosophie und Theologie* 54 (2007): 215–23.

Austin, J. L. *How to Do Things with Words*, edited by J. O. Urmson and Marina Sbisà. 2nd ed. Cambridge, MA: Harvard University Press, 1975.

Auwers, Jean-Marie. "Grégoire de Nysse, interprète du Psautier: À propos d'une récente édition de texte." *Ephemerides theologicae Lovanienses* 80 (2004): 174–80.

Ayres, Lewis. *Nicaea and Its Legacy: An Approach to Fourth-Century Trinitarian Theology*. Oxford: Oxford University Press, 2004.

Baker, David L. "Typology and the Christian Use of the Old Testament." *Scottish Journal of Theology* 29 (1976): 137–57.

Barnes, Michel René. "The Visible Christ and the Invisible Trinity: Mt. 5:8 in Augustine's Theology of 400." *Modern Theology* 19 (2003): 329–55.

Barnes, Timothy David. *Athanasius and Constantius: Theology and Politics in the Constantinian Empire*. Cambridge, MA: Harvard University Press, 1993.

Barr, James. "Childs' Introduction to the Old Testament as Scripture." *Journal for the Study of the Old Testament* 16 (1980): 12–23.

———. *Holy Scripture: Canon, Authority, Criticism*. Oxford: Oxford University Press, 1983.

———. "Jowett and the 'Original Meaning' of Scripture." *Religious Studies* 18 (1982): 433–37.

Bartholomew, Craig G. *Reading Ecclesiastes: Old Testament Exegesis and Hermeneutical Theory*. Analecta Biblica 139. Rome: Pontificio Istituto Biblico, 1998.

Bates, Matthew W. *The Hermeneutics of the Apostolic Proclamation: The Center of Paul's Method of Scriptural Interpretation*. Waco: Baylor University Press, 2012.

Beeley, Christopher A. *The Unity of Christ: Continuity and Conflict in Patristic Tradition*. New Haven: Yale University Press, 2012.

Behr, John. *The Nicene Faith*. Vol. 2, in two parts, of *Formation of Christian Theology*. Crestwood, NY: St Vladimir's Seminary Press, 2004.

———. "The Rational Animal: A Rereading of Gregory of Nyssa's *De Hominis Opificio*." *Journal of Early Christian Studies* 7 (1999): 219–47.

Billings, J. Todd. *Calvin, Participation, and the Gift: The Activity of Believers in Union with Christ*. Oxford: Oxford University Press, 2007.

Blackwell, Albert L. *The Sacred in Music*. Louisville: Westminster John Knox, 1999.

Bockmuehl, Markus. *Seeing the Word: Refocusing New Testament Study*. Grand Rapids: Baker Academic, 2006.

Boersma, Gerald P. *Augustine's Early Theology of Image: A Study in the Development of Pro-Nicene Theology*. New York: Oxford University Press, 2016.

———. "Augustine's Psalter as *Vox Totius Christi*." *Cithara* 55, no. 1 (2015): 27–34.

———. "Baptismal Identity in Ambrose's *De Isaac*." Forthcoming.

———. "Participation in Christ: Psalm 118 in Ambrose and Augustine." *Augustinianum* 54 (2014): 173–97.

Boersma, Hans. "The Church Fathers' Spiritual Interpretation of the Psalms." In *Living Waters from Ancient Springs: Essays in Honor of Cornelis Van Dam*, edited by Jason Van Vliet, 41–55. Eugene, OR: Pickwick, 2011.

———. *Embodiment and Virtue in Gregory of Nyssa: An Anagogical Approach*. Oxford Early Christian Studies. Oxford: Oxford University Press, 2013.

———. *Heavenly Participation: The Weaving of a Sacramental Tapestry*. Grand Rapids: Eerdmans, 2011.

———. "Joshua as Sacrament: Spiritual Interpretation in Origen." *Crux* 48, no. 3 (2012): 23–40.

———. *Nouvelle Théologie and Sacramental Ontology: A Return to Mystery*. Oxford: Oxford University Press, 2009.

———. "'Numbed with Grief': Gregory of Nyssa on Bereavement and Hope." *Journal of Spiritual Formation and Soul Care* 7 (2014): 46–59.

———. "Nuptial Reading: Hippolytus, Origen, and Ambrose on the Bridal Couple of the Song of Songs." *Calvin Theological Journal* 51 (2016): 227–58.

———. "Preaching through Many Voices: Caesarius of Arles on Genesis 18." *Crux* 50, no. 3 (2014): 2–10.

———. "Reconnecting the Threads: Theology as Sacramental Tapestry." *Crux* 47, no. 3 (2011): 29–37.

———. "Sacramental Interpretation: On the Need for Theological Grounding of Narratival History." In *Exile in Biblical Studies and Theology: A Dialogue with N. T. Wright*, edited by James M. Scott. Downers Grove, IL: IVP Academic, forthcoming.

———. *Sacramental Preaching: Sermons on the Hidden Presence of Christ*. Grand Rapids: Baker Academic, 2016.

———. "The Sacramental Reading of Nicene Theology: Athanasius and Gregory of Nyssa on Proverbs 8." *Journal of Theological Interpretation* 10, no. 1 (Spring 2016). 1 30.

———. "Spiritual Imagination: Recapitulation as an Interpretive Principle." In *Imagination and Interpretation: Christian Perspectives*, edited by Hans Boersma, 13–33. Vancouver: Regent College Publishing, 2005.

———. "Up the Mountain with the Fathers: Evangelical *Ressourcement* of Early Christian Doctrine." *Canadian Theological Review* 1 (2012): 3–22.

———. *Violence, Hospitality, and the Cross: Reappropriating the Atonement Tradition*. Grand Rapids: Baker Academic, 2004.

Böhm, Thomas. "The Exegesis of Arius: Biblical Attitude and Systematic Formation." In *Handbook of Patristic Exegesis: The Bible in Ancient Christianity*, edited by Charles Kannengiesser et al., 687–705. Leiden: Brill, 2006.

Boulton, Matthew Myer. *God against Religion: Rethinking Christian Theology through Worship*. Grand Rapids: Eerdmans, 2008.

Bouteneff, Peter. *Beginnings: Ancient Christian Readings of the Biblical Creation Narratives*. Grand Rapids: Baker Academic, 2008.

Brakke, David. *The Gnostics: Myth, Ritual, and Diversity in Early Christianity*. Cambridge, MA: Harvard University Press, 2010.

Brannan, Rick, et al., eds. *The Lexham English Septuagint*. Bellingham, WA: Lexham, 2012.

Brecht, Martin. *Martin Luther*. Vol. 3, *The Preservation of the Church, 1532–1546*. Translated by James L. Schaaf. Minneapolis: Augsburg Fortress, 1999.

Briggs, Richard. *The Virtuous Reader: Old Testament Narrative and Interpretive Virtue*. Grand Rapids: Baker Academic, 2010.

Brown, David. "A Sacramental World: Why It Matters." In *The Oxford Handbook of Sacramental Theology*, edited by Hans Boersma and Matthew Levering, 603–15. Oxford: Oxford University Press, 2015.

Buchanan, George Wesley. *The Gospel of Matthew*. Vol. 1. Lewiston, NY: Mellen, 1996.

Bucur, Bogdan G. "Justin Martyr's Exegesis of Biblical Theophanies and the Parting of the Ways between Christianity and Judaism." *Theological Studies* 75 (2014): 34–51.

————. "Theophanies and Vision of God in Augustine's *De Trinitate*: An Eastern Orthodox Perspective." *St Vladimir's Theological Quarterly* 52 (2008): 67–93.

Burrus, Virginia. "'The Passover Still Takes Place Today': Exegesis, Asceticism, Judaism, and Origen's *On Passover*." In *Asceticism and Exegesis in Early Christianity: The Reception of New Testament Texts in Ancient Ascetic Discourses*, edited by Hans-Ulrich Weidemann, 235–45. Göttingen: Vandenhoeck & Ruprecht, 2013.

Byassee, Jason. *Praise Seeking Understanding: Reading the Psalms with Augustine*. Grand Rapids: Eerdmans, 2007.

Caldecott, Stratford. *Beauty for Truth's Sake: On the Re-enchantment of Education*. Grand Rapids: Brazos, 2009.

Cameron, Michael. *Christ Meets Me Everywhere: Augustine's Early Figurative Exegesis*. New York: Oxford University Press, 2012.

————. "The Emergence of *Totus Christus* as Hermeneutical Center in Augustine's *Enarrationes in Psalmos*." In *The Harp of Prophecy: Early Christian Interpretation of the Psalms*, edited by Brian Daley and Paul R. Kolbet, 205–26. Notre Dame, IN: University of Notre Dame Press, 2015.

Catechism of the Catholic Church. 2nd ed. Vatican City: Libreria Editrice Vaticana, 2000.

Cerrato, J. A. *Hippolytus between East and West: The Commentaries and the Provenance of the Corpus*. Oxford: Oxford University Press, 2002.

Chappuzeau, Gertrud. "Die Auslegung des Hohenliedes durch Hippolyt von Rom." *Jahrbuch für Antike und Christentum* 19 (1976): 45–81.

Chenu, Marie-Dominique. *Nature, Man, and Society in the Twelfth Century: Essays on New Theological Perspectives in the Latin West*. Translated and edited by Jerome Taylor and Lester Little. Toronto: University of Toronto Press, 1998.

Childs, Brevard S. "Toward Recovering Theological Exegesis." *Pro Ecclesia* 6 (1997): 16–26.

Clark, Elizabeth A. *Reading Renunciation: Asceticism and Scripture in Early Christianity*. Princeton: Princeton University Press, 1999.

————. "Uses of the Song of Songs: Origen and the Later Latin Fathers." In *Ascetic Piety and Women's Faith: Essays on Late Ancient Christianity*, 386–427. Studies in Women and Religion 20. Lewiston, NY: Mellen, 1986.

Clayton, Allan Lee. "The Orthodox Recovery of a Heretical Proof-Text: Athanasius of Alexandria's Interpretation of Proverbs 8:22–30 in Conflict with the Arians." PhD diss., Southern Methodist University, 1988.

Collins, John J. *The Bible after Babel: Historical Criticism in a Postmodern Age*. Grand Rapids: Eerdmans, 2005.

Coyle, J. Kevin. "Mani, Manicheism." In *Augustine through the Ages: An Encyclopedia*, edited by Allan Fitzgerald and John C. Cavadini, 520–25. Grand Rapids: Eerdmans, 1999.

Cutrone, Emmanuel J. "Sacraments." In *Augustine through the Ages: An Encyclopedia*, edited by Allan Fitzgerald and John C. Cavadini, 741–47. Grand Rapids: Eerdmans, 1999.

Daley, Brian E. "Is Patristic Exegesis Still Usable? Reflections on Early Christian Interpretation of the Psalms." *Communio* 29 (2002): 185–216.

———. "Training for 'the Good Ascent': Gregory of Nyssa's Homily on the Sixth Psalm." In *In Dominico Eloquio: In Lordly Eloquence: Essays on Patristic Exegesis in Honor of Robert Louis Wilken*, edited by Paul M. Blowers et al., 185–217. Grand Rapids: Eerdmans, 2002.

Daly, Robert J. Introduction to "Treatise on the Passover (*Peri Pascha*)." In *Treatise on the Passover and Dialogue of Origen with Heraclides and His Fellow Bishops on the Father, the Son, and the Soul*, by Origen. Translated and edited by Robert J. Daly. Ancient Christian Writers 54. New York: Paulist Press, 1992.

Daniélou, Jean. *The Bible and the Liturgy*. Liturgical Studies 3. Notre Dame, IN. University of Notre Dame Press, 1956.

———. *From Shadows to Reality: Studies in the Biblical Typology of the Fathers*. Translated by Wulstan Hibberd. London: Burns & Oates, 1960.

Dawson, John David. *Christian Figural Reading and the Fashioning of Identity*. Berkeley: University of California Press, 2002.

Deferrari, Roy Joseph. Introduction to *Saint Ambrose: Theological and Dogmatic Works*, by Ambrose. Translated and edited by Roy Joseph Deferrari. Fathers of the Church 44. Washington, DC: Catholic University of America Press, 1963.

De Lubac, Henri. *Catholicism: Christ and the Common Destiny of Man*. Translated by Lancelot C. Sheppard and Elizabeth Englund. San Francisco: Ignatius, 1988.

———. "Hellenistic Allegory and Christian Allegory." In *Theological Fragments*, translated by Rebecca Howell Balinski, 165–96. San Francisco: Ignatius, 1989.

———. *History and Spirit: The Understanding of Scripture according to Origen*. Translated by Anne Englund Nash with Juvenal Merriell. San Francisco: Ignatius, 2007.

———. *Medieval Exegesis: The Four Senses of Scripture*. Vol. 2. Translated by E. M. Macierowski. Grand Rapids: Eerdmans, 2000.

———. "Typology and Allegorization." In *Theological Fragments*, translated by Rebecca Howell Balinski, 129–64. San Francisco: Ignatius, 1989.

Dodaro, Robert. *Christ and the Just Society in the Thought of Augustine*. Cambridge: Cambridge University Press, 2004.

Doerfler, Maria E. "Entertaining the Trinity Unawares: Genesis xviii in Western Christian Interpretation." *Journal of Ecclesiastical History* 65 (2014): 485–513.

Donovan, Mary Ann. *One Right Reading? A Guide to Irenaeus*. Collegeville, MN: Liturgical Press, 1997.

Dreyfus, François. "Divine Condescendence (*synkatabasis*) as a Hermeneutic Principle of the Old Testament in Jewish and Christian Tradition." *Immanuel* 19 (1984/1985): 74–86.

Drobner, Hubertus R. "Skopos – σκοπός." In *The Brill Dictionary of Gregory of Nyssa*, edited by Lucas F. Mateo-Seco and Giulio Maspero, translated by Seth Cherney, 681–82. Supplements to Vigiliae Christianae 99. Leiden: Brill, 2010.

Dupré, Louis K. *Passage to Modernity: An Essay in the Hermeneutics of Nature and Culture.* New Haven: Yale University Press, 1993.

Falls, Thomas B. Introduction to *The First Apology; The Second Apology; Dialogue with Trypho; Exhortation to the Greeks; Discourse to the Greeks; The Monarchy or The Rule of God*, by Justin Martyr. Translated and edited by Thomas B. Falls. Fathers of the Church 6. Washington, DC: Catholic University of America Press, 1948.

Faulkner, Quentin. *Wiser Than Despair: The Evolution of Ideas in the Relationship of Music and the Christian Church.* Westport, CT: Greenwood, 1996.

Fee, Gordon D. "Wisdom Christology in Paul: A Dissenting View." In *The Way of Wisdom: Essays in Honor of Bruce K. Waltke*, edited by J. I. Packer and Sven K. Soderlund, 251–79. Grand Rapids: Zondervan, 2000.

Fiedrowicz, Michael. General introduction to *Expositions of the Psalms 1–32*, by Augustine. Edited by John E. Rotelle. The Works of Saint Augustine: A Translation for the 21st Century III/15. Hyde Park, NY: New City, 2000.

———. General introduction to *On Genesis: A Refutation of the Manichees; Unfinished Literal Commentary on Genesis; The Literal Meaning of Genesis*, by Augustine. Edited by John E. Rotelle. The Works of Saint Augustine: A Translation for the 21st Century I/13. Hyde Park, NY: New City, 2002.

———. Introduction to *On Genesis: A Refutation of the Manichees*, by Augustine. Edited by John E. Rotelle. The Works of Saint Augustine: A Translation for the 21st Century I/13. Hyde Park, NY: New City, 2002.

Fowl, Stephen E. *Engaging Scripture: A Model for Theological Interpretation.* Malden, MA: Blackwell, 1998.

———. "Virtue." In *Dictionary for Theological Interpretation of the Bible*, edited by Kevin J. Vanhoozer, 837–39. Grand Rapids: Baker Academic, 2005.

Fowl, Stephen E., and Lewis Ayres. "(Mis)reading the Face of God: The Interpretation of the Bible in the Church." *Theological Studies* 60 (1999): 513–28.

Froehlich, Karlfried, trans. and ed. *Biblical Interpretation in the Early Church.* Philadelphia: Fortress, 1984.

Gadamer, Hans-Georg. *Truth and Method.* Translated by Joel Weinsheimer and Donald G. Marshall. 2nd ed. New York: Crossroad, 2004.

Gil-Tamayo, Juan Antonio. "Akolouthia – ἀκολουθία." In *The Brill Dictionary of Gregory of Nyssa*, edited by Lucas F. Mateo-Seco and Giulio Maspero, translated by Seth Cherney, 14–20. Supplements to Vigiliae Christianae 99. Leiden: Brill, 2010.

Goldingay, John, and David F. Payne. *A Critical and Exegetical Commentary on Isaiah 40–55*. International Critical Commentary. 2 vols. London: T&T Clark, 2006.

Greene-McCreight, Kathryn. *Ad Litteram: How Augustine, Calvin, and Barth Read the "Plain Sense" of Genesis 1–3*. Issues in Systematic Theology 5. New York: Lang, 1999.

Greidanus, Sidney. *Sola Scriptura: Problems and Principles in Preaching Historical Texts*. 1970. Reprint, Eugene, OR: Wipf & Stock, 2001.

Griffiths, Paul J. *Song of Songs*. Brazos Theological Commentary. Grand Rapids: Brazos, 2011.

Grypeou, Emmanouela, and Helen Spurling. "Abraham's Angels: Jewish and Christian Exegesis of Genesis 18–19." In *The Exegetical Encounter between Jews and Christians in Late Antiquity*, edited by Emmanouela Grypeou and Helen Spurling, 181–203. Jewish and Christian Perspectives 18. Leiden: Brill, 2009.

Hahn, Scott W., and Benjamin Wiker. *Politicizing the Bible: The Roots of Historical Criticism and the Secularization of Scripture 1300–1700*. New York: Herder & Herder / Crossroad, 2013.

Hainsworth, John. "The Force of the Mystery: Anamnesis and Exegesis in Melito's *Peri Pascha*." *St Vladimir's Theological Quarterly* 46 (2002): 107–46.

Hall, Christopher A. "Creedal Hermeneutics: How the Creeds Can Help Us Read the Bible." In *Serving God's Community: Studies in Honor of W. Ward Gasque*, edited by Susan S. Phillips and Soo-Inn Tann, 109–206. Vancouver: Regent College Publishing, 2014.

Hanson, R. P. C. *Allegory and Event: A Study of the Sources and Significance of Origen's Interpretation of Scripture*. 2nd ed. Louisville: Westminster John Knox, 2002.

Harrison, Carol. "Enchanting the Soul: The Music of the Psalms." In *Meditations of the Heart: The Psalms in Early Christian Thought and Practice; Essays in Honour of Andrew Louth*, edited by A. G. Andreopoulos, Augustine Casiday, and Carol Harrison, 205–23. Studia Traditionis Theologiae: Explorations in Early and Medieval Theology 8. Turnhout, Belgium: Brepols, 2011.

Harrisville, Roy A., and Walter Sundberg. *The Bible in Modern Culture: Baruch Spinoza to Brevard Childs*. 2nd ed. Grand Rapids: Eerdmans, 2002.

Heine, Ronald E. "Appendix: The Interpretation of Names in the Genesis and Exodus Homilies." In *Homilies on Genesis and Exodus*, by Origen. Translated and edited by Ronald E. Heine. Fathers of the Church 71. Washington, DC: Catholic University of America Press, 1982.

———. "Hippolytus, Ps.-Hippolytus and the Early Canons." In *The Cambridge History of Early Christian Literature*, edited by Frances M. Young, Lewis Ayres, and Andrew Louth, 142–51. Cambridge: Cambridge University Press, 2004.

———. Introduction to *Gregory of Nyssa's Treatise on the Inscriptions of the Psalms*, by Gregory of Nyssa. Translated and edited by Ronald E. Heine. Oxford: Clarendon, 1995.

————. Introduction to *Homilies on Genesis and Exodus*, by Origen. Translated and edited by Ronald E. Heine. Fathers of the Church 71. Washington, DC: Catholic University of America Press, 1982.

Hildebrand, Stephen M. *The Trinitarian Theology of Basil of Caesarea: A Synthesis of Greek Thought and Biblical Truth*. Washington, DC: Catholic University of America Press, 2007.

Hill, Jonathan. "Gregory of Nyssa, Material Substance and Berkeleyan Idealism." *British Journal for the History of Philosophy* 17 (2009): 653–83.

Hill, Robert C. "*Akribeia*: A Principle of Chrysostom's Exegesis." *Colloquium* 14, no. 1 (1981): 32–36.

————. Introduction to *Commentary on the Psalms: Psalms 1–72*, by Theodoret of Cyrus. Translated by Robert C. Hill. Fathers of the Church 101. Washington, DC: Catholic University of America Press, 1986.

————. Introduction to *Homilies on Genesis 1–17*, by John Chrysostom. Edited by Robert C. Hill. Fathers of the Church 74. Washington, DC: Catholic University of America Press, 1986.

————. "On Looking Again at *Sunkatabasis*." *Prudentia* 13 (1981): 3–11.

————. "St. John Chrysostom and the Incarnation of the Word in Scripture." *Compass Theology Review* 14, no. 3 (1980): 34–38.

Hirshman, Marc G. *A Rivalry of Genius: Jewish and Christian Biblical Interpretation in Late Antiquity*. Translated by Batya Stein. Albany: State University of New York Press, 1996.

Huijgen, Arnold. "Divine Accommodation in Calvin: Myth and Reality." In *The Myth of the Reformation*, edited by Peter Opitz, 248–59. Refo500 Academic Studies 9. Göttingen: Vandenhoeck & Ruprecht, 2013.

Hunter, David G. "The Virgin, the Bride and the Church: Reading Psalm 45 in Ambrose, Jerome, and Augustine." In *The Harp of Prophecy: Early Christian Interpretation of the Psalms*, edited by Brian Daley and Paul R. Kolbet, 149–74. Notre Dame, IN: University of Notre Dame Press, 2015.

Irvine, Martin. *The Making of Textual Culture: 'Grammatica' and Literary Theory, 350–1100*. Cambridge Studies in Medieval Literature 19. Cambridge: Cambridge University Press, 1994.

Jenson, Robert W. *Song of Songs*. Interpretation: A Bible Commentary for Teaching and Preaching. Louisville: Westminster John Knox, 2005.

Johnson, Julian. *Who Needs Classical Music? Cultural Choice and Musical Value*. Oxford: Oxford University Press, 2002.

Jowett, Benjamin. "On the Interpretation of Scripture." In *Essays and Reviews*, 330–433. 9th ed. London: Longman, Green, Longman and Roberts, 1861.

Kannengiesser, Charles. *Athanase d'Alexandrie évêque et écrivain: Une lecture des traités "contre les Ariens."* Théologie historique 70. Paris: Beauchesne, 1983.

Kaplan, Jonathan. *My Perfect One: Typology and Early Rabbinic Interpretation of Song of Songs.* Oxford: Oxford University Press, 2015.

Kärkkäinen, Veli-Matti. *One with God: Salvation as Deification and Justification.* Collegeville, MN: Liturgical Press, 2005.

Kelly, J. N. D. *Early Christian Creeds.* 3rd ed. New York: Routledge, 2014.

———. *Golden Mouth: The Story of John Chrysostom, Ascetic, Preacher, Bishop.* Ithaca, NY: Cornell University Press, 1995.

Kimelman, Reuven. "Rabbi Yoḥanan and Origen on the Song of Songs: A Third-Century Jewish-Christian Disputation." *Harvard Theological Review* 73 (1980): 567–95.

King, J. Christopher. *Origen on the Song of Songs as the Spirit of Scripture: The Bridegroom's Perfect Marriage-Song.* Oxford: Oxford University Press, 2005.

Kloos, Kari. *Christ, Creation, and the Vision of God: Augustine's Transformation of Early Christian Theophany Interpretation.* Leiden: Brill, 2011.

Knapp, Henry M. "Melito's Use of Scripture in *Peri Pascha*: Second-Century Typology." *Vigiliae Christianae* 54 (2000): 343–74.

Knight, Mark. "*Wirkungsgeschichte*, Reception History, Reception Theory." *Journal for the Study of the New Testament* 33 (2010): 137–46.

Kolbet, Paul R. "Athanasius, the Psalms, and the Reformation of the Self." In *The Harp of Prophecy: Early Christian Interpretation of the Psalms*, edited by Brian Daley and Paul R. Kolbet, 75–96. Notre Dame, IN: University of Notre Dame Press, 2015.

Lavery, Karen DeCrescenzo. "Abraham's Dialogue with God over the Destruction of Sodom: Chapters in the History of the Interpretation of Genesis 18." PhD diss., Harvard University, 2007.

Lawson, R. P. Introduction to *The Song of Songs: Commentary and Homilies*, by Origen. Translated and edited by R. P. Lawson. Ancient Christian Writers 26. New York: Newman, 1956.

Lee, Philip J. *Against the Protestant Gnostics.* New York: Oxford University Press, 1987.

Leemans, John. "After Philo and Paul: Hagar in the Writings of the Church Fathers." In *Abraham, the Nations, and the Hagarites: Jewish, Christian, and Islamic Perspectives on Kinship with Abraham*, edited by Martin Goodman, George H. van Kooten, and Jacques T. A. G. M. van Ruiten, 435–48. Leiden: Brill, 2010.

Leithart, Peter J. *Athanasius.* Grand Rapids: Baker Academic, 2011.

———. *Deep Exegesis: The Mystery of Reading Scripture.* Waco: Baylor University Press, 2009.

———. "Jesus as Israel: The Typological Structure of Matthew's Gospel." http://www.leithart.com/pdf/jesus-as-israel-the-typological-structure-of-matthew-s-gospel.pdf.

Levering, Matthew. *Participatory Biblical Exegesis: A Theology of Biblical Interpretation.* Notre Dame, IN: University of Notre Dame Press, 2008.

Lienhard, Joseph T. *Contra Marcellum: Marcellus of Ancyra and Fourth-Century Theology*. Washington, DC: Catholic University of America Press, 1999.

Longenecker, Richard N. *Biblical Exegesis in the Apostolic Period*. 2nd ed. Grand Rapids: Eerdmans, 1999.

Longman, Tremper, III. "Song of Songs." In *Dictionary for Theological Interpretation of the Bible*, edited by Kevin J. Vanhoozer, 758–61. Grand Rapids: Baker Academic, 2005.

Louth, Andrew. *Discerning the Mystery: An Essay on the Nature of Theology*. Oxford: Clarendon, 1983.

———. "'Heart in Pilgrimage': St Augustine as Interpreter of the Psalms." In *Orthodox Readings of Augustine*, edited by George E. Demacopoulos and Aristotle Papanikolaou, 291–304. Crestwood, NY: St Vladimir's Seminary Press, 2008.

MacIntyre, Alasdair. *After Virtue: A Study in Moral Theory*. 1981. Reprint, London: Bloomsbury Academic, 2011.

Malcolm, Noel. "*Leviathan*, the Pentateuch, and the Origins of Modern Biblical Criticism." In *"Leviathan" after 350 Years*, edited by Tom Sorell and Luc Foisneau, 241–64. Oxford: Clarendon, 2004.

Mannermaa, Tuomo. *Christ Present in Faith: Luther's View of Justification*. Edited and introduced by Kirsi Stjerna. Minneapolis: Fortress, 2005.

Marcus, Joel. "Israel and the Church in the Exegetical Writings of Hippolytus." *Journal of Biblical Literature* 131 (2012): 385–406.

Margerie, Bertrand de. "Saint Gregory of Nyssa Theoretician of Biblical Connections or Chains: *Skopos, Theoria, Akolouthia*." Translated by Leonard Maluf. In *Introduction to the History of Exegesis*. Vol. 1, *The Greek Fathers*, 213–39. Petersham, MA. St. Bede's, 1991.

Martens, Peter W. "Origen against History? Reconsidering the Critique of Allegory." *Modern Theology* 28 (2012): 635–56.

———. *Origen and Scripture: The Contours of the Exegetical Life*. New York: Oxford University Press, 2012.

———. "Revisiting the Allegory/Typology Distinction: The Case of Origen." *Journal of Early Christian Studies* 16 (2008): 283–317.

Mateo Seco, Lucas F. "Tunics of Hide." In *The Brill Dictionary of Gregory of Nyssa*, edited by Lucas F. Mateo-Seco and Giulio Maspero, translated by Seth Cherney, 768–70. Supplements to Vigiliae Christianae 99. Leiden: Brill, 2010.

Mattox, Mickey Leland. "*Sancta Domina*: Luther's Catholic Exegesis of Sarah." In *"Defender of the Most Holy Matriarchs": Martin Luther's Interpretation of the Women of Genesis in the* Enarrationes in Genesin, *1535–1545*. Studies in Medieval and Reformation Traditions 92. Leiden: Brill, 2003.

McClean, John. "Perichoresis, Theosis and Union with Christ in the Thought of John Calvin." *Reformed Theological Review* 68 (2009): 130–41.

McConvery, Brendan. "Hippolytus' Commentary on the Song of Songs and John 20." *Irish Theological Quarterly* 71 (2006): 211–22.

Meredith, Anthony. "God-Fittingness in Gregory of Nyssa." *Studia Patristica* 18 (1989): 507–15.

Mitchell, M. M. "John Chrysostom (c. 347–407)." In *Dictionary of Major Biblical Interpreters*, edited by Donald K. McKim, 571–77. Downers Grove, IL: IVP Academic, 2007.

Moberly, R. W. L. "'Interpret the Bible Like Any Other Book'? Requiem for an Axiom." *Journal of Theological Interpretation* 4 (2010): 91–110.

Mosser, Carl. "The Greatest Possible Blessing: Calvin and Deification." *Scottish Journal of Theology* 55 (2002): 36–57.

Murphy, Roland E. "Patristic and Medieval Exegesis—Help or Hindrance?" *Catholic Biblical Quarterly* 43 (1981): 505–16.

Naidu, Ashish J. *Transformed in Christ: Christology and the Christian Life in John Chrysostom*. Princeton Theological Monograph Series 188. Eugene, OR: Pickwick, 2012.

Nichols, Aidan. *Lovely, Like Jerusalem: The Fulfillment of the Old Testament in Christ and the Church*. San Francisco: Ignatius, 2007.

Nielsen, J. T. *Adam and Christ in the Theology of Irenaeus of Lyons: An Examination of the Function of the Adam-Christ Typology in the Adversus Haereses of Irenaeus, against the Background of the Gnosticism of His Time*. Assen, Netherlands: Van Gorcum, 1968.

Norris, Richard A. *The Song of Songs: Interpreted by Early Christian and Medieval Commentators*. The Church's Bible. Grand Rapids: Eerdmans, 2003.

O'Keefe, John J. "Theodoret's Unique Contribution to the Antiochene Exegetical Tradition: Questioning Traditional Scholarly Categories." In *The Harp of Prophecy: Early Christian Interpretation of the Psalms*, edited by Brian Daley and Paul R. Kolbet, 191–203. Notre Dame, IN: University of Notre Dame Press, 2015.

O'Keefe, John J., and R. R. Reno. *Sanctified Vision: An Introduction to Early Christian Interpretation of the Bible*. Baltimore: Johns Hopkins University Press, 2005.

O'Loughlin, Thomas. "The Mysticism of Number in the Medieval Period before Eriugena." In *The Perennial Tradition of Neoplatonism*, edited by John J. Cleary, 397–416. Ancient and Medieval Philosophy I/24. Leuven, Belgium: Leuven University Press, 1997.

Pabst, Adrian. *Metaphysics: The Creation of Hierarchy*. Interventions. Grand Rapids: Eerdmans, 2012.

Parry, Robin A. *The Biblical Cosmos: A Pilgrim's Guide to the Weird and Wonderful World of the Bible*. Eugene, OR: Cascade, 2014.

Patterson, Richard D. "Metaphors of Marriage as Expressions of Divine-Human Relations." *Journal of the Evangelical Theological Society* 51 (2008): 689–702.

Perhai, Richard J. *Antiochene* Theōria *in the Writings of Theodore of Mopsuestia and Theodoret of Cyrus.* Minneapolis: Fortress, 2015.

Phipps, William E. "The Plight of the Song of Songs." *Journal of the American Academy of Religion* 42 (1974): 82–100.

Provan, Iain. "Canons to the Left of Him: Brevard Childs, His Critics, and the Future of Old Testament Theology." *Scottish Journal of Theology* 50 (1997): 1–38.

Pusey, Edward. *An Historical Enquiry into the Causes of the Rationalistic Character Lately Predominant in the Theology of Germany.* London: Rivington, 1828.

Radner, Ephraim. "The Faith of Reading: Keble and Scriptural Interpretation." In *Hope among the Fragments: The Broken Church and Its Engagement of Scripture,* 79–90. Grand Rapids: Brazos, 2004.

Reno, R. R. "Series Preface." Brazos Theological Commentary on the Bible. http://www.brazostheologicalcommentary.com/about/series-preface/.

Richard, Marcel. "Une paraphrase greque résumée du Commentaire d'Hippolyte sur le Cantique des Cantiques." *Le Muséon* 77 (1964): 137–54.

Rondeau, Marie-Josèphe. "Exégèse du Psautier et anabase spirituelle chez Grégoire de Nysse." In *Epektasis: Mélanges patristiques offerts au Cardinal Jean Daniélou,* edited by Jacques Fontaine and Charles Kannengiesser, 517–31. Paris: Beauchesne, 1972.

Rosenberg, Randall S. "The Drama of Scripture: Reading Patristic Biblical Hermeneutics through Lonergan's Reflections on Art." *Logos* 11 (2008): 126–48.

Rowell, Lewis Eugene. *Thinking about Music: An Introduction to the Philosophy of Music.* Amherst: University of Massachusetts Press, 1984.

Rylaarsdam, David. *John Chrysostom on Divine Pedagogy: The Coherence of His Theology and Preaching.* Oxford: Oxford University Press, 2014.

Schultz, Richard L. "Isaiah, Book of." In *Dictionary for Theological Interpretation of the Bible,* edited by Kevin J. Vanhoozer, 336–44. Grand Rapids: Baker Academic, 2005.

Scott, Mark S. M. "Shades of Grace: Origen and Gregory of Nyssa's Soteriological Exegesis of the 'Black and Beautiful' Bride in Song of Songs 1·5." *Harvard Theological Review* 99 (2006): 65–83.

Seitz, Christopher R. *Figured Out: Typology and Providence in Christian Scripture.* Louisville: Westminster John Knox, 2001.

Sheridan, Mark. *Language for God in Patristic Tradition: Wrestling with Biblical Anthropomorphism.* Downers Grove, IL: IVP Academic, 2015.

Shuve, Karl. "Irenaeus's Contribution to Early Christian Interpretation of the Song of Songs." In *Irenaeus: Life, Scripture, Legacy,* edited by Sara Parvis and Paul Foster, 81–89. Minneapolis: Fortress, 2012.

———. *The Song of Songs and the Fashioning of Identity in Early Latin Christianity.* Oxford: Oxford University Press, 2016.

Silvas, Anna M. *Macrina the Younger: Philosopher of God*. Medieval Women: Texts and Contexts 22. Turnhout, Belgium: Brepols, 2008.

Simonetti, Manlio. *Biblical Interpretation in the Early Church: An Historical Introduction to Patristic Exegesis*. Translated by John A. Hughes. Edited by Anders Bergquist and Markus Bockmuehl. Edinburgh: T&T Clark, 1994.

Smith, J. Warren. *Passion and Paradise: Human and Divine Emotion in the Thought of Gregory of Nyssa*. New York: Crossroad, 2004.

Smith, Yancy. *The Mystery of Anointing: Hippolytus' Commentary on the Song of Songs in Social and Critical Contexts*. Gorgias Studies in Early Christianity and Patristics 62. Piscataway, NJ: Gorgias, 2015.

Spitzer, Leo. "Classical and Christian Ideas of World Harmony: Prolegomena to an Interpretation of the Word 'Stimmung,' Part I." *Traditio* 2 (1944): 409–64.

Stapert, Calvin. *A New Song for an Old World: Musical Thought in the Early Church*. Grand Rapids: Eerdmans, 2007.

Steiner, George. *Real Presences*. Chicago: University of Chicago Press, 1989.

Stewart-Sykes, Alistair. Introduction to *On Pascha: With the Fragments of Melito and Other Material Related to the Quartodecimans*, by Melito of Sardis. Translated and edited by Alistair Stewart-Sykes. Popular Patristic Series 20. Crestwood, NY: St Vladimir's Seminary Press, 2001.

———. *The Lamb's High Feast: Melito, "Peri Pascha," and the Quartodeciman Paschal Liturgy at Sardis*. Leiden: Brill, 1998.

Sutcliffe, E. F. "St. Gregory of Nyssa and Paradise." *Ecclesiastical Review* 4 (1931): 337–51.

Toom, Tarmo. "Was Augustine an Intentionalist? Authorial Intention in Augustine's Hermeneutics." *Studia Patristica* 70 (2013): 185–93.

Torjesen, Karen Jo. "'Body,' 'Soul,' and 'Spirit' in Origen's Theory of Exegesis." *Anglican Theological Review* 67 (1985): 17–30.

Trakatellis, Demetrios. *The Pre-existence of Christ in the Writings of Justin Martyr*. Missoula, MT: Scholars Press, 1976.

Treier, Daniel J. *Introducing Theological Interpretation of Scripture: Recovering a Christian Practice*. Grand Rapids: Baker Academic, 2008.

Tyson, Paul. *Returning to Reality: Christian Platonism for Our Times*. Eugene, OR: Cascade, 2014.

Tzamalikos, Panayiotis. *Origen: Philosophy of History and Eschatology*. Supplements to Vigiliae Christianae 77. Leiden: Brill, 2007.

Urbach, Ephraim E. "The Homiletical Interpretations of the Sages and the Expositions of Origen on Canticles, and the Jewish-Christian Disputation." In *Studies in Aggadah and Folk-Literature*, edited by Joseph Heinemann and Dov Noy, 247–75. Scripta Hierosolymitana 22. Jerusalem: Magnes, 1971.

Vaggione, Richard Paul. *Eunomius of Cyzicus and the Nicene Revolution.* Oxford: Oxford University Press, 2000.

Van den Hoek, Annewies. "Etymologizing in a Christian Context: The Techniques of Clement of Alexandria and Origen." *Studia Philonica Annual* 16 (2004): 122–68.

Vanhoozer, Kevin J. "Introduction: What Is Theological Interpretation of the Bible?" In *Theological Interpretation of the Old Testament: A Book-by-Book Survey*, edited by Kevin J. Vanhoozer, 15–28. Grand Rapids: Baker Academic, 2008.

———. "Providence." In *Dictionary for Theological Interpretation of the Bible*, edited by Kevin J. Vanhoozer, 641–45. Grand Rapids: Baker Academic, 2005.

Von Rad, Gerhard. *Old Testament Theology.* Vol. 2, *The Theology of Israel's Prophetic Traditions.* Translated by D. M. G. Stalker. New York: Harper & Row, 1962.

Webster, John B. *Holy Scripture: A Dogmatic Sketch.* Cambridge: Cambridge University Press, 2003.

———. "*Ressourcement* Theology and Protestantism." In *Ressourcement: A Movement for Renewal in Twentieth-Century Catholic Theology*, edited by Gabriel Flynn and P. D. Murray, 482–94. Oxford: Oxford University Press, 2012.

Weinandy, Thomas G. "Athanasius's Letter to Marcellinus: A Soteriological Praying of the Psalms." In *Jesus: Essays in Christology*, 396–401. Ave Maria, FL: Sapientia, 2014.

Westhaver, George. "The Living Body of the Lord: E. B. Pusey's 'Types and Prophecies of the Old Testament.'" PhD diss., Durham University, 2012.

Wilken, Robert Louis. "Augustine." In *The Sermon on the Mount through the Centuries*, edited by Jeffrey P. Greenman, Timothy Larsen, and Stephen R. Spencer, 45–46. Grand Rapids: Brazos, 2007.

———. "Melito, the Jewish Community at Sardis, and the Sacrifice of Isaac." *Theological Studies* 37 (1976): 53–69.

Wilken, Robert Louis, with Angela Russell Christman and Michael J. Hollerich, eds. *Isaiah: Interpreted by Early Christian and Medieval Commentators.* The Church's Bible. Grand Rapids: Eerdmans, 2007.

Williams, Daniel H. *Tradition, Scripture, and Interpretation: A Sourcebook of the Ancient Church.* Grand Rapids: Baker Academic, 2006.

Wink, Walter. *Cracking the Gnostic Code: The Powers in Gnosticism.* Society of Biblical Literature Monograph Series 46. Atlanta: Scholars Press, 1993.

Wood, Susan K. *Spiritual Exegesis and the Church in the Theology of Henri de Lubac.* Grand Rapids: Eerdmans, 1998.

Wright, N. T. *The Climax of the Covenant: Christ and the Law in Pauline Theology.* Minneapolis: Fortress, 1992.

Young, Frances M. *Biblical Exegesis and the Formation of Christian Culture.* Cambridge: Cambridge University Press, 1997. Reprint, Peabody, MA: Hendrickson, 2002.

————. "Sexuality and Devotion: Mystical Readings of the Song of Songs." *Theology & Sexuality* 14 (2001): 80–96.

Zachhuber, Johannes. "Once Again: Gregory of Nyssa on Universals." *Journal of Theological Studies* 56 (2005): 75–98.

Zimmermann, Jens. *Recovering Theological Hermeneutics: An Incarnational-Trinitarian Theory of Interpretation.* Grand Rapids: Baker Academic, 2004.

NAME INDEX

ANCIENT AND MEDIEVAL WRITINGS INDEX

SCRIPTURE INDEX

SUBJECT INDEX